MEDIEVAL MONASTICISM

Medieval Monasticism traces the Western Monastic tradition from its fourth century origins in the deserts of Egypt and Syria, through the many and varied forms of religious life it assumed during the Middle Ages. Hugh Lawrence explores the many-sided relationship between monasteries and the secular world around them. For a thousand years, the great monastic houses and religious orders were a prominent feature of the social landscape of the West, and their leaders figured as much on the political as on the spiritual map of the medieval world. In this book many of them, together with their supporters and critics, are presented to us and speak their minds to us. We are shown, for instance, the controversy between the Benedictines and the reformed monasticism of the twelfth century and the problems that confronted women in religious life. A detailed glossary offers readers a helpful vocabulary of the subject.

This book is essential reading for both students and scholars of the medieval world.

C. H. Lawrence is Professor Emeritus of the University of London, UK. His previous publications include *St Edmund of Abingdon* (1960); *Matthew Paris and St Edmund* (1996); *The Friars: The Impact of the Mendicant Orders on Medieval Society* (2001) and *The Letters of Adam Marsh* (ed. and translated 2006–10).

The Medieval World

Series editors: Warren C. Brown, Caltech, USA and
Piotr Górecki, University of California, Riverside, USA

MEDIEVAL MONASTICISM

Forms of religious life in Western Europe in the Middle Ages

Fourth edition

C. H. Lawrence

 Routledge
Taylor & Francis Group

LONDON AND NEW YORK

First published in 1984 by Longman Group Ltd
Second edition published in 1989 by Longman Group UK Limited
Third edition published in 2001 by Pearson Education Limited
This edition published in 2015

by Routledge
2 Park Square, Milton Park, Abingdon, Oxon OX14 4RN

and by Routledge
52 Vanderbilt Avenue, New York, NY 10017

Routledge is an imprint of the Taylor & Francis Group, an informa business

First edition published in 1984 by Pearson Education Ltd
Third edition published in 2001 by Routledge

British Library Cataloguing-in-Publication Data
A catalogue record for this book is available from the British Library

Library of Congress Cataloging-in-Publication Data
Lawrence, C. H. (Clifford Hugh), 1921–
    Medieval monasticism : forms of religious life in Western Europe in
the Middle Ages / C. H. Lawrence. — Fourth edition.
        pages cm
    Includes bibliographical references and index.
    1. Monasticism and religious orders—History—Middle Ages, 600–1500.
I. Title.
    BX2470.L39 2015
    271.0094′0902—dc23
    2015000988

ISBN 13: 978-1-138-85403-1 (hbk)
ISBN 13: 978-1-138-85404-8 (pbk)

Typeset in Bembo
by Apex CoVantage, LLC

CONTENTS

LIST OF IMAGES

PUBLISHER'S ACKNOWLEDGEMENTS

The publisher would like to thank Clive Hicks and The Getty Research Library for granting permission to reproduce copyright material.

PREFACE TO THE FIRST EDITION

History is a language of explanation. This book has grown out of the experience of years spent endeavouring to explain to students the presence and function of monasteries in the medieval world. Huge though the literature of the subject is, indeed because it is so vast, it seemed to me that there was use for a short study that traced the growth of the Western monastic tradition as a whole in its social context, from its origins in late antiquity down to the later Middle Ages. This unifying purpose is my justification for the title; for although I have included the friars, they were not, properly speaking, monks, nor were the Brethren of the Common Life or the members of other fringe groups who figure in the later chapters. But the Mendicant Orders and the other religious movements of the later Middle Ages were nevertheless offshoots of the same monastic tradition and would be unintelligible without reference to it.

In the course of writing, I have often been aghast at my presumption in attempting to survey such a vast and rich manifestation of the human spirit in the compass of one short book. Drastic selectivity has been forced upon me both by the scale of the subject and by the limitations of my own scholarship. I am conscious that Spain gets scanty treatment and that, although I have written about the Military Orders, the other monks of *Outremer* should also have had a place in the story.

I have done my best to indicate my literary debts in the chapter endnotes. Other intellectual debts are less easy to define. Like all workers in this field, I owe much to the teaching and inspiration of the late David Knowles; also to a kind of infused understanding derived from the conversation of the late Father Daniel Callus. To me he always seemed to personify the essence of the ideal of the scholar-friar. I should like to acknowledge with gratitude the help of my wife, who encouraged me to write the book and cast a judicious eye over each chapter as it was finished.

PREFACE TO THE SECOND EDITION

In this edition I have tried to incorporate, either in the text or the notes, some of the new work that was not available to me when the first edition went to press. Besides this, retirement from the frenetic distractions that afflict all universities in these times has given me the chance to deal at length with some themes in which I have long had a special interest, such as the relationship of the monasteries to the world of the schoolmen. I have also taken the opportunity to repair some obvious omissions. Thus, for instance, Heloise, who had only the briefest of walk-on parts in the first edition, has been brought on to full stage among the abbesses.

I should like to record here my thanks to Dom Anselme Davril of Fleury and Fr Norman Tanner for helpful comments that prompted me to rewrite two passages, and to Miss Sheelagh Taylor and Mrs Joan Wells, who typed the greater part of the text for me.

PREFACE TO THE THIRD EDITION

In this edition I have done my best to take account, either in the text or the endnotes, of some of the new work that has appeared in print since the publication of the second edition eleven years ago. The extreme difficulty, even in retirement, of keeping abreast of ongoing scholarship over such a wide field has further impressed upon me the temerity of my original enterprise. At all events, I must recognise that a third edition represents the terminus of this particular journey. Perhaps this is the place to record one of the circumstances that moved me to undertake it in the first place. While wandering in France during a university vacation soon after the end of the Second World War, travelling by country buses, I came upon the ancient abbey of Fleury Saint-Benoît. I had read of its links with Anglo-Saxon England in the tenth century, but I was surprised to find it occupied once more by Benedictine monks, whose guest-master, the late Père Wulfram, received me with great kindness and installed me in a cell looking on to the nave of the church. I was even more astonished to be shown in the crypt a large gilded reliquary containing some meagre remains that were said to be those of St Benedict himself. The strangeness of this encounter, and the warmth of the hospitality I received from the community in the days that followed – which included a place among the monks to sing the night office in that superb romanesque choir – are memories which have never been far from my mind when studying monastic history. One day in a corner of the monastic kitchen, as Père Wulfram plied me with an elaborate boiled concoction which he believed to be English tea, he said to me, 'You must write about us when you return home.' This book began partly as a belated response to that request.

PREFACE TO THE FOURTH EDITION

In this edition I have endeavoured to give fresh emphasis to the theme of monastic reform, which preoccupied the minds and writings of many religious leaders of the twelfth century, and directed so many efforts to seek institutional change and to experiment with new forms of religious life.

ABBREVIATIONS USED IN THE NOTES

AA SS	*The Acta Sanctorum* of the Bollandists
AFH	*Archivum Franciscanum Historicum*
AFP	*Archivum Fratrum Praedicatorum*
ALKG	*Archiv für Literatur- und Kirchengeschichte des Mittelalters*, ed. H. Denifle and F. Ehrle, 6 vols (Berlin, Freiburg, 1885–92)
ASOC	*Analecta Sacri Ordinis Cisterciensis*
Canivez	*Statuta Capitulorum Generalium Ordinis Cisterciensis*, ed. J. Canivez (Louvain, 1933ff)
CCM	*Corpus Consuetudinum Monasticarum*, ed. K. Hallinger (Siegburg, 1963ff)
CSEL	*Corpus Scriptorum Ecclesiasticorum Latinorum* (Vienna and Prague, 1866ff)
DHGE	*Dictionnaire d'Histoire et de Géographic Ecclésiastique*
Friedberg	*Corpus Iuris Canonici*, ed. E. Friedberg, 2 vols
Habig	*St Francis of Assisi, Omnibus of Sources*, ed. Marion A. Habig, 3rd edn (Chicago, 1973)
JEH	*Journal of Ecclesiastical History*
Mansi	*Sacrorum Conciliorum Nova et Amplissima Collectio*, ed. J. D. Mansi (Florence, 1759–98)
MGH SS	*Monumenta Germaniae Historica, Scriptores*
MGH SSRM	*Monumenta Germaniae Historica, Scriptores Rerum Merovingicarum*
MOFPH	*Monumenta Ordinis Fratrum Praedicatorum Historica*
PG	*Patrologia Graeca*, ed. J. P. Migne
PL	*Patrologia Latina*, ed. J. P. Migne
Rev. bén	*Revue bénédictine*

RS   *Chronicles and Memorials of Great Britain and Ireland in the Rolls Series*

Schroeder   *Disciplinary Decrees of the General Councils*, ed. H. J. Schroeder (1937)

1

THE CALL OF THE DESERT

Christian monasticism made its earliest traceable appearance in Egypt and Palestine towards the end of the third century. In its primitive form it was a way of life adopted by solitaries, or anchorites, who lived in the desert. The word 'monasticism' itself derives from the Greek word *monos*, meaning 'alone': monks were people, mostly lay people, who had withdrawn from society to pursue the spiritual life in solitude. As Jerome, one of the early Western converts to the monastic life, explained to another convert, Paulinus of Nola, 'If you wish to perform the office of a priest, live in cities and townships, and make the salvation of others the gain of your soul. But if you desire to be what is called a monk, that is a solitary, what are you doing in cities, which are after all the dwelling places not of solitaries, but of the many?'[1]

Some monks, in time the majority of them, lived in organised communities of their own kind; but the first in time whose footprints we can trace were the hermits. By the fourth century, the desert of Nitria, on the western edge of the Nile delta, and the wilderness of Judea were peopled by scattered colonies of hermits. For the most part these people were not clergy but lay Christians, who had migrated into the solitude of the waste places from the urban society of late antiquity.

Writers on the subject, both ancient and modern, have suggested two alternative explanations for the movement. Some, including Jerome (*c.* 331–420), have claimed that the first Christian anchorites were refugees who sought safety in the desert from the persecution launched against the Church under the regime of Decius and Diocletian. Others have argued that the movement was a symptom of a softening of the moral fibre of the Christian community after Constantine had given peace to the Church in 313. Seen from this angle, the asceticism of the desert solitaries represented a reaction by finer spirits against the laxer standards and the careerism that crept into the Church once imperial approval had given it respectability and brought it endowments. The advent of large numbers of merely nominal Christians, which followed upon public recognition of Christianity, impelled those who were more deeply committed to the religious life to separate themselves from their congregations. Both these explanations have some basis in our sources, but neither is completely satisfying in itself.

Ascetical withdrawal from the world – that is, the renunciation of marriage, personal property, and the ordinary pleasures and comforts of life, in order to discipline the senses and free the mind for supernatural contemplation – is a feature of other world religions besides Christianity. Buddhism has its monks; and Judaism, which is not conspicuously ascetical in its ethos, had its Essene tradition, which modern archaeology has done much to elucidate. The study of the Dead Sea Scrolls and excavation of the Qumran site have revealed the existence of a Jewish ascetical settlement at the time of Christ that displayed many of the characteristics of a later Christian monastery.

There was also an ascetical tradition in Greco-Roman philosophy, represented by the Stoics and the Neoplatonists, which counselled the man who aspired to perfect wisdom to avoid the distractions of marriage and social intercourse and live the life of a recluse. As we can see from the career of St Augustine, this pagan image of the sage or philosopher as a recluse exercised a powerful influence over the minds of educated Christians who had been schooled in the classical tradition. Augustine had been a teacher of rhetoric. But the earliest Christian anchorites were not for the most part highly educated men, and we must look elsewhere for the source of their inspiration.

Christian renunciation of the world was rooted in the Gospel. The earliest of the Gospel narratives, that of St Mark, begins in the desert with the prophetic voice of the Baptist crying in the wilderness. Before beginning his public ministry, Christ was led by the Spirit into the desert, where he fasted for forty days. Ecclesiastical tradition saw in this a parable of the conflict within the soul of the Christian: the quest for God involved separation from the world and the conquest of sensuality and human ambition. One of the passages in the Gospels that launched many ascetics on their spiritual career was the invitation of Jesus to the rich young man who asked, 'What must I do to be saved?' He was told, 'Keep the commandments; love your neighbour as yourself.' But he was not satisfied: he had done all this, or so he claimed, and he pressed for more. And in reply he received the devastating advice, 'If you would be perfect, go, sell what you possess and give to the poor, and you will have treasure in heaven; and come, follow me.'

In fact, the desert monks were responding to a vocation which they found in the Christian tradition – to follow the 'evangelical counsels', to renounce property and ordinary human ties in the quest for spiritual perfection. They accepted the challenge of total surrender to Christ through the abandonment of worldly goods and prospects. But the quest for perfection involved more than this. Renunciation was only the beginning of the journey of the monk. His ultimate goal was union with God through prayer. But man's predicament since the Fall made the journey of the soul to God a hard one. Original sin had left man's reason darkened and his senses in disorder. Human passions choked the life of the spirit. Thus the newness of life, of which the Gospel spoke, could only be realised in this life by the continual mortification of the natural appetites and the progressive purification of the mind. In the solitude, beyond the frontiers of human society and freed from its distractions and temptations, a man might through grace achieve that detachment from created things that led him in prayer to the supreme encounter with God.

In the first centuries of the Christian era, before Constantine proclaimed the peace of the Church, the ascetical spirit of renunciation was fostered by periodic persecution and the very real possibility of martyrdom. Many Christian congregations contained individual ascetics of both sexes, who renounced marriage and devoted themselves to a life of prayer and service to the deprived. This form of idealism was kept alive, too, by the expectations of the early Church, which stressed the need to live in constant readiness for the hour of divine judgement and the second coming of the Lord, an event that was believed to be imminent: '. . . the appointed time has grown very short; from now on, let those who have wives live as though they had none, and those who buy as though they had no goods, and those who deal with the world as though they had no dealings with it. For the form of this world is passing away.'[2] But the passage of time gradually dampened the urgency of this appeal. In the fourth century, the change from persecution to imperial recognition of the Church brought a sense of security and creeping worldliness in its train, and in this situation those who hankered for a more intense religious commitment were increasingly attracted by the idea of total withdrawal from the community.

The pull of the desert gained added force from the popular esteem that was accorded to the solitary holy man. For as the age of the martyrs passed into historical memory, their role as the heroes of the faith was increasingly occupied in the eyes of devout Christians by the monks. These were the new confessors, 'the athletes of God', who had renounced the security of property and the ordinary comforts of hearth and home to conquer the spirit of the world and scale the heights of contemplative prayer. As Sulpicius Severus wrote of St Martin of Tours, protagonist of the monastic movement in fourth-century Gaul, 'to fast, to keep unceasing vigil, to lacerate the flesh, this also is a martyrdom'.[3] He was echoed in the ninth century by Abbot Smaragdus of Verdun: 'Let no man say, brethren, that in our times there are no combats for martyrs. For our peace has its martyrs also.'[4]

The deserts to which the early ascetics were drawn were those of Egypt, Syria, and Judea. Egypt, in fact, was the cradle of the monastic movement, which gradually spread into all the lands penetrated by the Church. It was on the fringe of the Western Desert, in the hinterland of the city of Alexandria, and in the fertile lands higher up the Nile valley, that there appeared in the course of the fourth century two variant modes of ascetical life, each of which became the source of a distinct and enduring monastic tradition. The first was the way of life adopted by the desert hermits – the eremitical life of the solitaries, which took its name from *eremos*, the Greek word for a desert. Its acknowledged leader and inspiration was St Antony (*c*. 251–356), a Coptic-speaking Christian of the Alexandrian region.

The other and commoner way was the cenobitical life, that is the ascetical life practised within an organised community or monastery, which Greek-speaking Christians called a 'coenobium' – from the word *koinos*, meaning 'common'. According to tradition, the originator of the Christian coenobium, the first fully communal monastery, was St Pachomius (*c*. 292–346), who established a community of monks beside the upper Nile somewhere about the year 320. These two, Antony the hermit and Pachomius the abbot, represent the twin fountainhead of two traditions – the eremitic and the cenobitic – which constantly inspired and reinvigorated distinct types of monastic organisation in the Middle Ages, both in Western Christendom and in the Byzantine East.

The fact that Egypt was the arena for the pioneers of Christian monastic life is readily explicable. It reflects the dominance of the east Roman provinces in the polity of the early Church, and particularly the leading role played by the church of Alexandria in the theological world of the patristic age. Christianity, after all, had arisen and made its first conquests in the teeming cities of the Eastern Empire. Alexandria, with its famous schools of Platonic philosophy and Jewish Rabbinic learning, was a major centre of Christian speculation, a forcing-ground of major heresies, as well as the territory of Clement of Alexandria, Origen and Athanasius, the three greatest of the Greek Fathers. Its large Christian population offered a fertile seed-bed for fresh interpretations of the Christian life. And the intellectual element in the early monastic movement should not be overlooked. For not all the ascetics who fled to the desert were simple and unlearned people. The writings of Origen (184–254) were circulated and read in the desert communities, and Origen, who had had himself castrated for the sake of the kingdom of heaven, provided an ascetical theology of total renunciation. The two worlds of ascetical retreat and doctrinal controversy constantly interpenetrated one another. Athanasius (*c*. 296–373), patriarch of Alexandria and hero of the struggle against the Arian heresy, when driven from his see, found a refuge among the monks of Pachomius. Later, Alexandria was invaded by mobs of excited monks demonstrating in the cause of orthodoxy.

The desert hermits

We do not really know when the flight to the desert began. Antony first embarked on the life of a hermit shortly before the year 270, but it seems that he had predecessors. The *Life of St Antony*, attributed to Athanasius, makes it clear that he was not the first of the anchorites. Athanasius tells us that when he experienced the call to the spiritual life, Antony renounced his inherited property, sought out an aged holy man living as a hermit on the fringe of the village and placed himself under his guidance; and during this phase of his ascetical training he was helped by other solitaries in the district. He was the heir of an already established ascetical tradition. But if he was not the originator of Egyptian monasticism, it was his life-story, as told by Athanasius, that provided the eremitical life with its first and most widely read manifesto and attracted a significant number of imitators. After his spiritual apprenticeship, he retired to live in a tomb within reach of his village. Then, as he attracted growing numbers of sightseers, he withdrew to a ruined fortress on the edge of the desert, and lived there in solitude for twenty years. At the end of this period he emerged as a charismatic teacher and leader of monks: 'from that time', says Athanasius, 'there were monasteries in the mountains and the desert was peopled with monks'.[5] In the final stage of his career he retreated from the growing pressure of his admirers to a remote oasis near the Red Sea, where he died in 356 at a great age.

The saga of Antony represents the earliest traceable age of Egyptian monasticism. By the time of his death, the mountain of Nitria to the west of the Nile delta and the inner desert of Scetis, forty miles to the south, had been settled by colonies of hermits. Similar settlements had also appeared in Palestine and Syria inspired, according to Jerome, by St Hilarion, who had been instructed in the ascetical life by Antony.[6] These colonies contained several hundred solitaries living in caves or huts out of sight, and generally out of earshot, of one another. A group of this kind was called a *laura*, a Greek word meaning a pathway or passage, and apparently derived from the common pathway that connected the caves in the mountain monasteries of Judea. At the centre of the settlement stood a complex of buildings, which included bakeries and a church, where the entire group of hermits gathered on Saturdays and Sundays for common prayer and the weekly celebration of mass. There was also accommodation for guests: something had to be done to provide for the constant flow of pious sightseers, some of whom might prove to be recruits to the hermitage. Even anchorites required a modicum of food and clothing to stay alive, and the leaders of the movement enjoined their disciples to work for their livelihood. Out of the raw materials available in the region of the Nile they produced baskets, mats, ropes and linen, which could be exchanged for basic necessities. The marketing of these products was left to agents in the local villages, so that the monks themselves could preserve their solitude.

The life of the anchorite was not structured for him by any monastic rule. The only form of community support was the weekly gathering for common prayer. The abbot, the father-figure who directed the group, was available for counsel. It was he who trained the neophytes, for it was a cardinal principle of ascetical teaching that the beginner should place himself under the guidance of an experienced instructor. But apart from this, the spirit of the *laura* was intensely individualistic: 'Except a man shall say in his heart', said Abbot Allois, 'I alone and God are in this world, he shall not find peace.'[7] The aspirant was taught how to brave the unbroken solitude of his cell, to meditate, and to engage in lonely combat with his own passions and illusions and with the demons of the waste places, who haunt the literature of the desert.

Fasting, deprivation of sleep, and other forms of bodily mortification were the standard weapons of the ascetic's armoury in his struggle for self-conquest. The novice's resolution was stiffened by tales of the feats accomplished by the heroes of this spiritual warfare. In about the year 420 Palladius wrote down what he had discovered about the lives of the desert anchorites in his *Lausiac History*. He had been a monk himself, though he could not stay the course. He still hankered after the fleshpots; but he garnered some good anecdotes from the brethren. One of these was about the Alexandrian Macarius (d. 393), a giant of the first generation among the hermits of Nitria. Macarius had heard of the superhuman austerities practised by the monks of Pachomius in the Theban desert of upper Egypt and he resolved to outmatch them. So he went to the monastery of Tabennesis, disguised as a man of the world, and sought admission as a novice. The abbot was doubtful of his staying powers in view of his advanced age, but was prepared to let him try. As Lent came on, Macarius observed that some of the brethren fasted for two days together, and one of them for a whole week, while others spent half the night standing in prayer. So he made his dispositions to outdo them all. He took up his stand in a corner, and remained there praying and plaiting mats, without food, drink or sleep, until Easter. This performance caused an outcry among the brethren, who complained to the abbot that this strange old man was making fools of them. But Pachomius fell to prayer, and it was revealed to him who his novice was. All the same, after thanking Macarius for knocking the conceit out of his youngsters, he gently asked him to leave: 'Now therefore return to the place from which you came; we have all been sufficiently edified by you.'[8]

The kind of competitive asceticism that drew a cool response from Pachomius seems to have been a characteristic of the eremitical movement in its early age. Later, wiser counsels prevailed. The classical masters of monastic spirituality discountenanced the more extravagant forms of mortification to be seen in the East. But spectacular feats by individual anchorites continued to excite veneration and feelings of awe among the people. Some of the wildest and most bizarre manifestations of the ascetical spirit appeared in the fifth century among the anchorites of Syria, who inhabited the desert in the region of Antioch and Chalcis. It was here that the most dramatic form of withdrawal from the world was personified by the weird figure of St Simeon the Stylite, who made his residence on top of a pillar, where he remained, exposed to sun and weather, for forty-seven years. Simeon commanded much admiration in the ecclesiastical world of his time, and he even had a few emulators, but his strange feat has no relevance for the history of the monastic tradition.

St Pachomius and the cenobitical life

The example of the desert hermits continued to inspire individuals and groups in the Middle Ages, but the vocation of the hermit was an extremely rare one. Man is a social animal. The life of the solitary was full of difficulties and hazards. Only the strong dare be lonely. Lesser mortals can all too easily sink into mental breakdown or despair. It was easier and safer to pursue the ascetical life of prayer with the support of a community engaged in the same task and within the reassuring framework of a Rule. This, the fully shared life of monks living in an organised community, appeared in upper Egypt almost as soon as the anchoritic movement. Its originator, according to tradition, was Pachomius (c. 292–346), another Coptic-speaking Egyptian, who had been a conscript in the Roman army before his conversion to Christianity. At first, in his quest for self-discovery he was drawn to the life of the anchorites; but after a time the need to organise and direct a colony of disciples that had settled round him persuaded him to create a collective establishment at Tabennesis, the site of a deserted village beside the upper Nile, in the region of the Egyptian Thebes. As recruits multiplied, fresh colonies were planted in the district, some for men, others for women. Each community had its own head, but Pachomius himself presided patriarchally over the whole congregation until his death.

The Pachomian monastery was a large community, numbering several hundred monks or nuns. According to Palladius, the great monastery where Pachomius himself lived, housed thirteen hundred men. Within the walls, which enclosed a wide precinct, a central focus was provided by a church, common refectory, and infirmary. There was also a guest-house, where the Rule required that visitors should be housed in comfort. The residences of the monks consisted of a series of simple houses, laid out with a functional precision reminiscent of the legionary camps Pachomius had known in his youth. Each house contained some twenty monks under the direction of a housemaster or prior, who was responsible for their instruction and spiritual guidance.[9]

The distinctive things about the life of the monastery were its fellowship – the daily round of collective worship in the oratory and the common meal – and an insistence upon total obedience to the commands of the superior. This surrender of personal will to that of a teacher, and the necessity of physical mortification, were things Pachomius himself had learned when, at the outset of his Christian life, he had placed himself under the direction of Palamon, an aged hermit, and both became cardinal principles of the Pachomian ascesis. Another axiom of the founder was the virtue of work. There could be only limited provision for intellectual activities in the Pachomian settlement. Many of the monks were, in any case, unlettered men of peasant origin, who had to be taught to read.[10] But all were required to do manual work. Manual tasks were prescribed because the product could be sold to support the monastery, and because work was a sovereign remedy for the mental state of 'accidie' – that insidious demon of the burning noonday which tempted solitary and cenobite alike to abandon his vocation through boredom and disgust. The Pachomian monks were grouped in their houses according to their skills. Most of them occupied themselves with manufacturing linen and making mats and baskets from the rushes of the Nile, which were ferried down the river to market – the boatmen figure prominently in the Rules of Pachomius. At regular times, the housemasters led the brethren to work in the cornfields and gardens surrounding the monastery, where the food of the community was grown.

St Basil

An important part in taming the ascetical idealism of the desert monks and integrating it into the organisation of the Church was played by St Basil of Caesarea. Basil represents a new kind of monastic convert. Unlike most of the Egyptian ascetics, he was a highly educated man from a professional family, educated in the schools of rhetoric at Caesarea and the academies of Constantinople and Athens. Drawn to the ascetical life, in the years 357–8 he set out on a tour of Palestine and Egypt in search of a spiritual director. He visited the eremitic colonies of Nitria and Scetis; but the deepest impression seems to have been made on him by the Pachomian communities in the Thebaid. On his return home, he retired to a remote place near Annesi in the north of Asia Minor, where he was joined by other hermits. But after experiencing the solitary life for a few years, he concluded that the organised life of the coenobium offered a better way, and he created a cenobitical community at Caesarea, which became a model for many other monasteries in Asia Minor.

As a writer, and in later years as bishop of Caesarea, Basil not only helped to bring the monastic movement under the control of the ecclesiastical hierarchy; he left a lasting mark upon the monastic tradition. He left no 'rule' in the sense of a blueprint for the interior organisation of a monastery, like the Rule of St Benedict. His so-called Longer and Shorter Rules are really a series of disconnected precepts or conferences, set out in the form of question and answer, the random harvest of the years he spent counselling the monks of Cappadocia and Asia Minor. But these, and his letters, reveal what he considered to be the essential principles on which a monastery should be based. In the first place it should be cenobitical – an integrated community. Basil's monks constitute a spiritual family living under one roof, a kind of villa-monastery, as opposed to the scattered *laura* of the desert hermits or the huge subdivided Pachomian colony. The significant thing is that, after touring the eremitical settlements of Judea and Egypt and himself trying his vocation as a solitary recluse, he reached the conclusion that the ascetical life followed in community was better than the life of the anchorite. The reason for this was that the community was based upon the social nature of man and alone provided the opportunity of fulfilling the Christian commandment to love one's neighbour: 'Charity seeks not her own. But the solitary life removed from all others has only one aim – that of serving the ends of the individual concerned. But this is manifestly opposed to the law of charity . . . We have been called in one hope of our calling, are one body and members of one another.' The defect of the solitary life was that it provided no occasion to practise the virtues of humility and patience or to perform practical works of mercy: 'If you live alone, whose feet will you wash?'[11] Basil did not totally reject the authenticity of the hermit's vocation; he recognised that the man who sought freedom in the desert to be alone with the Alone was fulfilling the first and greatest of the commandments, which was to love God; but he regarded the eremitical life as a less perfect fulfilment of the Gospel counsels than the life of the monk in community, where the spiritual gifts of the more advanced members might be passed on to others.

Basil left his mark upon monastic thinking in other ways. His conception of obedience to the head of the community was more subtle and far-reaching than that of Pachomius, and it represented an important refinement of the ascetical tradition. The novice was to renounce his own will and obey the superior in everything, in spirit as well as in act, on the model of Christ, who was 'obedient unto death'. There was no room in Basil's monastery for the individualism and the spectacular ascetical feats of the Egyptian anchorites. The only kinds of mortification allowed were those that the superior had authorised. It was only thus that the fanatic who was bent on taking the kingdom of heaven by storm could be saved from falling into the pit of pride. There is a rationality and moderation in Basil's ascetical teaching that is the hallmark of a cultivated Greek intelligence.

Another theme of Basil's teaching that was to be influential was his insistence upon the virtue of work in the monastery. Work was a means of perfecting the soul as well as supporting the community and providing for the poor. He would have the novice taught a trade, if he did not possess one when he joined the community, preferably one of the sort that produced marketable essentials, such as agriculture, weaving, or shoemaking. Perhaps it was from the monks of the Thebaid that Basil derived his high regard for manual work – it was not a probable inclination for a highly educated Greek. At all events, it was a doctrine that made a deep imprint upon the minds of subsequent monastic legislators.

Although he left no systematic Rule, Basil's collected counsels for the ordering of a cenobitical community gave him a unique status in the Eastern Church, where he came to be regarded as the father of Orthodox monasticism. Nevertheless, despite his preference for the cenobitical life, in the monastic world of the Byzantine Empire the eremitical tradition continued to hold a prominent place in practice and public esteem, alongside that of the organised coenobium. A long series of Orthodox ascetical theologians, from St Maximos the Confessor in the seventh century to St Gregory Palamas in the fourteenth, bears witness to the persistence of the desert ideal. The major centres of Orthodox monasticism, such as the peninsula of Mount Athos, in northern Greece, and the rocky canyons of the Meteora in Thessaly, were peopled by anchorites living in caves as well as by thousands of monks living in cenobitic communities.[12]

The desert tradition transmitted to the West

Knowledge of the monastic movement, which spread across the eastern provinces of the Empire during the fourth century, was transmitted to western Europe through various channels. Interest was awakened by the dissemination of literature about the desert monks, by migration to the West of refugee bishops like Athanasius and of individual ascetics like Cassian, and by accounts brought back by pilgrims and pious sightseers.

It was the literature of Egyptian monasticism that brought the first flood of converts. More than any others, the work that made the deepest and most long-lasting impression upon Western readers was the *Life of St Antony* by Athanasius. He explains that he has written it to give encouragement to the brethren across the seas. And the strange ferment it caused must have fully satisfied his expectations. It was quickly translated into Latin, and by the year 374 Evagrius of Antioch, the friend and patron of Jerome, had improved on the earlier verson with a more elegant translation, for, as he explained, 'a literal translation from one language to another occludes the sense and strangles it, as couchgrass does a field of corn'.[13] It was read with passionate interest in Christian circles at Rome and Milan and at Trier, where the imperial court was located. It was in his house at Milan, in the summer of 386, that Augustine heard an account of it from a visitor who had come from Trier; and it was the story of the desert anchorites that stirred his conscience and brought on the crisis of his conversion. He was only one of the first of a long line of Western Christians who were to fall under the spell of the Antonian desert.

In the course of the following decades, other literary accounts of the lives of the Desert Fathers became available to Latin readers. Stirred by the success of Evagrius, Jerome wrote a colourful *Life of Paul the Hermit*, and translated the Rules of Pachomius. His friend Rufinus of Aquileia, who had settled in a monastery at Jerusalem, translated the *History of the Monks in Egypt* from Greek into Latin. Like the *Lausiac History* of Palladius, this was an account written by a monk – a member of Rufinus's own community – who had made a pilgrimage to Egypt and gathered recollections from the aged anchorites on the spot. There were other travellers, too, who extracted literary capital from their tours of Nitria and the Thebaid, like Postumianus, who supplied Sulpicius Severus with anecdotes about the desert monks for the first book of his *Dialogues*, which he wrote in 430. As time went on, a mass of oral tradition accumulated and gradually assumed written form in the various versions of *Apophthegmata* or Sayings of the Fathers – collections of maxims which circulated in Greek and Coptic and were eventually translated into Latin. But more faithfully than anywhere else, the ethos of the desert and the teaching of the famous abbots were encapsulated in the *Conferences* of the Scythian-monk John Cassian.

About the year 385 Cassian left his monastery at Bethlehem in the company of Germanus to tour the monastic settlements of Egypt. He stayed at Nitria and

Scetis, and sat at the feet of the veterans in their cells. He was a good listener, and years later, when the violent controversy over the theology of Origen had driven him from the East, he settled in the south of Gaul and sat down to distil the wisdom of the anchorite-abbots for the benefit of Western readers. In these conferences the reader is given the freedom of the cells of Scetis and is allowed to listen to the aged masters of the contemplative life talking about their experience. Of course, memory is an incorrigible improver. We cannot be sure how much Cassian's recollections improved upon the discourses of the Egyptian abbots, for twenty-five turbulent years intervened before he committed them to writing. But the work became a classic of Latin spirituality – part of every monk's essential reading. Cassian was the maestro whose writing taught St Benedict and his successors the ascetical lore of the East. His *Conferences* provided an inexhaustible treasury of axioms and reflections on the techniques and trials of the interior life of prayer; and the *Institutes*, a treatise he wrote for a community of monks he helped to found at Apt in Provence, contained the first body of instruction on the cenobitic life to be produced in western Europe. Together these two works did much to form the spirit and shape the pattern of early Western monasticism; and they continued to provide daily food for meditation in the cloisters of the Middle Ages.

The first Western monks

According to Jerome, it was the visit of Athanasius to Trier and Rome during his years of exile (335–7 and 339–46) that gave Western monasticism the kiss of life. Certainly, he was an enthusiastic propagandist for the ideals of the Egyptian monks; but the process of cross-fertilisation between the two traditions was too complex to be the work of a single individual.[14] Probably Hilary of Poitiers (*c.* 315–67) played just as big a part in transplanting Eastern monastic practices to the lands of the Western Empire. Hilary had been driven into exile in Asia Minor by the ascendancy of the Arian heresy at the imperial court, and during his enforced travels he must have encountered the monastic movement. On his return, he sponsored a group of ascetics in his episcopal city of Poitiers, and he became the patron and mentor of St Martin of Tours, who settled in Gaul about the year 360.

Martin is the first major figure in Gallic monasticism. He had had a career in the Roman army before his conversion. Having decided to adopt the life of an anchorite, he installed himself in a cell near Milan, where he remained until the hostility of the Arian bishop persuaded him to migrate to Gaul. The reputation of Hilary drew him to Poitiers, and it was at Ligugé, in the vicinity of the town, that he settled in a hermitage, which became a focal point for like-minded souls. Martin's association with Hilary made him widely known and led to his appointment to the see of Tours, but his elevation to the episcopate in no way diminished his devotion to the monastic life. Even as a bishop he persisted in maintaining the life-style of a hermit; and after the year 372 he organised his disciples as a colony

Rutilius spoke for the cultivated pagans. But even Christian society at Rome remained cool towards the practice of ascetical withdrawal from society that was advocated by Jerome.[18] Despite the promotion by Athanasius and the example of St Martin, many bishops regarded the monastic movement with mistrust. This was heightened by the conspicuous and sometimes violent part played by monks in the theological controversies that rent the Eastern Church. The increasingly public role that the monks were assuming seemed to pose a threat to the hierarchical order of the Christian community. In 451 the Council of Chalcedon decreed that monasteries were subject to the jurisdiction of bishops, whose approval must be obtained for any new foundations, and insisted that monks should not interfere in ecclesiastical business.[19]

The mistrust was not all on one side. In the East, the monastic movement had sprung up alongside the secular Church, but independently of it. The communities of Nitria could call on the sacramental services of priests from the vicinity, but the movement did not derive its inspiration from clerical leadership. As was explained by the monk who wrote the earliest Coptic *Life of Pachomius*, 'our father did not want clerics in his monasteries for fear of jealousy and vain glory'. Although he was deeply versed in the Scriptures, Pachomius remained a layman, and he hid himself away when Athanasius on one of his visits to the Thebaid proposed to ordain him.[20] 'The monk', wrote Cassian, 'ought to flee women and bishops';[21] and he warned the brethren against the diabolical temptation of seeking clerical office out of a desire to bring spiritual help to others. The author of the *Life of St Romanus*, the fifth-century founder of the monastery of Condat in the Jura, was even fiercer. He reserves some of his best invective for monks who get ordained: 'gaining clerical office out of rabid ambition, they are straight away inflated with pride and exalt themselves, not only over their worthier contemporaries but even over their elders – mere youths, who for their juvenile vanity ought to be put in their place and whipped'.[22] Ecclesiastical office was regarded as part of that world of secular distractions that the monk had renounced.

All the same, unless it was to suffer the fate of all fringe movements, monasticism had to be domesticated and brought under the roof of the institutional Church. Its authenticity as a divinely ordained paradigm of the Christian life had to be recognised. It needed episcopal approval and encouragement. Athanasius had already pointed the way. At the height of the Arian dispute, when forced to abandon his see, he had found a refuge among the monks of the Thebaid and had become an admirer and devoted friend. Augustine, after his elevation to the African see of Hippo, lent his immense authority to the idea that the proper lifestyle for a bishop was monastic. And the *Life of St Martin* pointed the same moral. Thus a dangerous dichotomy between the ascetical movement and the ecclesiastical hierarchy was averted. Several monasteries of Gaul and Italy attracted the patronage and protection of bishops. Early in the fifth century, communities of clergy following a monastic regime were serving bishops at Vercelli and Aquileia, and at Rome the liturgical offices in the Lateran basilica were executed by a community of monks – the first of a group of basilican monasteries – under papal patronage.[23]

In fact, despite Cassian's warning, monasteries came to be a favoured recruiting ground for zealous pastors. Honoratus left Lérins to become bishop of Arles, and in 429 he was followed in the see by Hilary, who had been one of his monastic disciples. In the following centuries the monk-bishop, from the Irish Aidan to the English Boniface, played a major role in evangelising the Germanic peoples of the North. Monasticism was thus integrated into the structure of the Church. But monks in general remained part of the lay section of the Christian community. It was some time before it became a common practice for those who entered a monastery to be ordained.

By the fifth century then, the ascetical tradition of the Eastern desert had been transmitted to the West. Monasticism had struck roots in Italy and southern Gaul. The writings of Cassian had supplied the Western ascetical movement with a theology. But it was not until the sixth century that the first treatises appeared that offered a coherent plan for a monastic community. The earliest of these were the Rules composed by Caesarius of Arles, St Benedict, and the unknown 'Master' who provided him with a literary model. Those of Caesarius were compiled in Gaul, those of Benedict and the Master in Italy. All of them drew deeply upon the oriental tradition.

Notes

1. *Epistulae, PL* 58, 583.
2. *I Cor.* vii, 29–31.
3. *Sulpicii Severi Epistulae, CSEL* 1, ii, 144. For Jerome, the monk's profession was a kind of second baptism; the austerity of the monastic life made it analogous to martyrdom: P. Antin, 'Saint Jerome' in *Théologie de la vie monastique (Théologie* 49, Vienna, 1961), pp. 191–9; J. N. D. Kelly, *Jerome: His Life, Writings and Controversies* (1975), pp. 138–40.
4. *Diadema Monachorum, PL* 102, 688.
5. *Vita S. Antonii, PG* 26, 866. For Antonian monasticism see Derwas J. Chitty, *The Desert a City* (1966), chapter 1, and the works there referred to.
6. For primitive monasticism in Palestine see Chitty, pp. 14–16.
7. *Apophthegmata Patrum, PG* 65, 134. For extracts from the Sayings of the Fathers in translation see Helen Waddell, *The Desert Fathers* (1936).
8. *Historia Lausiaca, PL* 73, 1116.
9. The Rules of St Pachomius are translated by A. Veilleux, *Pachomian Koinonia* II (Kalamazoo, Michigan, 1981), pp. 141–67; for the Lives of St Pachomius *ibid.* vol. 1.
10. Veilleux II, p. 166.
11. *Regulae Fusius Tractatae, Interrrogatio vii, PG* 31, 934; translated in W. K. Lowther Clarke, *The Ascetical Works of St Basil* (1925). See also the same author's *St Basil the Great* (1913); and B. Gain, *L'église de Cappadoce au IVe siècle d'après la correspondance de Basile de Césarée (Orientalia Christiana Analecta* 225, Rome, 1985).
12. On the Byzantine monastic tradition see J. M. Hussey, *Church and Learning in the Byzantine Empire 867–1185* (1937); D. M. Nicol, *Meteora: The Rock Monasteries of Thessaly* (1963).
13. *Evagrii ad Innocentium prologus, PL* 73, 125–6.

14. For the process by which the monastic lore of Egypt and Syria was transmitted to the West see R. Lorenz, 'Die Anfänge des abendländischen Mönchtums im 4. Jahrhundert', *Zeitschrift für Kirchengeschichte* 77 (1966), pp. 1–61; Owen Chadwick, *John Cassian* (1950).

15. *Sulpicii Severi Dialogi* i, CSEL 1, ii, 186.

16. Kelly, pp. 129–40.

17. *Claudii Rutilii Namatiani De Reditu Suo*, ed. L. Mueller (Leipzig, 1870), 11. 440–8. For a translation see H. Isbell, *The Last Poets of Imperial Rome* (1971), p. 233.

18. Kelly, pp. 104–15.

19. *Decrees of the Ecumenical Councils*, ed. G. Alberigo and N. Tanner (Georgetown, 1990) I, p. 89.

20. Veilleux I, pp. 47–8, 51–2.

21. *Instituta* xi, 18, CSEL 17, 203. On Cassian's view of clerical office as a form of temptation see *Collationes* i, 20; CSEL 13, 31.

22. *Vita S. Romani* in *Vie des pères du Jura*, ed. F. Martine (*Sources chrétiennes* 142, Paris, 1968), p. 262. The whole question of the relationship of the early monastic movement to the ecclesiastical hierarchy has been investigated by P. Rousseau, *Ascetics, Authority and the Church, in the Age of Jerome and Cassian* (1978).

23. G. Jenal, *Italia Ascetica atque Monastica. Das Asketen und Mönchtum in Italien von den Anfängen bis zur Zeit der Langobarden* (Stuttgart, 1995) I, pp. 134–6. This is now the authoritative account of early monastic foundation in Italy.

2

THE RULE OF ST BENEDICT

St Benedict and his biographer

For many centuries in the medieval West the Rule for Monks composed by St Benedict provided the standard pattern of monastic observance. Richly endowed, and sometimes exploited by lay rulers, the great Benedictine abbeys came to occupy a prominent position in the social landscape of Europe as land-owning corporations, ecclesiastical patrons, employers of labour, and centres of learning. But we have to be on our guard against a tendency to project the images of a later period backwards upon the earlier age when the Rule was only slowly establishing its reputation. In his own day, St Benedict (c. 480–550), the patriarch of Western monks, was a quite obscure Italian abbot, and we know surprisingly little about the origins of his Rule.

In many ways the first half of the sixth century, when he lived, is a bad period for literary sources. The Roman Empire in the West had been succeeded by a cluster of unstable barbarian kingdoms ruled by Germanic warlords. Italy had been subjected to a century of settlement by the Ostrogoths, at the end of which the peninsula was plunged into a prolonged and destructive war by Justinian's effort to recover it for the East Roman Empire. Siege and counter-siege had gone far to reducing the city of Rome to ruins, inhabited by a much shrunken population. During this troubled period the West produced little in the way of historical writing that could be compared with the literary histories of antiquity. 'Among all our people', lamented Gregory of Tours, when he took up his pen to fill the gap, 'there is not a man to be found who can write a book about the happenings of today.' By contrast, Gregory's contemporaries produced a rich crop of 'biographies' in the literary genre that had been pioneered by St Athanasius and Sulpicius Severus – the hagiographical Lives of saints, designed to promote their cultus and stimulate popular devotion. It is to a work of this kind that we owe what little we know about the author of the Benedictine Rule.

We depend in fact upon a single source – a *Life of St Benedict* written by Pope Gregory the Great about the year 593–4,[1] some forty-five years after Benedict's death. Attempts have sometimes been made to reconstruct a kind of identikit character study by examining his Rule, but modern textual criticism has shown most such efforts to be worthless: the very passages that were once thought to express the personal ideas of the author have been shown to be derivative. For St Benedict's life-story we have no alternative but to rely upon the 'biography' which constitutes the second book of Gregory's *Dialogues*. These are a collection of Lives of Italian abbots and bishops cast, according to a well-established literary convention, in the form of dialogues between a questioner and his informant.

It was the *Dialogues* that launched the cultus of St Benedict, for the book enjoyed immense popularity in the Middle Ages; and it is the earliest reference to him that we have. It evidently contains all that was known about him in Rome at the end of the sixth century; possibly rather more than was known. For Gregory's work is a piece of hagiography. It represents Benedict as both a holy man and a powerful wonder-worker or thaumaturge. His prayers conjure a spring from a barren cliff-top, enable his disciple, Maurus, to run on the surface of a lake, and restore to life children who have died by mishap. By contrast with the miraculous matter, there is a shortage of verifiable detail and a frustrating absence of chronological landmarks, except perhaps for an alleged visit of Cassino by the Goth Totila shortly before his entry to Rome.[2] These failings, and the lack of any contemporary source to corroborate Gregory's account, have caused some scholars to dismiss it as a work of allegory or pure fiction, and even to question the historical existence of St Benedict.[3]

Such comprehensive scepticism is unjustified. We must not allow Gregory's concern with miracles to distort our evaluation of his work. His purpose in writing the *Dialogues* was, of course, didactic; and the miraculous anecdotes were an integral part of his message. His object was to record and celebrate the conquests made by Christian asceticism in Italy in the early decades of the sixth century, when the country was under Gothic rule – to show that Italy, too, had its saints and heroes of the ascetical life, like Egypt. In fact, he was doing for Italy what Sulpicius had done for Gaul in the previous century, and the work of Sulpicius suggested a literary model. There, too, were to be found anecdotes about holy abbots and, as the centre-piece, an extended *Life of St Martin*. The heroic saga of the Desert Fathers was being repeated in Gaul. Gregory's *Dialogues* carried the same message for Italy. The Roman population, impoverished and humiliated under a barbarian regime, and further demoralised by plague and by Justinian's short-lived *reconquista*, was to understand that it had not been abandoned by God. The sanctity of its monks and bishops, and the marvels God had worked for them, were grounds for hope in the future. The theme gained added poignancy from

Gregory's own regret for his lost monastic vocation and his lament for the collapse of the old social order.

Thus miraculous signs were essential to Gregory's purpose. The more sophisticated part of Gregory's readership, consisting of the clergy and monks, would have recognised their symbolic significance. For less cultivated readers, they simply accorded with a popular conviction, widespread in late antiquity, that the holy man wielded mysterious powers over the forces of nature. For the historian, the important part of the miracle stories is their context, and there is no reason think this was fictitious. Gregory, after all, was writing oral history for a live Italian readership. If his readers were to accept his message, he could neither invent the topographical setting of the anecdotes, nor could he invent personalities who had existed within living memory. Author and reader alike were surrounded by the visual evidence of the recent past. Cassino and Subiaco were lying ruinous and deserted, as St Benedict had prophesied. There were still living those who could remember the life at Cassino before the Lombards burnt it, and who had known the founder. Some of them are named by Gregory as the source of his information.

Gregory tells us that Benedict was born in central Italy in the province of Nursia – the conventional date of 480 is pure surmise – and was sent to Rome for his education in liberal letters. But, distressed by the debauched life of his fellow-students, he abandoned the schools, 'knowingly ignorant and wisely untaught', and fled with his nurse to the village of Afide, some twenty miles away. From there he withdrew to the solitude near Subiaco, a deserted spot in the Sabine Hills, where he lived in a cave for three years. In ascetical tradition, this initial retreat into solitude became a topos – a necessary phase in the process of dissociation from society and the reorientation of the personality towards God.

During this time Benedict was supplied with bread by a monk named Romanus from a nearby monastery, who also instructed him in the practices of the ascetical life. Gradually, disciples settled round him, and he organised them into groups of twelve, appointing an abbot over each group. Finally, he migrated to the hilltop of Monte Cassino which towers above the Via Latina midway between Rome and Naples, and there he constructed a fully cenobitical monastery, which he directed for the rest of his life.

He died, Gregory seems to indicate, some time between the years 546 and 550, and was buried at Cassino. In the *Dialogues* Gregory makes only a single reference to St Benedict's Rule: 'He wrote a Rule for monks remarkable for its discretion and the lucidity of its language. If anyone wishes to know more about his life and conversation, he can find all the facts of the master's teaching in this same institution of the Rule, for the holy man could not teach otherwise than he lived.'[4] This is the earliest known reference to the Rule and it is all that Gregory has to say about it. He may himself have read it, but there is nothing else in the *Dialogues* to show that he had done so.[5]

The Rule and its sources

Among the innumerable manuscripts of the Rule, the earliest extant is probably one that was copied in Anglo-Saxon England about the year 750, which is now at Oxford in the Bodleian Library. But a more precious copy is one that survives in a manuscript of Saint-Gall. This is a copy made at Aachen early in the ninth century from a codex that Theodemar, the abbot of Monte Cassino, had sent to Charlemagne. Charles had written to request an authentic text for use in his dominions, and the codex that Theodemar sent him was copied at Cassino from the manuscript that was believed to be St Benedict's own autograph. It seems then that we have in the Saint-Gall manuscript a text derived at only one remove from the author's original – a rare thing for a widely disseminated text of such antiquity.

Although we cannot be sure when Benedict compiled it, there are internal signs that the work in its existing form was not composed all at once, but was amended and expanded over a period of some time in the light of his experience. This is indicated by a number of dislocations in the logical sequence of the subject-matter and by the fact that the last seven chapters appear to have been added to the original conclusion as an afterthought. The Rule in fact consists of a prologue and seventy-three chapters, and, apart from the occasional discontinuities in the argument, it sets out a coherent and detailed plan for the organisation of a monastic community. The monastery it describes is a fully cenobitical society, living in a single building or complex of buildings, under the direction of an abbot, who is elected by the brethren. Those who seek admission to it are required to pass a year in the noviciate to test their suitability and perseverance. Following this, they totally renounce all personal property, and take vows binding them to observe the rules of the monastic life and to remain in the community until death.

The prologue and first seven chapters of the Rule comprise an exhortatory treatise on the ascetical life, explaining its aims and the characteristic virtues the monk should strive to cultivate, foremost among which are obedience and humility. The following thirteen chapters contain detailed instructions for the order of divine service – the regular round of prayer, readings, and psalmody, which constituted the framework of the monk's day. After this there is a series of chapters dealing with such constitutional matters as the election of the abbot and the role of other monastic officers, regulations for the hours of sleep, manual work, and reading, and for meals; and intercalated among these various instructions is a penitential code, which lays down penalties for breaches of the monastic discipline. Much attention is given to the reception and training of recruits. It is impossible to do justice in a few words to the wealth of detail and the subtlety of insight contained in Benedict's treatise. Some of his cardinal ideas will be examined below. As a whole, the Rule offered a realistic and eminently practical guide both to the government of a cenobitical community and to the spiritual life of the monk.

Although internal evidence suggests that the Rule was composed in the years soon after 535, we know very little about the circumstances in which St Benedict worked. The sources of his teaching pose a special problem. One thing at least has been made clear by modern critical scholarship: it is no longer possible to regard the Rule as the isolated work of an original genius. It formed one of a group of closely interrelated monastic Rules that were composed in Italy and southern Gaul in the first half of the sixth century. Close to it in time were the two Rules – the one for women and the other for men – written by Caesarius of Arles (*c.* 470–542).

Like most Gallic bishops of his time, Caesarius was an offspring of the Gallo-Roman aristocracy. He had taken monastic vows at Lérins as a lad of twenty, but his health could not stand the life. He was sent to Arles, where he went to the schools and the bishop, who was a relative of his, ordained him. But his heart remained at Lérins. They had to drag him out of hiding to make him a bishop; but years later, he compensated for his lost vocation by founding and overseeing a community of nuns outside the walls of the city. It was for them that he wrote the first and longer of his Rules after persistent nagging by their abbess.[6]

The document he produced consisted of a rather disorganised collection of precepts and an order of psalmody for use in the divine office. Many of the instructions on such matters as the noviciate, the renunciation of personal ownership, and lifelong stability, were cardinal principles adopted by St Benedict, and there are verbal echoes in the Rule which suggest that he knew the work of Caesarius. But the borrowing was not all in one direction. Caesarius knew Cassian's *Institutes* and the Rules of Pachomius, and he had clearly read the Italian *Rule of the Master*, a text which, as we shall see in a moment, provided Benedict with his major literary source. These complex literary relationships show that in the sixth century Italy and Provence formed part of a single monastic world, united by a common body of ascetical doctrine.

Some of the literary products of this milieu have been identified by modern scholarship, such as the Rule for monks composed by Eugippius.[7] Eugippius was abbot of a monastery at Lucullanum near Sorrento. His other work, a *Life of St Severin*, was written some twenty years before St Benedict founded his community at Cassino. It was probably in one of the monasteries south of Rome that, soon after the year 500, an unknown abbot wrote the *Rule of the Master.*[8] It is now generally accepted by scholars that this text was St Benedict's chief literary source.

Benedict's debt to the anonymous Master was a heavy one. He derived from him not only most of his basic principles and organisational details; some of the most famous passages in the Rule, such as the chapters on obedience and the grades of humility, were taken over verbatim; and many other passages were transplanted with little change. In fact, all the essentials of St Benedict's Rule are to be found in the work of his unknown predecessor who, to judge by his liturgical instructions, was writing some forty years earlier. Appropriation of other people's work without acknowledgement was commonplace among medieval writers. To us it is plagiarism; to them it was a mark of humility and deference to superior wisdom. When Benedict decided to compile a book of instruction for his monks at Cassino it would have seemed perfectly natural to model his Rule on a treatise composed by some other acknowledged and admired veteran of the ascetical life.

St Benedict emerges then not as a solitary genius with a unique gift for monastic legislation, but rather as the representative of a school of ascetical teaching current in sixth-century Italy, which derived its primary inspiration from Egypt. He does not stand alone. Behind him we can dimly discern a shadowy company of abbots and hermits inhabiting the hill-places east and south of Rome and the offshore islands, who were linked to one another by personal contact and the exchange of books. Nevertheless, it was his Rule, and not that of the anonymous Master, that gradually won universal recognition in western Europe. What were the reasons for this?

Gregory's biography was certainly a major factor. It made him famous and aroused interest in the Rule. But its success cannot be explained solely by Gregory's propaganda. The intrinsic merits of Benedict's treatise can have been no less important in promoting its circulation. For he was no slavish copyist. Both structurally and stylistically his Rule is better than the model he used. He and the Master both wrote in the *lingua vulgaris* – the native Latin spoken and written in southern Europe in the sixth century, as opposed to the literary Latin of the classical age. But Benedict's language, where he is not copying from his source, is terser and his phraseology is more finely chiselled than the Master's. It is tinged with the juridical vocabulary of the law courts.[9] Again and again he arrests and pleases the reader with a lapidary phrase or epigram: 'Idleness is the enemy of the soul'; 'Wine is certainly not suitable for monks'; or 'Let nothing have precedence over divine service.' By contrast, the Master's treatise is rather verbose, rambling, and poorly co-ordinated.

It was not only stylistically that Benedict improved on his source. His thought is more refined and his argument is less cluttered with irrelevant detail. Also, at several points where he is discussing the government of the monastery, he reveals a more genial spirit than the Master's and a greater tolerance of human weakness. 'We hope', he writes, 'we shall ordain nothing that is harsh or burdensome.'[10] In both treatises the sheet-anchor of the community is the personality of the abbot, and here both authors were clearly influenced by Roman notions of paternal authority. But the authority of Benedict's abbot is less autocratic. In decision-making he is instructed to solicit the opinion of the whole community, including its most junior members, whereas the Master insists that no one is to proffer advice unless it is asked for. And Benedict's abbot is elected by the brethren, whereas the Master's abbot is given the power to designate his successor. Unquestioning obedience to the will of the superior is demanded by both Rules, but Benedict tempers this doctrine with a repeated emphasis upon the bond of mutual love between head and members. All in all, his Rule is gentler and more humane than its prototype.

The monk's profession according to the Rule

St Benedict's idea of the monastic life is completely cenobitic. His community of monks is a spiritual family living under one roof, or at any rate round one patio, under an abbot who is father to the community – in fact, a villa–monastery. Indeed, the classical layout of the Benedictine abbeys and priories of the Middle Ages was descended from the plan of the Roman country villa of late antiquity.

Following the Master, Benedict allows for the vocation of the hermit; but he obviously considers it a rare one, fraught with particular dangers. Those who are called to it must first undergo their training by sharing the life of the monastic community – 'who not in the first fervour of the ascetical life, but in the daily testing of the monastery have been taught to fight the devil, and go out well armed from the battle-line of the brethren to the solitary combat of the desert'.[11] The military imagery is a pervasive feature of early monastic literature. The spiritual life of the monk was a ceaseless warfare against demons, who roved the world seeking to exploit the weaknesses of man's fallen nature. The anchorite needed to be well equipped for his lonely confrontation with the rulers of the world's darkness.

Benedict's cautious approval of hermits was not lost on his disciples of later times. It was not unusual for a Benedictine abbey of the Middle Ages to have one or two members of its community who were living as hermits at some remove from the parent monastery. As late as the fourteenth century, the cathedral priory of Durham dispatched a series of monk-solitaries to occupy a cell on the island of Inner Farne, off the Northumbrian coast. But it was not for people like this that Benedict composed his Rule. He was writing for the cenobites – 'the brave race who conduct their warfare subject to a Rule and under an abbot'.[12]

There are several hints in the Rule that he had a wider monastic public in mind than his own community at Cassino. But although he included advice for other communities living in different conditions from his own, he did not envisage anything that could be called a monastic order. The kind of monastery described by the Rule was an autonomous unit, economically self-supporting, and having no constitutional links with any other religious house. A man who sought to become a monk must needs knock on the gate of a particular community and if, after a period of trial lasting not less than a year, he was admitted to membership, he promised to remain in that establishment until his death.

The ritual set out in the Rule for receiving new brethren throws much light on Benedict's thoughts. The postulant was not to be allowed easy entry. He had to persist in his request for four or five days before the door was opened to him, and he had then to complete a year's probation in the cell of the novices. If he stayed the course, he made his profession in the oratory in the presence of the assembled community. He took a vow of stability, undertaking to persevere in the same house for the rest of his life, a vow to embrace the religious life, and a vow of obedience. He then prostrated himself before each member of the community in turn. If he had any property, he was required either to distribute it to the poor or to confer it on the monastery by a solemn deed of gift.

Benedict's insistence on the need for stability was not novel. 'A monk out of his enclosure', said St Antony, 'is a fish out of water.' And Caesarius agreed with him. What was new was the incorporation of the principle into the monk's vows. Its importance for Benedict is apparent from the fierceness with which he condemns the *gyrovagi* – the wandering monks, who were constantly on the move, trading on the hospitality of other houses, 'concerning whose wretched way of life it is better to be silent than to speak'. The Master had been less reticent: his Rule includes a Rabelaisian picture of the gluttonous wanderers descending upon their impoverished host and picking him bare before moving on. The professional guest – whether he was a wandering monk or a vagabond clerk – was a constant nuisance to the medieval Church. For centuries bishops and councils fulminated against him in vain.

Benedict's uncharacteristic sharpness on the subject is understandable: the wanderer not only disrupted the cohesion of the brethren by his restlessness; by abusing hospitality he exploited one of the most solemn obligations imposed by the Rule, for Benedict insisted that a monastery should receive a guest as though he were Christ himself. A guest-house was an adjunct of every abbey. Of course, a monk might be sent elsewhere under higher orders without detriment to the general principle of stability. So Abbot Hadrian was dispatched to England by the pope with Archbishop Theodore of Tarsus to make sure he introduced none of his dubious Greek customs into the English Church, and the Irish monks, who were notorious wanderers, evangelised Northumbria and planted monasteries across the face of Europe from Saint-Gall to Bobbio.

Another feature of Benedict's thought that is highlighted by the instructions for novices is his thoroughly Roman insistence upon the absolute sovereignty of a written Rule. The law of Rome was a written law – at the time that the Rule was taking shape in his mind the jurists of the Emperor Justinian were busy codifying the great mass of classical legislation and jurisprudence. So it was that he ordained that the would-be monk should have the Rule read to him repeatedly during the year of his noviciate, and after two months he was to be told, 'Here is the law under which you wish to fight; if you can observe it, enter; if you cannot, depart freely.'[13] In other monasteries the customs of the house were determined by the superior; but in Benedict's plan the Rule is sovereign, and even the abbot is allowed no discretion to depart from it. He is warned of his duty to maintain it in every detail. Because the Rule reflected the social customs and liturgical practices of the sixth century, there were bound to be later modifications. But the essence of Benedict's idea impressed itself upon the Western ascetical tradition. Men came to think of monks as people whose religious life was governed by a written code: the monastic life came to be described as the 'regular life' – life according to a Rule.

When the monk made his profession he was required to renounce personal ownership completely: 'from that day he will not even have proprietorship of his own body'.[14] All property was held by the community in common. The individual must regard nothing as his own. Even the possession of a stylus and writing-tablets required the abbot's permission. Property is an extension of personality. Its renunciation was a radical act of self-negation that the Gospel had commended to those who sought spiritual perfection. But it did not involve destitution where it was made within the context of a society enjoying corporate ownership.

Benedict makes it clear that he expected a monastery to possess buildings and land. He assumes that in most cases the labour on the estate will be performed by tenants or servants, though where poverty forced the monks to help gather the harvest they are told to do so without grumbling, 'for then are they truly monks when they live by the labour of their hands as the Apostles and Fathers did before them'.[15] But it is unlikely that he visualised monasteries possessing great wealth. Monks were *ex professo* 'the poor of Christ', and as such they attracted support from pious benefactors. Yet the poverty of the individual living in a spacious and wealthy institution tended to be psychological rather than material. Centuries of landed endowment turned many abbeys into rich and powerful corporations, displaying all the characteristics of group acquisitiveness. Was wealth on this scale compatible with the Rule? In the twelfth century, the question was put to Cluny by St Bernard and other monastic reformers. 'In saying any property', writes Peter the Venerable defensively, 'the Rule makes no exception. Monks hold these things in a quite different way . . . they exist as having nothing, yet possessing all things.'[16] It was a stock answer. But the question could not be so easily silenced in a society where those vowed to personal poverty enjoyed the security and comfort of palatial surroundings and good food, while most of those in the outside world were living at subsistence level.

Following the teachings of the Eastern masters, Benedict makes obedience the cardinal principle of the monastic life. Along with stability and 'conversion of ways', it was the subject of the monk's threefold vow. Its significance for Benedict is shown by its place in the opening words of the Rule: 'Hear, O son, the precepts of the master: so that by the labour of obedience you may return to Him from whom, through the sloth of disobedience, you fell away.' So the monk's task was to undo the primeval act of man's disobedience to the divine will by modelling himself on Christ, who 'was obedient unto death'. The monastic life began with the intention to renounce self-will and to place oneself under the will of a superior, who represented the person of Christ. What was demanded was not mere outward conformity, but the inner assent of the will to the commands of the abbot. Obedience must be prompt, willing, and without murmuring. The sixty-eighth chapter of the Rule raises the question of what a brother should do if he is ordered to undertake something too burdensome or impossible. He is told he should receive the command gently and obediently; and if the task required seems utterly beyond his powers, he is to explain patiently to his superior the reason for his inability to carry out the instruction, but without resisting or contradicting. If, after his explanation, the superior persists, the monk is to obey, trusting in the help of God. The conundrum was a classical one in the training of ascetics. Total docility to the will of the master was the essential safeguard against spiritual pride.

It followed from such an uncompromising doctrine of obedience that the personality of the abbot was the linchpin of the monastic community. St Benedict's abbot cannot lawfully command anything that is contrary to the law of God or to the Rule, but otherwise his discretion is absolute. He can appoint and dismiss subordinates, allocate punishments, and direct the relations of the monastery with the outside world as he thinks best. The Rule urges him to take the advice of the brethren before making policy decisions, but he is not bound by it. Constitutionally then, St Benedict's monastery is a paternal autocracy tempered only slightly by an obligation to listen to advice.

Nevertheless, the abbot is much more than an absolute ruler. He has a pastoral role towards his community. He is the teacher, confessor, and spiritual guide of his monks. This side of his role is illuminated by Benedict's instructions for Lenten observance. Each monk is to decide what form of mortification he is going to undertake; he must then propose it to the abbot and only undertake it with his permission. Thus, by performing his ascetical acts under obedience the monk is protected against spiritual pride or complacency. As the pastor of his community, the abbot is reminded that at the Judgement he will have to render account for their souls. The Rule constantly warns him against ruling tyrannically or harshly. He is to regard himself as the servant of the brethren rather than their master; he should study to make himself loved rather than feared.

The authoritarian character of the regime is softened not only by St Benedict's insistence upon governing with counsel but also by his provisions for selecting the head of the monastery. The abbot is to be chosen by the brethren themselves and, usually, it is implied, from their own number. Even the most junior member of the community is to be considered eligible if his prudence and learning make him suitable. Once elected, the abbot is presented to the bishop for consecration, and he holds office for life. Benedict allows for active intervention by the bishop or by neighbouring abbots only in an emergency situation, where a lax or disorderly community has elected a candidate who is obviously unworthy. In such a case, they may have an abbot imposed upon them, but otherwise the choice remains with the monks.

In a community of any size the abbot would need assistants to help him govern the monastery. The Rule refers to a provost or prior, and several other officers – deans, a cellarer, who is in charge of provisioning the establishment, a gatekeeper, a novice-master, and brethren to manage the guest-house and the infirmary. Benedict's main concern here seems to be to preserve the monarchic regime of the abbot from any dilution. All the monastic officers are to be chosen by him and directly subordinated to him.

In the great Benedictine abbeys of the Middle Ages, where the abbot was a prelate constantly taken from his community by public duties and the need to supervise daughter-houses, the effective head of the brethren was the claustral prior. But in the Rule St Benedict contemplates the prior with some misgiving as a possible source of discord: 'some there be, puffed up with the malignant spirit of pride, who reckon themselves second abbots'.[17] He prefers a system of deans, each of whom is placed by the abbot in charge of a group of ten monks. The deans were, so to speak, non-commissioned officers – name and rank were in fact derived from the imperial army, and the system was adopted in the Pachomian monasteries of Egypt. The Abbot Smaragdus, commenting on the Rule in the ninth century, observed that the deans were not merely rulers of their sections; they were their spiritual mentors and should know the inmost thoughts of their charges. Smaragdus wrote from experience, for the system was still practised in the Carolingian monasteries, but it hardly outlived him. In the reformed abbeys of the eleventh century, the devolution of authority followed different lines, determined by economic and administrative convenience.

The monk's life according to the Rule

'We must', wrote Benedict in his preface, 'create a *scola* for the Lord's service.' In the language of the sixth century the word *scola* had a military as well as an academic sense. It meant a special regiment or *corps d'élite*. In the early Middle Ages the borgo of Rome – the region of the city that lay outside the Aurelian walls between St Peter's and the Tiber – was defended by *scolae* or units of militia, supplied by the various nationalities settled in the district. Benedict was using the word in this sense. His monastery was not a place of quiet retreat or leisure, nor a school in the academic sense; it was a kind of combat unit, in which the recruit was trained and equipped for his spiritual warfare under an experienced commander – the abbot. The objective was the conquest of sensuality and self-will so as to make a man totally receptive to God.

For this purpose the Rule prescribed a carefully ordered routine of prayer, work, and study, which filled the day, varying only according to the liturgical year and the natural seasons. It was a regime of strict discipline but, wrote Benedict, casting an eye over his shoulder at the fiercer austerities of the Eastern ascetics, there was to be 'nothing harsh or burdensome'. His was 'a little Rule for beginners'. And in fact the timetable made no intolerable demands. It allowed eight hours of sleep in the winter and six hours, with an afternoon siesta, in the summer. The allowance of food, if not lavish, was adequate. The eating of meat was forbidden except to the sick, but a meal could include two or three dishes of cooked vegetables, with bread and a measure of wine. If, however, the brethren lived in a region where wine was not to be had, they were to accept the fact without grumbling. 'We read', observed Benedict, 'that wine is certainly not for monks'.[18] Yet here, as elsewhere in the Rule, he was willing to make concessions to human weakness.

The first task of the monastic life was prayer in common – the singing of divine service in the oratory, what Benedict calls the Work of God or *Opus Dei*. This provided the basic framework of the day and everything else was fitted round it. Following the Rule of the Master, but with significant variants, Benedict gives elaborate instructions for the celebration of these daily services, which are of great interest to the historian of Christian worship, as they are the earliest detailed description of the divine office that we have. It had long been the common practice in the greater churches to conduct public prayers daily at dawn and in the evening; these were the offices of Lauds and Vespers. By St Benedict's time, the monastic communities had added to these services and evolved a daily round of eight offices that were recited in common at certain hours of the day.

The monk's routine of worship began during the hours of darkness, at 2 a.m. or shortly after that time in winter, and at 3 a.m. or shortly after in summer, with the singing of the office of Vigils or Nocturns (later called Matins). Lauds was sung at first light, and there followed the relatively short offices of the day, sung at the first, third, sixth, and ninth hours, and the evening office of Vespers. The day ended with the brief office of Compline, which was sung at sundown or before retreating to bed. The night office was the longest and most elaborate of the services. It was divided into parts called Nocturns, each of which consisted of six psalms and four lessons together with responseries, or meditative verses, relating to the subject of the lessons. On Sundays and major feast-days the night office contained three Nocturns, and it must have taken nearly two hours to complete; on ferial days it would have lasted a little less than an hour.

Benedict's Rule laid down detailed instructions for the order of psalmody so as to ensure that the entire psalter was recited in the course of each week. The lessons were drawn from the Bible and the Scriptural commentaries of the Fathers and the recorded acts of the martyrs. In the course of the following centuries the office was greatly elaborated, musically as well as textually, but the basic pattern as it is outlined in the Rule persisted and came to be the standard framework of daily worship in the Western Church. Its traces are clearly visible in all the service-books, Protestant as well as Catholic, that are derived from the medieval tradition.

Rather surprisingly to the modern reader, the Rule, which provides in such detail for the daily prayer of the community, has only a few and incidental references to eucharistic prayer. This was because the order of the eucharistic liturgy was determined by the bishop; it was not something on which an abbot could legislate. And St Benedict was observing the custom of the early Church, which was still maintained in his time, by which the celebration of mass was reserved to Sundays and feasts of the Lord.

As the whole community would attend the weekly eucharist, the monastery would not need more than one or two men in priest's orders to celebrate mass. Those to be ordained for this purpose by the bishop were to be selected by the abbot. Those chosen are sternly warned against arrogance: they are to do nothing except on the abbot's instructions and they must remain in the rank already assigned them in the community. Benedict assumed that the majority of the community – possibly the abbot himself among them – would not be ordained. In this he reflected a common assumption of the early monastic world. Monks were not clergy. Gregory the Great considered clerical office to be incompatible with the monastic profession. 'No man', he wrote to the bishop of Ravenna, 'can both serve under ecclesiastical obedience and also continue under a monastic rule, observing the strict regime of a monastery when he is obliged to remain in the daily service of the Church.'[19] He must choose one or the other. A clerk might, of course, become a monk, but if he did so, he must cease to exercise his priestly functions outside his monastery.

For all this, Gregory was prepared to use monks for the task of evangelising the barbarian peoples of northern Europe; and the pressing needs of the mission made it necessary to relax his principle in order to provide the newly converted peoples with the sacraments. Perhaps for this reason it became a growing practice in the seventh century to ordain men in Western monasteries.[20] But the ancient tradition died hard: it was not until 826 that a Roman synod required abbots to be ordained to the priesthood.[21] The Gregorian principle was sometimes resuscitated for polemical purposes. As late as the twelfth century, Theobald of Etampes reminded Archbishop Thurstan of York that monks were not permitted to preach to the people, to baptise, or to absolve penitents.[22] In fact, they were expressly forbidden to exercise the pastoral care or to celebrate mass in public churches by the First Lateran Council of 1123.

The community did not go back to bed after Nocturns; there was a short interval, after which the office of Lauds was sung at first light, and then the office of Prime followed at sunrise. The monks then processed out of choir and went about the day's work. The timetable varied like the tides in response to the rhythm of the seasons. The computation of time that was followed was that of classical antiquity, which was still observed in the sixth century. By this reckoning the periods of daylight and darkness were each divided into twelve hours of equal length. Thus in winter the night hours would be longer than sixty minutes, and the day hours would be correspondingly short; conversely, in summer the day hours would be long, and the night hours short. The job of getting everybody out of bed at the correct time for the night office and ringing the bells for the canonical hours must have posed problems before the advent of the mechanical clock in the fourteenth century. Before this, water clocks and hour-glasses were widely used. Some monastic customaries recommend astronomical observation as a check during the night hours. Clearly, somebody had to stay awake during the night to rouse the community at the proper time. In the Master's Rule the duty falls upon each tithing of the brethren in turn. They watch the clock in pairs, lest one of them should fall asleep, and when the hour comes, they go to the abbot's bed and say 'Lord, open thou my lips', tapping his feet gently until he wakes.[23]

Outside the hours of community prayer the Rule divided the monk's day into periods of manual work and periods of reading. The summer timetable, which began at Easter, allocated upwards of seven hours to work and three hours to reading; in winter the period of work was shortened and the time for reading increased. In the longer summer days the Rule provided for two meals, the first shortly after midday and the second in the early evening; whereas the winter timetable allowed only a single meal, which was served at about 2.30 in the afternoon, or later still in Lent. No talking was permitted during meals; the brethren ate in silence while a member of the community read to them. Silence, in fact, was enjoined at all times, but especially during the night hours.

The thing most conspicuously absent from the Rule is any provision for leisure. 'Idleness', Benedict observes severely, 'is the enemy of the soul.' His insistence upon the value of manual work is in the Eastern monastic tradition. It had an ascetical as well as an economic function; it kept men humble, and it provided for the material wants of the community. Any of the monks who were craftsmen were to ply their skill at the abbot's discretion, and their artefacts might be sold. The rest of the community would go to work in the fields or be occupied with house duties. Benedict's careful balance between periods of manual work, prayer and study, was destroyed by later developments of the Middle Ages. The addition of a daily chapter mass and the increasing elaboration of the liturgical offices, which reached its climax at Cluny, encroached upon the rest of the day; and the acquisition of great estates meant that growing numbers of monks in the Benedictine abbeys were preoccupied with managerial tasks. But Benedict's simple plan offered a model that later monastic reformers constantly sought to revive.

What did St Benedict intend his monks to read during the many hours of each week that were allocated to study? Did the phrase he used – *lectio divina*, or sacred reading – include literary or intellectual pursuits? Here was one of the enigmas of the Rule over which later commentators spilt much ink. The ninth century was an age of learned abbots, when the Benedictine monasteries of the Meuse and the Rhineland played a major role in transmitting the literary culture of antiquity to the medieval world. In fact, until the scholastic movement of the twelfth century, most of the leaders in the world of learning were monks. But did this tradition represent an authentic interpretation of St Benedict's plan? In the seventeenth century, Rancé, the founder of the Trappist reform, had no doubt that it did not, and charged the learned Benedictines of St Maur with subversion of the Rule: 'St Benedict and the whole of antiquity is on my side . . . what is called study has only been established at a period of relaxation.'[24] Rancé displays all the blind rigidity of the self-appointed dogmatist; and the chief merit of his shrill polemic was that it provoked the great monk-scholar Jean Mabillon to write his magnificent apologia for monastic scholarship. Nevertheless, from the viewpoint of the sixth century, Rancé had a point.

Churchmen of the sixth century displayed an ambivalent attitude towards classical letters. Christianity had conquered the Empire, but the pagan deities which haunted the poets and orators of antiquity were still too close to be trifled with. Venus and the Muses were dangerous beguilements for the men who had heard the Gospel call to renunciation. It was this that gave the *coup de grâce* to the ancient schools of rhetoric. They had lingered on in Italy and Gaul after the collapse of the imperial civil service, only to be finally smothered under a cloud of ecclesiastical disapproval. But the poets and orators were not so easily exorcised. The Latin Fathers who railed against them most had been reared on them, and their prose betrays their debt on every page. There were some who sought a reconciliation, like the old Roman aristocrat, Cassiodorus, who was a contemporary of St Benedict. After serving the Ostrogothic king, Theodoric, he retired to a monastery which he had created on his own estate at Vivarium, in southern Italy, and composed a programme of studies for his monks which included the classical orators and the logic of Aristotle. The programme was to be divided into two parts, or *Institutes* – one of divine and one of secular letters – and, as he explains, the purpose of studying the pagan classics was to equip the student for a better understanding of the sacred Scriptures.[25] It was the strategy Augustine had approved: as the Israelites had plundered the Egyptians before they fled, Christian education might exploit the classics for its own purposes.

The *Institutes* of Cassiodorus were much read, but his educational scheme did not win general approval among early monastic legislators. The learned leisure of Vivarium owed more to the classical tradition of the scholar-recluse than it did to the ascetical spirit that was blowing from the East. That spirit was more faithfully encapsulated in Jerome's account of a dream he had after he had decided to embrace the ascetical life. He was on his way to the Syrian desert to become a monk, but he could not bring himself to leave his Cicero out of his luggage. One night, during a bout of illness, he dreamed he was brought before the divine seat of judgement and asked his profession. His protestation that he was a Christian produced the stern response: 'Thou liest. Thou art no Christian, but a Ciceronian; where the heart is, there is thy treasure also.' And he was sentenced to a cruel flogging.[26] In his fright he vowed never to read the pagan authors again, and for some years at least he seems to have kept his promise.

The anecdote, which was intended to warn one of his spiritual protégés off reading Horace and Virgil, is a paradigm of the attitude of the early monastic world towards the classics. Apart from the Old and New Testaments, the only works that St Benedict expressly commends to his monks are the books of the Catholic Fathers, the Lives of the Fathers, Cassian, and the Rules of St Basil. It is the ascetic's quintessential library. His phrase 'divine reading' by implication excludes the pagan classics. His instructions for the issue of books to the community imply that the purpose of reading is to acquire food for meditation. Every year, at the beginning of Lent, each monk received a codex from the library, which he was expected to read in its entirety, without skipping pages. The ritual was maintained at Canterbury in the eleventh century, in Lanfranc's day: the books for Lenten reading were laid out on a carpet in the centre of the chapter-house; the books of the previous year were returned, and anyone who had failed to finish his volume prostrated himself and confessed his fault.[27]

Yet even in St Benedict's cloister there had to be some study of the classics. The Rule provides for child-oblates, donated to the monastery by their parents. The practice already existed in the time of the anonymous Master. The principle was stated by the Council of Toledo in 633: 'a person is made a monk either by his own profession or by his father's piety. Whichever it be, all such are forbidden to return to the world.'[28] In the Rule the parents make the vows on the child's behalf, wrap his hand in the cloth used for the mass offerings, and, as it were, place him in the offertory plate, together with a suitable gift to provide for his maintenance. So boys, aged seven and upwards, formed a normal group in the Benedictine communities of the early Middle Ages. In the eighth-century commentary of Paul the Deacon, they are shepherded about the house in crocodile formation by a posse of masters, and are required to take their place in choir for all the offices. They had, of course, to be taught their letters through the standard grammars of Priscian and Donatus, which provided a fair anthology of the Latin poets. The classics might be dangerous fare, but they could not be wholly dispensed with in educating the young. Thus, of necessity, the monastery contained a school, but it was a school for child-monks, which did not normally admit pupils from outside.

St Benedict's Rule did not deny entry to men from any class of society. But in practice the requirements of the monastic life as he described it restricted adult recruitment to those social groups that were educated. In the following centuries the foundation and endowment of monasteries was largely the work of the princes and aristocracy in the Germanic kingdoms, and the recruitment of monks was largely from the same class. The practice of child-oblation, distressing though it may be to the mind of a modern parent, became increasingly popular. Among landed families it offered a welcome means of providing for surplus children, who could not be endowed without a dangerous partition of the family estate. It was equally valued as a way of providing for girls for whom no suitable marriage alliance could be found. Thus the child-oblates were a major source of recruitment to the medieval monasteries. Once donated, they were committed for life.

Sentiment turned against child-oblation in the twelfth century. The Cistercians refused to accept children – though more out of a desire to avoid the worldly entanglements involved than from any appreciation of child psychology – and before the end of the century the canon law had decreed that no person could be permanently committed to the monastic life until he had attained his majority and freely taken vows as an adult.[29] But in the heyday of Benedictine monasticism the practice produced some remarkable people. The Northumbrian Bede, 'Candle of the Church' and proto-historian of the English people, and Eadmer, the precentor of Christ Church Canterbury and biographer of St Anselm, were both reared in the cloister from childhood. So too was Matilda, the abbess of Quedlinburg, a daughter of the Emperor Otto I, who had been veiled at the age of eleven, but who in a national crisis proved herself able to rule a kingdom in the absence of her nephew. After the twelfth century it was still permissible to accept children for education in the cloister as long as they were not committed to the monastic profession before they reached adulthood. But from this time the numbers of children in monastic houses dwindled rapidly, and there seems no doubt that the ending of child-oblation was one of the reasons for the reduced size of Benedictine communities in the later Middle Ages.

St Benedict's Rule provided a model for a close-knit, well-organised ascetic community, following a carefully planned routine of prayer, work, and study. Although the writer's debts to the ascetical teaching of the East are obvious, what gave his scheme its distinctive character was his concern for the essentially Roman virtues of stability, order, and moderation. It was a wise and reassuring prescription for religious groups recruiting their members from the intelligentsia of later antiquity. Amid the debris of classical civilisation, in a world grown barbarous, violent and unpredictable, Benedict's monastery offered an enclave of peace and order. But it was vulnerable, and the survival of his institution was by no means assured. Some twenty years after his death, the Lombards broke into Italy and carried devastation through the peninsula. The military presence left by Byzantium was too weak to offer any effective resistance. In 577 Monte Cassino was sacked and its monastic buildings were burned down. Benedict's other foundations at Subiaco and Terracina suffered the same fate. The monks at Cassino scattered. Some went to Rome, where the pope offered them a refuge at San Pancrazio, one of the satellite monasteries of the Lateran basilica. The site at Cassino remained ruinous and deserted for the next hundred and forty years.

Elsewhere also the Lombardic settlement seems to have arrested the development of Italian monasticism for nearly a century. Revival came in the seventh century with the advent of a Catholic dynasty to Lombardy and the conversion of the dukes of Benevento. The rulers of the eighth century became fervent patrons of monks, and monastic life burgeoned in a new spring. It was in this period that the great abbey of Nonantola in Emilia was founded by a relative of King Aistulf (749–56), and monks from Bobbio planted olives in the coastlands of Liguria.[30] But the fate of Benedict's Rule after the sack of Cassino is a mystery. It is obvious from Pope Gregory's reference that it was known at Rome at the end of the sixth century, yet there is no evidence of any monastery in the city following the Rule nor, significantly, is there evidence of a cultus of St Benedict at Rome, either in iconography or church dedication, before the tenth century. In the shorter term the future of the Rule lay in fact, not in Italy, but north of the Alps in the Germanic kingdoms, and above all in Gaul.

Notes

1. *PL* 66, 126–204; modern edition by A. de Vogüé, *Les Dialogues de Grégoire le Grand* (*Sources chrétiennes*, 251, 260, 265, Paris, 1978–80).
2. The story of Totila's visit and St Benedict's alleged prophecy of his entry to Rome has literary antecedents in the Lives of the Fathers and the Life of St Martin which throws some doubt on its historical authenticity, see P. A. Cusack, 'Some literary antecedents of the Totila encounter in the second Dialogue of Pope Gregory I', *Studia Patristica* 12 (1975), pp. 87–90. On the allegorical sense of the anecdotes in the *Dialogues* see W. F. Bolton, 'The suprahistorical sense of the anecdotes in the Dialogues of Gregory I', *Aevum* 33 (1959), pp. 206–13, and J. H. Wansborough, 'St Gregory's intentions in the stories of St Scholastica and St Benedict', *Rev. bén* 75 (1965), pp. 145–51. In his introduction to the *Dialogues* I (*Sources Chrétiennes* 251, Paris, 1978), A. de Vogüé rejects a comprehensively sceptical approach to the historical matter in the *Dialogues*, and distinguishes between narration and Gregory's tropological exposition. I agree with him.
3. Gregory's authorship of the *Dialogues* has been contested by Francis Clark, *The Pseudo-Gregorian Dialogues*, 2 vols (Leiden, 1987). His theory that the work is a forgery of the seventh century has not, however, found favour with most authorities on the period, see discussion and references in R. A. Markus, *Gregory the Great and his World* (1997), pp. 15–16.
4. *PL* 66, 161.
5. It was argued by K. Hallinger in 'Papst Gregor der Grosse und der heilige Benedikt', *Studia Anselmiana* 42 (Rome, 1957), pp. 231–319, that Gregory's letters concerned with monastic matters display no acquaintance with the Rule and in some respects are contrary to it, implying that he probably had not read it. But subsequent critics pointed out echoes of the Rule in his commentary on the book of Kings, see Markus, *op. cit.* p. 69, n. 6.
6. *Sancti Caesarii Arelatensis Opera*, ed. G. Morin (Maredsous, 1942) II, pp. 129–30. On the sources and teaching of Caesarius see W. E. Klingshirn, *Caesarius of Arles. The Making of a Christian Community in Late Antique Gaul* (1994).
7. A. de Vogüé, 'La règle d'Eugippe retrouvée', *Revue d'ascétique* 47 (1971), pp. 233–65.
8. Text edited by A. de Vogüé, *La Règle du Maître*, 3 vols (*Sources chrétiennes* 105, Paris, 1964–5). For the discussion surrounding this document see M. D. Knowles, *Great Historical Enterprises and Problems in Monastic History* (1963), pp. 137–95; de Vogüé, 'Saint Benoît en son temps: règles italiennes et règles provençales au VIᵉ siècle', *Regulae Benedicti Studia* I (Rome, 1972), 170–93; Marilyn Dunn, 'Mastering Benedict: monastic rules and their authors in the early medieval West', *English Historical Review* 105 (1990), pp. 567–83.
9. Christine Mohrmann, 'La langue de Saint Benoît', *Sancti Benedicti Regula Monachorum*, ed. P. Schmitz (Maredsous, 1955), pp. 9–39.
10. The Rule, prologue. The edition used here is that of Philibert Schmitz (Maredsous, 1946), based upon the manuscript of Saint-Gall. English readers will find a convenient edition with translation by Justin McCann (1951). More recent scholarly editions are those by de Vogüé in *Sources chrétiennes*, 181–2 (Paris, 1972–77), R. Hanslik in *CSEL* (1977), and J. Chamberlin (Toronto, 1982), with translation.
11. The Rule, c. 1.
12. *Ibid.*, c. 1.
13. *Ibid.*, c. 58.
14. *Ibid.*, c. 58.
15. *Ibid.*, c. 48.
16. *The Letters of Peter the Venerable*, ed. G. Constable (Cambridge, Mass., 1967) I, p. 84.
17. The Rule, c. 65.
18. *Ibid.*, c. 40.

19. *Gregorii I Papae Registrum Epistolarum* I, ed. P. Ewald and L. M. Hartmann (*MGH*, 1891), pp. 281–2. See on this question T. McLaughlin, *Le très ancien droit monastique de l'occident* (*Archives de la France monastique* 30, Ligugé, 1935), pp. 116–28.

20. J. A. Jungmann, *Missarum Solemnia* (Paris, 1956) I, p. 267. N. Brooks argues in *The Early History of the Church of Canterbury* (1984), p. 89, that the needs of the Gregorian mission to England were a direct cause of the practice.

21. *MGH Concilia* II, 2, p. 578.

22. R. Foreville and J. Leclercq, 'Un débat sur le sacerdoce des moines au XIIe siècle', *Studia Anselmiana* (4th ser.) 41 (1957), pp. 52–3. For the conciliar prohibition see I Lateran c. 17: Mansi XXI p. 285.

23. *La Règle du Maître* II, pp. 172–3.

24. *Lettres de Armand Jean le Bouthillier de Rancé*, ed. B. Gonot (Paris, 1846), p. 226.

25. *Cassiodori Senatoris Institutiones*, ed. R. A. B. Mynors (1937), pp. 68–9.

26. *Epistulae, PL* 58, 22, 30; J. N. D. Kelly, *Jerome* (1975), p. 42.

27. *The Monastic Constitutions of Lanfranc*, ed. M. D. Knowles (1951), p. 19.

28. *Corpus Iuris Canonici*, ed. Freidberg c. 20, q. 1 c. 3 (col. 844).

29. The principle seems to have been established by a decretal of Celestine III (1191/98) which laid down that a boy offered to a monastery by his father was free to leave on attaining his majority; only a solemn vow taken as an adult made him a monk: *X III, 31 c. 14*. See discussion by W. M. Plöchl, *Geschichte des Kirchenrechts* II (Vienna, 1962), p. 253. In 1222 the Council of Oxford decreed that no one was to be received as a monk under the age of eighteen: F. M. Powicke and C. R. Cheney, *Councils and Synods* IIi (1964), p. 122.

30. G. Penco, *Storia del Monachesimo in Italia* (Rome, 1961), pp. 110–25.

ascetical ideal of exile for the sake of Christ, had driven him to quit his monastery to evangelise areas that were still semi-pagan. In or about the year 591 he landed in Gaul with twelve companions, and made his way to the court of Childebert in Burgundy to seek the king's collaboration. He was first allocated a wild spot at Annegray in the Vosges. Recruits flowed in to people the new foundation of Luxeuil – the most illustrious Celtic monastic establishment on the Continent – and its creation was followed shortly afterwards by that of Fontaine. But this promising start to the Irish missionary enterprise was placed in hazard when Columbanus fell from favour at court.

The role of moralist at Merovingian courts was a dangerous one. The outspokenness of Columbanus about the sex-life of the young King Theuderic gained him the enmity of the formidable Queen Brunhild, the king's grandmother, and she had him expelled from Burgundy. He narrowly escaped being transported back to Ireland, but resumed his wanderings. He visited the Neustrian court at Soissons, and then moved on over the Vosges into Swabia. By Lake Constance he parted from his faithful companion, Gallus, whose cult centre grew into the great abbey of Saint-Gall, and made his way into Italy. He was graciously received at the court of the Lombard King Agilulf and granted a site in the Apennines at Bobbio, where he created his last monastic colony. It was there that he died and was buried in 615.

Like Luxeuil and Saint-Gall, Bobbio became a focus for expatriate Irish monks and scholars. Columbanus was, in fact, the spearhead of the first invasion of the Continent by the culture of Celtic Christianity. The impact of his advent upon the religious life of Gaul was like that of a spring tide bursting into a stagnant pool. His foundations excited a wave of religious enthusiasm among the Frankish aristocracy and inaugurated a new era of growth for Gallic monasticism. To understand the sources that energised this growth it is necessary to turn to the development of monastic life in the Celtic lands.

Early Irish monasticism

We do not know how or when organised monasticism reached Ireland. It may have been imported from Britain or from Gaul or even directly from the east Mediterranean. The weight of evidence has forced modern scholars to abandon the old notion that the Anglo-Saxon invasion and settlement severed the Celtic Christians of western Britain and Ireland from contact with continental Christianity. Missionaries from both Britain and Gaul had played a part in evangelising Ireland; there is also evidence that monastic life existed in Wales and Strathclyde in the fifth century, and that individual ascetics moved freely between the Celtic lands and the Continent.

The mission of St Patrick, who died in 461, created in Ireland a Roman episcopal organisation like that existing in Gaul. The evangelization of the Irish people reached a high point in the mission of St Patrick who, before his death in c.461 had assured the continuity of his work by ordaining many clergy and appointing bishops. Before the end of the century St Brigit had formed her monastery at Kildare. But the great age of monastic foundation in Ireland was the sixth century. Hagiographical tradition ascribed the cardinal role to St Finnian, 'master of saints', who was led by an angel to the site of Clonard, where he constructed the cell that became the nucleus of his famous monastery.[5] Clonmacnoise, Clonfert, Terryglass and many other monasteries claimed foundation by saints who had been disciples of Finnian at Clonard. In the same period, St Columba (Colmcille) founded Derry and Durrow and planted a colony of monks on Iona off the coast of Pictland; St Comgall founded Bangor; and towards the end of the century, St Kevin founded Glendalough.

The inspiration for these ascetical colonies came ultimately from Egypt, but we do not know how it travelled from there. In some ways their mode of life resembled what we know of St Martin's semi-eremitical establishments in the west of Gaul, and perhaps it was from there rather than from the west of Britain that the pattern was derived. The Irish monastery was like a walled city. The whole settlement was enclosed by a rampart of earth and stones, within which monks lived singly or in small groups in detached huts, made either of wattle or of stones morticed in a characteristic beehive fashion. The crudity of the building technique imposed limitations of scale, and larger monasteries like Bangor and Clonmacnoise, which were unable to house the whole community in a single building for liturgical purposes, contained several relatively small churches; kitchen, guest-house, and other offices were also housed in separate structures. Each settlement was an autonomous unit, presided over patriarchally by a presbyter-abbot – a monk in priest's orders.

These were cenobitical communities, but they also made room for anchorites on their fringe. Cassian's teaching that the contemplative life of the hermit was superior to the cenobitical life found a receptive ear in early Irish culture, and the Celtic monastic movement embraced a strong anchoritic tradition. A text called the *Catalogus Sanctorum Hiberniae*,[6] now recognised to be a compilation of the ninth century, divides the early saints of Ireland into three orders and assigns the highest place in the spiritual hierarchy to the third order – the anchorites. Not only monks, but Celtic abbots and bishops, moved freely and often from community life to solitude. The *Life of St Columbanus*, written by Jonas of Bobbio, describes him from time to time quitting his monks at Luxeuil and living alone in a cave. During one of these eremitic spells, it was revealed to him that several of the brothers had fallen ill, and he hurried back to the monastery to care for them.[7] When St Cuthbert at the end of his life withdrew from the community on Lindisfarne to settle in a hermitage on the island of Inner Farne, he was following a well-recognised Celtic practice. The pull of the desert – 'the wave cry, the wind cry, the vast waters of the petrel and the porpoise' – that sounds so strongly in Celtic hagiography, peopled many desolate islands and rocks round the coasts of Ireland and northern Britain with hermits. In some places their derelict stone huts and oratories are still visible.

No Irish monastic rule is known earlier than the Rule of St Columbanus. This, together with his penitential and sermons, give us a glimpse of the spirit that governed Celtic monastic practice. These documents, in fact, describe an ascetical regime so harsh and uncompromising that they chill the blood. For Columbanus, the life of the monk was a heroic and unremitting warfare to conquer his own self-will and sensuality:

> The chief part of the monk's rule is mortification . . . Let the monk live in a community under the discipline of one father and in the company of many . . . Let him not do as he wishes, let him eat what he is bidden, keep as much as he has received, complete the tale of his work, be subject to him whom he does not like. Let him come weary and as if sleep-walking to his bed, and let him be forced to rise while his sleep is not yet finished. Let him keep silence when he has suffered wrong. Let him fear the superior as a lord, love him as a father, believe that whatever he commands is salutary for himself.[8]

This austere programme is underpinned by a penitential of merciless severity. A brother who drops food or spills drink while serving is to do penance in church, lying prostrate and motionless during the singing of twelve psalms; breaking the rule of silence at meals is to be punished with six lashes; forgetting prayer before or after work, twelve lashes; smiling during the divine office, six lashes; using the words 'mine' or 'thine', six lashes; contradicting the words of another, fifty lashes.[9]

This ferocious discipline obviously reflects the conditions of a violent and turbulent society; but its object here was to hurry the monk up the steep road to the unitive experience of God, which was the crown of the contemplative's efforts. Columbanus explained it in the letter he wrote from his impending exile, addressed to the brethren he had been forced to leave at Luxeuil. He writes tearfully and in haste, for a messenger has come to say that the ship to carry him back to his own country is loaded and ready to sail: 'Keep to the highway of perfection . . . we must pass by the royal road to the city of God through affliction of the flesh and contrition of the heart; through the toil of the body and the humiliation of the spirit; if you remove the battle, you remove the crown as well.'[10]

The tone of this advice is echoed in Celtic hagiographical literature. The saints perform heroic acts of mortification; they recite the Psalter standing in icy waters, or stand for long periods in prayer with arms outstretched like a cross, an exercise known as the crossfigill; Kevin of Glendalough was said to have maintained the posture for seven years, unsleeping and motionless, so that the birds nested in his upturned hands;[11] they fast continuously, and use bare rocks for bolsters. On the other hand, there are hints in the Lives that the regime in the Irish monasteries was in reality more compassionate towards human weakness than the penitentials suggest. In the midst of the ascetical heroics, glimpses of a gender and more humane spirit break through, of the abbot's solicitude for his monks to see they are not overworked and are properly fed, of the love of animals and an appreciation of the natural world.

The Irish monks seem to have been free from the dread of the pagan classics that afflicted Jerome and Gregory the Great. Latin was taught in the Irish monasteries of the seventh century, and it was not only the Latin of the Scriptures and the Fathers. The Latinity of Columbanus, who had taught the monks of Bangor before embarking on his continental odyssey, shows reminiscences of Virgil, Ovid, and Juvenal, as well as the Christian poets.[12] By the seventh century, their enthusiasm for learning and their zeal for teaching had made the monastic schools of Ireland the most famous in Europe. Bede referred to them with awe. They were also important centres of book production. Children were brought up in the monastery to copy texts in the distinctive half-uncial script that was transmitted by the Irish missionaries to Anglo-Saxon England and by migratory monks to the scriptoria of Saint-Gall, Bobbio, and many other Irish monastic colonies on the Continent.

St Columba was an accomplished scribe. Adamnan, who wrote his Life nearly a century later, tells us that at Durrow, when there was drought, they carried the books written in Columba's own hand into the fields and opened them, so as to induce rain.[13] The tenth-century author of the *Life of St Comgall* has a pleasing story of one of the boys in the monastery who was learning to write; but his writing was so appalling that nobody could tell whether it was a human script or meaningless marks made by the claws of a bird. His teachers despaired; but Comgall blessed his eyes and hands, and after that he made fine progress until he surpassed all the other scribes of his time.[14] It was the fusion of this tradition of Irish calligraphy and love of zoomorphic animal forms with the artistic tradition of northern Britain, after the Celtic mission to Northumbria, that was to produce the great series of illuminated Gospel books, like the Echternach Gospels, the Book of Kells, and the Lindisfarne Gospels, which are the supreme monuments of Hiberno-Saxon art.

Historians have long puzzled over the peculiarities of the monastic structure that developed in the Irish Church. The Church of the early centuries had modelled its organisation upon the administrative structure of the Roman Empire. In Gaul, as in other lands of the old Empire, diocesan organisation rested upon monarchic bishops, who were city-based. Everywhere the bishop's see was located in the old Roman *civitas* – an arrangement that was expressly authorised by the Council of Chalcedon in 451. Monasticism had developed in the West alongside, and in close connection with, this urban episcopal structure. Monasteries of men and women were founded in or adjacent to cities, and were under the supervision of bishops. But Ireland had never been within the Empire and lacked any urban life that could provide a basis for a Roman diocesan structure. It was a pastoral society, bonded together by the ties of tribe and kindred, thus lacking the kind of social base for the episcopal organisation that existed on the Continent. As in Anglo-Saxon Britain, where Roman urban life had disappeared, the area of a bishop's jurisdiction was that of the tribal settlement and diocesan boundaries were fluid. Co-existing with this episcopal organisation was that of the tribal monastery presided over by a presbyter-abbot. Several monasteries, like Columba's foundations at Durrow and Derry, acquired extensive territorial empires, comprising not only daughter foundations, but lands, churches, and in some cases missionary colonies, like Iona, across the Irish sea. A monastic empire of this type was called a 'paruchia', and it constituted a pastoral unit, subject to the authority of the priest-abbot of the founding house. Bishops continued to play an essential role both alongside and within this structure. In the course of the sixth century a number of them adopted the monastic life themselves and located their sees within a monastery. In this case, the bishop exercised within the paruchia the sacramental powers of his order, while sharing governmental authority with the priest-abbot. In some cases the roles of bishop and abbot were united in the same person, as happened at Armagh.[15]

One kind of organisation based upon collaboration between bishop and abbot can be seen in sixth-century Northumbria, which was evangelised by Irish monks from Iona. St Aidan was called from Iona by King Oswald to preach the Gospel in his kingdom. Aidan was, in fact, a tribal bishop, attached to the territory of the heathen Angles. As a monk in the Irish tradition, he chose to locate his see in a monastery on the offshore island of Lindisfarne. He resided on the island and followed the regime of the monastery when he was not occupied with one of his prolonged missions on the mainland. The domestic affairs of the monastery and its spiritual direction were left to the abbot. In Ireland, by the eighth century most episcopal sees had been merged with monastic paruchiae.

This monastic church structure was peculiar to the Celtic lands. It existed in sixth-century Wales as well as Ireland and parts of northern Britain; but it made no headway on the Continent against the long-established Roman episcopal organisation. In Britain, its further development was arrested by the Synod of Whitby (664), where Colman of Lindisfarne representing the Irish mission, and Wilfrid of Ripon the Roman, argued out the case for their respective traditions, and King Oswiu declared for the Roman party. Ostensibly, the object of the conference was to settle the Easter controversy – the two traditions differed over the dating of Easter because the Celts still adhered to an older system of computation which Rome had abandoned. But behind this frontal issue lay deeper differences, not of doctrine, but of culture and ecclesiastical organisation.

The monastic organisation of the Celtic Church, so different from that of Rome, was rooted in the socio-political structure of Irish society. The ascetical movement of the sixth century had found its recruits chiefly among the aristocracy, and the wave of monastic foundations was largely the work of fervent princes. It provided an outlet for their religious zeal without diminishing the property or power base of local dynasties. The monastery was the spiritual focus of the tribe or kindred group. The ruling dynasty which endowed it with a portion of the family lands retained a continuing interest in its property. The abbot was normally a member of the dynasty, and his successors were also co-arbs or co-heirs of the founder's family. The paruchia of the monastery was not only an area of spiritual jurisdiction where the abbot held sway; it also reflected the political dominance of the founding dynasty.

The place of Iona in the polity of the Celtic Church is a conspicuous case. Its founder, St Columba, was a prince of the Ui Neill, the most powerful dynasty in northern Ireland. Iona was to be the royal cult centre for the Scottish kingdom of Dalriada, an Irish colony ('Scotus' was the medieval term for an Irishman) established in Argyll, on the edge of the Pictish kingdoms. As the evangelisation of the Picts and the northern Angles proceeded at the hands of monks from Iona, the paruchia of the monastery expanded eastwards, and it came to hold a position in the Celtic churches of Britain analogous to that of a metropolitan see in southern Europe. But it continued to be, as it had begun, a spiritual base for Scottish colonisation of the territory of the Picts. A century after Columba's death Adamnan, the abbot, was still a member of the ruling Irish dynasty of the Ui Neill.

Columbanus and the Merovingian nobility

This special relationship between the monastery and its founding dynasty helps to explain the success of St Columbanus and his disciples in promoting Irish monasticism in Gaul. From the outset Columbanus directed his mission to the Merovingian court and he made his most influential conquests among the court aristocracy. This was the area of society from which Luxeuil, despite the severity of its regime, chiefly recruited its monks.[16] It became a focus from which the ideals and usages of Celtic monasticism were widely diffused on the Continent, and in the seventh century it stimulated a wave of monastic foundations which went forward under the enthusiastic patronage of kings and queens and members of the Frankish nobility. Part of the attraction the Columbanian type of monastic organisation must have had for this class lay in its independence from episcopal control and the continuing control that the founding family might exercise over the landed property of the monastery and over its choice of abbot.

Within a few years of the death of Columbanus, Luxeuil had mitigated the deterrent effects of his fearsome penitential by tempering it with the gentler and more humane Rule of St Benedict and it was this 'mixed rule' of Luxeuil that was introduced into the many abbeys that adopted the new model. Like Lérins in an earlier age, Luxeuil was a nursery of monk-bishops. At least eleven of its monks were appointed to Gallic sees in the course of the seventh century.[17] Besides these products of the cloister, the chief agents in promoting the ideals of

Columbanian monasticism were secular bishops, like Audoenus of Rouen – the St Ouen of hagiographical tradition – and St Eligius of Noyon, who had previously held high office at the Neustrian court of Paris.

Audoenus was the son of an Austrasian nobleman who had sheltered Columbanus during his exile from Burgundy, and his childhood encounter with the holy *émigré* inspired a lifelong devotion to the ascetical life. Audoenus became *Referendarius* (Secretary) to King Dagobert, and with the king's assistance he founded a monastery at Rebais in Brie in 635 which was modelled on Luxeuil. After 640, when he was appointed to the see of Rouen, a new field was opened to him. 'If anyone would know', wrote his hagiographer excitedly, 'how many monasteries for either sex have been founded by him and under his episcopate, let him perambulate his diocese and marvel at the throngs of monks; he might think he was in Egypt.'[18] St Wandrille, Jumièges, Pavilly, and Fécamp all owed their existence to his patronage and to the favour of the king, which he was in a position to tap. Enthusiasm for the monks of Columbanus seems to have gripped the whole family of Audoenus; two of his brothers collaborated with him in the foundation of Rebais, and one of them, Ado, established the famous double monastery of Jouarre on his portion of the family estates in the valley of the Marne.

The family of Audoenus were typical of members of the Frankish court aristocracy who responded with enthusiasm to the inspiration of Columbanus and his disciples. In their activities as monastic founders they had the active encouragement of the Merovingian kings, who seconded their efforts with charters of confirmation and grants of immunity. But royal assistance was not confined to ratifying the acts of others. Several women of the reigning dynasty also played a conspicuous role in promoting Columbanian monasticism of the kind practised at Luxeuil. Direct royal sponsorship reached a climax in the activity of Queen Balthild, the wife of Clovis II, who ruled the joint kingdom of Neustria and Burgundy. Balthild is a startling instance of the tendency of the Merovingians to follow their fancy in choosing their brides from the lower strata of society. She came of an obscure Saxon family settled in Britain. She had been sold into slavery as a girl and had been acquired by Erchinoald, the mayor of the Neustrian palace. According to her hagiographer, Erchinoald was much taken with her and offered her marriage; but Clovis, the son and heir of King Dagobert, snapped her up instead – 'a reward for her humility', adds the writer unctuously.[19] She did much for the family of her adoption; she bore her husband three subsequent rulers, and her posthumous career as a royal saint conferred on the dynasty a valuable aura of supernatural approval. It was possibly a mixture of piety and policy that made her the devoted friend of zealous churchmen like Audoenus and St Eloi, and the patroness of monks, for ecclesiastical support could be invaluable in reinforcing the position of a legitimate wife.[20]

Both during her husband's lifetime and after his death in 657, when she presided matriarchally over the conjoint kingdom as regent for her son, Chlotar III,

Balthild worked steadily to promote the monastic customs of Luxeuil. It was through her efforts that the 'mixed rule' of Luxeuil was imposed upon the royal abbey of Saint-Denis. She also used her influence with many of the bishops to introduce the same regime to the loosely structured communities that served the basilicas housing the tombs of the saints, so that Saint-Martin of Tours, Saint-Germain of Auxerre, Saint- Médard of Soissons, Saint-Pierre-le-Vif of Sens, and Saint-Aignan of Orleans all became regular monasteries following the 'mixed rule' of St Columbanus and St Benedict. Shortly after 657 she founded and endowed the abbey of Corbie and peopled it with monks from Luxeuil. But her darling was the abbey of nuns at Chelles. The original convent there had been established on a royal villa by Clotilde, queen of the first Clovis; but Balthild refounded and rebuilt it on a grander scale. The first abbess, Bertille, and a community of nuns were imported from Jouarre. In the end a political upheaval that was probably connected with her policy of monastic endowment forced her to relinquish power;[21] and the Wagnerian drama of her life ended in the peace of Chelles, where she took the veil and lived out her remaining years humbly under the abbess she had appointed.

The double monasteries of Gaul

Both Chelles and Jouarre were double monasteries, housing communities of men and women within the same enclosure.[22] They formed part of a group of aristocratic foundations for women that sprang up in the north-east region of Gaul in the three decades following the death of St Columbanus. The double monastery was not, of course, a mixed society. It consisted of separate communities of men and women living in proximity, in most cases using a common church for the liturgical offices, and directed by a single head. There was a precedent for the arrangement in the early monasticism of the East. Both Pachomius and St Basil had organised communities of nuns in the vicinity of their houses of monks for the purpose of mutual support. The point of the arrangement was that the female communities required the liturgical and sacramental ministrations of priests; the male community also provided help with manual tasks and managerial skills that were thought to be beyond the capacity of women.

The Columbanian double monasteries of seventh-century Gaul were essentially communities of nuns to which communities of monks were attached in order to provide priests and heavier manual services. The head of the joint congregation was invariably an abbess. Although the inspiration for these foundations had come from the mission of Columbanus, he himself did nothing to provide religious institutions for women, nor was there any clear precedent for double monasteries in Celtic lands.[23] The initiative came from the same court circles that created the abbeys for men. The regime of Luxeuil provided the model for observance, and encouragement seems to have come from Eustace and Walbert, the two abbots who succeeded Columbanus at Luxeuil.

The proprietary attitude of the founding families towards these establish-ments is vividly displayed in the matriarchal abbesses who ruled autocratically over both their male and female subjects. The contemporary *Rule of a Father for Virgins*, which may have been the work of Walbert of Luxeuil, gives the abbess much the same role as a male abbot, including the power to hear the confessions of her nuns and to absolve them. 'An abbess', writes the author significantly, 'ought to be noble in wisdom and holiness, as well as noble by birth.'[24] The noble abbesses of Merovingian hagiography are learned and masterful women with the authority and self-assurance that society regarded as their birthright. Through them and the successors they appointed from their own kindred, the families which had endowed monasteries out of their own land continued to retain an interest in the property. The apotheosis of the abbess after death at the hands of the hagiographers provided the family with a domestic saint – a *Hausheiliger* – who enhanced its standing with a special kind of sacral prestige.[25] This was the role that St Gertrude, the abbess of Nivelles, discharged for the Carolingian family of Austrasia, which provided mayors of the palace before they aspired to the throne.

Nivelles in Brabant was the earliest of the family's monastic foundations. It was constructed and endowed by Itta, the wife of Pippin the Elder, after her husband's death in 640. Itta appointed her daughter, Gertrude, as its first abbess, while continuing to direct the abbey's external affairs herself. Gertrude organ-ised it as a double monastery following the 'mixed rule' of Luxeuil. That she intended it to be a Columbanian establishment following Celtic liturgical cus-toms is evident from the fact that she sent to Ireland for monks to come and instruct the sisters in the chant. She was also determined to infect her nuns with the Irish zest for letters: she sent agents to Rome to buy books to educate them, being herself, writes her hagiographer, almost an entire library of sacred lore.[26] Like other aristocratic abbesses, she appointed her successor, choosing her niece, whom she had educated in the abbey. Gertrude's powerful figure so dominated the imagination of her community that ten years after her death she reappeared to rescue the house from a crisis. A fire had broken out. The community had abandoned all hope of saving the buildings; and the nuns had taken refuge out-side the enclosure, when the monk-steward of the estates caught sight of the familiar figure, clothed in her habit, standing, it seemed, on the summit of the refectory roof, and battering back the insolent flames with her veil.[27]

The mixed rule in Gaul and Spain

The 'mixed rule' of St Benedict and St Columbanus that was followed by both monks and nuns in the newly founded Gallic monasteries of the seventh cen-tury derived its authority from the example of Luxeuil. The first reference to this hybrid regime, in the foundation diploma of Solignac, indicated that it was adopted at Luxeuil under Walbert, who became abbot in 629.[28] We do not know enough about the observance of Luxeuil at this period to say with confidence which features of the Benedictine Rule were adopted; but it is a reasonable assumption that the successors of Columbanus preferred St Benedict's gentler penitential system as well as various practical directions for the management of the community that the Rule of St Columbanus ignored.

The same regime of a 'mixed rule' prevailed in the monasteries of seventh-century Spain. There, too, following the conversion to Catholicism of the Visigothic king, Recared, in 589, monasticism flowered under the warmth of royal patronage and monks played an active role in evangelising the people. The customs followed in the Spanish cloisters were a pastiche of Eastern traditions and the Rules of Leander and Isidore of Seville. The so-called *Regula Communis*, a seventh-century compilation attributed to St Fructuosus of Braga, presupposes the existence of double monasteries, not unlike those of Gaul. Isidore's Rule, which had a wide circulation, shows the impress of St Benedict, but the Benedictine Rule penetrated the peninsula only slowly and relatively late. It was evidently known, but it was many centuries before it was adopted as an exclusive model by some of the abbeys in the north of Aragon and the Spanish March.[29]

How knowledge of the Italian Rule reached the northern kingdoms of the Franks remains a historical puzzle; but is is clear that through the spiritual colonies of Luxeuil knowledge and appreciation of it were gradually disseminated among the bishops and ascetical communities of northern and central Gaul. The spread of the Benedictine conception of the monastic life was closely associated with the cultus of St Benedict, and somewhere about the end of the seventh century this gained added impetus from a sensational relic theft, which brought the bones of the patriarch himself to a Frankish monastery. The perpetrators and immediate beneficiaries of this furtive translation were the monks of Fleury abbey, the modern Saint-Benoît-sur-Loire.

Fleury was founded in 651 by Leodebodus, the abbot of Saint-Aignan of Orleans, and it was richly endowed with land by Chlotar III and Theuderic III. But the days of its fame began with its acquisition of St Benedict. The great romanesque basilica erected over the shrine in the eleventh century still stands by the rapid waters of the Loire as an eloquent memorial to its importance as a major cult centre of northern Europe. The eighth-century tradition, represented in its most reliable form by Paul the Deacon, contained only a few facts about the translation. These were that a party of monks from the Orleannais came to Monte Cassino, which had lain deserted and ruinous for the past century, disinterred the bones of St Benedict and his sister, St Scholastica, and carried them back to their homeland.

This sparse stock of information was copiously improved by Adrevald of Fleury in the ninth century. He wrote a *History of the Translation of St Benedict*, which proved a welcome model to other monasteries anxious to authenticate the acquisition of their patron saints.[30] Adrevald attributed the plan of retrieving the relics to Abbot Mommoleus of Fleury, who sent a party over the Alps to find

St Benedict's tomb. They were joined in the enterprise by a party dispatched by the bishop of Le Mans, who wanted the body of St Scholastica. There was the classical *mise-en-scène*: the unsuccessful search for the graves, miraculous guidance to the spot, a night break-in and a dramatic flight home from the pursuit of the pope and the Lombards. The monks of Monte Cassino, of course, later contested the authenticity of the translation, and medieval pilgrims had a choice between two St Benedicts. But Adrevald was widely read; and the fact that the author of the Benedictine Rule had chosen Gaul as his final resting place was of much significance for the development of Gallic monasticism. The Franks had taken possession of St Benedict; and it was in the Frankish realms that the Rule eventually acquired its authoritative status as the standard norm of monastic observance.

Notes

1. *The History of the Franks*, trans. Lewis Thorpe (1974), p. 152.
2. *Sanctae Radegundae Vita, MGH SS RM*, II, pp. 366–7.
3. *MGH Auctorum Antiquissimorum*, IV, p. 289. On Radegunde's manner of life at Holy Cross see Joan M. Peterson, 'The spirituality and miracles of St Radegunde' in *Monastic Studies*, ed. Judith Loades (1990), pp. 36–8.
4. *The History of the Franks*, p. 526.
5. On Irish monastic foundation in general see J. Ryan, *Irish Monasticism, its Origins and Early Development* (1972); A. C. Thomas, *Britain and Ireland in Early Christian Times, AD 400–800* (1971). For an evaluation of the sources see J. F. Kenney, *The Sources for the Early History of Ireland, I Ecclesiastical* (New York, 1929), Kathleen Hughes, *Early Christian Ireland: Introduction to the Sources* (1972). Among the most valuable modern studies are those of Kathleen Hughes, *The Church in Early Irish Society* (1966); and M. Dillon and Nora Chadwick, *The Celtic Realms* (1967); also Nora Chadwick, *The Age of the Saints in the Early Celtic Church* (1963); T. M. Charles-Edward, *Early Christian Ireland* (2000).
6. Text in A. W. Haddan and W. Stubbs, *Councils and Ecclesiastical Documents* (1869–78) II, p. 292. See discussion of its date and significance by Kathleen Hughes, *The Church in Early Irish Society*, pp. 69–70.
7. *Vitae Columbanae abbatis discipulorumque eius auctore Iona, MGH SS RM IV*, pp. 75, 76–8.
8. *Sancti Columbani Opera*, ed. G. S. M. Walker, *Scriptores Latini Hiberniae* II (1957), pp. 140–2.
9. *Ibid.*, pp. 142–68.
10. *Ibid.*, pp. 26–36.
11. L. Gougaud, *Christianity in Celtic Lands*, trans. M. Joynt (1932), p. 95.
12. On the literary culture of St Columbanus see M. Manitius, *Geschichte der Lateinischen Literatur des Mittelalters* (1911–31) I, p. 181; Walker, *op. cit.*, introduction; and *Columbanus: Studies on the Latin Writings*, ed. M. Lapidge (1997). M. Richter, *Bobbio in the early Middle Ages: the legacy of Columbanus* (Dublin, 2008).
13. *Adamnan's Life of Columba*, ed. and trans. A. O. and M. O. Anderson (1961), pp. 450–2.
14. *Vitae Sanctorum Hiberniae*, ed. C. Plummer (1910), II, p. 13.
15. On relations between bishops and the monastic paruchiae see Kathleen Hughes, *op. cit.* (1966), pp. 79–90.
16. The best account of the spread of Columbanian monasticism in Gaul is by F. Prinz, *Frühes Mönchtum im Frankenreich* (Munich, Vienna, 1965), pp. 121–41. I am especially indebted to this work.

17. Prinz, *op. cit.*, p. 123.
18. *Vita Audoini MGH SS RM*, V p. 557. On the foundations of Audoenus and his family see Prinz, pp. 124–7.
19. *Vita Sanctae Balthildis, MGH SS RM*, II pp. 482–3; cf. the *Vita Eligii, ibid.*, pp. 32, 37–8,41,48.
20. A point made by Prof. Janet Nelson in her stimulating study of the careers of Brunhild and Balthild in *Medieval Women*, ed. D. Baker (*Studies in Church History, Subsidia* I, 1978), pp. 31–77. On Balthild's monastic patronage see E. Ewig, 'Das Privileg des Bischofs Berthefrid von Amiens für Corbie u. die Klosterpolitik der Königin Balthild', *Francia* I (1973), pp. 62–114.
21. Ewig, *op. cit.*, p. 109, who points out that the conversion of the basilican churches into monasteries involved loss of control and of valuable property by the bishops.
22. On Jouarre and the other women's foundations see G. A. Rohan Chabot, Marquise de Maille, *Les cryptes de Jouarre* (Paris, 1971), and Prinz, pp. 142–5. On double monasteries, Mary Bateson, 'The origin and early history of double monasteries', *TRHS* new ser. xiii. (1899), pp. 137–98; Margaret Deanesly, *The Pre-Conquest Church in England* (1961), pp. 199–207; and the studies in *Doppelklöster und andere Formen der Symbiose männlicher und weiblicher Religiosen im Mittelalter*, ed. K. Elm and M. Parisse (*Berliner Historische Studien* 18, Berlin, 1992).
23. The argument of Mary Bateson and J. Ryan that St Brigid's Kildare was a double monastery has not found favour with modern Celtic scholars.
24. *Regula cuiusdam Patris ad Virgines, PL* 88, 1069.
25. Prinz, pp. 489–503.
26. *Vita Sanctae Gertrudae, MGH SS RM*, II p. 458.
27. *Ibid.*, p. 406.
28. Prinz, p. 268.
29. A. L. Coude, 'La diffusión de la Regula Benedicti en la.Peninsula ibérica' in *Regula Benedicti Studia* I (1972), pp. 297–325. On early monasticism in Spain see M. Cocheril, *Ètudes sur le monachisme en Espagne et en Portugal* (Lisbon, 1966); and the monumental modern study of Antonio L. Conde, *San Benito y los Benedictinos*, 7 vols (Braga, 1993).
30. *MGH SS*, XV, pp. 474–7. For Adrevald and his work see W. Goffart, 'Le Mans, St Scholastica, and the literary tradition of the translation of St Benedict', *Rev. bén* 77 (1967), pp. 107–41; P. J. Geary, *Furta Sacra: Thefts of Relics in the Central Middle Ages* (Princeton, 1978), pp. 146–9.

4

ENGLAND AND THE CONTINENT

Roman and Celtic foundations

It must have been the aristocratic tone of the women's abbeys of northern Gaul, as well as their reputation for asceticism and learning, that commended them to the notice of the nobility in the Anglo-Saxon kingdoms of Britain. Bede had heard that for lack of suitable nunneries nearer home, Earcongota, the daughter of King Earconberht of Kent, had become a nun at Faremoutiers-en-Brie; and he reports that many girls of the English nobility were sent to Chelles, Andelys and other Gallic monasteries to be educated and in some cases to enter the religious life.[1] Abbess Hilda, who was related to the royal family of Northumbria and who had been baptised by Paulinus together with the rest of the Northumbrian court, had a sister at Chelles. She had intended to go to Chelles herself until Aidan undertook her spiritual direction, and by so doing saved her for English monasticism and the English Church.

In seventh-century Britain the three traditions, Roman, Gallic and Irish, met together and fused. Monastic life grew step by step with the conversion of the heathen English to Christianity and, as the life of Hilda shows, it recruited among first-generation converts. Britain was the field of two missionary efforts – that of Augustine dispatched from Rome by Pope Gregory the Great, and the Celtic mission sent from Iona at the request of King Oswald of Northumbria; and two distinct monastic traditions were planted in their wake. Augustine and his companions had been monks before setting out on the mission to Kent, and besides erecting a cathedral at Canterbury he founded a monastery dedicated to Saints Peter and Paul outside the city – the later St Augustine's abbey – which became the mausoleum of the first archbishops and the early kings of Kent. Probably the original role assigned to the monks of this establishment was that of maintaining the round of liturgical offices at the nearby cathedral, on the model of those monasteries at Rome that were satellites of the patriarchal basilicas.[2] We know nothing of its observance at this early period, but it is a fair assumption that it followed the customs of Gregory's foundation on the Coelian Hill, from which Augustine himself had come.

It has often been suggested that Augustine imported the Rule of St Benedict into England and that the abbey outside Canterbury was the first Benedictine foundation outside Italy.[3] However, there is no evidence for this. The suggestion rests upon the mistaken notion that St Andrew's on the Coelian Hill and other monasteries in Rome had adopted the Benedictine Rule. In fact, the usages of the Roman monasteries of the seventh century were various and eclectic. Some were Greek communities following the tradition of St Basil; others, which had sprung up as satellites round the patriarchal basilicas of the city, used the liturgical order of the basilicas they served, and their internal regime, as it is revealed by the early Roman *Ordines*, was determined by the varying experience of their founders. The Rule of St Benedict was known at Rome, but there is no evidence that any Roman monastery adopted it as an exclusive model before the tenth century.[4]

The first great burst of English monastic foundation followed Aidan's mission to Northumbria. True to the tradition of the Celtic Church, he set up his missionary see in a monastery on the island of Lindisfarne, which King Oswald had granted him in 635. Although he was an active bishop with a diocese that covered the whole of Northumbria, he continued to live the life of a monk, retreating periodically to Lindisfarne, where the community was governed not by him but by an abbot, and even on occasion withdrawing to a hermitage on the island of Inner Farne.

The rule of life followed at Lindisfarne was that established by Columba at Iona. And the same Celtic observance presumably governed the other northern monasteries that sprang from the headwater of Aidan's mission: Melrose, Gateshead, and Hartlepool, all founded by Aidan; Ripon, which originated as a colony of Melrose; and Lastingham, which was founded by Cedd, the apostle of the East Angles, who had been a monk at Lindisfarne. The strategy of the missionaries from Iona was the same as that of Columbanus in Gaul: they addressed themselves initially to the court aristocracy, and monastic foundation went forward with the active collaboration of the Northumbrian kings, who provided the landed endowment. The main effort of Iona was concentrated on the north; but a number of Celtic monasteries were planted in the southern kingdoms by Irish missionaries from elsewhere. Fursey, an Irish princeling who, like Columbanus, had taken a vow to spend his life as a pilgrim for love of Christ, was welcomed by the East Anglian King Sigebert, and given the old Roman shore-fort at Burgh castle in Suffolk, where he erected a monastery. Malmesbury in Wessex was also an Irish foundation.

One of the most striking results of the links between English royal courts and the women's abbeys of northern Gaul was the introduction of double monasteries of the Gallic type into England. The author of the *Life of Bertila*, abbess of Chelles, reports that she received requests from England to send teachers, women as well as men, to give instruction in the religious life and in the construction of monasteries.[5] Like their Gallic counterparts, the English double monasteries of the seventh century were primarily nunneries to which communities of men were attached, and they were governed by abbesses. In England also they were aristocratic foundations, housing the daughters and dowagers of kings and ruled by abbesses of noble blood. Wimborne in Dorset was founded and directed by two sisters of King Ine of Wessex. St Mildred, the founder and abbess of Minster-in-Thanet, came from the royal family of the Hwicce. St Etheldreda, the founder of Ely, herself the daughter of a king, had been queen of King Ecgfrith of Northumbria.

At court Etheldreda encountered Bishop Wilfrid and came under the influence of his domineering personality. Under his direction she adopted an ascetical style of life and resolved to become a nun. According to Bede, Ecgfrith tried without success for twelve years to persuade her to consummate the marriage.[6] He never forgave Wilfrid, but in the end he allowed her to take the veil at Coldingham. The double monastery she constructed at Ely was built on her own land, which was a dower from a previous marriage. Coldingham, where she was trained in the religious life, was governed by Abbess Aebbe, who was her aunt and a sister of King Oswiu.

No rule in use by an English monastery of the seventh century is known to survive. But the prototype of the English double monasteries was the Columbanian double monastery of Gaul, and the customary they followed was probably the 'mixed rule' of Saints Columbanus and Benedict that was observed at Chelles and Faremoutiers. The Irish element is certain. Hilda, successively abbess of Hartlepool and Whitby, had been trained in monastic observance by Aidan. And Coldingham, which was to be a nursery of royal saints and abbesses, had Irish monks. It was an Irish member of the community who complained to Aebbe that her nuns were eating and gossiping in their cells when they should have been at prayer, and wasting their time weaving fine clothes. He predicted the abbey would be punished by fire, like Nineveh.[7] And it was. But the story is Bede's, and we need not take the accusation of laxity too seriously. The double monasteries may not have conformed to the fiercely ascetical standards of Columbanus, but they had inherited the Hiberno-Frankish tradition of religious fervour and learning, and they stood high in contemporary esteem.

The royal abbesses of Anglo-Saxon England, like their sisters in Gaul, ruled with the imperious self-assurance conferred on them by their birth, and many of them exerted an influence far beyond the confines of their monasteries. St Hilda's regime at Whitby, from its foundation in 657 until her death in 680, made it one of the most vital and creative centres of English Christianity in the generation before Bede. She had renounced the world but had not been forgotten by it. Bede wrote that kings and princes came to her for advice.[8] It was indicative of the prestige of her abbey in Northumbrian society that King Oswiu chose it as the venue for the momentous synod of 664 that settled the Easter Controversy in favour of the Roman party and determined the future course of the English Church.

Whether it was for political reasons or out of loyalty to those who had trained her in the Celtic tradition, in the controversy Hilda sided with the spokesmen for the Irish practice and remained a stubborn opponent of Wilfrid. But her involvement in ecclesiastical politics was less important than the direction she gave to her monastic community. She vigorously promoted education and learning in the abbey. Her enlightened regime thus performed a vital service by educating clergy for what was still a missionary church operating in an oral society. Five monks of her community in fact became bishops. Probably it was her perception of the cathechetical possibilities of religious epic that made her quick to befriend and encourage the peasant poet, Caedmon. When late in life he discovered his gift for song, she persuaded him to join the monastery and had him compose poems – transmitted orally, for he never learned to write – on the great Biblical themes of creation and redemption. Both as an intellectual centre and as a focus for pastoral activity Hilda's Whitby stood faithfully in the Irish monastic tradition.

Wilfrid claimed he had been the first to organise an English monastery entirely on the basis of the Rule of St Benedict. The monastery was Ripon, and Wilfrid had been given it to rule after Abbot Eata and a group of the Irish monks had left it rather than conform to Roman customs. Wilfrid regarded enforcement of the Benedictine Rule as part of his campaign 'to root out the poisonous weeds planted by the Scots'.[9] His residences in Rome and Gaul had given him a taste for grandeur and a contempt for the insular traditions of the Celts. He had effectively pleaded the case for conformity with Roman practice at the Synod of Whitby. After 669, as bishop of Northumbria, his state was kingly; and something of his magnificence rubbed off on Ripon and the sister abbey he founded at Hexham in *c.* 670. The straggling monastic colonies of the Irish, with their humble structures of drystone or timber, must have looked barbarous to the eye that had feasted on the spacious Christian basilicas of Rome. At both Rippon and Hexham Wilfrid embarked on elaborate building operations, which included the erection of stone churches, the crypts of which still survive with their narrow passages encased by great blocks of ashlar. There seems no reason to doubt the claim of his biographer and devoted chaplain, Eddius Stephanus, that Ripon and Hexham were the first Benedictine monasteries in England in the sense that their customary was based exclusively upon the Rule. But it was not a model immediately imitated by other monastic founders of the seventh century. Knowledge of the Rule was gaining ground, and it might be referred to for guidance on practical matters such as the procedure for electing an abbot; but in general, monastic customaries were still eclectic.

Wearmouth and Jarrow

This conjunction of *Romanitas* with the monastic traditions of Gaul and Ireland can be seen in the two famous foundations of Benedict Biscop at Wearmouth and Jarrow. Like Wilfrid, Biscop belonged to the Anglian court nobility and was an inveterate traveller. At twenty-five he abandoned everything and set out on pilgrimage for Rome.[10] He stayed a while at Lérins, where he learned the discipline of the regular life and took monastic vows. But Rome repeatedly drew him like a magnet. He returned to England in 669 in the company of Archbishop Theodore, and was placed in charge of the abbey of Saints Peter and Paul at Canterbury. But within a couple of years he was off to Rome again in search of books and relics. The great Northumbrian monastery he began building on the north bank of the Wear in 674 was erected on land given him by King Ecgfrith. To help him in the enterprise and to govern the new community he obtained the assistance of another young nobleman, Ceolfrith, who was a monk at Ripon. Some years later, Biscop erected a sister monastery at Jarrow on the Tyne, and colonised it with monks brought from Wearmouth under the headship of Ceolfrith. An original inscription, incised in Roman capitals and miraculously preserved above the chancel arch of the existing church at Jarrow, records that it was dedicated to St Paul on 23 April, in the fifteenth year of King Ecgfrith and the fourth year of Abbot Ceolfrith – the year 685.

The dedication of Biscop's twin foundations to Saints Peter and Paul, the patron saints of the Roman Church, was an outward sign of their spiritual and cultural affinity with Rome. In the course of his constant travels, he brought back numerous trophies of pilgrimage – books from Rome to stock the libraries and scriptoria of both houses, and paintings and relics for their churches. He also persuaded John the arch-cantor of St Peter's to come to Wearmouth to instruct his monks in the Roman chant and liturgical use. For the buildings he imported masons and glaziers from Gaul, who knew how to build 'according to the Roman fashion that he loved'. Modern excavation of the sites has revealed constructional techniques and architectural features, such as lathe-turned baluster shafts and flooring material in *opus signinum*, derived from sub-Roman Gaul. Investigation of the layout of the monastic buildings is inconclusive, but indicates a single axial plan that differed from both the clustered enceinte of the Irish monasteries and the classical Benedictine arrangement round a square cloister garth.[11]

Were Biscop's foundations Benedictine abbeys in the proper sense of the term, as has often been claimed? We cannot be sure. He demonstrated his own devotion to St Benedict by adopting his name when he entered the religious life. He knew the Rule and expressly commended it to his two communities as an authoritative guide to be followed when they had to elect a new abbot. Moreover Ceolfrith, Biscop's friend and travelling companion of many journeys, had come from Wilfrid's Ripon, where the observance was based exclusively upon the Benedictine Rule. Yet in Bede's *Life of Biscop* there seem to be counter-indications that the observance of Wearmouth and Jarrow was not confined within the framework of the Rule. The regime was devised by Biscop and, like other monastic founders of the seventh century, his method of compiling a customary was eclectic: 'You are not to think', he told the brethren when he was dying, 'that I produced these ordinances from my own untutored heart. In fact, what I transmitted to you to be observed for the health of your souls, were all the best things I learned from seventeen monasteries in the course of my long wandering and frequent pilgrimage.'[12] This valedictory speech seems to conflict with St Benedict's severe insistence on the undiluted sovereignty of his written code. But for all its merits, the Rule of St Benedict was not comprehensive; even later monasteries that were governed by it required a customary to regulate many details of daily observance. Understood in this sense, Biscop's words are compatible with a monastic regime which accorded the Rule the status of constitutional law.

Biscop's concern that his monks should follow the Rule in their procedure for choosing a new abbot marks a significant desire to eliminate one of the prevalent features of Celtic and Frankish monasticism. St Benedict's abbot was not a co-arb or member of the founder's kindred; he was elected by the brethren solely on grounds of his personal suitability. This was what Biscop wanted, instead of a choice dictated by considerations of kindred. It was evidently to safeguard this freedom of choice from any outside pressure that he obtained a privilege of Pope Agatho for Wearmouth, which was later confirmed by Pope Sergius and extended to Jarrow. But it was a long time before this precocious ideal made any headway in northern Europe. It collided with the determination of aristocratic dynasties to retain their control over foundations which had been endowed out of their family estates. Less than fifty years after Biscop's death, the debilitating effect of this domination by founder's kindred was already making itself felt in the monastic movement of Northumbria. In a letter written towards the end of his life to his friend, Archbishop Egbert of York, Bede laments the decline of religious fervour; he attributes much of the trouble to the growth of kindred monasteries, in which the founders assumed the role of abbot while living in the establishment with their wives and families.[13] In England, as in Gaul, the Germanic aristocracy had a way of adapting the ascetical movement to fit their own requirements.

Of course the supreme monument to Benedict Biscop's twin foundations was Bede (*c.* 672–735). His parents, who lived in the vicinity, had given him to Wearmouth as a child-oblate at the age of seven. Shortly after its foundation he was transferred to Jarrow, and there he spent the rest of his life, never stirring outside the monastic enclosure except for a belated visit to York to see his old pupil, Archbishop Egbert, and possibly a visit to Lindisfarne – for his description of the island and its tides has the smell of sense-perception about it: 'I have spent all my life in this monastery, applying myself with all my might to the study of the Scriptures; and, in the midst of observing the discipline of the Rule and the daily care of singing in the church, it has always been my delight to learn or to teach or to write.'[14] This testament of a lifetime of peace, fulfilment and joy comes at the end of his *Ecclesiastical History of the English People*, which he finished in 731, four years before his death. It is followed by a list of thirty-five works he had written, including commentaries on the books of the Old and New Testaments, homilies and letters, two books on chronology, a martyrology, and a history of the abbots of his own monastery. His treatises on chronology were widely read and copied, and his homilies found their way into the night office of the Western Church; but it is the *Ecclesiastical History* that historians have always gratefully singled out as his masterpiece. Its wealth of detail, its concern for accuracy and documentary evidence, and the classical clarity of its Latin style, make it an astonishing achievement in view of the limitations of time and place within which the author had to work. Without it our knowledge of early Anglo-Saxon England would be immeasurably poorer.

The purpose of the *Ecclesiastical History* was avowedly didactic. Its object was to show that God had chosen the English race to receive the light of the Gospel; and a subsidiary theme, but an important one, was the reception by the English of orthodox Roman Christianity. Writing in a Northumbrian monastery a generation after the Synod of Whitby, Bede was preoccupied with the conflict between the Celtic and Roman traditions which had come to a head over the dating of Easter. His account of the synod, which he placed at the centre of the *Ecclesiastical History*, is one of the best pieces of reportage that the eighth century has to offer. Although he disliked the British and disapproved of the Celtic deviations from Roman practice, he fully appreciated the heroic role the Irish monks had played in the conversion of the heathen English. He wrote with enthusiasm about Columba and Aidan, and showed much interest in the monastic life at Lindisfarne. But the real warmth of his admiration was reserved for St Cuthbert – the monk trained by the Irish at Melrose, who came to accept the Roman Easter and who, as bishop of Lindisfarne, reconciled the two traditions.

The Anglo-Saxon monks on the Continent

The resolution of the conflict not only closed a sore that was draining the strength of the Northumbrian Church; it opened a new phase in the monastic history of Europe. The marriage of the two traditions gave direction and impetus to a new missionary effort by English monks on the Continent. English churchmen felt a hankering for the conversion of their heathen kindred in Frisia and Germany. And the monks who undertook the task took with them the notions of *Romanitas* they had acquired in England – of the normative value of Roman custom and the centrality of the see of St Peter in the ecclesiastical cosmos.[15] They also carried with them a devotion to the Rule of St Benedict. The first objective of their efforts was the evangelisation of Frisia.

Wilfrid had initiated the enterprise when he stayed for some months in Frisia in 678 on his journey to Rome. But the hero of the Frisian mission was Willibrord, a monk who had been trained in Benedictine observance and devotion to Rome at Wilfrid's Ripon. From Ripon he had migrated to Ireland after Wilfrid's downfall, and there he came under the influence of Egbert, another English émigré who had been attracted across the sea by the fervour of the Irish monks and the reputation of the Irish schools for learning. Egbert was an adherent of the Roman tradition. It was he who in the end persuaded Iona, last bastion of Celtic insularity in Britain, to accept it. But he had absorbed the ideals of Irish asceticism and missionary zeal and he hankered for the penitential life of the pilgrim. In 690 he managed to fulfil his ambition vicariously by sending Willibrord with eleven companions to evangelise Frisia.

The Frisian mission advanced under the patronage and protection of Pippin II, the Carolingian, who as mayor of the palace effectively ruled in place of the Merovingian monarch. The strategy of the missionaries was shaped by their Northumbrian training. Educated in the monastic schools of Wilfrid and Egbert, Willibrord sought and obtained papal sanction for his work; with the collaboration of Pippin he got the pope to create a new ecclesiastical province based on his mission station at Utrecht, and was himself consecrated its first bishop by Pope Sergius. And the pope conferred on him the pallium – the yoke of white wool that had first been placed on the tomb of St Peter and symbolised the authority delegated by St Peter's vicar to the bishop of a metropolitan see.

The same strategy was adopted by St Boniface, an English monk who followed in Willibrord's footsteps and evangelised Thuringia. Boniface was not from Northumbria; he was a Wessex man, given to the monastic life in childhood and reared first at Exeter and then at Nursling near Southampton. But his missionary career exhibited the same loyalties that the northern monks had shown to the Benedictine Rule and the traditions of Rome. He, too, went to Rome to seek an apostolic mandate for his work from the pope. Before he left Rome his Saxon name, Wynfrith, was changed by the pope to that of Boniface, a Roman martyr whose church stood on the Aventine Hill. Later, when he returned to Rome to be consecrated bishop by Gregory II, he took an oath to St Peter and his vicar to 'uphold the faith and purity of holy catholic teaching' and 'to agree to nothing that is opposed to the unity of the universal Church, but in all things I will show, as I have said, complete loyalty to you and to the welfare of your church'.[16] Like Willibrord before him, he received the pallium, which was sent him in 732, signifying the creation of a new ecclesiastical province for Germany.

This re-exportation to northern Europe of the Anglo-Saxon idea of Roman ecclesiastical order had momentous consequences for medieval Christendom. After establishing the episcopal organisation of the German Church, Boniface was invited by the rulers of Austrasia and Neustria, Carloman and Pippin III, to help reorganise the Church in their dominions. Thus the Frankish Church was brought into a direct constitutional relationship with the Roman see and the path was laid for the future expansion of papal jurisdiction. Boniface was also a primary agent in forging the political alliance between the young Carolingian dynasty and the papacy that paved the way to the creation of the medieval Empire.

The long-term results of the Anglo-Saxon mission were as important for Western monasticism as they were for the secular Church. It had been a monastic enterprise from the start, and this monastic character was maintained by a steady stream of recruits, both men and women, who came from English monasteries to join the mission. Workers in Germany were kept in touch with the brethren at home by the exchange of letters. 'I thank you for the presents and vestments you have sent,' writes Boniface to an English abbess; 'as for copying out the passages of Scripture you asked me for, please excuse my remissness – I have been so much occupied with preaching and travelling about that I could not find time to complete it.'[17] From Bishop Daniel of Winchester he begs the copy of the Prophets that belonged to his old abbot, Winbert, because the text is written in large clear letters; for 'such cannot be procured in this country, and with my failing sight it is impossible for me to read small abbreviated script'.[18] For an instant a bridge is thrown across twelve and a half centuries, and one sees the flickering oil wick and the monastic settlement in the menacing forest, where the monk, Sturmi, constructed a fence every night round his mule to protect it from being eaten by wild beasts. The missionaries not only drew comforts and reinforcements from the English abbeys; as their work advanced they made recruits to the monastic life among the newly converted peoples, and several major foundations sprang from the mission. These were all given the Benedictine Rule for their model.

These spiritual colonies of Anglo-Saxon England on the Continent owed their creation to collaboration between the monk-missionaries and the Carolingian dynasty. Echternach, in the region of Trier, was erected by Willibrord in place of a small existing convent and on land given by Pippin II and his wife, Plectrudis. It provided him with a welcome refuge at times when it was going hard with the Frisian mission. The presence of English monks at the abbey in the eighth century, alongside their German brethren, is visually attested by the manuscripts produced in its scriptorium. The best known of these, the Echternach Gospel Book, now in the Bibliothèque Nationale at Paris, is a superb monument of the Northumbrian school, illuminated and written in the characteristic half-uncial script of the Hiberno-English monasteries.

The most illustrious of Boniface's foundations was Fulda in Hesse. It was constructed in 744 with the co-operation of Carloman of Austrasia. The story of the foundation is vividly told in the Life of the Bavarian monk, Sturmi, who became its first abbot. After Sturmi had spent some weeks in the forest prospecting for a site, he reported his chosen location back to Boniface, who made straight for the court of Carloman to ask for a royal grant. The hagiographer hints that other landowners besides the king had an interest in the area, and so 'a charter of this gift was ordered to be drawn up, signed by the king's own hand; and all the nobles in the vicinity of Grapfelt were summoned and asked to follow the king's example, if by any chance they possessed any property in that quarter . . . the donation was accordingly confirmed by all and passed from the possession of men into the possession of God'.[19] But a further act was necessary if God was to enjoy undivided possession: there were still the claims of the bishop. To meet these, Boniface obtained a privilege from Pope Zachary I, which exempted the abbey from all episcopal jurisdiction and placed it under the direct jurisdiction of the Apostolic See.

Fulda exemplified in a special way the two poles of Anglo-Saxon monastic loyalty. Its observance was to be strictly modelled on the Benedictine Rule. Sturmi was sent to the fountain-head at Cassino, now repopulated with monks, to imbibe the spirit of the Rule, so that he could return and instruct the brethren. The other English feature was exemplified by the papal privilege of exemption, which accorded with the ideas of Roman authority implanted in their disciples by Wilfrid and Benedict Biscop. Boniface had chosen Fulda to be his place of burial. After his martyrdom in Frisia at the hands of some enraged pagans, local enthusiasts tried to retain his body. But it was well known that the will of the saints was as impossible to frustrate after death as it was in life: the bier became immovable until they placed it on a barge to carry it up the Rhine on the first stage of its journey to Fulda. It was an appropriate mausoleum for a monk who had instructed the Carolingian dynasty in the merits of St Benedict's Rule and the all-powerful authority of St Peter. Later events showed they had learned their lesson well. They invoked the authority of St Peter's vicar to dismiss the last of the Merovingian kings and rule in their stead; and at their direction the Benedictine Rule was imposed as a norm upon monasteries throughout their northern dominions.

Notes

1. *Historia Ecclesiastica* iii, 8. The best text, with translation, will be found in B. Colgrave and R. A. B. Mynors, *Bede's Ecclesiastical History of the English People* (1969). Page references are to this edition.
2. N. Brooks, *The Early History of the Church of Canterbury: Christ Church from 597 to 1066* (1984), pp. 91–2.
3. Thus P. Schmitz, *Histoire de l'ordre de Saint Benoît* (Maredsous, 1942), I, p. 38; and J. Godfrey, *The Church in Anglo-Saxon England* (1962), p. 153.
4. On the observance of Roman monasteries at this period see G. Ferrari, *Early Roman Monasteries* (*Studi d'Antichità Cristiana* 23, Vatican, 1957).
5. *MGH SS RM* VI, p. 106; cited by D. Baltrusch-Schneider in *Doppelklöster und anderen Formen der Symbiose männlicher und weiblicher Religiosen im Mittelalter*, ed. K. Elm and M. Parisse (*Berliner Historische Studien* 18, Berlin, 1992), pp. 63–4.
6. *Historia Ecclesiastica* iv, 19.
7. *Ibid.* iv, 25.
8. *Ibid.* iv, 23.
9. *The Life of Bishop Wilfrid by Eddius Stephanus*, ed. B. Colgrave (1927), p. 99.
10. For Benedict Biscop and the foundation of Wearmouth and Jarrow see A. H. Thompson, *Bede, Life, Times and Writings* (1935), pp. 60–101; and P. Hunter Blair, *The World of Bede* (1970), pp. 155–99.
11. Rosemary Cramp, 'Monkwearmouth and Jarrow, the archaeological evidence' in *Famulus Christi. Essays in Commemoration of the Thirteenth Centenary of the Birth of the Venerable Bede*, ed. G. Bonner (1976), pp. 5–18.

12. *Venembilis Baedae Opera Historica*, ed. C. Plummer (1896), pp. 374–5.
13. *Epistola ad Ecgbertum, ibid.*, pp. 415–16.
14. *Historia Ecclesiastica* v, 24.
15. On the Frisian mission see W. Levison, *England and the Continent in the Eighth Century* (1946), pp. 45–69.
16. *Die Briefe des heiligen Bonifatius*, ed. M. Tangl, *MGH Epistolae* Berlin 1916, No 16; trans. C. H. Talbot, *The Anglo-Saxon Missionaries in Germany* (1954), p. 70.
17. Talbot, *op. cit.* p. 84.
18. *Ibid.*, p. 118.
19. *Ibid.*, p. 189.

5

THE EMPEROR AND THE RULE

The religious motives for endowment

When King Carloman granted fiscal immunities to the monks of Granfelden, he explained the reason for his grant was 'that thereby we may merit pardon from the eternal giver of rewards, and that it may please them to pray perpetually for the stability of our kingdom and in every way to give faithful assistance to our governance'.[1] The same formula was used by his brother, Charlemagne, in a privilege he gave to Lorsch abbey in 772.[2] The stereotyped language of these royal diplomas indicates the complex attitudes – the mixture of piety and policy – that moved the Carolingians, like other secular rulers, to promote monasticism in their realms.

As with all monastic benefaction, the primary motive was that of safeguarding the soul of the benefactor and the souls of his relatives. Medieval rulers shared with their people current doctrinal assumptions about the economy of salvation. These assumptions included the ideas of vicarious merit and the need to make satisfaction or reparation for sin. The merit that accrued to an individual through prayer and good works could be applied to other people, and not only to living people but also to the dead. This concept played a crucial role in medieval religious practice. To found and endow a community of monks was to ensure for the donor an unceasing fund of intercession and sacrifice which would avail him and his relatives both in their lifetime and after death.

The concern with vicarious merit was associated with the belief that people could, and should, make satisfaction for their sins. Repentance attracted divine forgiveness, but without satisfaction it was not enough; compensation must be paid to the wronged party, and in the case of sin, the wronged party was God. The concept of satisfaction was fostered by the early medieval penitentials. These extraordinary documents belong to the same mental world as the barbarian law codes, with their elaborate tariff of monetary compensations for offences against persons and property. They were primarily manuals compiled for the guidance of priests who had to hear confessions and allocate appropriate penances. Private auricular confession and the use of a penitential were both features of monastic life. It seems that these practices were first extended to Christians living in the secular world by the Celtic Church, and that the Irish monk-missionaries transported them to the Germanic peoples of England and the Continent. Columbanus composed a penitential for the secular clergy and laity as well as for monks. And under the influence of the Irish treatises, penitentials were also compiled in England and circulated by the Anglo-Saxon missionaries abroad. From the eighth century lay people were exhorted to confess their sins at least once a year, and a penitential treatise became part of the stock-in-trade of a priest.

The penitentials laid down a nicely graduated scale of satisfactory penances appropriate to every sin. Thus, in the seventh-century penitential attributed to Archbishop Theodore of Canterbury, a priest or deacon who vomits on account of drunkenness is assigned forty days of penance; a layman who commits the same offence is allocated fifteen days; fornication with a virgin involves a year's penance; homicide, seven years; and so forth.[3] During his period of penance the sinner was required to fast on bread, salt, and water, and to abstain from the sacraments; if a married man, he must abstain from conjugal intercourse. A year of penance involved performing these ascetical exercises for three Lents – three periods of forty days each.

Medieval piety was haunted by the menace of these terrifying documents. The careless could easily accumulate more than a lifetime of canonical penance. What if the sinner should die without having completed his penance? Moralists of the twelfth century declared that the outstanding balance of satisfaction had to be made up in purgatory. But in earlier centuries, before the doctrine of purgatory had been fully articulated, it seemed doubtful whether the penitent who died without having discharged his debt could be saved. The best hope lay in the possibility of commutation or substitution: periods of canonical penance might be commuted to alms-giving, pilgrimage, or other recognised good works. This was the basic conception underlying the medieval indulgence. Indulgences remitted a stipulated period of canonical penance and were attached to specified works of piety such as visiting a shrine or contributing to the building of a church. Alternatively, a penitent might find helpers who could perform the acts of satisfaction on his behalf.

These features of the medieval penitential system in part explain the eagerness of princes and others to found and endow monasteries. A gift to a monastery was of itself a meritorious act which might remit a long period of penance. More important, the monks, through their penitential life of continual prayer and fasting, acted as surrogates for their benefactor; they performed the satisfaction on his behalf. Moreover, as a deathless society established in perpetuity, they would continue to render him this service until the end of time. These considerations are expressed with uncommon directness in the preamble of the charter with which Duke William III of Aquitaine signified the foundation of Cluny in the year 909:

> Desiring to provide for my own salvation while I am still able, I have considered it advisable, indeed most necessary, that from the temporal goods conferred upon me I should give some little portion for the gain of my soul . . . which indeed seems attainable by no more suitable means than that, following the precept of Christ: 'I will make his poor my friends' (Luke xvi, 9), and making the act not a temporary but a lasting one, I should support at my own expense a congregation of monks. And this is my trust, this my hope, that although I myself am unable to despise all things, nevertheless by receiving those who do despise the world, whom I believe to be righteous, I too may receive the reward of the righteous.[4]

We have here the primary motivation behind the attention that the Carolingian rulers of the eighth and ninth centuries gave to the endowment and protection of monasteries: in the words of Carloman's charter, they hoped in this way to merit pardon. This also explains the concern of secular-minded princes and magnates for the cause of monastic reform, which is a recurrent theme of Charlemagne's capitularies. The prayers and mortifications of holy men would be efficacious with God. But clearly to a benefactor who hoped to participate in the merit acquired by a monastic community, to reap the spiritual divdends as it were, a community of lax and negligent monks was a poor investment.

Social convenience

Besides these spiritual advantages, the patron of a monastery looked to obtain temporal benefits from his foundation. We have already seen how the royal and noble dynasties of seventh-century Gaul used monasteries to make provision for members of their families who could not otherwise be accommodated. Surplus male children who could not be adequately set up in land without a dangerous diminution of the dynastic estate, and women of the family for whom no suitable marriage alliance could be found, could be placed in monasteries, where they might live with the dignity and esteem that was proper to their rank. In many cases they were given to the monastery as children, together with an endowment in land. The abbeys of the Carolingian age were used in this way by the Frankish nobility, and not least by the ruling dynasty itself. The heads of the richer and more illustrious establishments were in many cases blood relations of the royal family. Fulrad, the abbot of Lobbes, was a grandson of Charles Martel; most of the abbots of Saint-Riquier in the ninth century were members of the family, including Charlemagne's son-in-law and three of his grandsons; and Charles's daughter, Rohaut, was abbess of Faremoutiers. 'Every high dignitary,' boasted the chronicler of Saint-Riquier, 'wheresoever he was in the kingdom of the Franks, rejoiced that he had a relative in this monastery'.[5]

The abbeys which housed these aristocratic communities tended to exclude postulants who were not of noble birth. The great Swabian abbey of Reichenau claimed as much when it petitioned the pope in 1029: 'in the monastery there have always been, and are, only monks of illustrious and noble birth . . . from its foundation there have been none but the sons of counts and barons'.[6] Nor was this social exclusiveness confined to the greater monasteries. Noble founders and benefactors, when they placed their children in a monastery, assumed that they would continue to enjoy the society of their own kind. When the bishop of Eichstätt confirmed the gift of a church to the small Bavarian nunnery of Monheim, he agreed that the benefactress should have the office of abbess among the sisters, and gave an undertaking that 'our successors shall see that the abbess has no permission to admit girls of base or ignoble birth to the monastery'.[7]

Public policy

Personal piety and social convenience were the primary motives that prompted rulers to encourage monasticism in their dominions, but they were not the only ones. There were also wider considerations of public policy. These, too, were referred to in the charters of the Carolingian dynasty; monks were assigned lands and privileges 'that they should pray perpetually for the stability of our kingdom and the safety of our country'. The safety of the realm depended upon the intercession of holy men. The monks were the spiritual counterpart of the secular armies which defended the realm against its enemies, especially against incursions by the heathen. Their prayers and sacrifices averted the wrath of God from the sins of the people and ensured God's blessing upon the king when he went into battle. But it was not only through the invisible services of prayer and fasting that the monks promoted the stability of the realm; the great abbeys on the frontiers of the Carolingian Empire performed an important role in colonising newly conquered territories. Both as landed corporations entrusted with clearance and settlement, and as mission stations for the evangelisation of lesser breeds without the law, they were vital agents of the Carolingian *Ostpolitik*.

Charlemagne made it a primary task of his regime to subjugate the warlike and heathen people of Saxony and to incorporate the area into the Frankish realm. This involved the destruction of German paganism and the forcible conversion of the Saxons to Christianity; for religious unity was the counterpart of political dominion; Roman Christianity was the common bond that united the different peoples of Western Europe in obedience to the Frankish ruler. It was here that the monks, alongside the bishops and secular clergy, had an essential role to play. When Charlemagne embarked upon the conquest of Saxony, he summoned an assembly at Paderborn to apportion the task of conversion, and the lion's share was assigned to the frontier abbeys of Hersfeld and Fulda. Abbot Sturmi, grown old and tired, spent his last days preaching to 'the depraved and perverse race',[8] destroying pagan temples, and building churches. The same kind of missionary role was performed in the south by Reichenau from its island fastness on Lake Constance. Its founder, St Pirminus, was a contemporary of St Boniface. He was a Visigoth who had come to the Frankish court as a refugee from southern Gaul, which was harassed by the Arabs; and Charles Martel sent him to plant monastic missions among the Alamans.

The importance of the abbeys as mission stations and centres of Frankish loyalty was reflected in the pattern of royal munificence. A few favoured monasteries in the central heartlands of the Frankish realm, like Saint-Denis, received generous gifts; but the most lavish land grants were reserved for the abbeys like Fulda, Hersfeld, and Lorsch, which lay east of the Rhine, and the abbeys of Aquitaine and Septimania, which were close to the Pyrenean frontier.[9]

Concern for the public as well as the private function of the monasteries explains the constant preoccupation of Carolingian legislation with the details of monastic discipline. The decrees of Frankish councils and the royal capitularies harp upon the duties of abbots towards their monks, the rights of postulants to be received without payment, the obligation of monks to maintain strict enclosure and to be zealous in observing the Rule, 'for tepidity is displeasing to God',[10] to avoid secular business, and to be obedient to their bishop. And from the German Council of 742 until the end of the century, the standard of practice for monks to which the decrees appeal is always the Rule of St Benedict. Charlemagne was convinced that the Rule offered the best plan for a well-ordered monastery; so much so that in 787 he sent to Cassino to ask Abbot Theodemar for an authentic copy of the text. This steady promotion through royal propaganda gave the Rule a unique status as the approved code of practice for the monasteries of the Frankish Empire.

Yet despite the cachet of royal approval and the growing adoption of the Rule in the lands east of the Rhine and in southern Gaul, it had still not superseded the 'mixed rule' and other forms of observance by the end of Charlemagne's reign. Customs consecrated by long usage, and traditions embalmed by the veneration of saintly founders, died hard in many of the Gallic abbeys. Not all were willing to swim with the tide. Under the old dispensation the difference between a community of monks and a body of secular canons, which was often called a 'monastery', was not always clear. One of the results of the Carolingian drive for order and uniformity in the affairs of the Church was to clarify the distinction. Those who took vows and followed the Rule of St Benedict were monks; other congregations of men and women who lived a communal life of a quasi-monastic kind were canons and canonesses. Thus the clergy who served the basilica of Saint-Martin at Tours, and who clung to the traditions of the past, came in the ninth century to be identified as secular canons. Some of the more famous women's abbeys, including Nivelles, Faremoutier, Chelles and Jouarre, went the same way and became houses of canonesses. The Benedictine Rule, which had made such spectacular progress in the outer territories of the Carolingian Empire, seems to have encountered more resistance in the central lands of Austrasia and Neustria. At Saint-Denis, in the time of Hilduin, a majority of the community were in favour of adopting the canonical life, and the minority who wanted to observe the Rule of St Benedict had to be hived off to a villa on the Oise. In the year 813 a synod of bishops meeting at Tours lamented that monasteries which had once observed the Rule were now lax in keeping it or had abandoned it entirely.[11]

It was not only pious conservatism that hindered the spread of regular Benedictine observance. Many of the older and richer abbeys suffered loss and demoralisation at the hands of their lay proprietors; and the greatest and most exploitive lay proprietor was the king. In this respect, royal practice fell short of the public and repeated avowals of approval for the Rule. The Carolingians extended royal proprietorship over the monasteries of the Frankish Empire; bishops and lay benefactors were encouraged to donate their foundations to the king, who could offer them effective protection. But proprietorship meant the right to dispose of the abbey and its property as the proprietor thought fit. Its endowments had been given to God, but God's bailiff was the temporal proprietor.

The very lavishness with which lands had been showered upon the monasteries made it inevitable that they would be made to support many secular purposes. Charlemagne was not prepared, any more than his father had been, to divert huge estates solely to the maintenance of relatively small groups of men and women vowed to a life of prayer and seclusion. He used the abbeys freely as a form of property with which he could reward loyal supporters and relatives or remunerate ministers.

This royal exploitation took two forms. In some cases a portion of an abbey's estates would be allocated as a fief to a royal vassal; the early Carolingians, hungry for land with which to reward loyal service, constantly appropriated monastic property in this way. It is to this practice that we owe the *polyptiques* – the early inventories of monastic estates and movable property, made at royal command, which have been of such value to economic historians. In other cases the king would grant the abbey totally to a lay vassal or relative. Just as the grant of a secular estate included both the land and the peasant tenants who worked on it, so the grant of an abbey as a 'benefice' or fief to a royal servant included both the lands of the monastery and the monastic establishment itself together with the monks, who were part of the human stock, as it were, of the estate. In this case the recipient of the grant became the lay abbot and could lay claim to most of the rights over the community that were assigned to an abbot by the Rule or by monastic custom. Most of those Charles favoured in this way seem to have been secular clerks, but under his successors the conferment of abbeys on laymen was not uncommon.[12]

Where an abbey was given to a layman or a clerk, the allocation of the property and income between the abbot and the monks was a matter for negotiation between the parties; so too was the division of responsibility for the direction of the community. The arrangement did not always work to the disadvantage of the monks. Alcuin, the English scholar and poet, whom Charlemagne invited from York to be schoolmaster of the palace school, was given six abbeys by his grateful royal master and pupil, including Saint-Martin of Tours; and although he was scathing about the 'rusticity of Touraine', he was an appreciative governor. 'I love your holiness,' he wrote to the community of Saint-Martin; 'I desire to be one of you.'[13] And in the end he had his desire: after years of struggling to educate the court, from the emperor downwards, he was allowed to retire in 796 to his favourite haven beside the Loire, where he ended his days. It must have been his care for the scriptorium of the abbey that made it one of the most famous centres of manuscript production in Europe at the end of the eighth century.

Although Alcuin was a clerk, not a monk, he loved the monastic life. But not all those to whom the king gave abbeys were equally sympathetic to the monastic ideal. A layman might exploit the lands of the monastery ruthlessly and disrupt the life of the community by moving his household, with women, servants and dogs, into the monastic buildings. Those royal abbeys that remained under the direct control of the king tended to fare better. Charlemagne (768–814) treated them as an integral part of the political structure, and himself appointed the abbots, whom he regarded as imperial functionaries. It was, of course, contrary to the express directions of the Benedictine Rule, which vested the election of the abbot in the monks of his community; but nepotism and political prudence did not invariably result in unsuitable appointments. Angilbert, Charles's son-in-law, whom he designated abbot of Saint-Riquier, seems to have felt a genuine, if belated, vocation to the monastic life, and he rebuilt the abbey and furnished the church on a magnificent scale, as well as restocking the library.[14]

At the end of Charles's reign then, the monastic landscape presented a chequered picture. The abbeys east of the Rhine, which had drawn their inspiration from the Anglo-Saxon missionary effort, contained flourishing Benedictine communities. In Aquitaine and the province of Lyons the Rule was gaining ground. But elsewhere there was a variety of practice; and there are indications that in the Frankish heartlands of Gaul and Lorraine the ideal of the cenobitical life was in recession. Charles's desire to see a single and uniform monastic observance serving the needs of the Frankish Empire was never realised. It was left to his son and successor, Louis the Pious (814–40) to take up the plan and carry it through to a successful conclusion. The emperor's agent in this was St Benedict of Aniane (c. 750–821), a monk from the south, who had become a zealot for the strict observance of the Benedictine Rule. Through the collaboration of these two men the Rule was imposed upon monasteries throughout the Carolingian dominions north of the Alps. So, by a development that St Benedict of Nursia could never have envisaged, his Rule was enforced by an act of state, and in this way it came to be the sole standard of monastic observance in the ninth century.

The Rule under imperial supervision

Louis's protégé – this second Benedict – was a member of the Gothic aristocracy of southern Gaul. His father, the count of Maguelonne in the March of Gothia, sent him to the court of the Frankish queen to be educated and apprenticed to arms. It was in Italy, on campaign with Charlemagne, that a narrow escape from drowning brought his interior searchings to a crisis and persuaded him to enter the cloister. In 774 he became a monk at Saint-Seine, near Dijon. At first the fierceness of his macerations moved the abbot to remonstrate, but he replied that 'the Rule of St Benedict was composed for beginners or the sick; he himself was striving to rise higher by following the Rules of the Blessed Basil and the Blessed Pachomius'.[15] The anecdote, which is told by Ardo, who was a disciple and uncritical admirer, conveys more than youthful conceit; there is in it a foretaste of the puritanical self-righteousness Benedict displayed later, when his single-minded enthusiasm caused him to ride roughshod over the traditions of a previous age. Even so, there must have been a warmth in his personality that is concealed in Ardo's austere portrait, for Alcuin, who met him at court, could write to him in terms of intimate friendship. Perhaps he mellowed with the years.

Being dissatisfied with Saint-Seine, Benedict left it to pursue the ascetical life on his own patrimony, in a cell beside the river Aniane. Faced with the task of organising disciples who gathered round him, he came to the conclusion that the Benedictine Rule was, after all, the best model for a cenobitical community; and it must have been at this time that he adopted the name of Benedict in place of his Gothic name of Witiza. In 782 he laid the foundations of a new monastery on the banks of the Aniane, which was to be the prototype of many others. In conformity with a growing practice, he gave the abbey and its estate to Charlemagne, who took it under his protection and removed it from the jurisdiction of count and bishop. Its exclusive code of observance was to be the Rule of St Benedict.

The rest of Benedict's life was spent in actively propagating knowledge and practice of the Rule with the zeal of a convert missionary. The hagiographer has probably inflated the list of southern monasteries reformed by him in the early years;[16] but it is clear that he came to be regarded as the leading exponent of the Rule in Provence and Gothia. These activities brought him to the notice of Charles's son, Louis, who was then king of Aquitaine, and he was given a commission to visit the abbeys of Aquitaine and instruct their monks in Benedictine practice.

When Louis succeeded his father to the Empire in 814, a much wider field of action was opened to Benedict. Louis saw in this single-minded zealot the vicar-general he needed to implement Charlemagne's plan for a uniform and universal pattern of monastic observance. He summoned him to court at Aachen, and in order to keep him within reach, he had a new abbey constructed for him in the valley of the Inde, a few miles from the imperial palace. Inde was to be more than a convenient residence for the emperor's monk-councillor; it came to have a central role in the monastic reform as the official model of Benedictine observance for all the imperial abbeys – a kind of ascetical staff-college, where abbots and monks could be sent to learn the approved practices, so that they could return home and instruct their communities. Benedict was given the authority of abbot-general over all the monasteries of Francia, situated in the lands between the Loire and the Meuse.

The programme of reform and standardisation was explained to two assemblies of abbots which met in the imperial chapel of Aachen, the first in August 816 and the second in July 817. In the course of debate these two synods, which were steered by Benedict, produced a series of decrees which received the assent of the emperor, and which were subsequently conflated into an imperial edict that became known as the Monastic Capitulary.[17] The general spirit of the Aachen ordinances is encapsulated in the opening decrees of the first synod: it was to be the literal observance of the Benedictine Rule, to the exclusion of all else. Every abbot present, on returning home, was to read and expound the Rule to his monks, and to take pains to see that it was meticulously implemented. Those monks who were able to do so, were to learn the Rule by heart. All present at the synod agreed to celebrate the divine office according to its instructions. The rest of the ordinances range over various other details of the regular life. Some dealt with trivialities, such as the custom of not shaving in Lent; others with more fundamental matters, such as the duty of abbots to share the life of the brethren. The object was to draw up a common customary that all would follow.

On some minor points the decrees of the second synod were less restrictive than those of the first. The Rule forbade the eating of flesh-meat except by the sick; did this prohibition include the flesh of birds? The first synod insisted that it did: monks were not to eat fowl, unless it was prescribed for the sick. But the second synod relaxed the prohibition for the Christmas and Easter seasons. The first synod followed the Rule in restricting the use of baths, while allowing bathing at Christmas and Easter; the second left the ordering of baths to the discretion of the prior. These minor emendations apparently reflect pressure by a more liberal group at the synod that wished to modify the rigorism of Benedict of Aniane.

There were dissenting voices. Some muffled echoes of the debate can be heard in the comments that Haito of Basel wrote for his monks of Reichenau. The synods decreed that abbots should share the life of their monks in table and dormitory; but 'in this matter', wrote Haito, 'I wish to avail myself of the authority of the Rule, which is not to be prejudiced by any new constitution'. As for forbidding abbots to eat with guests by the monastery gate, he had eaten with guests from time to time, but in the abbot's auditorium, and 'this practice we wish to keep, unless it be more clearly forbidden'. The synod had forbidden the eating of fowl, 'though', he observes tartly, 'it is not forbidden by the authority of the Rule'.[18] Haito was not the only one who had reservations. The plan for the rebuilding of Saint-Gall, drafted for Abbot Gozbert shortly after the synods, included a separate house and kitchen for the abbot, and a bath-house for the monks.[19] Probably the straitjacket Benedict of Aniane sought to impose was not accepted by many establishments without some modification.

All the same, the Aachen decrees were not just an expression of pious hopes. Active steps were taken to enforce them. Special *missi* were appointed by the emperor to visit monasteries and inquire whether the decrees were being observed. Each house was required to send representatives to Inde to reside for a period and learn the observance so that they could return home and instruct their own communities. The primitive and cumbersome apparatus of the Carolingian state was now harnassed to the task of imposing a uniform pattern of life on all the imperial monasteries. The outcome of this effort was that throughout northern Europe the Rule of St Benedict became for the first time the sole norm of observance for monks.

Paradoxically, in bringing about this standardisation, Benedict of Aniane set Western monasticism on a new path which increasingly diverged from the Rule. For one thing, the autonomy of each community in the management of its internal affairs was now curtailed by the overriding authority of the abbot-general, which was backed by the power of the secular government. Also, the interpretation that Benedict of Aniane placed upon the Rule was coloured by Gallic practices of the early ninth century, which departed in significant ways from the intentions of St Benedict and upset the symmetry of his original model. The most obvious of these changes were the large number of additions to the divine office described in the Rule. 'It is not to be believed', wrote Theodemar of Cassino to Charlemagne, 'that it would displease the blessed father Benedict, but rather would it gratify him, if anyone cared to add anything over and above what he ordained for the divine praises'.[20] And Angilbert evidently agreed with him: his *Ordo* for Saint-Riquier provided for three monastic choirs, each of a hundred monks and thirty-four boys to maintain a continuous round of psalmody, litanies, solemn processions, and the celebration of at least thirty masses daily at the different altars.[21]

These and other ritual developments of the time were accepted by Benedict of Aniane and were prescribed by the Aachen decrees. In addition to the sevenfold office of the day, monks were now required to chant additional psalms before the night office and visit the numerous altars in procession, and to recite the office of the dead daily. Besides these services, the community or chapter mass was now celebrated daily after the office of terce, and it was a growing practice for individual monks to celebrate 'private' masses on the numerous altars that were coming to be a feature of monastic architectural design.

This elaboration of liturgical prayer meant that a lengthening part of the monk's day was spent in choir. And the pace set by Benedict of Aniane was to be quickened in the tenth and eleventh centuries by the musical elaboration of the chant and the virtuosity of monastic authors in the composition of new tropes, proses and sequences for the feasts of the saints. In this way the old equilibrium between prayer, work and study, that the Rule advocated, was destroyed. The divine office, which had always been a central point in the life of the monk, now became almost his exclusive occupation. There was little time left for manual work. The monastery employed servants for that purpose. The skills of the monk were more appropriately used in singing the divine praises. The idea that the perfect execution of the liturgy was the characteristic function of a Benedictine community had its origin in the reforms of the ninth century. It was an idea that accorded well with the notions of lay benefactors. This was the unceasing stream of prayer which, it was hoped, would bear them and their relatives into heaven. It was primarily to maintain this vital service that they gave landed endowments and offered their children as reinforcements for the ranks of the spiritual militia.

One of the major objects of the Aachen decrees had been to enforce stricter rules of enclosure. St Benedict had warned of the dangers that beset the souls of the brethren when business took them beyond the walls of the monastery. The ideal monk was Brother Ratpert, the historian of Saint-Gall, who rarely put a foot outside the cloister and feared going out like death, so that he needed only two pairs of shoes a year.[22] The other side of the problem was how to keep the outside world from filtering into the cloister. It was with this in mind that the assembly at Aachen decreed that there should be no school in the cloister other than that for the child-oblates. Secular clerks and lay people were excluded. The intention of the prohibition was to preserve the peace and segregation of the monastic enclosure. It did not stop a monastery from acting as the proprietor and director of an external school outside its walls. We know from Ekkehard that Saint-Gall had both a claustral school and an external school in the ninth century, and that monks taught in both of them.[23] But the more austere spirits were opposed to this kind of arrangement; it was safer to leave the conduct of the external school in the hands of a secular master appointed by the monks.

Although Benedict of Aniane wanted monks to disengage from secular education, he was eager to promote study in the cloister. But the learning he wanted was confined to what was implied by the *lectio divina* of the Benedictine Rule – the Scriptures, Origen, Augustine, and Jerome, and, above all, Gregory the Great, master of monks and mystics. This was the syllabus he prescribed for his disciple, Garnier. It was a programme designed to enlarge understanding of the dogmas of faith, and so to lead to contemplation.[24] 'All progress comes from reading and meditation', wrote Abbot Smaragdus in the *Monks' Diadem*;[25] but the only reading he recommends is that of Scripture. It was a narrower and more exclusively monastic culture than Alcuin had purveyed at the palace school or than Einhard had acquired at Fulda before the reformers got into the saddle.

The change is reflected in the literary product of the ninth-century monasteries. The cosmopolitan society of scholars, grammarians and poets that Charlemagne assembled from all parts of Europe made his court a major centre of literary activity, most strikingly in the composition of Latin verse.[26] The monasteries, too, were centres of scholarship and book production. In the libraries of Lorsch,

Saint-Gall and Saint-Amand, Virgil, Horace, Juvenal, and Cicero rubbed shoulders with the weightier and more numerous tomes of the Fathers.[27] Learned abbots like Rhabanus Maurus, the schoolmaster of Fulda, and Walafrid Strabo, his pupil, who became abbot of Reichenau, wrote living poetry besides Biblical commentaries and works of ascetical theology. But as a whole, the monastic contribution to the Carolingian renaissance largely lay in the transmission, collection, and preservation of the past rather than in new creation. Copies of classical authors, commentaries on the books of the Bible, mainly distilled from the Latin Fathers, and anthologies of patristic texts, were the most characteristic works that emerged from the scriptoria of the Carolingian abbeys. The ninth century also saw the composition of the earliest commentaries on the Benedictine Rule – those of Smaragdus and Hildemar, which became classics of monastic literature. The compilation of *florilegia*, or anthologies of the Fathers, was unoriginal work, but in the end it served a wider purpose than its authors could have foreseen: the patristic anthologies of the ninth century provided a ready-made compost in which the schoolmen of a later age were able to grow strange plants as yet undreamed of.

Collapse and dispersal

Benedict of Aniane died in 812, and the organisation he had brought into existence did not outlive him for very long. Italy had never been brought within the orbit of his reform programme.[28] In the Germanic lands of the Empire, there is evidence of the *missi* conducting monastic visitations in the 830s, but the system collapsed with the disintegration of imperial authority. It was not just the problem of enforcement that caused the plan to wither in the opening bud; the conditions of the ninth century blighted monastic life. Monasteries, unlike wealthy lay landowners, were unarmed and defenceless communities. They could only survive in a violent society as long as they had the patronage and effective protection of strong rulers; and in the dominions of the later Carolingians this condition ceased to exist.

The civil war between the sons of Louis the Pious, and the troubled period that followed the partition of the Empire in 843, led to the widespread secularisation of abbeys. The reformers had never succeeded in eliminating the practice of appointing lay abbots, and during the years of upheaval the contestants distributed abbeys freely among their aristocratic followers as a way of rewarding loyal service. The Frankish bishops upbraided Charles the Bald in 844 for having committed 'even some more especially venerable places, against all authority and reason and the custom of your fathers, to the care and power of laymen. They sit in the midst of priests and Levites like abbots and make rules for their life and conversation.'[29] The resulting exploitation of monastic lands and buildings disrupted regular observance and impoverished the monks, who either dispersed or adopted the easier-going life of individual canons, and joined in dividing the spoils.

Political instability and lay exploitation were not the only enemies of organised monastic life. The monks had to face more frightening foes in the heathen Vikings and the Saracens. In the ninth century Christian Europe was under siege. Ireland, England, and the north of Gaul were ravaged by the Northmen. Abbeys situated near the coasts or on the inland waterways of these areas were sitting targets. Lindisfarne, Clonfert and Clonmacnoise were among the first to be sacked. The more accessible abbeys near the coast of northern Gaul and along the valleys of the Seine, the Meuse, and the Loire fell victims to the onslaught of the predators. The monasteries of the Rhône valley and southern Italy suffered the same fate at the hands of the Arabs, who had established themselves in the Maritime Alps as well as in Spain and Sicily. In 883 they burned Cassino and slaughtered the monks, leaving it deserted for the next sixty years.

Communities of some of the ravaged abbeys escaped the raiders and dispersed. Others kept together and maintained a precarious existence as refugees, like the monks of St Philibert of Noirmoutier, who fled from the Danes in 836. Some years later Charles the Bald made them a grant of land to serve as a refuge from 'attack by the cruel Northmen'.[30] They were sheltered, in fact, in five successive monasteries before finding a permanent home at Tournus thirty-nine years later. Their saga was paralleled by that of the monks of Lindisfarne, who fled to the mainland from a second Danish attack, taking the body of St Cuthbert with them, and wandered in Northumbria with their precious freight for seven years until they found a residence at Chester-le-Street. Such enforced migrations were commonplace at this period.

Before the end of the century, regular monastic observance had almost disappeared from western Gaul and England. Alfred of Wessex lamented over the destruction of the Anglo-Saxon abbeys and their libraries. He provided endowments for the Old Minster at Winchester and a few other houses in which he had a family interest, and according to Asser he founded the nunnery of Shaftesbury and appointed his daughter, Aethelgifu, as its first abbess;[31] but a full-scale monastic revival had to await more settled times. In the east German lands, religious observance and scholarship survived at Fulda and Saint-Gall; and Reichenau remained an island of peace and learning under the gentle abbacy of Walafrid Strabo, whose poetry kept his herb-garden green for all posterity.

The situation in other parts of Gaul is indicated by the experience of St Odo, as described by his biographer. As a young man, the son of a Frankish knight, Odo was comfortably installed in a canonry at Tours, when a reading of the Rule of St Benedict convinced him he should become a monk. With a like-minded friend he set out in search of a monastery where the Rule was observed, but they traversed most of Francia without finding one. Odo returned home frustrated; but his friend travelled further afield and eventually discovered what they had been looking for in the remote abbey of Baume, on the west side of the Jura. It was a monastery where the observance of Benedict of Aniane had survived. Its abbot was Berno, a Burgundian, who had been called in to restore regular life there in accordance with the Aachen decrees. The friend sent back the news, and both he and Odo took the habit there.

Some years later, in 909, when Duke William III of Aquitaine decided to found a monastery on his Burgundian estates, he sought the advice of Abbot Berno. Duke and abbot set off together to reconnoitre a suitable spot, and Berno chose the richly wooded valley of Cluny. William protested that the site was his favourite hunting ground, but Berno was inexorable: 'which will serve you better at the Judgement, O Duke, the prayers of monks or the baying of hounds?' So William yielded, and Berno became the first abbot of the new foundation. He thus became a link between the Carolingian programme of reform and the monasticism of Cluny, which was to dominate the religious life of the next two hundred years.

Notes

1. *Die Urkunden der Karolinger*, ed. E. Mühlbacher, *MGH Diplomata* (1906) I, pp. 57–8.
2. *Ibid.*, pp. 86–7.
3. *Poenitentiale Theodori*, ed. A. W. Haddan and W. Stubbs in *Councils and Ecclesiastical Documents* (1871) iii, pp. 173–203; cf. texts edited by L. Bieler, *The Irish Penitentials (Scriptores Latini Hiberniae)* V (1963).
4. *Receuil des chartes de l'abbaye de Cluny*, ed. A. Bruel (Paris, 1876) i, pp. 124–8.
5. *Chronique de l'abbaye de Saint-Riquier*, ed. F. Lot (Paris, 1894), pp. 118–19.
6. A. Schulte, *Der Adel und die deutsche Kirche im Mittelalter*, 2nd edn (Stuttgart, 1922), p. 3 & n.
7. *Ibid.*, p. 114.
8. *Vita Sancti Sturmi*, *MGH SS* II, pp. 366–77.
9. J. Semmler, 'Karl der Grosse und das Fränkische Mönchtum' in *Karl der Grosse* ii: *Das geistige Leben*, ed. B. Bischoff (Düsseldorf, 1965), pp. 255–89. This is the best modern account of Charlemagne's monastic policy.
10. Thus the general capitulary for the *missi* of 802: *MGH Leges* II: *Capitularia Regum Francorum*, ed. A. Boretius (1881) i, p. 94.
11. *MGH Concilia*, ed. A. Werminghoff (1906) II, p. 290.
12. E. Lesne, *Histoire de la propriété ecclésiastique en France* (Lille, 1926) ii, *passim*; P. Schmitz, *Histoire de l'ordre de Saint Benoît* (Maredsous, 1942) i, pp. 80–90. As against Lesne, it has been argued that the lay abbot does not appear before the reign of Louis the Pious: F. Felten, 'Laienäbte in der Karolingerzeit' in *Mönchtum Episkopat und Adel zur Gründungszeit des Klosters Reichenau*, ed. A. Borst (Constance, 1974), pp. 397–431. On Louis's appointment of lay abbots see Rosamond McKitterick, *The Frankish Kingdoms under the Carolingians* (1983), pp. 115–22.
13. *MGH Epistolae* IV, p. 94.
14. *Chronique de Saint-Riquier*, p. 53.
15. *Vita Benedicti Abbatis Anianensis*, *MGH SS* XV, p. 202.
16. O. G. Oexle in *Forschungen zu monastischen und geistlichen Gemeinschaften im Westfränkischen Bereich* (Munich, 1978), p. 151, argues that the abbey of Île- Barbe was organised according to the Benedictine Rule by Archbishop Leidrad of Lyons in *c.* 802 and that, contrary to the statements of Ardo, Benedict of Aniane had no part in it. In Oexle's view the range and importance of Benedict's work has been exaggerated.
17. The original texts of the Aachen decrees have now been clarified and newly edited by Semmler in *CCM* I (1963), pp. 451–68, 471–81. Semmler has shown that the so-called *Capitulare Monasticum*, ed. A. Boretius in *MGH Capitularia* (1883) I, pp. 343–9, is

a document produced in *c.* 818–19 by conflating the capitularies containing the decrees of both the first and second synods: 'Zur Überlieferung der monastischen Gesetzgebung Ludwigs des Frommen', *Deutsches Archiv zur Erforschung des Mittelalters* 16 (1960), pp. 309–88.

18. Haito's commentary is contained in the so-called Statutes of Murbach, *CCM* I (1963), pp. 443–8.
19. W. Horn and E. Born, *The Plan of St Gall* (1979) i, p. 24.
20. *MGH Epistolae* IV, p. 511.
21. *Chronique de Saint-Riquier*, pp. 70–1; see discussion by J. Hubert, 'Saint-Riquier et le monachisme bénédictin en Gaulle à l'époque carolingienne' in *Il monachesimo nell'alto medioevo* (Spoleto, 1957), pp. 293–309.
22. *Casus S. Galli, MGH SS* II, pp. 94, 97.
23. See *The Plan of St. Gall* i, p. 24 & n.
24. Cf. J. Leclercq, F. Vandenbroucke, and L. Bouyer, *The Spirituality of the Middle Ages* (1968), pp. 77–8.
25. *Diadema Monachorum, PL* 102, 597.
26 Mary Garrison, 'The emergence of Carolingian Latin literature and the court of Charlemagne' in *Carolingian Culture: emulation and innovation*, ed. Rosamond McKitterick (1994), pp. 111–38.
27. Monastic library catalogues of the ninth century list only a few classical authors, who are heavily outnumbered by Christian writers of the patristic age, see Giles Brown, 'The Carolingian Renaissance', *ibid.*, pp. 35–7. For a survey of ninth-century monastic scholarship see McKitterick, *op. cit.* pp. 200–27.
28. G. Penco, *Storia del monachesimo in Italia* (Rome, 1961), p. 170.
29. *MGH Capitularia Regum Francorum* II, p. 115.
30. *Receuil des actes de Charles II le Chauve*, ed. G. Tessier (Paris, 1943) I, No. 91; cited by Jane Martindale, 'The kingdom of Aquitaine and the dissolution of the Carolingian fisc' in *Francia, Forschungen zur Westeuropäischen Geschichte* (1984) 11, p. 163 & n.
31. *Alfred the Great: Asser's Life of King Alfred and Other Sources*, trans. & ed. Simon Keynes and Michael Lapidge (Penguin, 1983), p. 105. Controversy over the authenticity of Asser, specifically in relation to Alfred's monastic foundations, has been renewed by A. P. Smyth, *King Alfred the Great* (1995), pp. 264–9.

6

THE AGE OF CLUNY

The rise of Cluny

'From this, the best seed', wrote Ralph Glaber, himself a pupil of Cluny, 'sprang an innumerable lineage of the Lord of Hosts, which is known to have filled a great area of the earth.'[1] There was much truth in Ralph's encomium. At the end of the eleventh century, at the height of its magnificence, Cluny was the head of a huge monastic empire containing many hundreds of dependencies and associated houses spread throughout western Europe. It was a nursery of zealous prelates and the mentor of pious princes. Its holy and learned abbots were prominent counsellors at the courts of popes and emperors. Before Leo IX ascended the papal chair at the end of 1048 and made Rome the headquarters of the so-called Gregorian Reform Movement, it was to Cluny that men looked for spiritual leadership and religious inspiration. Even after its heyday was past and its creativity and confidence had begun to ebb, it remained a powerful force in the ecclesiastical and political establishment of the twelfth century.

All this lay in the future. In the tenth century Cluny stood for the restoration of Benedictine monastic life, largely as it had been understood by Benedict of Aniane a century earlier. As a house that was dedicated to reviving strict observance of the Rule, it was not unique. It had spiritual parentage in Baume and St Martin of Autun; and it also had important contemporaries. Within a few years of its foundation, a monastic revival was sponsored in Flanders by the count, Arnulf I. He found an enthusiastic collaborator for his purpose in Gerard of Brogne, a young nobleman who had adopted the ascetical life and created a monastery on his own patrimony at Brogne. Under the count's active patronage, he restored Benedictine observance, first at Saint-Bavo of Ghent and St Peter's on Mount Blandin, and then at the other Flemish abbeys of Saint-Bertin, Saint-Amand and Saint-Omer.

A similar revival, but one of wider dimensions, began in Lorraine in the year 933, when the abbey of Gorze was reformed by John of Gorze and archdeacon Einold, acting under the authority of the bishop of Metz. Gorze in turn became corner-stone of a large federation of reformed abbeys in Germany. The striking thing about the promoters of the monastic revival of the tenth century is that they worked independently of each other in the different areas, apparently expressing a common need felt by individual ascetics and their lay patrons and that, despite differences of organisation, all three groups derived their inspiration and forma-tive ideas from the work of Benedict of Aniane.

Cluny was given the basic organisation of its internal regime by Berno, its first abbot. It was also to him and Duke William that it owed a feature of its con-stitution that enabled it to preserve its identity and provided the base on which its later greatness was built: it was granted a degree of autonomy that was still uncommon for a monastic establishment. William's foundation charter expressly authorised the monks to choose their own abbot after Berno's death, without interference by any outside persons either lay or ecclesiastical. The abbot and community were to have sole and undivided control over their properties, free from intrusion by any secular power, including William's own.

In order to guarantee this immunity William resorted to a device which a number of other founders had adopted in the previous fifty years: he vested the proprietorship of the establishment in the Apostles Peter and Paul and placed it under the immediate protection of the Apostolic See. In recognition of this special relationship, the abbey was to pay a *census* or tribute of ten solidi every five years to maintain lights burning round the shrine of St Peter in Rome. Recent work has shown that this arrangement was not as original as was once believed.[2] Other benefactors had donated their monastic foundations to St Peter. In any case, the invocation of the bishop of Rome as protector of the monastery can have been an act of little more than symbolic significance at this time, for the tenth-century popes, immersed in the dynastic politics of Rome, appeared to lack either the will or the means to defend their distant protégés. What made the case of Cluny different was that the bond with Rome later developed into a special relationship of mutual advantage, which enabled the abbey to achieve its unique position of independence, prestige and power. This development was largely the work of a series of exceptionally gifted men who ruled Cluny for the next hundred and forty years.

In this respect, Duke William's self-denying ordinance in granting the monks complete freedom to elect their abbot was a provision of crucial importance. In fact, this freedom, which the earlier reformers had struggled for in vain, was not exercised in the way specified by the Rule; for Berno and the three abbots who followed him designated their successors. But it was a primary factor in establishing the Cluniac ascendancy. It produced in St Odo (926–44), St Mayeul (965–94), St Odilo (994–1048), and St Hugh (1049–1109), four spiritual leaders of genius, each of whom in his own way stamped his imprint not only upon the regime of Cluny but also upon the religious life of his age.

Much that was characteristic of the Cluniac ideal was the creation of Odo, who was brought from training the novices at Baume to succeed Abbot Berno. He gave the monastic vocation a new theology and a new sense of mission. The vision of the world he communicated in his *Occupation of the Mind* – a prolonged meditation written in hexameters – was unrelievedly sombre. The evils of society seemed convincing evidence that the end of the world and the Day of Judgement were at hand. For the great mass of mankind, which was enslaved by concupiscence, there seemed to be little hope. The only safe route to salvation lay through repentance, conversion and entry into the monastic life. Monks were the Pentecostal Church created and renewed by the Holy Spirit. If they utterly renounced the world and were faithful to their calling, they were already living in paradise: the great silence that engulfed the cloister was a participation in the eternal silence of God; and the monk was united to God through the practice of unbroken prayer.[3] This conviction that the restored Benedictine life was the only authentic fulfilment of the Christian vocation was at the heart of the appeal that Cluny made to the society of its time.

To his disciples and admirers Odo himself seemed a living embodiment of the Benedictine ideal. He taught the message of renunciation with an evangelical fervour: 'He found me at Rome,' wrote Brother John, his biographer, 'trapped in the toils of earthly desires, and in his compassion he landed me in his net like a fish.'[4] He observed the Rule meticulously. Some wag in the cloister nicknamed him 'Ditcher' because he went about keeping constant custody of his eyes, with his head bowed and his eyes fixed on the ground. Two of the practices he inculcated in his monks came to be regarded as distinctive marks of early Cluniac observance: the keeping of silence at all times, and the continual use of vocal prayer. Not only in choir during the offices, but wherever he went and whatever he was doing the monk was enjoined to recite the psalms. Brother John recalled an incident that occurred during one of their many journeys across the Alps. A gang of robbers was lying in wait for travellers. But the leader of the gang was astounded at the unusual spectacle of a cortege moving with bowed heads and ceaselessly chanting psalms. 'I never remember seeing men like these', he muttered. And he would not let his men attack them.[5] Another of Odo's disciples, Brother Godfrey, had learned the lesson of silence so well that he lost the community one of its horses. While the party was in Rome, he had been set to guard the horses, which had been put to grass overnight. Rather than shouting to the sleeping watchmen during the hours of the Greater Silence that followed Compline, he allowed a thief to mount one of the animals and ride off with it.[6]

In terms of buildings and material goods Cluny was still poor in Odo's time. He saw the first church completed, but when the bishop of Mâcon came to consecrate it, the monks were embarrassed by his large entourage as they lacked the wherewithal to feed everybody. Their dilemma was solved, according to Brother John, by the providential appearance of a wild boar, which came and banged on the door of the church with its trotters; having failed to gain admittance, he lay

FIGURE 6.1 The Abbey of Saint Benoît-sur Loire
© Arnaud Chicurel/Hemis/Corbis

down across the entrance and obligingly offered his body to the spears of the epis-copal knights. Yet despite these humble circumstances, the reputation of Cluny as a model of Benedictine observance was spreading, and Odo received invitations from princes and bishops to undertake the reform of other monasteries.

The old abbeys of Fleury and Romanmôtier were among the first of a whole series of French monasteries in which he restored regular observance. It was to authorise and promote his mission of monastic reform that in 931 he obtained from Pope John XI a most significant privilege. The vows that a monk took bound him for life to the particular community that had accepted him; transfer to another community was contrary to the spirit of the Rule, and required the sanction of higher authority. Pope John's privilege offered a ladder of escape from this rule by authorising Cluny to accept from any other monastery a refu-gee who was in search of a stricter observance. Odo obtained the same privilege for Déols, and a few years later for Fleury as well. These bulls in effect conferred official recognition on the Cluniac reform and authorised its expansion.

It was Odo's regime and his own charismatic personality that set Cluny on the path to European status. He was a figure on the European stage himself. By con-stantly seeking papal approval for his work of monastic renewal he developed the special relationship with Rome at a time when papal influence in the churches of northern Europe was at low tide. His reputation beyond France was strik-ingly demonstrated by the fact that only twenty-five years after the foundation of Cluny he was invited by the secular ruler of Rome to undertake the reform of the monasteries in the city and in the Roman duchy. Rome at this time was ruled by the Senator Alberic, son of the notorious Lady Marozia and head of the dynasty of Theophylact. Most of the Roman monasteries had been secularised by this period. The establishments which served the patriarchal basilicas of the city and the imperial abbey of Farfa in the Sabina were occupied by married secular canons.

Alberic has not had a kindly press from historians of the Church. It has been argued that he sponsored the monastic revival for very worldly reasons: the resumption and reallocation of ecclesiastical lands that had fallen into the hands of rival families would serve to strengthen the hold of his own dynasty upon the duchy. Certainly, he was not above foisting his own son, the profligate and half-illiterate John XII, upon the papacy in order to perpetuate the family's fortunes. Whatever his motives, he placed his authority behind Odo, who embarked upon his task in 936. During the following years Odo made six prolonged stays in the city. He introduced Cluniac observance to St Paul's-without-the-walls and to Farfa, and presided over the newly founded abbey of St Mary's, constructed among the groves of the Aventine hill out of one of the palaces Alberic had donated for the purpose.[7] None of the Roman monasteries was placed in a relationship of dependence upon Cluny at this date, and Odo's reforming work was not long-lasting. But it impressed upon the capital of Christendom the fact that Cluny was the recognised standard-bearer of the regular Benedictine life.

The extension of the Cluniac family that Odo had begun was continued by Mayeul, whose life-history resembled Odo's in many ways. He too had come to the monastic life as an adult. He was already an archdeacon when he knocked on the doors of Cluny. He had been to the schools and acquired a love of the philosophers and poets, which he afterwards renounced so fiercely that he would neither read them nor suffer others to read them: 'the divine poets are sufficient for you; what need to pollute yourselves with the voluptuous eloquence of Virgil?'[8] But the reading habit never left him, and even in the saddle he rode with an open book in his hand. As abbot he was constantly in demand to reform other monasteries, which involved him in frequent and prolonged absences from Cluny, and his Life, written by Brother Syrus, is filled with anecdotes of his journeys to and from Italy. On one occasion he was seized by Saracens while crossing the Alps and had to be ransomed. He was a familiar figure at Rome and a welcome guest at the imperial court, where he won the admiration of the dowager Empress Adelaide. She asked him to introduce the Cluniac observance to the new foundation of San Salvatore at Pavia; and when the Roman See fell vacant, she and her son, Otto II, urged him to accept the papacy. But he refused the distinction of being the first Cluniac pope, saying he did not relish the ways of the Roman people and, in any case, he was not willing to desert the monastic life and the monks under his care.

The Cluniac empire

The missionary zeal and energy of Odo and Mayeul placed Cluny at the centre of the monastic map of Europe. But it was the regime of Odilo and Hugh that gave it a great spiritual empire. The extraordinary reign of these two men, both of whom were long-lived, lasted for a hundred and fifteen years. Slight in build and ascetical, always gentle and perceptive in his relations with his monks, Odilo was for Fulbert of Chartres 'the archangel of monks'. He had a capacious mind and humane sympathies which make him one of the most attractive figures in the gallery of Cluniac saints.[9] Like his predecessor, a constant traveller in the cause of monastic revival and reform, he was friend and counsellor to popes and kings and moved with assurance in the courts of Europe.

It was through Odilo's tireless efforts that the first outlines of Cluny's monastic empire began to emerge. Besides abbeys in France, Italy, and Spain which accepted Cluniac customs, a growing number of monasteries were donated to Cluny by their patrons and these remained direct dependencies in the sense that the abbot of Cluny was their head. The process of forging a Cluniac order was taken a stage further by the privilege of exemption which Odilo obtained from the papacy. Like the previous abbots, he assiduously courted papal support for the monastic reform. And he used his influence at Rome to extricate Cluny from diocesan authority. In 998 he procured a privilege from Pope Gregory V to the effect that no bishop might celebrate mass or ordain anyone at the abbey except by the abbot's invitation. The final step towards autonomy was taken in 1024 when Odilo secured from John XIX a grant of complete exemption from the jurisdiction of the bishop of Mâcon, which placed Cluny under the direct authority of the Roman See. And this exemption extended to monks of Cluny wherever they resided. This effectively freed all the dependencies of Cluny from episcopal oversight and left them under the sole supervision of the abbot of Cluny.

The need to supervise the dependent houses and appoint their superiors kept Odilo continually on his travels in the later years. But Cluny was where his heart lay, and he always tried to get back there for major festivals. He revelled in its triumphs, as he happily contemplated the growing numbers of novices and the monks from elsewhere who had come to study the observance. 'How festively he would stand,' wrote Jotsaldus, his pupil and biographer, 'in the middle of that holy choir, looking to left and right at the new plantation which was his crown',[10] as the head of a college might from the vantage-point of high table survey a new intake with pleasure and surmise.

Success and mounting fame had brought the abbey a flood of endowments. The stringency of the early days was forgotten, and the exalted grandeur of the Cluniac ideal was beginning to take palpable shape in magnificent buildings. In order to accommodate increasing numbers Mayeul had replaced the church of Odo's time with a new and grander building. Odilo set about reconstructing the community's domestic premises. He was a great builder – he renewed everything, wrote Jotsaldus, except the walls of the church. A new dormitory and refectory were built, and a guest-house divided into two sections, with beds for forty-five men and thirty women. But the major source of his pride was the cloister, which he rebuilt with piers of marble procured from Provence and shipped up the Rhône and Saône, and embellished with animated sculptures. 'He used to boast,' says Jotsaldus, 'that he found it made of wood and was leaving it marble, like Octavious Caesar who, as the historians say, found Rome brick and left it marble.'[11]

With the assumption of the abbacy by Hugh, Cluny entered on its last and greatest period of expansion. The year 1049, when his reign began, was also a milestone in the history of the secular Church. It saw the arrival in Rome of the emperor's cousin, Bruno of Toul, who as Pope Leo IX, inaugurated a new style of papal goverment. The first year of Leo's pontificate proved in fact to be an *annus mirabilis* for the growing party of high-minded churchmen who were pressing for the reform of abuses and an end to the secularisation of ecclesiastical offices. Following a brisk drive to restore clerical discipline in Rome, he set off to make his presence felt north of the Alps. Assemblies of bishops and abbots were summoned to meet him at Reims and Mainz. The prelates who attended were examined on the circumstances of their appointments and were asked whether they had paid money for their offices. Those who admitted having done so were disciplined; absentees were declared suspended from office; the disobedient were excommunicated; and new canons were promulgated. This burst of activity indicated that the pope had stepped into the leadership of the reform movement. It inaugurated a new phase in which the papacy demanded an ever more active and interventionist role in the affairs of local churches and called in question the domination of the Church by secular rulers. It was significant that Leo's synod at Reims was cold-shouldered by the king of France. The pope's attack on simony had thrown down the first challenge to lay control of ecclesiastical offices that was to lead to the Investiture Contest.

Cluny, by its idealism, its assertion of spiritual autonomy, and its constant appeal to papal protection, had helped to create the necessary spiritual climate in which the reform movement could flourish, and it could hardly avoid being drawn into the ensuing conflict between the papacy and secular rulers.

Thanks to the status won by his predecessors, Abbot Hugh entered at once into a European role. And his birth and his own talents equipped him well for the part. He was born to the purple – the son of a count of the Brionnais, with family connections among the higher aristocracy of Aquitaine and Burgundy.[12] He had entered the noviciate of Cluny in his early teens. Odilo, who was no respecter of persons but a good judge of managerial capacity, appointed him prior at the age of twenty-two. His devotion to the Rule and his successful management of the abbey's external affairs during Odilo's later years marked him out as the obvious successor. He was a tall, well-built man, with an impressive physical presence. His shrewd judgement was combined with an urbanity and perceptiveness that attracted confidences from others. He had all the mental and personal gifts of the successful executive, which contended in his soul with the deeply ingrained humility of the monk: 'the flesh wanted it', he answered with utter candour when, with other abbots, he was asked at the Council of Reims how he had obtained the abbacy, 'but the mind and rational part refused it'.[13] He read much, but he seems to have felt no urge to authorship; his talents lay elsewhere, in planning, directing, and building. Intense bodily mortification and constant prayer had enabled him to sublimate personal ambition into an unflagging will to promote the monastic ideal and enhance the grandeur of Cluny. His zeal in supervising the dependent houses of the order made him a constant traveller, and he was a familiar figure to many of the French and Italian bishops as well as a welcome visitor to the courts of the emperor and the king of France. While he was prior, he had already met and won the confidence of the Emperor Henry III, and he later accepted the invitation to be godfather to the future Henry IV. It was this long-established association of the leaders of Cluny with the imperial family, as well as their carefully cultivated links with the papacy, that obliged them to assume a role in the investiture struggle.

For many of the aims and ideals of the Gregorian Reform movement the Cluniacs were bound to feel a profound empathy. They wholeheartedly endorsed that part of the reform programme that aimed at purifying the Church from abuses and rescuing it from exploitation by lay rulers. The fact that they owed their own freedom from lay interference and episcopal jurisdiction to the favour of St Peter and his vicar made them natural allies of the papacy in its struggle to assert its spiritual authority over Christendom. On the other hand, the spread of Cluniac monasticism owed much to the enthusiasm of pious princes; and their long history of collaboration with lay rulers, especially with the German imperial family, disposed the leaders of Cluny to adopt a cautious attitude to the more radical of the hierocratic claims made by Gregory VII.[14] Their dilemma is apparent from the part played by Abbot Hugh in the bitter struggle between Gregory and Henry IV of Germany.

Gregory had been a monk himself, possibly at St Mary's on the Aventine, which had links with Cluny, and he admired the Cluniac ideal. Hugh was a friend to whom he looked for moral support in the darkest days of his struggle. In 1075 he poured out his heart to him in a long letter written in a mood of deep depression and discouragement over the violent opposition to his decrees on clerical celibacy and lay investiture.[15] But Hugh was also godfather and counsellor to King Henry; and this made it impossible for him to remain aloof from the dispute. So he bent all his efforts to bring about a reconciliation. He was, in fact, one of the chief architects of the dramatic meeting between the pope and emperor-elect at Canossa in 1077. He was present at the negotiations, and attested the oath Henry swore to implement the terms of the concordat.

FIGURE 6.2 Vézelay Abbey: the storiated capital of the mystic mill
Photograph by Clive Hicks

Six years later, when the German army was investing Rome and Gregory was trapped in the Castel Sant'Angelo, Hugh was allowed to cross the lines in a last but unsuccessful attempt to mediate between Henry and the pope. The fact that he managed to retain the trust and affection of both the contestants throughout the struggle is a tribute to his detachment and diplomatic skill. But ultimately, of course, the interests as well as the ideal of Cluny were bound to align it with the Gregorian papacy. If Hugh felt a painful division of personal loyalties, he never wavered in his support for the papal programme of reform, and he served Gregory well as papal legate in France. Other Cluniac monks also served at the papal Curia; and the old alliance was consummated in 1088 when a former grand prior of Cluny, Odo, the cardinal bishop of Ostia, was elected pope as Urban II.

In the course of Hugh's abbacy, which lasted for sixty years, Cluny touched the peak of its power and social esteem. Urban II was only the most conspicuous of a stream of Cluniac monks who were recruited to the ranks of the episcopate. It was during Hugh's regime, too, that a vast and complex network of relationships began to emerge between Cluny and its dependencies which has baffled the descriptive powers of modern historians. New foundations that were colonised by monks from Cluny were organised as priories immediately dependent upon the mother-house, which appointed the superior of each house, who was often drawn from Cluny itself. Hugh also brought pressure to bear upon abbeys reformed by Cluny to accept reduction to the status of priories. Those old and wealthy abbeys, like Vézelay and Moissac, that were allowed to retain their abbatial status, were subject to the control of the abbot of Cluny, who either appointed their heads or supervised the election of their abbots. Some of the subject abbeys and priories were themselves the parents and overseers of families of dependent monasteries. Moissac, in Gascony, acquired a cluster of houses in Catalonia. And the priory of La Charité, situated in the upper valley of the Loire, had a far-flung family of seventy dependencies, which included five foundations in post-Conquest England. Besides the host of monasteries that stood in a relationship of direct or indirect subordination to Cluny, there was a shifting circle of satellite establishments which were drawn into the organisation after accepting Cluniac observance, but subsequently regained their independence. Others again adopted Cluniac practice without ever surrendering their autonomy.

These differing degrees of association were to be seen in most parts of Europe by the end of the eleventh century. In the duchy of Rome, the ancient abbey of Farfa was restored to Cluniac observance with the help of Odilo, but it never became constitutionally subordinated to Cluny. By contrast, during the regime of Hugh a whole series of dependent priories were founded in north Italy at Lodi, Pontida, and in the region of Milan. In Germany, the major focus of Cluniac influence was the Swabian abbey of Hirsau, which adopted Cluniac observance after 1079 under the leadership of Abbot William of Hirsau – it was he who got Ulrich, the prior of Zell, to compile a customary for him; but Hirsau itself was never directly affiliated to Cluny.

In Spain, Cluny acquired a group of subject monasteries after 1072, thanks to the enthusiastic patronage of Alfonso VI of Leon-Castile. Cluniac penetration of the Spanish kingdoms began in the time of Odilo, when Sancho the Great sent monks to Cluny to learn the observance and introduce it to the abbey of San Juan de la Peña in Aragon. The personal links with the royal dynasty forged by Odilo were strengthened in Hugh's time by the marriage of his niece to

Alfonso VI. Alfonso gave several monasteries to Cluny, but its practices and ethos were disseminated in Spain not so much through its subject priories as through the abbeys which adopted its customs without becoming dependencies. Chief among these was the royal abbey of Sahagun in Leon, which Alfonso forced to accept the customs of Cluny in 1080, together with a Cluniac monk as abbot. Sahagun became in fact the major agency by which Cluniac observance was introduced to the religious communities of Leon-Castile.

This ramshackle spiritual empire was not an order in the proper sense of the term. It was a vast spatial extension of St Benedict's idea of a monastery as a family community living under the personal direction of a father-abbot. All Cluniac monks, wherever they lived, were in theory members of the community of the mother-house itself. When they visited Cluny, they were entitled to take their place in chapter with the residents. Postulants who had been admitted to any house of the congregation, once they had completed their noviciate, were sent to make their profession to the abbot of Cluny or alternatively awaited his visitation of their own monastery. He was the spiritual father of all Cluniac monks everywhere. It was a theory that stretched St Benedict's model to breaking-point. For although Odilo and Hugh were indefatigable travellers and visitors of the daughter-houses, any real supervision of such a huge congregation was obviously beyond the capacity of one man. As time went on, the relationship between the mother-house and the dependencies lost the intimacy of a filial bond and assumed some of the colour of feudal lordship that existed in the secular world. The role of the abbot of Cluny became that of a distant potentate, to whom every house of the congregation owed obedience and to whom it looked for protection. The outward sign of this subjection was the annual tax or *census* paid to Cluny by each of its daughter-houses.

The Cluniac empire lacked an effective organisation because it was not the outcome of any clearly formulated design. Its colonies were acquired piecemeal in the course of two centuries through unsolicited donations and requests for help. It owed its existence chiefly to the enthusiasm of lay magnates, who either sponsored new foundations or donated abbeys in their possession with an appeal, not always happily endorsed by their monks, for the introduction of Cluniac observance. Two cases illustrate the different ways in which additions were made to the Cluniac family.

One of these was the case of Fleury, which came into the hands of Abbot Odo about the year 930. It was an acquisition of special and symbolic significance as it contained the body of St Benedict. It was a royal abbey, but Odo's biographer tells us that the Robertian king Rudolf I gave it as a reward for service to Count Elisiard. Elisiard was an admirer of Cluny and offered the abbey to Odo to be reformed. But the community did not share Elisiard's enthusiasm. When Odo arrived with a heavy escort of two counts and two bishops, he found the doors barred against him. The monks waved royal privileges which promised they should never be ruled by a superior from another congregation;

and some of them retreated to the roof of the cloister, from which they pelted the visitors with brickbats.

Odo, who was a peaceable but persistent man, allowed the siege to continue for three days; then, unescorted and unnoticed, he placed a ladder against an inconspicuous corner of the wall and quietly let himself into the enclosure. He was received without violence, and his gentle persuasiveness prevailed on the monks to accept him as their abbot. According to Brother John, their change of heart was prompted by a threat from a personage more exalted than either count or bishop: one of the brethren, returning from duties outside the cloister, was confronted by the Blessed Benedict himself who gave him a frightening message for the community: 'Since they will allow me no rest, I am departing from this house, and know that I shall not return to this place until I bring from Aquitaine a man after my own heart.'[16] Thus Fleury passed into the Cluniac family through the collaboration of St Odo with the wishes of a lay proprietor. It seems that its links with Cluny remained purely personal, through the appointment of its abbots. Odo did no more than restore strict observance. The early eleventh-century customary of Fleury, which contains some variants from Cluniac practice, indicates that he did not impose all the practices of Cluny upon his newly acquired abbey.[17]

A different case was that of Lewes in Sussex, which was a new foundation. Cluny began to penetrate England after the Norman Conquest, though the initiative came from the king and the Anglo-Norman nobility and not from Abbot Hugh, who showed no great eagerness to extend his monastic family across the Channel. In fact he declined a request from King William to supply him with monks for English abbeys in return for an annual payment to Cluny. The foundation of Lewes priory, the first of the English Cluniac houses, was the result of an initiative by William de Warenne, the first Norman earl of Surrey. After the turmoil of the Conquest and settlement, William, accompanied by his English wife, Gundrada, set out on a pilgrimage to St Peter's in Rome. They made a leisurely progress through France and stopped at Cluny, where they were royally received and entertained in the palatial building Odilo had designed for noble guests.[18] The warmth of the hospitality and the splendour of the liturgical life made a deep impression on them, and they sought and obtained from the community the privilege of confraternity.

On returning home, the earl and countess determined to create a Cluniac priory at Lewes, close to the castle which was the head of their lordship. They petitioned Abbot Hugh to send monks, promising to donate to the proposed foundation the newly built stone church of Lewes and an endowment big enough to support a community of twelve. But Hugh at first demurred. As he had told King William, he was disinclined to send monks to an alien country across the sea, where supervision would be impossible. The earl and countess persisted, however, and in the end they prevailed on Cluny to send a small party consisting of a prior and three monks, and the work of erecting the priory could begin. Lewes in fact came to hold a privileged position as one of the five major priories of the Cluniac congregation. Its heads were appointed by the abbot of Cluny, and in the twelfth century one of its priors, Hugh III, became head of the mother-house itself. The circumstances of its foundation are only remarkable in that they typify the way in which the unsolicited efforts of lay magnates added fresh colonies to the empire of Cluny.

The Cluniac ideal

What was it about the Cluniac life that evoked such an eager response from the leaders of eleventh-century society? The Cluniac message that the secular world was irremediably sinful and that the life of the monk was the only sure route to salvation struck a deeply responsive chord in the minds of men who were oppressed by the need to make satisfaction for their sins and fearful of the impending Day of Judgement. Cluny, as St Hugh wrote to King Philip of France, was the refuge of the penitent; let the king therefore resign his earthly kingdom while there was still time and lay hold on the eternal kingdom by ending his days as a monk.[19] 'Acknowledging the enormity of my sins,' runs the charter of a benefactor, 'and at the same time fearing the dread condemnation of the reprobate, and mindful of the greatness of God's mercies, I fly to the harbour of safety.'[20] Arnaldus, the author of the charter, donated both himself and his church to the abbey, where he purposed to take the habit. To those who could not commit themselves in this way (and King Philip was one of them), the best hope lay in winning the remission of sins by sharing in the merits of Cluny through association. This could be achieved by the gift of property or of children. A child-oblate provided a kind of living investment in the monastic community from which a family hoped to reap rich spiritual rewards. At Cluny, the *nutriti* reared in the cloister were trained up to sing the elaborate services with a professional expertise that was hard for an adult convert to master.

The repetitious formulas alluding to the burden of sins and the terror of the Last Judgement, which recur again and again in the hundreds of charters of donation written during the abbacies of Odilo and Hugh, reveal the mind and handiwork of the monk draftsman; but there can be no doubt that they echoed the sentiments of the donors themselves. They hoped to render satisfaction for their offences by sharing in the observances of the monks. One of the surest and most coveted means of accomplishing this was to be received into confraternity. This was a form of association that communities of different monasteries granted one another on request. The monks of two houses connected in this way prayed for one another, and deceased members of either community were commemorated in both establishments. The privilege was also open to individual benefactors, both clerical and lay. From the ninth century onwards, it was sought by individuals of every class in ever-increasing numbers.

An application for confraternity was considered by the community in chapter, and if it was granted, the applicant was brought into the chapter and inducted by a special form of words. In effect, he or she was made a participant in all the spiritual benefits of the monastery, and on the death of the confrater the community celebrated the full office of the dead for the deceased as it did for its own monks. The rich and influential often obtained confraternity in several abbeys. In the year 929, Coenwald, the bishop of Worcester, visited a number of German abbeys with a commission to present gifts from the English king, Athelstan. At Saint-Gall, after placing an offering of money on the altar of the basilica, he was received into confraternity by the brethren; and at the same time he asked for the names of King Athelstan, Archbishop Wulfhelm, seven of his suffragan bishops, and a number of others, to be inscribed with his in the register of confraters.[21]

The names of confraters and benefactors were written in a *Liber Vitae*, or Book of Life, which was placed on the high altar during the celebration of mass so that those in it, too numerous to be named individually, might be commemorated in the eucharistic prayer. These books, in which fresh names were constantly being inserted, are eloquent witnesses to the belief of medieval people in the efficacy of the intercessory prayer of the Cluniac monks. One of them, compiled at Marcigny during the abbacy of St Hugh and continued at the small priory of Villars-les-Moines in the diocese of Lausanne, contains as many as ten thousand names.[22]

The observance with which benefactors were so eager to associate themselves was the unending round of psalmody and vocal prayer. It was this that averted the anger of God from sinful and forgetful men and made reparation on behalf of the living and dead. The liturgical life of Cluny satisfied this deeply felt need to a degree that had never been achieved before. Our knowledge of the liturgical practice of medieval monasteries is chiefly derived from customaries. These, which survive in increasing numbers from the end of the tenth century onwards, were treatises setting out detailed regulations for every part of the monastic day. They filled out and supplemented the more general instructions contained in the Rule. Customaries were widely circulated and copied, and were the primary means of preserving uniformity of practice among different houses of the same congregation. Thus one of the earliest customaries of Cluny is a copy that was made in the time of Abbot Odilo for the Italian abbey of Farfa.[23] It reveals a timetable in which choir duties occupy the greater part of the monk's day – perhaps as much as eight hours on festival days. This was much longer than the time allocated to the divine office in the Rule of St Benedict.

In much of its liturgical practice Cluny had simply adopted and developed the legislation of St Benedict of Aniane and the Aachen decrees. Additions to the canonical hours, such as the recitation of the Matins of the Dead and the office of All Saints following the night office, were already established practice in the ninth century; so too was the custom of celebrating two community masses every day. The prolongation of services was a trend that had been going on for centuries. At Cluny it was given a further push by the constant addition of psalms for benefactors and lengthening of the lessons recited at the night office – in the two weeks preceding Lent, the entire books of Genesis and Exodus were chanted at Matins. Another growth factor was the multiplication of saints' days on which the longer night office of twelve lessons was celebrated. 'In Lent', observes the customary of Ulrich grimly, 'the psalmody is extremely prolix.' On some days it must have been almost continuous. On Good Friday, after the office of Prime, the community retired barefooted to the cloister and recited the entire Psalter. Besides this, the customaries lay down elaborate rules for processions to the altars with cross, candles, incense and reliquaries.

For this endless solemn celebration of the liturgy the efforts of Odilo and Hugh had provided an architectural setting of incomparable magnificence. Odilo had reconstructed the abbey's domestic buildings on a grand scale. Hugh set about replacing Mayeul's church with a third and still bigger building, a huge basilica 531 feet in length and 100 feet in height, constructed on the plan of a patriarchal cross, with four transepts, five major towers, and five chapels radiating from the ambulatory of the choir.[24] The grandeur of Hugh's design caught the imagination of Europe. Subventions were received from Henry I of England and Alfonso VI of Leon-Castile, who exacted the money from his newly conquered Muslim subjects; the Empress Matilda presented the bells. The work was begun in 1088. By October 1095 the altars of the chevet were ready to be consecrated by the Cluniac pope, Urban II, who had come to France to preach the First Crusade; and in 1130 Innocent II dedicated the whole church. All but a fragment, a transept, of Hugh's great church has gone, but something of the harmonious masses of the design and the richness of its historiated capitals can be seen from its imitators at Paray-le-Monial and La Charité-sur-Loire, and from the debris of sculptured capitals housed in the old granary building. The marble sculptures of Odilo's cloister have vanished, but they live on, forever encapsulated in the vivid denunciation of St Bernard:

> in the sight of the brethren reading in the cloister, what is that ridiculous monstrosity doing? What is that deformed beauty and that beautiful deformity? those unclean monkeys? those ferocious lions? those battling knights? those monstrous centaurs? those huntsmen sounding their horns? Here are several bodies under a single head; there a quadruped with the head of a serpent; there a fish with the head of a quadruped . . . on all sides one sees such a rich and amazing variety of forms that it is more pleasing to read the marbles than the manscripts.[25]

It was all a disgraceful aberration from the austere simplicity of the Rule. But Bernard was the spokesman of a new monastic age which was in search of apostolic poverty and was in the process of rejecting the Cluniac model. In Hugh's day, the great choir with its high altar hung with orphreys and lit by a forest of

FIGURE 6.3 The exterior of Paray-le-Moniale (twelfth century)

Photograph by the author

candelabra, surmounted by the gold pyx studded with precious stones, which was the gift of Henry of Blois, bishop of Winchester – 'a special lover of his mother, the church of Cluny'[26] – and the splendour of the liturgy it housed, seemed to most of those who saw it to be a symbol of the glory of heaven, expressing in palpable form the highest realisation of the monastic ideal.

Cluny was the spiritual Everest in a landscape containing many peaks. Its far-flung network was only one of several monastic associations which derived their inspiration from the Carolingian revival directed by St Benedict of Aniane. In the course of the tenth and early eleventh centuries many ruined abbeys were repeopled with monks, new foundations were made, and fresh congregations sprang into existence. Some of these took their pattern of monastic life from Cluny while remaining outside the Cluniac empire; others followed a distinct, if not very different type of Benedictine observance, given them by the mother-house of their own congregation.

Among the groups that were influenced by Cluny, but not of it in any constitutional sense, was the large constellation of reformed monasteries which received their customs from Saint-Bénigne of Dijon. Its animator was an Italian, William of Volpiano, who ranks among the greatest ascetical revivalists of his age. It is observable, and perfectly understandable, that most of the reformers were men who had come to the monastic life as adults. Often they were clerks, who had absorbed the best of the learning the schools of the time had to offer. The oblate, educated in the cloister and trained from childhood in the habits of obedience and conformity, was less likely to question the accepted norms of his establishment than was a recruit from the outside world, who had formed his ideals independently. But William of Volpiano was the exception. He had been placed as a child in the monastery of Lucedio near Vercelli. The stimulus that made him a reformer came from a meeting with Mayeul, which drew him to Cluny. In 989 he was sent to reform Saint-Bénigne of Dijon, where he introduced the customs of Cluny. For the next forty years, as abbot of St Bénigne, he worked to extend the Benedictine revival in northern Italy, where he founded the famous Piedmontese abbey of Fruttuaria. But the area of his most impressive achievement was Normandy. In 1001, at the invitation of Duke Richard II, he took a party of monks from Dijon to Fécamp, where he restored regular observance. In the following years the reform was extended to the Norman abbeys of Saint-Ouen, Jumièges, and Mont-Saint-Michel; and the duchy became famous for the quality of its monastic life. It was to the customary of William's congregation that Herluin, the convert-knight, looked for the guidance of the humble group of monks he gathered at Bec in the year 1034.

In Catalonia Cluny had little direct influence. There the monastic revival of the early eleventh century, which followed the ravages of the Muslim conqueror, al-Mansur, stemmed from the abbeys of Cuxa and Ripoll, They were ruled jointly by the famous Abbot Oliva, who founded a dependent priory of Ripoll to serve the sanctuary of the Blessed Virgin at Montserrat. Later in the century, Ripoll was absorbed into the spiritual empire of St Victor of Marseilles, which formed a large congregation of subject abbeys extending from the Midi into northern Spain.

Gorze and the German revival

Apart from a few outposts across the English Channel, the Cluniac empire was largely confined to the Romance-speaking lands. In the east Frankish lands which were gradually welded into the medieval kingdom of Germany, the monastic revival of the tenth century was led from the abbey of Gorze, near Metz. Gorze had been founded in the eighth century by St Chrodegang of Metz, but monastic life had ceased there and it was much dilapidated when in 933 Adalbero, the bishop of Metz, gave it to John of Gorze and the Archdeacon Einold of Toul, so that they could restore Benedictine observance at the abbey. Helped by the enthusiastic patronage of bishops and German princes, the reform of Gorze was imported into St Maximin of Trier, St Vanne of Verdun, and other abbeys of Lorraine. And from Lorraine it was transmitted both to revived monasteries and to new foundations in Hesse, Swabia and Bavaria.

The major role in spreading the Gorzer observance in Bavaria was played by St Wolfgang of Regensburg. He had abandoned his post as *scholasticus* to the cathedral school of Trier to take the monastic habit at Einsiedeln, but the cloister could not hold him for long. In 971 he set off to evangelise Hungary. The following year his friendship with members of the Bavarian ducal house brought him to the see of Regensburg. His first step was to introduce the customary of Gorze to the monastery of St Emmeram, which he separated from the bishopric; and from this base, he restored Benedictine life to a series of Bavarian abbeys and founded several monasteries for women.

In Germany and the Empire Gorze played a role in the Benedictine revival similar to that of Cluny in France, but with a difference. The monks of Gorze followed an elaborate liturgical routine derived, like that of Cluny, from the reform of St Benedict of Aniane, but Gorze had developed a tradition of its own quite independently of Cluny.[27] Its lectionary was different, and so were its liturgical ceremonies. It is in the customaries of the Gorzer group that we encounter for the first time the Easter play of the Sepulchre – the dramatisation of liturgical song, played out during the night office, which marks the birth of medieval drama. It was unknown at Cluny; but the common customary of the English monks, which was compiled in 970, has it – the fruit of Dunstan's residence at Ghent, where he came into contact with the Gorzer tradition. In the English *ordo* for Nocturns in the night of the Resurrection, three monks wearing albs and carrying incense, advance slowly up the church towards the place where a sepulchre had been prepared, step by step, as though searching for something; and when they draw near, 'he that is seated there shall begin to sing softly and sweetly, "Whom do you seek in the sepulchre, O worshippers of Christ?"'[28]

Organisationally, the family of monasteries that sprang from the Gorzer reform had little in common with the centralised patriarchal structure of the Cluniac empire. The Lotharingian and German reformers owed much to the patronage of the imperial house and to the active sponsorship of bishops. Unlike Cluny, they did not seek large-scale exemptions from episcopal jurisdiction. Nor did they attempt to reduce newly reformed abbeys and daughter foundations to dependent status. German abbeys that received the customs of Gorze retained their autonomy. No abbot east of the Meuse claimed the kind of suzerainty exercised by the abbots of Cluny. Instead the monasteries of the Gorzer tradition developed 'filiations' or associations of houses grouped round the abbeys from which they had received their common customary. These groups were not linked to their mother-houses by juridical bonds. They were primarily associations of prayer or confraternities which provided services at death for each and every monk of the congregation. So, besides Gorze itself, St Maximin of Trier, Fulda, which had the customs of Gorze imposed upon it by the Emperor Henry II, Einsiedeln, and the Bavarian abbeys of St Emmeram and Niederaltaich, all became the nuclei of congregations of coequal monasteries.

The English revival of the tenth century

Cluny and Gorze represented two distinct traditions, both of which derived their interpretation of the Benedictine life from the reform of Benedict of Aniane and the Aachen decrees. Both traditions played a part in shaping the form taken by the monastic revival in tenth-century England. Social pressure and foreign invasion had combined to cut short the first spring of monasticism in the Anglo-Saxon kingdoms. Practically no organised monastic life survived the Danish invasions of the ninth century. Monastic lands had been appropriated, and those monastic buildings that were not deserted and ruinous were occupied by groups of married secular clergy. The impact upon learning of the loss of these monasteries and their libraries, which Alfred lamented in his translation of *The Pastoral Care*, is eloquently attested to by the low standard of Latinity displayed in diplomas, even those written by royal and episcopal clerks in the last decades of the ninth century.[29]

The way for a revival was prepared by individual ascetics who found it necessary to go to the Continent to fulfil their vocation. One of these was Archbishop Oda, who came to the see of Canterbury in 942. He had previously gone to Fleury to take the monastic habit, and he sent his nephew, Oswald, there to become a monk, so initiating a connection with the ancient abbey on the Loire that influenced the whole course of the English movement. On being recalled to take up the bishopric of Worcester in 961, Oswald became one of the three leading promoters of the monastic revival, and it was from Fleury that he summoned Germanus, another English monk, to be the first abbot of a new foundation at Westbury-on-Trym. There were also personal links with the Lotharingian reform. St Dunstan, who became the chief architect of the revival, spent an instructive period of exile at Blandinium in Ghent, which had accepted the customs of Gorze. This process of cross-fertilisation later bore fruit in the common customary agreed by all the English abbots in 970.

The English revival was pre-eminently the work of three determined men: St Dunstan, St Ethelwold, and St Oswald.[30] But it could not have been accomplished without the active support of the Wessex kings. The movement began when King Edmund gave Dunstan, who was the son of a Somerset thegn and a relative of the royal family, the old abbey of Glastonbury, where he had been educated. Dunstan repaired the monastic buildings and recruited a community of monks who vowed to follow the Benedictine Rule. His disciples included Ethelwold, who was to prove himself the most austere and dynamic of the reformers. Dissatisfied with the observance at Glastonbury, Ethelwold hankered to search out his ideal on the Continent, but King Eadred diverted him from his planned flight abroad by giving him the derelict monastery of Abingdon to restore.

The momentum of the movement suffered a check during the crisis of Eadwig's short reign, when Dunstan was forced into exile and was sheltered by the monks of St Peter's in Ghent. But the accession of the young King Edgar in 959 gave the reformers the enthusiastic and powerful patron they needed to pursue their project. Dunstan was recalled to be bishop of Worcester, and from there was quickly translated, first to London, and then in 960 to Canterbury. Ethelwold, who had been the king's mentor, was appointed to the see of Winchester, where he took the drastic step of expelling the married secular canons from the Old Minster and installing a community of monks brought from Abingdon. And, at Dunstan's suggestion, Oswald was summoned home from exile to take up the see of Worcester.

With the force of the king behind it the monastic revival now made rapid progress. The two restored abbeys at Glastonbury and Abingdon, and Oswald's foundation at Westbury-on-Trym, became the power-houses of the movement, each of them sending out groups of monks to people and restore ruined houses or to found new ones. The community of Abingdon supplied monks for a group of new foundations made by Ethelwold in East Anglia, including Medehamstede (later Peterborough), Ely, Thorney, and Croyland. Westbury colonised a group of houses in the West Midlands, including Worcester, Pershore, Ramsey and, at one remove, Winchcombe. Glastonbury supplied monks for Bath, Malmesbury, Sherborne, and, at a later stage, for Westminster. Besides the monasteries for men, several abbeys of nuns were either restored or newly founded, among them the larger and richly endowed establishments at Romsey, Shaftesbury, Wilton, and the Nunnaminster at Winchester. One by-product of the revival, rare outside England, was the cathedral monastery – communities of monks who took the place of a cathedral chapter that was normally occupied by secular clergy – which was introduced at Winchester, Worcester, and Sherborne, and some decades later at Canterbury. In these cases the place of the abbot in the community was held by the bishop, but for most purposes its effective head was the claustral prior.

All the English monasteries followed the Benedictine Rule, but within the common framework there was much variety of practice stemming from the differing background and experience of the founders. It was therefore thought desirable to compile a single uniform customary which all would observe. So an assembly of abbots and abbesses was summoned to meet at Winchester under the presidency of the king in 970, and an agreed code of observance was drawn up, called the *Regularis Concordia*.[31] According to Aelfric, the *Concordia* was the work of Ethelwold. We know in fact very little about the circumstances that produced it or why it was thought necessary. The desire for a nationwide uniformity of monastic observance and the idea that the king should be its patron and guardian, a notion quite foreign to the Rule of St Benedict, was a product of the Carolingian reform of the ninth century and a society that accorded a sacral role to kingship.

The programme of monastic life set out in the *Concordia* is that of the Aachen decrees, derived from the traditions of Cluny and Gorze. As was to be expected, the leaders of the English movement looked to the Continent for guidance in interpreting the Rule. The preface to the document, in fact, acknowledges the help given by monks who had been summoned from Fleury and Ghent to advise the synod. The timetable of the monastic day as set out conforms to the continental practice of the tenth century in making the execution of the liturgy the chief task of the monk. The additions to the divine office adopted at Cluny are included in the instructions of the *Concordia*, but at some points the document follows the Lotharingian tradition: the order for the last three days of Holy Week and the week following Easter is that used by the Gorzer congregation. The Easter play of the Sepulchre within the night office is apparently derived from the same source. A special feature of the customary is the emphasis upon the role of the king as patron and protector. It was agreed that psalms and prayers for the king and queen should be recited after all the liturgical hours except Prime. In this way the abbots acknowledged the bond of mutual service that existed between the English monasteries and the monarchy.

The monastic renaissance could not, in fact, have been accomplished without the constant support and collaboration of the Wessex kings. The endowment of minsters restored to monastic use involved the resumption of church lands which had been secularised or appropriated by secular canons, and this could only be done by acts of royal power. Besides the forcible bestowal of alienated lands and churches, the king in many cases endowed abbeys with important franchisal privileges which gave them seignorial jurisdiction over the population of large areas. The abbots of Medehamstede, for instance, were granted jurisdiction over eight of the hundreds of Northamptonshire, and in this area the hundred courts were presided over by the steward of the abbey.

Not all the nobility shared Edgar's enthusiasm for the monastic revival, and after his death there was a brief insurrection by a group of families which had suffered loss through the king's largesse.[32] But the gains made in his reign could not now be reversed. Despite the problems caused by renewed Danish invasions, King Aethelred maintained the policy of restoring lost lands to monastic houses and enriching them with fresh endowments. The Old Minster at Winchester, Abingdon, St Alban's, Ely, and the nunnery of Shaftesbury, all benefited from his favour,[33] and the new foundation of Eynsham, sponsored by the ealdorman, Aethelmar, was reinforced by royal conformation.[34] Cnut's role in the foundation of Bury St Edmunds is doubtful,[35] but he showed himself an enthusiastic patron of the monasteries, not least by his practice of nominating abbots to English bishoprics. By the eve of the Norman Conquest, though something of the initial fervour of reform had cooled and the intoxicating sense of pioneering a great revival had been lost, the Benedictine abbeys had struck long and deep roots in the social landscape of southern England.

The English revival had drawn much of its inspiration from Cluny. Yet before the end of the eleventh century new kinds of religious organisation were rising to challenge the Cluniac ascendancy. Some of the best minds of the time were turning away from a life dominated by corporate ritual in search of a simpler form of ascetical life which allowed more opportunity for private prayer and reflection and which was less involved with the secular world. Behind the imposing façade of Cluny itself, there were signs of malaise, which became plain for all to see following the death of St Hugh. His successor, Pons of Melgueil, became the focus of a European scandal.

According to Peter the Venerable, Abbot Pons had resigned in 1122 to go on pilgrimage to the Holy Land; but he reappeared three years later, during Peter's abbacy, at the head of a mob of runaway monks and, with the help of malcontents in the community, seized the abbey, which was barricaded and subjected to an orgy of plunder and violence before Peter regained possession. Authority moved in with the assistance of the secular arm. Pons was summoned to Rome, was excommunicated, and died in 1126 in the prison of Pope Honorius II. This startling rebellion has been regarded by some scholars as the nemesis of the open-door policy followed by St Hugh. In his later years the probationary period of the noviciate had been reduced to as little as a single week. The fact that Pons found allies in the cloister could be explained by this and by Cluniac propaganda, which may well have attracted numbers of adult recruits with no aptitude for the religious life.

There is no doubt that there had been relaxations in the last years of Hugh's long regime. But recent studies have rehabilitated Pons to some extent and related his fall to broader developments in the monastic world, which were in turn reflected in divisions within the papal Curia.[36] Peter the Venerable, an admirer of the Carthusians and a friend of St Bernard, was attuned to the new ascetical spirituality of the twelfth century; he was known in monastic circles to be a reformer, and he sought to make changes in the observance at Cluny that aroused the opposition of the traditionalists in the community.[37] It was this group of dissidents that attempted to restore Pons, alleging in fact that he had never resigned the abbacy. They hoped to thwart Peter's efforts to restore some of the earlier austerity to Cluniac practice. Significant though it was, the rebellion headed by Pons did not herald the decline of Cluny; it continued to attract patrons and recruits throughout the twelfth century. The crisis of 1122–26 was a symptom not of decadence, but of the challenge the new ascetical ideals were offering to the traditional version of the Benedictine life.

Notes

1. *Radulphi Glaber Historiarum Libri Quinque*, ed. J. France (1989) iii, pp. 124–5.
2. For a modern discussion of the charter and its precedents see H. E. J. Cowdrey, *The Cluniacs and the Gregorian Reform* (1970), pp. 8–15.
3. On Odo's doctrine of the monastic life see R. Morghen, 'Monastic reform and Cluniac spirituality' in *Cluniac Monasticism in the Central Middle Ages*, ed. Noreen Hunt (1971), pp. 11–28; and K. Hallinger, *ibid*, pp. 29–55.
4. *Vita S. Odonis, PL* 133, 45.
5. *Ibid.*, 71.
6. *Ibid.*, 60.
7. On Odo's work at Rome see E. Sackur, *Die Cluniacenser in ihrer kirchlichen und allgemeingeschichtlichen Wirksamkeit* (Halle, 1892–94) i, pp. 99–114; and B. Hamilton, 'Monastic revival in tenth-century Rome' in *Studia Monastica* (1962) iv, pp. 35–68.
8. *Vita S. Maioli, PL* 137, 752.
9. See the *Vita S. Odilonis* by his pupil, Jotsaldus, in *PL* 142, 897–940. For a striking modern portrait see R. W. Southern, *The Making of the Middle Ages* (1953), pp. 158–9.
10. *PL* 142, 906.
11. *Ibid.*, 908. For the buildings of Cluny see J. Hourlier, 'Le monastère de Saint Odilon, *Studia Anselmiana* 50 (Rome, 1962), pp. 5–21. The authoritative monograph is that of K. Conant, *Cluny: Les églises et la maison du Chef d'Ordre* (Mâcon, 1968).
12. On Hugh's regime see Noreen Hunt, *Cluny under St Hugh 1049–1109* (1967).
13. *Vita S. Hugonis, PL* 159, 865–6.
14. Cowdrey, *op. cit.*
15. *Registrum Gregorii VII*, ed. E. Caspar, *MGH* (1920) ii, 49.
16. *Vita S. Odonis*, 80.
17. Anselme Davril, 'Un coutumier de Fleury du début du XIe siècle': *Rev. bén.* 76 (1966), pp. 351–4, and Dom Anselme's edition of the customary in *CCM* VII (1984). L. Donat in 'Recherches sur l'influence de Fleury au Xe siècle', *Études Ligériennes d'histoire médiévale* (Auxerre, 1975), pp. 165–74, remarks on the close association of Fleury with the Lotharingian reform and suggests it was the source of the customs of Gorze.
18. According to a thirteenth-century tradition, they were warned to proceed no further as the war between the pope and the emperor had made the passage of the Alps unsafe. This and other details are derived from the spurious foundation charter of Lewes, printed in W. Dugdale, *Monasticon* (edn 1825) v, pp. 12–13. This was shown to be a forgery by C. T. Clay in *Early Yorkshire Charters* viii, *The Honour of Warenne* (Yorkshire Archaeological Society Record Series vi, 1940), pp. 59–62; but the historical material used by the forger is apparently derived from an earlier and genuine narrative.
19. *Epistolae, PL* 159, 9302.
20. *Receuil des chartes de l'abbaye de Cluny*, ed. A. Bruel (Paris, 1876) iv, no. 3063.
21. *Councils and Synods with Other Documents relating to the English Church*, I, part i, ed. Dorothy Whitelock (1981), pp. 41–3.
22. J. Wollasch, 'A Cluniac necrology from the time of Abbot Hugh' in *Cluniac Monasticism, op. cit.*, pp. 143–90.

23. *Liber Tramitis Aevi Odilonis Abbatis*, ed. P. Dinter in CCM X (1980). On the liturgical practice of Cluny see G. de Valous, *Le monachisme clunisien des origines au XVe siècle* (Ligugé-Paris, 1935) i, pp. 327–72.

24. Conant, *op. cit.*, and *idem, Carolingian and Romanesque Architecture 800–1200* 3rd edn (1979), pp. 185–221.

25. From Bernard's Apologia: *S. Bernardi Opera*, ed. J. Leclercq, C. H. Talbot and H. Rochais (Rome, 1959) III, p. 106; English trans. M. Casey (Kalamazoo, 1970).

26. E. Berger, *Notices sur divers MSS de la Bibliothèque Vaticane. Richard le Poitevin* (Bibl. des Écoles françaises d'Athènes et de Rome 6, Paris 1879), p. 126.

27. The distinctive liturgical tradition of Gorze and its independence of Cluny were vindicated by K. Hallinger's monumental study *Gorze-Kluny*, 2 vols, *Studia Anselmiana* 22–25 (Rome 1950–51); on the organisational differences see particularly vol. ii, pp. 765–80.

28. *The Regularis Concordia*, ed. T. Symons (1953), p. 50.

29. N. Brooks, *The Early History of the Church of Canterbury* (1984), pp. 171–4.

30. For the history of the English revival see M. D. Knowles, *The Monastic Order in England*, 2nd edn (1963), and the studies in *Tenth-Century Studies*, ed. D. Parsons (1975).

31. On the sources of the *Concordia* see T. Symons in *Tenth-Century Studies*, pp. 37–59.

32. D. J. V. Fisher, 'The anti-monastic reaction in the reign of Edward the Martyr', *Cambridge Historical Journal* 10 (1950–2), pp. 254–70.

33. P. H. Sawyer, *Anglo-Saxon Charters, an Annotated List* (1968), nos 836, 839, 891; 876, 897; 888, 916; 907, 919; 850, 899.

34. *Ibid.*, no. 911.

35. Antonia Gransden, 'Traditionalism and continuity during the last century of Anglo-Saxon monasticism', *JEH* 40 (1989), pp. 159–207. On Cnut's patronage of the monastic Church see Frank Barlow, *The English Church 1000–1066* (1963), pp. 72–5.

36. H. V. White, 'Pontius of Cluny, the *Curia Romana* and the end of Gregorianism in Rome', *Church History* 27 (1958), pp. 195–219; and G. Tellenbach, 'Der Sturz des Abtes Pontius von Cluny und seine geschichtliche Bedeutung' in *Quellen u. Forschungen aus italienischen Archiven* 43–3 (Tübingen, 1963), pp. 13–55, where the rough treatment of Pons at Rome is related to a conflict between Cluny and the bishop of Mâcon.

37. Giles Constable, 'The monastic policy of Peter the Venerable', *Pierre Abélard, Pierre le Vénérable: Colloques internationaux du centre national de la recherche scientifique*, no. 546 (Paris, 1975), pp. 119–42.

7

THE CLOISTER AND THE WORLD

Bare ruined choirs and empty cloisters kindle the imagination of a modern visitor, but cannot satisfy it. To anyone standing on the floor of the dormitory at Fontenay and glancing down the night-stairs into the transept of the great church, it is easy to visualise the cowled figures, hands hidden in the voluminous white sleeves, scurrying down for the night office. From the stone pulpit high up in the wall of the roofless refectory of Fountains one can look down upon a ghostly congregation of bowed heads. Yet it is hard to recapture the experience and atmosphere of daily life in a medieval cloister. Our documents can conjure up for us the exterior activities of the monastic routine; but ultimately, the inwardness of it eludes us. Our sources cannot penetrate the interior experience of the individual that energised and gave meaning to a pattern of life built round a belief in the omnipresence of the supernatural and in the power and necessity of constant prayer, and to which the modern secular world offers us no key.

How exactly did monks spend their day? Here we have to make distinctions of time and place. Although the Rule of St Benedict constituted a thread of continuity through the centuries, the domestic arrangements and assumptions of a monastic community were no more static than those of the society that surrounded it. The experience and mental furniture of a Benedictine monk living in the fifteenth century would have been different from those of a monk of the twelfth century, and the life-style and expectations of both would have differed from those of a monk living in a Carolingian abbey of the eighth century. Let us try to reconstruct the daily round in a Benedictine establishment towards the close of the eleventh century.

There is much to be said for selecting this point in time. Letters and monastic chronicles provide us with occasional glimpses over the walls of the enclosure; but the most systematic information about the occupations that filled the monk's day

FIGURE 7.1 The exterior of the lay brothers' refectory, with dormitory above, at Fountains Abbey

Photograph by the author

comes from the customaries, and these survive in substantial numbers from the two centuries between 1050 and 1250. These were treatises recording the customs and established practices of particular monasteries. They were compiled to supplement or fill out the general instructions of the Rule and contained detailed regulations for the celebration of the divine office and for every activity that occupied the monastic day, as well as listing the duties assigned to the various officers of the community. One of the primary objects of these compilations was to secure uniformity of observance in houses belonging to the same congregation; so they were widely circulated, carefully preserved and periodically amended. Uniformity of practice was the avowed motive for the composition of the *Regularis Concordia* – the common customary agreed by the monks of tenth-century England; and a similar intention must have underlain the customary, or so-called statutes, that Archbishop Lanfranc gave to the cathedral priory of Christ Church Canterbury, soon after 1070, for they were copied in other cathedral monasteries of Norman England.

Some of the fullest of these rule-books are those written in the eleventh century as a guide to the customs of Cluny. One of them was compiled by a monk of the Italian abbey of Farfa, who had been sent to Cluny by his abbot to learn the usages and report back home.[1] Another was compiled by Ulrich, himself a monk of Cluny. He had been on a visit to the Swabian abbey of Hirsau about the year 1075, and during his stay, his host, Abbot William, had plied him with questions about Cluniac practice. So on returning home Ulrich wrote up the customs of his abbey for William's benefit and also, unforeseeably, for ours.[2] Together these two treatises provide us with a fairly detailed guide to the pattern of life at Cluny under the regime of Odilo and St Hugh. We have already drawn upon them in describing some of the features of Cluniac observance. All the customaries give elaborate instructions for the celebration of the divine office at the various seasons of the year, but omit much that we should like to know. Nevertheless, they do enable us to reconstruct in some detail the routine of daily life in a great Benedictine abbey of the eleventh century.

The daily round

Both the brethren and the children slept in the common dormitory, fully clothed in their habits except for cowl and scapular. This may have been no hardship on winter nights in an unheated stone building, but it must have been uncomfortable in summer. It was the rule at Cluny that even on the hottest nights no more than feet or arms might be uncovered. At some time between 2 and 3 a.m., depending upon the time of year, the community was roused by the bell. They rose, pulled the covers over their beds, put on night-shoes and cowl – a monk, explains Ulrich, must not enter the lavatory (which connected with the far end of the dormitory) with head uncovered, for the cowl conferred anonymity – and then, while the bell continued to ring, they made their way down the stairs which led directly into the church and took their places in the choir to sing the night office of Nocturns (now called Matins) and Lauds. A monk who was not in choir in time for the preliminary prayers, which were said when the bell ceased to ring, had to confess his fault and ask pardon in chapter. The adult monks were followed into the choir by the boys, shepherded by their master; and after them came the novices, who slept in their own quarters. When they had arrived the service could begin. Engulfed in a cavern of darkness broken only intermittently by the pools of light shed by lanterns and candelabra, the cantors began the chant.

Staying awake during the lengthy readings of Nocturns was evidently a problem for some. The Cluny customary provides for a lantern-bearer to perambulate the choir to make sure that everybody is awake. If he comes upon a monk who has fallen asleep during the lessons, he does not speak, but gently waves the lantern to and fro close to his face until the sleeper wakes. Although the day began in the early hours of the morning, it was not unduly long as the community retired for the night at dusk. The longer summer days were punctuated by a siesta that was allowed in the afternoon. At some periods of the year the community would go back to bed after singing the Lauds of the dead and rest until the bell woke them again at first light. Then they returned to the church to sing Prime – the first service of the day. After this there was an interval, which in summer might last three hours or more, before the bell rang for the short office of Terce, the service of the third hour, sung at about 9 a.m. During this period the monks changed into their day-shoes, washed hands and face at the lavabo, which was situated in the cloister, and occupied themselves with reading or the business affairs of the house.

As St Benedict had intended, vocal prayer at the canonical hours formed the framework of the monastic day. There were the three short services of Terce, Sext, and Nones, the last two sung respectively at about midday and three in the afternoon, and the rather longer evening office of Vespers; and the day concluded at dusk with the brief service of Compline – the prayer for 'a quiet night and a perfect end'. But as we have seen, by the eleventh century the relatively simple liturgical scheme of the Rule had been greatly enlarged by the addition of further services – the offices of the dead and of All Saints, by additional psalms and freshly composed hymns and sequences for the ever-growing number of saints' days. The community now attended two masses daily: the 'morning mass' celebrated immediately after Terce, and the high mass that followed the office of Sext at about midday. Besides these, there were the private masses murmured at side-altars in the early hours before daybreak, for by this period it had become the practice to ordain a high proportion of monks to the priesthood. The practice was reflected in the monastic architecture of the tenth and eleventh centuries – churches were provided with increasing numbers of altars and side-chapels, where individual monks could offer private masses for benefactors.

At major festivals the rituals of the liturgy were enriched with added magnificence. On the vigils of Christmas, Easter, and Pentecost, the church and cloister were decorated with foliage and flowers, and the brethren were woken for the night office by the pealing of all the bells. The high altar was illuminated by masses of candles, the cantors wore gorgeous copes, and during Nocturns two priests circulated incensing the altars and members of the community. When Matins was finished, the solemn mass of the feast was celebrated, heralded by a peal of bells, and following this the night services were completed by the singing of Lauds. The monks could then return to bed to snatch what sleep they could before daybreak.

It is impossible for the modern student to assess the psychological impact upon the individual of these interminable hours spent daily in communal vocal prayer and liturgical rituals. How much of the participation was simply mechanical? It is significant that some of the most reflective minds of the period rejected the Cluniac pattern of observance and that the new orders of the twelfth century cautiously pruned the traditional monastic liturgy. Even at Cluny, Peter the Venerable reduced the 'hateful multiplicity of familiar psalms', and composed a new hymn for the feast of St Benedict that was shorter than the old one 'on account of the boredom of the singers'.[3]

Outside choir, the most important assembly point of the day was the chapter. Following the morning mass, the community processed out of the church into the chapter-house. The brethren sat on the gradines – the tiers of benches round the walls – and the abbot or prior presided. After the reading of a lesson and a chapter of the Rule, the head of the house delivered a conference or sermon. Business matters concerning the community might then be discussed. This was also the occasion when individuals who had committed breaches of the Rule confessed their faults or were accused by others, and were assigned penances. The boys met in a chapter of their own. There, Ulrich explains, those who have blundered in singing the psalmody, misbehaved in any way, or simply fallen asleep during the services, are stripped of cowl and frock and beaten by their master with willow rods. Harsh, but no harsher than the treatment children expected to receive in the outside world. It was a general conviction in medieval society that constant beating was indispensable for the proper education of the young.

After chapter, which would have ended towards 10 a.m., there was a clear period that could be devoted to work or study, lasting until the bell rang for Sext, about midday. Work was a part of the monk's routine expressly enjoined by St Benedict. There were always tasks to be performed in the offices and workshops of the monastery. But the abbeys of the eleventh century employed servants for the menial jobs. In a major establishment such as Cluny, or the cathedral priory of Canterbury, which contained upwards of a hundred monks, as much as half of the community might be occupied with administrative duties, either inside or outside the enclosure. The management of the monastery's estates necessarily involved the periodic absence of a number of monks. Those who were not occupied in administration spent the hours outside choir in reading, copying books in the scriptorium, or in artistic work. The manual labour prescribed by the Rule had by now become largely ritualised. 'To tell the truth,' says the maestro in Ulrich's customary, 'it amounts to nothing more than shelling the new beans or rooting out weeds that choke the good plants in the garden, sometimes making loaves in the bakery'.[4] On days when it is done, after holding a shorter chapter than usual, the abbot says 'Let us proceed to manual labour.' All then process out, the boys leading, to the garden. Psalms are sung, and after a spell of weeding, the procession reforms and returns to the cloister.

The virtual elimination of manual work in favour of intellectual activities was partly the result of the great elaboration of the monk's liturgical duties. Far more of his day was spent in choir than St Benedict had envisaged; and choir duties were physically exhausting as well as time-consuming. The change also reflected changing social assumptions. Tilling and hewing were work for peasants and had servile associations. Peter the Venerable argued that the delicate hands of his monks, who came from social classes unfamiliar with toil, were more suitably employed furrowing parchment with pens than ploughing furrows in fields. It was one of the objects of the Cistercians and other reformers of the twelfth century to reinstate manual labour in the monk's timetable and to assert its spiritual significance. But it was a reversal of the prevailing trend, in which the Benedictine houses did not in general follow the reformers.

The importance of reading in the life of the monk was underlined by the generous amount of time allocated to it in the Rule; and it was symbolised by the annual issue of books for private reading at the beginning of Lent. At Cluny, the keeper of the book-store, in accordance with the Rule, had the books laid out on a carpet that was spread on the floor of the chapter-house. A list of the books issued the previous year and their recipients is read out. On hearing his name, each monk hands back his book and receives another. Anyone who has not finished his book confesses his fault and asks pardon. Lanfranc's constitutions describe an identical ritual at Canterbury. A chance survival in the customary of Farfa abbey of a list of sixty-three books issued to the monks one Lent in the mid-eleventh century gives us a momentary glimpse of the reading tastes of one community.[5] Most of the books fall into the expected categories of devotional works and ascetical theology – Cassian, Smaragdus's commentary on the Rule, Lives of the saints, and the Scriptural commentaries of the Fathers from Jerome to Gregory the Great, as well as the later commentators like Bede, Alcuin and Rhabanus Maurus. But the list also includes an interesting selection of historical works, the *History* of Josephus, the *Ecclesiastical History* of Eusebius, an anonymous *History of the English*, which must be Bede, and more surprisingly, the secular Roman history of Livy, a work that was not widely known at this period. The reading of history was regarded as an improving spiritual exercise. As John of Salisbury observed in the twelfth century, through studying the chronicles of the past, men came to perceive the invisible working of God.

A significant part of the book-holdings in a Benedictine library were likely to have come from donations. When Odo became a monk at Baume he took with him a hundred books, which were probably transported in due course to Cluny. Medieval library catalogues, like the great catalogue of Canterbury cathedral priory which was compiled in the thirteenth century, sometimes list the books under the names of donors. Nevertheless, a proportion of the library's stock had to be supplied by the monastery's own scriptorium.

The work that went on in the scriptorium or writing-room was vital to the interior life of the monastery and it also provided an important service to the outside world. At any given time several monks were likely to be engaged in copying texts or composing books of their own. Sometimes they worked in the northern walk of the cloister alongside the church, but often a separate room off the cloister was allocated to the task. The ninth-century plan of Saint-Gall provides for a spacious scriptorium above the library, with seven writing-desks. The first charge on the workers in the scriptorium was the reproduction of the books needed for the services in choir and the readings in the refectory – the antiphoners, tropers, missals and lectionaries. An equally important task was the provision of grammars for the education of boys in the cloister and the multiplication of books to stock the library.

Most of the energies of monks engaged in writing would be devoted to making copies of approved texts or standard authorities. If exemplars were needed, they could be borrowed from other monasteries. Since pen, ink, and parchment were the sole materials of production, books took a long time to make and they were rare and costly objects in the medieval world. Men used them as security for loans, and they were often passed on by pious bequest – they figure conspicuously in the wills of bishops and other higher clergy. A complete Old Testament, which was generally sold with the standard gloss, might cost more than the total annual stipend of a country priest. A whole flock of sheep would be needed to provide the parchment for it. Understandably, therefore, some abbeys demanded a deposit before lending books. 'Send by the bearer of these present letters', writes Peter the Venerable to the monks of the Grande Chartreuse, 'or by some other trustworthy person securities for the books I have sent – not as a pledge for their better preservation, but so that the orders of our father St Hugh relating to such loans may be observed.'[6]

It was not only the humble copyists of texts who worked in the scriptorium of course. The regulated leisure of the cloister offered the ideal conditions for authorship. The evidence lies in the product. The monastic writing-office was the factory that, until the twelfth century, produced the great majority of the literary works, secular as well as sacred, that filled the libraries of the Middle Ages. Abbo of Fleury (d. 1004), grammarian, mathematician, historian, and hagiographer to Fulbert of Chartres ('the most famous master of all France'), held that, after prayer and fasting, the practice of literary composition did most to bridle the lusts of the flesh.[7]

Although the community itself had first call on the resources of the scriptorium, monastic scribes also provided important services for the outside world. Both in France and pre-Conquest England, early rulers who possessed no organised chanceries of their own made use of the scriptoria of the abbeys to write their letters and diplomas. Abbot Hilduin of Saint-Denis was arch-chaplain to Louis the Pious, and the abbey supplied the emperor with a writing-office. But besides such periodic help to princes, the monasteries performed an essential service for the world of letters by reproducing books to order for scholars or secular patrons. Some houses acquired a reputation for the technical excellence of their calligraphy and the beauty of the illumination and miniature painting with which they decorated their manuscripts. It was, of course, a source of income to the monastery; the person who ordered the book paid for the labour, and sometimes he supplied the necessary parchment. Canon Hillin of Cologne, when he commissioned a text of the four Gospels from the tenth-century workshop of Reichenau abbey, apparently sent the monks the parchment already cut and made up into quires.[8]

Reichenau in the tenth century, like St Augustine's Canterbury in the twelfth, was famous for the sumptuous quality of its painted manuscripts. But the monks produced utilitarian copies of texts as well as the more colourful display books. In fact, until the rise of the university stationers in the thirteenth century, who specialised in the rapid reproduction of cheap texts for use in the schools, the monasteries had a virtual monopoly of book production. As time went on, however, the pressure of demand made it necessary to supplement the efforts of the monk copyists by employing professional scribes, who were paid a salary or pro rata wages out of the monastic coffers.

The monastic timetable allocated two periods of the day to reading or writing, one in the morning hours before the midday office, and the second in the afternoon between Nones and Vespers. The hour of dinner – the main meal of the day – varied according to the season. In the summer months, beginning with Easter, it was eaten soon after midday following the high mass; and there was a second meal in the evening after Vespers. In the shorter days of winter the timetable allowed for only a single meal, which was served rather later in the afternoon, but some other form of solid refreshment or a drink of wine was given before Compline and departure to bed. Meals, like other activities, had their ritual. After washing their hands, all entered the refectory, where places were allocated by strict rules of seniority, and remained standing until the arrival of the abbot or prior, who pronounced or chanted the blessing and presided at the high table. The meal was served and eaten in silence except for the voice of the lector who read to the community from a lectern or pulpit.

The preservation of silence in which prayer and reflection could flourish was one of the primary aims of all monastic observance. After the morning chapter and after dinner in the afternoon there were periods of the day when conversation was permitted in the cloister. The calefactory – the chamber off the cloister with the great fireplace, where chilled bodies could be warmed before retreating to bed – was also a meeting point for chatting. But in church, refectory, and dormitory, silence was perpetually observed, broken only by the chant and the public reading by the lectors. Some latitude was allowed to individual officers of the community engaged in business or to the head of the house who might be entertaining guests in his own quarters; but with Compline all talking had to cease. The silence of Cluny in the early days was proverbial. An elaborate sign- language, a kind of deaf-and-dumb alphabet, evolved so that a monk could express his needs without speaking. 'The novice must needs learn the signs with diligence,' explains Ulrich, 'for after he has joined the community he is very rarely allowed to speak.' A request for bread was indicated by a circular motion made with the thumb and first two fingers of both hands; fish was signified by a motion of the hand simulating the tail of a fish moving through water; trout was the same, but in addition the finger was drawn from eyebrow to eyebrow (a sign indicating that even if no meat was eaten at Cluny, the table did not lack some variety); to ask for milk, the lips were touched with the little finger, 'because thus does an infant suck'.[9] A monk who wanted to confess and receive absolution approached a priest of his choice and, standing before him, indicated his wish by drawing his right hand from his scapular and placing it on his chest; whereupon the priest would rise and lead him into the chapterhouse to hear his confession.

The rules of silence must have done something to mitigate what strikes a modern student as one of the most oppressive aspects of life in a medieval monastery – the total lack of privacy. It was not only that the individual slept, ate, and moved about in the constant company of others; even such humdrum personal activities as shaving and taking baths were closely supervised communal exercises. Shaving was reserved for the eve of major festivals, so that during the last days of Lent before Easter the community must have presented an exceedingly shaggy appearance. At Cluny the razors were kept locked in a cupboard beside the entrance to the dormitory, to be produced when a general shave took place. The brethren sat in lines along the cloister wall and passed round the razors and bowls. The operation was preceded by the recitation of psalms and collects. At St Augustine's Canterbury, the monks shaved one another but, as the chronicler explained, the wounds they inflicted on each other's faces by their inexpert hands were so bad that Abbot Roger of Chichester imported lay barbers to do the job.[10]

The Benedictine Rule urged that bathing was a practice to be discouraged except for those who were sick. The medieval customaries commonly ordained baths three times a year, before the festivals of Christmas, Easter, and Pentecost, but always with the proviso that those who did not wish to participate need not do so. Lanfranc's constitutions for Canterbury lay down an elaborate procedure for the provision of baths before Christmas. The brethren assemble in the cloister and wait until the senior monk in charge of the operation calls them in groups to the bath-house. There each monk undresses and enters a cubicle shielded by a curtain where he takes his bath in silence. And even this moment of solitude was not to be prolonged: 'when he has sufficiently washed, he shall not stay for pleasure, but shall rise, dress and return to the cloister',[11] An unmistakable air of anxiety hangs over the whole proceeding.

It would be a mistake, of course, to suppose that the monks themselves felt oppressed by the lack of solitude. Medieval society did not afford the individual much opportunity to be alone, unless he retreated to a hermitage. Peasant families occupied one-room dwellings separated, in many cases, from their livestock by only a partition. Townsmen lived in narrow congested houses; and rural knights lived and ate in halls surrounded by family, bailiffs, and retainers. Continuous company was the normal lot. The privacy we take for granted is the product of a more affluent society. As Heloise reminded Abelard when she was trying to dissuade him from marriage, only the very rich had houses with many rooms where a thinking man might find solitude, and scholars were not usually wealthy.[12]

The customaries set out an orderly routine covering every hour of the day and night. They made it clear what everyone had to do and when he was required to do it. What they cannot tell us, however, is the extent to which the Rules were observed at any given time. The history of most monasteries that were long-lived reveals alternating periods of strict observance and relaxation. Much depended upon the quality of the superior. Under an easy-going or senile abbot discipline tended to disintegrate. There were always those in a community who were ready to take advantage of such a situation. For, as long as the practice of child-oblation continued, a fair proportion of monks in the Benedictine houses had been drafted. Some, when they reached adulthood, were able to rise to the ideal that had been wished upon them by their parents; others obviously sought to create a comfortable life for themselves in a predicament from which medieval society offered no escape, except for a very few who managed to extricate themselves by obtaining a parish living.[13] Nor were all adult postulants motivated by a simple enthusiasm for the ascetical life. Some sought admission because the monastic habit offered them the best prospect of status and security. Young clerks who had attended the schools, but who lacked the family connections or patrons necessary to obtain a benefice, might choose the monastic profession as an alternative career.

Apart from the question of lax observance, the customaries by their very nature convey a deceptive impression of peaceful and undisturbed routine. Yet this was a condition few communities can have enjoyed for very long. The erection of monastic buildings, which look homogeneous to the casual eye of the modern visitor, often took several generations. In a thriving establishment there was a constant process of rebuilding and enlargement. During the eleventh century there can have been few periods when the claustral peace of Cluny was not disturbed by the sound of hammer and chisel, the creaking of hoists and the clatter of workmen. The even tenor of monastic life was often disrupted, too, by natural mishaps and by the violent intrusion of the outside world. A wealthy landed corporation could not hope to insulate itself entirely from the turmoils of war and political upheaval. Canterbury cathedral priory, like other English monasteries, suffered disturbance of its internal harmony after the Norman Conquest by the forcible importation of an alien prior and a group of Norman monks; and for some years racial animosity and cultural differences drove the two sections of the community apart. The life of the priory was also disrupted by the wholesale building operations that followed the Conquest. Its church was twice rebuilt in the course of the next sixty years, only to be devastated in 1174 by a fire which left the monks without a usable choir for more than a decade. Such mishaps were almost commonplace. But community life underwent a gradual erosion which was less the consequence of catastrophes like this than of forces that sprang from the internal administration of the monastery itself.

Monastic tasks and their distribution

As St Benedict had envisaged, the abbot found it necessary to appoint a number of subordinate officers from among the brethren to assist in the management of the monastery's affairs. By the eleventh century a fairly elaborate chain of devolved authority had come into being in the greater Benedictine houses. The special task to which each official was assigned was called an 'obedience' and he himself was referred to as an 'obedientiary'. In the first place there was the prior. Although the abbot appointed all his subordinates, as head of a religious community that was also a great landed corporation, he was a prominent person with public responsibilities that frequently took him away from the monastery. He might be absent for long periods in the service of king or pope or on the business of his own congregation. When he was at home, he was expected to entertain important visitors at his table. All this tended to separate him from the routine life of his monks; and during the twelfth century it became normal practice for the abbot to have his own house, with hall, kitchen, and chapel, within the enclosure. This development meant that the responsibility for maintaining regular life and discipline in the cloister fell increasingly to the abbot's second-in-command, the claustral prior. The bigger houses had more than one prior. At Cluny, where the abbot was constantly on his travels visiting his far-flung dependencies, there was a grand prior, charged with the general management of the abbey's properties and its relations with the external world, a claustral prior to oversee the internal life of the community, and second and third priors to help him. There were also roundsmen, called *circatores*, whose role was to tour the premises during periods of work and reading and ensure that there was no disorder or idle gossiping.

The various administrative departments of the establishment were entrusted to a lengthening chain of obedientiaries. The precentor or cantor was responsible for training the monks in the chant and the proper celebration of the liturgy and also, since he had to ensure a supply of choir-books, for supervision of the scriptorium. The sacrist had the duty of looking after the fabric of the church, the altars and sacred vessels, and he had care of the shrines – a heavy duty in abbeys that boasted famous relics and attracted a large number of pilgrims. The novice-master had the care and training of the novices. The almoner was entrusted with the task of dispensing food and other forms of relief to the poor.

Feeding the hungry and clothing the naked was an evangelical precept that was reiterated in the Rule, and most monasteries took it seriously. Pious confraternities distributed alms to the needy, and many towns endowed hospices to shelter lepers, but monastic alms-giving was the only regular form of poor-relief that existed in medieval society. At Cluny the almoner was assigned a portion of the tithes from the churches in the abbey's possession to enable him to meet the demands of his office. There was a daily distribution of bread and wine and twelve pies, weighing three pounds each, from the monks' kitchen. On Quinquagesima Sunday, all the poor who cared to come were fed with a meal of salt pork. Besides giving food, the almoner also provided hospitality for poorer pilgrims and clerks who arrived on foot. And his charity was not confined to callers. According to Ulrich, he was expected to make a weekly tour of the township to seek out any who were sick and in need of food or medicaments. It was a practice that Lanfranc enjoined on the almoner of Christ Church Canterbury.[14]

The normal recipients of alms were the poor who congregated at the monastery gate. Thus in many cases the porter or gate-keeper acted as the almoner's deputy for alms distribution. At Beaulieu abbey in the thirteenth century, the porter was instructed to issue loaves and leftovers from the refectory to those begging at the gate on three days a week, and to offer hospitality in the hospice each night to not more than thirteen poor men. On Christmas Eve he was to give hospitality to as many poor people as there were monks in the abbey. On Maundy Thursday he was to admit the same number and give each of them a penny. But the almoner's ordinance distinguished between the deserving and the undeserving poor: the porter was told to issue the daily dole during time of harvest only to those unable to work – the sick and the aged, boys and pilgrims; women thought to be prostitutes were to be given nothing, except in time of famine.[15] Famine following on harvest failure would bring large crowds of the starving and destitute to the gates of monasteries. In normal times, bread, ale or wine, occasional pittances (a share of the special dishes enjoyed by the monks on anniversaries), and discarded clothes, were the staple commodities of monastic alms-giving.

The monk-chamberlain saw to the provision and laundering of clothing for the brethren. The supply of food, drink, and fuel for the community and its guests was the business of the cellarer. 'He should be sober and no great eater', urges St Benedict with understandable anxiety. Much of his time was taken up with the transport, checking, and storage of provisions from the abbey's estates. It was common practice to allocate to his use the buildings off the west range of the cloister for storage purposes.

Another sensitive appointment was that of the infirmarian. He had charge of what was, in effect, a parallel establishment, usually situated a little to the east of the main complex, containing its own dormitory, hall, chapel, and suites of private rooms. It was a monastery in cameo. This was because it had not only to house and nurse monks who were sick, but also to provide a permanent rest-home for those who were too old and infirm to take full part in the routine of the monastery. It might also be called upon sometimes to furnish quarters for the head of the house in retirement. As the Rule restricted the eating of meat to the sick, in times of strict observance the refectory in the infirmary was the only place in the monastery where meat was served.

In a great abbey like Cluny one of the heaviest tasks was that of the guest-master. He was in fact running what was, by twelfth-century standards, a first-class hotel, providing accommodation, meals, and stabling facilities, for a continual stream of visitors which included prelates, princes, and members of the higher nobility. The guest-house built by Odilo was a palace with a frontage of one hundred and thirty-five feet, containing forty-five beds for male guests and, in another wing, thirty beds for their ladies; but it was reserved for visitors who came on horses; those arriving on foot were assigned to a less grand establishment under the infirmarian's jurisdiction.[16] As time went on, the senior obedientiaries, who had the heaviest responsibilities, delegated part of their task to subordinate officers, so that it came about that an ever-larger proportion of the community was involved in administrative or supervisory duties. Thus the sacrist was assisted by a subsacrist and in some cases by a separate warden of the shrine, who was needed to manage the throng of pilgrims attracted to a monastic church that housed the relics of a famous saint. Some of the cellarer's duties were distributed among a kitchener in charge of the catering, a refectorer, a gardener, and a woodward.

Although all the obedientiaries owed their appointment to the abbot, in practice they acquired a large degree of independence in the administration of their offices. This was the outcome of a growing tendency to divide the properties of the abbey in such a way that a proportion of lands, tithes, and offerings was allocated to maintaining each office. This subdivision was encouraged by the habits of benefactors, who often made pious bequests to support specific departments such as the almonry – a favourite object for charitable bequests – the infirmary, or the guest-house. It gave each of the major obedientiaries control over a portion of the monastery's property and over the income from it. It was a practice fraught with dangerous implications both for regular observance and for financial stability. It meant that a group of monks were not only preoccupied with internal administration, but were also involved in managerial responsibilities that frequently took them away from the monastery, for estate management necessitated inspecting distant properties, interviewing bailiffs, hearing accounts, and attending courts. It was thus necessary to exonerate obedientiaries from regular attendance in choir, a duty that St Benedict had insisted was the first priority in the life of a monk: 'Let nothing take precedence over the divine office.'[17]

The devolution of authority and economic decision-making could also have damaging financial consequences. In the course of the twelfth century bad housekeeping or financial adventurism by individual monastic officers got some abbeys into serious debt. Cluny, whose estates were under the control of twenty-three monk-deans, was in financial difficulties when Peter the Venerable was elected abbot in 1122. Excessive expenditure and mismanagement of the demesne manors had made it hard to keep the abbey supplied with regular provisions. It had to be rescued from this predicament by a reorganisation of the abbey's farms and by generous financial help from one of its former monks, Henry of Blois, the brother of King Stephen and now bishop of Winchester.[18] Crises like this were common among the Benedictine houses. In the thirteenth century there was a general move by ecclesiastical authorities – most observable by bishops in the course of visitation – to improve the situation by re-establishing central control over monastic finances. This was done by pressing each house to appoint a monk-treasurer and to set up a central exchequer, through which all income and disbursements had to pass, and by requiring an annual audit of accounts.

Recruitment

Although monks had in principle withdrawn from the world, the monastery was an organism whose roots were deeply embedded in the social landscape. Many of the older Benedictine houses were situated in, or on the fringe of towns, and were intimately involved in civic life. At Bologna, the ancient abbey of Santo Stefano still carries on its twelfth-century facade an open-air brick pulpit, the outward and visible sign of a pastoral role it discharged to the surrounding city. Those richly endowed abbeys that were founded in the countryside usually became the nuclei of new townships, created by the need of a large monastic community for goods and services and the demands of a constant stream of visitors.

The most obvious and immediate link between the cloister and the world outside it lay in its sources of recruitment. Throughout the eleventh and twelfth centuries new monasteries were founded and the monastic population continued to increase. The rising number of monks and nuns was a dimension of the general population increase that most parts of western Europe experienced during this period. In the second half of the period, growth was most conspicuous among the new orders of Cistercians and canons regular. Figures for the Benedictines are hard to obtain before the thirteenth century and have been variously interpreted.[19] Some abbeys suffered a marked fall in numbers after the eleventh century; others, after a phase of rapid expansion which was often the result of local circumstances, settled down to a steady level of recruitment, filling vacancies caused by death, which continued with little change for the next two hundred years. Canterbury cathedral priory, for instance, experienced a boom in applicants in the two generations that followed the Norman Conquest, which can be explained by the dispossession of many English landed families and the destruction of their worldly prospects. Thus by 1120 the number of monks at the priory, which was about sixty in the time of Archbishop Lanfranc, had risen to one hundred and twenty. Thereafter numbers declined to about eighty and remained at about this level during the thirteenth century.

FIGURE 7.2 Canterbury Cathedral cloisters
© Bildarchiv Monheim GmbH/Alamy

Here, as elsewhere, the relative constancy of numbers over a long period of time indicates not so much a shortage of recruits as a determination of monastic chapters to match numbers to material resources. With this end in view, both Cluny and Cîteaux in the thirteenth century assigned to each house of their order a fixed quota of monks – a *numerus clausus* – which was not to be exceeded. Numbers at Cluny touched their maximum of about three hundred by the death of St Hugh. He seems to have admitted all who applied, without much regard to their character or suitability; but his successors found it necessary to adopt a more discriminating policy over admissions. By 1250 the community contained about two hundred monks, and it seems to have remained at roughly that level for the next hundred years.[20]

Who were these people and where did they come from? As we have seen, the children donated by their parents formed one section of the monastic population. But the new orders of the twelfth century generally declined to accept child-oblates, and although the Benedictines continued to take them, the children formed a declining proportion of black-monk communities also at this period. Peter the Venerable regarded them as a potential source of trouble, and he reduced the number of boys at Cluny to six. The surge of new recruits to the cloister thus consisted largely of adult postulants, both clergy and lay people.

The scarcity of systematic records makes it difficult to generalise about their social origins. Some establishments, like the Swabian abbey of Reichenau, boasted of their social exclusiveness, but this was far from being the general situation. The requirement of noble birth as a qualification for entry was commoner in the men's monasteries and cathedral chapters of Germany than it was elsewhere. The leading figures in the Cluniac empire were men of aristocratic birth, but the rank and file were trawled from a more varied background. Most Benedictine houses appear to have recruited from their own locality and to have admitted men without distinction of birth, provided they could bring some form of endowment with them. The only class debarred was that of the unfree. But the property requirement, even if it was small, obviously meant that most recruits came from the ranks of middling landowners and better-off townspeople. One reservoir of recruits, about which we know too little in this early period, may have been provided by the local schools in monastic ownership. The chronicler of Bury St Edmunds tells us that his hero, abbot Samson of Bury, got his early education at the abbey's school in the borough, where he was taught by Master William of Diss, a secular clerk, who waived the fees for his impoverished pupil.[21] We have no means of telling how many others made their first and most decisive contacts with the cloister through this channel.

Canterbury cathedral priory provides an illuminating case history of a large and wealthy Benedictine establishment which drew a significant number of recruits from the local township. The surviving rent-rolls reveal that in the twelfth century many Canterbury families gave a relative to the cathedral monastery.[22] Those monks who can be identified, including some of the senior obedientiaries, were children of the more substantial town families – those of the borough reeves and the wealthier tradespeople, such as goldsmiths and mercers. The endowment they brought with them when they took the habit consisted in many cases of quite modest properties – a house or a plot of land within the city walls. Some of these recruits were evidently late converts to the monastic life. One of them, a monk named Henry, was the father of Hamo, the reeve of Canterbury. Another late convert, a leading citizen named John Calderun, retired to the cloister about the year 1176, while his wife was still living. He arranged for her maintenance by contracting with the priory to supply her with a daily corrody or pension of food from the monks' kitchen and a periodic provision of clothes. Thus many of the monks had relatives among the townspeople, including, in some cases, sons as well as brothers and sisters.

Possibly Calderun represented a category of recruits that was familiar to most monasteries – that of the aged, the ailing or terminally ill, the death-bed converts. An unquiet conscience and belief in the efficacy of the intercession of monks for the living and dead prompted numbers of clergy and lay people to seek admission to the noviciate in their last years *ad succurendum* – to obtain the help of a monastic community in making their peace with God and to have the benefit of the prayers, especially the office of the dead, that the community offered for its own members. The prospect of a perpetual commemoration made burial in the monastery a coveted privilege. Princes and patrons who obtained it might hope for interment in the monastic church close to the spot where the blessed sacrifice of the mass was offered daily. Such was Queen Blanche of Castile, the widow of Louis VIII and regent of France, who in her last days took the veil of a Cistercian nun, and was duly buried in the nuns' choir at Maubuisson.[23] Lesser folk who made their dispositions in time could look for burial in the monks' graveyard. The monastic reformers of the twelfth century were generally opposed to the acceptance of these death-bed converts, whose residence in the community was necessarily brief and whose vocation was questionable. But the repute of the Cistercians for devout observance made them a specially desirable refuge for old and ailing penitents. Clairvaux, in particular, attracted numerous retired bishops, some of them former monks of the order and others secular clergy, like John Bellesmains (d. 1204), who got papal permission to resign the see of Lyons in order to die in the abbey, though he was never a professed monk.[24]

The social and economic role

The Canterbury muniments give us some insight into the close economic ties that existed between a large monastery and a medieval township. By the twelfth century the priory had acquired through gift or purchase the lordship of nearly half the houses in the town and its suburbs, and the rent from these properties constituted a steady though minor element in its income. The economic converse of the priory's role as landlord was its function as employer. It provided a livelihood for a large number of the city's residents. On its payroll there were, besides upwards of a hundred domestic servants employed in the precincts, a multitude of professional people and craftsmen who provided it with specialist services, such as attorneys, physicians, goldsmiths, masons, and plumbers. There were, too, a group of residents who derived support from the priory in the form of a corrody or pension. Some of these were permanent lodgers in the priory.

At a later period, corrodies came to be a serious drain on monastic resources. Kings and other patrons occasionally required monks to provide a pension, or board and lodging on the premises, for retired clerks, domestic servants and soldiers. This form of exploitation, for which the monastery usually received no compensation, became more frequent in the thirteenth century. In England the practice reached a peak in the reigns of Edward I and Edward II. But there also existed corrodies of a different sort, which were purchased by the recipients. In twelfth-century Canterbury we meet a number of townspeople who have granted the cathedral priory a house or rent from a property in return for an undertaking to provide them with daily food and a cash allowance for the duration of their lives; sometimes the contract includes the privileges of confraternity and burial within the priory precinct. Frequently the purchaser would, like John Calderun of Canterbury, include his wife or others in the benefits purchased.

Canterbury was not unusual in this. From the twelfth century onwards, most monasteries granted corrodies to lay people, commonly in the form of an allowance of food and drink from the monastic kitchen; sometimes clothing was included in the benefits, sometimes accommodation within the monastic complex. In the Cistercian abbeys, those lodgers who were unmarried were often housed in the infirmary of the lay brothers.[25] Many of those who bought corrodies, either with a cash sum paid in advance or with a grant of property were men of means, who were still active at the time of purchase.[26] They were seeking an endowment for themselves on retirement or for their wives in their widowhood. In effect they were buying an annuity or endowment policy, and the monastery was discharging the role of an insurance company. Sometimes the beneficiary was a lay servant of the monastery, who was granted a corrody without payment as a reward for service, as was done for the porter at Canterbury cathedral priory. But inevitably the majority of corrodians were middle-class people who could afford to secure their future.

The town of Canterbury predated the foundation of the cathedral priory. As it was a royal borough, the monastery had no governmental responsibilities towards it. In this respect it differed from many of the satellite towns that grew up round the Benedictine abbeys in England and on the Continent. Population centres like these had been created by the needs of the monastery for servants, craftsmen and retailers, and the land they occupied had formed part of the original endowment of the monks. Where an abbey possessed the relics of a famous saint, the original nucleus of the settlement was augmented by pilgrim traffic, which in turn attracted innkeepers and trade. In such cases, where the abbey had given birth to the settlement, it was landlord of the entire town and acquired all the advantages and duties that went with medieval landlordship. It not only collected the rents and managed the leasing of the urban properties and controlled the market; also like secular landlords, it had seignorial jurisdiction over the tenants, held the borough court, and took the profits of justice.

By the year 831, the great abbey of Saint-Riquier had spawned a dependent township containing some 2,500 houses, all of them leased from the abbey.[27] A similar situation existed at Bury St Edmunds, where a township had sprung up round the abbey founded some twenty-five years before the Norman Conquest. The monastery had sole and undivided jurisdiction over the borough. Several of the obedientiaries drew rents from properties within the town, but the lion's share of the spoils was divided between the cellarer and the sacrist. The cellarer held the lordship of the manor of Bury, which included receipts from mills and from the sale of pasture rights as well as the right to the proceeds of the manorial court. The sacrist had control over the borough; he received rents from urban houses, dues from the market, and tolls levied upon all merchandise passing in and out of the town, and the profits of the portman moot or borough court. He also had the appointing of the reeves or bailiffs who administered the township on his behalf.

Rent from urban properties constituted part of the income of most Benedictine houses, but the primary form of endowment from which they derived their income was land. In the early Middle Ages, the abbeys were richly endowed with estates by their princely founders, and these initial grants were augmented by gifts from kings and members of the higher nobility. But by the twelfth century the heyday of monastic endowment was past. Small gifts and bequests continued to be made, but as population growth pressed upon natural resources and ever more land was brought under the plough, the area of cultivable land available for charitable use diminished; and the lay aristocracy became more concerned with preserving their family inheritance, and more cautious about giving parts of it away.

Nevertheless, the estates of the more ancient abbeys were often huge in extent and, as a result of piecemeal acquisition, they tended to be situated in widely scattered areas. These properties were managed in much the same way as the great estates belonging to secular lords. The land was worked by the servile labour of serfs or villeins – peasant smallholders who owed week-work for their tenements and whose bodies were at the disposal of the landlord. A proportion of the manors that made up the estate was leased to tenants, who paid the monastery a fixed rent in cash or kind. The remaining manors were retained in demesne – in other words they were exploited directly by the monastery, which consumed the produce and sold any of it that was surplus to the needs of the monks. The primary role of the demesne manors of a great abbey was to supply the table of the monks and to feed the army of servants and guests. In order to ensure more regular supplies, Peter the Venerable reorganised the demesne manors of Cluny so that each group specialised in a particular product – some supplied wheat for the white bread, some rye for the bread of the lower orders; others specialised in producing cheese, beans, or wine. Each manor was made the sole supplier of its particular produce for a given period of time. Lourdon supplied bread-corn for February and March; Mazille had to supply all the oats required for the horses at Cluny for a single night; Jully and Saint-Hippolyte had to supply the abbey with wine.[28]

As landlords, monasteries were subject to the same economic forces as secular lords and responded in much the same way. After about the year 1180, population growth and the corresponding growth of demand caused a continuing rise in the price of agricultural produce and land values throughout northern Europe. Most landlords responded to these trends by recovering leases and extending their demesne lands so as to produce large surpluses for sale and reap the profits of the rising market. 'Yesterday I would have given sixty marks to recover that manor,' shouted Abbot Samson of St Edmunds gleefully, when they reported the death of one of the abbey's tenants, 'but now the Lord has freed it.'[29] The raising of a cash crop was becoming a major preoccupation. In the thirteenth century, Christ Church Canterbury organised its demesne manors into groups round a number of centres where the corn crop could be concentrated for bulk sale and shipment round the coast or abroad. The historian of its estates described them in this period as 'a federated grain – factory producing for the market'.[30]

The remarkable thing is that as money and exchange came to play an ever-greater role in the agrarian economy, increasing numbers of landowners got into a chronic condition of debt. And the monasteries were no exception. Cluny was in almost constant debt after 1140, and by the end of the century La Charité and Monte Cassino were in a similar plight. In England, France, and Italy, monastic indebtedness is a recurrent theme of the chronicles and visitation records of the thirteenth century. The scarcity of financial records, and the complexity of those that do survive, make it difficult to unravel the causes of the problem. It does not admit of any single explanation. Lavish expenditure on building, the incessant drain of hospitality, and the burden of corrodies, were obviously contributory factors. Some houses that engaged in trade got into financial difficulties by raising loans on the security of a future grain or wool crop, which subsequently failed to come up to expectations. But the malaise was more persistent and deep-seated than this.

Grain prices – a fairly accurate barometer for the state of an undeveloped economy – reveal that the period 1180–1300 was a time of prolonged inflation.[31] This underlying trend was responsible for many of the political problems of thirteenth-century governments, whose efforts to meet rising costs by taxing the property of their subjects encountered stiffening resistance. Monasteries were among the big spenders most affected by fluctuations in prices. A great abbey containing upwards of a hundred monks and perhaps double that number of servants, and feeding a continuous stream of important guests, was a major consumer of goods and purchaser of services. Its attempts, in an age of growing affluence but persistent inflation, to keep up with contemporary standards of living enjoyed by the upper classes meant a steadily widening gap between expenditure and income. It was this chronic financial problem, rather than a shortage of postulants, that imposed limits upon the number of recruits accepted by the greater Benedictine establishments.

Feudal obligations

The possession of land conferred both privileges and public responsibilities. The kings who endowed the ancient Benedictine abbeys with great estates expected temporal returns as well as spiritual dividends from their investment. Abbots were enfeoffed with their lands in return for services. Like the king's lay vassals, they owed their lord suit of court – the obligations of attendance at the royal court and council – and military service. They could also expect to be used from time to time as royal judges, ambassadors, or inspectors-general. Charlemagne and his successors constantly used abbots as imperial *missi*, charged with the duty of visiting counties, investigating the conduct of counts and other agents, and ensuring that the emperor's instructions contained in the capitularies were being implemented.

It was the Carolingians, too, who began the practice of requiring abbots to supply contingents of mounted soldiers for the royal army. These contingents were raised from the tenants who had been enfeoffed on the abbey's estates. Early in the ninth century, the abbey of Saint-Riquier was supplying the imperial army with a force of one hundred knights. The contingents provided by the German abbeys, together with those raised by the bishops, constituted the mainstay of the armies that the Saxon and Salian emperors led across the Alps in the tenth and eleventh centuries. In the summer of 981 Otto II, who had been residing at Rome for some months, decided to embark upon the conquest of southern Italy, which was under mounting attack by the Saracens. For this purpose he needed to strengthen his army, and he summoned the prelates of Germany to bring reinforcements. A surviving list of the military quotas supplied on this occasion shows the abbot of Saint-Gall leading forty knights to join the emperor; the abbots of Lorsch and Weissenburg set off each with fifty knights, and the abbot of Reichenau with sixty; the abbot of Fulda also supplied a contingent of sixty, but he apparently left it to someone else to lead them and himself stayed at home. The abbots and bishops together provided Otto with a reinforcement of 1,504 knights, as against only 586 supplied by his lay vassals.[32]

In the same way, a group of royal abbeys in north-eastern France supplied the Capetian kings with troops. There are traces of this kind of military obligation in late Anglo-Saxon England; but it was only after the Norman Conquest that the English Benedictine abbeys were subjected to the full impact of the feudal customs that had developed on the Continent. The Conqueror assessed their lands for specified quotas of armed knights. The archbishop of Canterbury, as titular abbot of the cathedral priory, had to supply sixty knights for the royal host. The abbots of Bury St Edmunds had to provide forty knights to garrison the royal castle at Norwich, ten at a time, throughout the year.[33] A few privileged establishments, like the Conqueror's foundation at Battle, were exempted from military service; otherwise, only monasteries that were not in the king's patronage and the houses of the new orders of the twelfth century, like the Cistercians, escaped the obligation. It was one of the strengths of Cluny that Duke William, its founder, had freed it from all secular ownership or patronage, and so from the burden of knight-service.

In the train of military service came the other incidents of feudal tenure. There were gifts or financial aids, demanded by the king to defray the cost of war or to meet some other crisis. Scutage – a cash commutation of military service – was sometimes exacted in place of knights. Most serious of all for monastic finances, was the application of the custom of escheat to the lands of an abbey on the death of an abbot: in this case, the estates of the abbey were treated like those of a lay vassal who had died without an adult heir, and were occupied by the king's bailiffs, who diverted the income that accrued from them into the royal coffers, until such time as a new abbot had been approved by the king and installed. In order to protect themselves against this threat to their livelihood and against the depredations of lay abbots, monastic bodies created a legal division between the property of the abbot and that of the monks. This device, which appears in the Carolingian age, had been adopted by most of the Benedictine abbeys by the end of the eleventh century. That portion of the estates that fed the community and supported the various offices of the monastery was separated from the lands of the abbot, and it was the abbot's portion alone that bore the burdens attached to military service and that was taken into the hands of the king's agents during the vacancy of the abbacy.

If the abbot was a tenant-in-chief, holding his land immediately of the king and owing knight-service for it, he was himself an overlord in relation to the knights enfeoffed on his estates. And lordship in a feudal society involved mustering troops, holding courts, litigating over property and services, exacting financial aids, and much else. It was a position manifestly at variance with the role assigned to an abbot by the Rule of St Benedict. In order to free abbots and monks from these distracting burdens, the abbeys of the Carolingian age appointed lay agents called advocates. Originally, the lay advocate was the abbot's representative in legal and business matters. He acted as general manager of his lord's estates, presided over the manorial and feudal courts in place of the abbot, and mustered and led the abbey's contingent of knights when they were called out on active service. Such functions could only be discharged by a man of some social standing, and advocates were commonly appointed from the ranks of substantial landowners or the lesser nobility of the area.

The English counterpart of the advocate was the lay steward of the estates, who figures in the chronicles and records of the Benedictine houses from the eleventh century onwards. It was clearly a position of influence and patronage, which afforded opportunities for personal enrichment; and many aristocratic families regarded it as a worthwhile prize. But the stewards of English monasteries never achieved the kind of power and independence that was gained by lay advocates on the Continent. In northern France and Germany in particular, in the troubled political conditions of the ninth century, the advocate's role became primarily a military one – that of defending his abbey and its property against predators – and the office was converted into a hereditary fief. In many cases, the advocate turned into an overmighty vassal, who dominated and preyed upon the property of the monastery he was supposed to protect.

Lay patrons

The religious and social motives that prompted kings and members of the nobility to found and endow monasteries have already been examined. The special rights and privileges that a founder acquired in the religious establishment he had nurtured did not die with him; they were transmitted to his descendants. This was how the position of lay patron originated: the patron was a descendant of the founder unless, as was not uncommon, the patronage had been taken over by the king. Princes and magnates tended to adopt a proprietorial attitude towards the abbeys and priories they or their families had founded and endowed. They regarded the property of their monasteries as being at their disposal, and took it for granted that they would designate the abbot or superior of the community in each case. But in the course of the eleventh and twelfth centuries these assumptions were challenged by the leaders of the Gregorian Reform movement.

Gregorian principles of ecclesiastical government and the growth and diffusion of canon law did much to erode the notion that lay lords could be proprietors of abbeys and churches. In the new climate of opinion, it was recognised that a layman could not own a monastery, and a founder's relatives had to be content with the role of patrons. This position, though less exploitative than that of proprietor, still conferred important privileges and provided possibilities of interference in the life of a monastery. The patron retained the right to consultation when a new abbot was to be elected; he could claim hospitality in the establishment for himself and his household; he might require the monks to provide corrodies, in the form of board and lodging or an annuity, for his dependants or retired servants; and, of course, he had a right to the spiritual privileges of burial in the precinct and to have the monks sing the Office of the Dead for his soul.

Not all patrons were princes, nor were all monasteries large establishments. In the twelfth century many of the lesser nobility and members of the knightly class, and also royal ministers, founded religious houses of modest size. The relationship between the patron and community of such a foundation was often one of mutual respect and even intimacy, as it was between the small Cambridgeshire priory of Barnwell and the Pecche family, who were its patrons in the thirteenth century. The monks were regarded as friends and country neighbours. The annalist of the priory displayed a lively interest in the family's affairs, faithfully recording marriages, births, and deaths; and when Gilbert de Pecche died in the East while on crusade, two of the monks went out to bring his body home for burial in the cloister.[34]

The most powerful and demanding patron a monastery could have was the king. In Germany and England kings had been the chief promoters of the tenth-century monastic revival, and so they assumed patronage of most of the older Benedictine abbeys. The Capetian kings who ruled in France from 987 brought with them to the crown a cluster of abbeys of which their family had been patrons, including the prestigeous establishment of Saint-Martin at Tours; and as the monarchy slowly extended the territorial range of its power, more monasteries were brought under its patronage. The relationship cut both ways of course. In a violent age, kings were potent and desirable protectors, and they often made princely gifts. But, conversely, royal abbeys were subjected to heavy demands. One of these was the occupation and exploitation of the abbot's estates to the financial benefit of the crown during a vacancy; another was royal control over the appointment of abbots. When their abbot died, the monks had to seek a licence from the king to proceed to an election; and although the formalities of election by the monks in chapter might be observed, until the thirteenth century they were often instructed whom to elect by the king's ministers.

One of the most onerous obligations was that of offering hospitality to the royal patron. The life of a medieval ruler was spent in a constant itinerary about his kingdom, and the greater abbeys situated on the habitual routes of the royal progress were frequently called upon to provide lodging for the king, his household and his numerous retinue. Saint-Denis, Saint-Vaast at Arras, and Saint-Médard at Soissons were among the most favoured residences of the later Carolingians, and the Capetian kings maintained the tradition. In Germany, the Saxon and Salian kings of the tenth and eleventh centuries used the strategically situated abbeys of Lorsch, Hersfeld, Fulda, and Reichenau as staging-posts with such regularity that at each of them a special palace was built – a *Klosterpfalz* – within, or adjacent to, the monastic complex, to house the royal household.[35] It was the same in England in the Norman and Angevin period. When the court was not residing at one of the king's rural palaces or at Westminster, it was to be found at one of the abbeys that lay on his usual routes across the southern counties and the Midlands – St Albans, Waltham, Bury St Edmunds, Hyde abbey at Winchester, Reading, and St Peter's abbey at Gloucester.

The abbeys not only served as convenient hostels for the royal household on its travels; they were also used as centres for national or regional assemblies. Few secular palaces, even those of the king, were big enough to accommodate a gathering of all the baronial tenants of the crown. A large abbey, with its church, chapter-house, and refectory, could provide the kind of accommodation that was needed, both for parley and for the rituals of crown-wearing and banquet. Thus

St Peter's Gloucester was a favourite venue for the annual assembly of magnates that the Norman kings summoned to meet the court at Christmas. In the same way Fulda, which lay at the focal point of the roads in medieval Germany, was often used by the Hohenstaufen kings as a meeting place of The *Hoftag*, or feudal assembly.[36] It was there, at the end of January 1147, that Conrad III set before the German aristocracy his proposal to embark on the Second Crusade.

The impact of such enforced hospitality upon monastic finances could be catastrophic; but there were usually compensations. The presence of the royal visitor offered a heaven-sent opportunity to secure new privileges or the confirmation of old ones; and gifts could be expected. The ancient Carolingian abbey of San Zeno, on the outskirts of Verona, owed much of its huge territorial wealth and its commercial privileges to gifts made by the Saxon emperors, who used it as a hostel when they descended into Italy from the Brenner pass.[37]

Relations with bishops and secular clergy

Lay patrons and guests were not the only channel of communication between the cloister and the world outside it. As an ecclesiastical institution a monastery was subject to the spiritual jurisdiction of the bishop within whose diocese it lay. In some cases, the bishop was the founder of the establishment and his successors continued to be its patrons. But apart from any such special relationship, the bishop had the right and duty to supervise all the religious houses in his diocese. He discharged this duty by overseeing and confirming the election of abbots or priors, by consecrating monastic churches and, if he was conscientious, by making periodic visitations. When he visited he was entitled to receive procuration, maintenance, that is, for himself and his entourage of clerks and servants. This was the canonical position as originally decreed by the Council of Chalcedon and as it was outlined in the imperial decrees of Charlemagne and his successors: the monastery was under the jurisdiction of the diocesan. It continued to be the norm in the centuries that followed. But in the course of time a number of Benedictine abbeys succeeded in obtaining special privileges which exempted them from episcopal supervision and placed them directly under the authority of the pope.

The privilege was always a rare one before the twelfth century. Bobbio and Fulda had it from early times. Odilo secured it for Cluny by a gradual process which was completed in 1024. In England it was gained by a handful of Benedictine abbeys – St Albans, St Augustine's Canterbury, Malmesbury, Evesham, and the two royal nurslings of Westminster and Battle. In the twelfth century claims to exemption multiplied. The Cistercian Order gradually negotiated it for all its houses. The effect of the privilege was to emancipate an abbey from the bishop's supervision and visitation. It could be inspected only by visitors appointed by Rome. Its abbot, when newly elected, had to seek confirmation from the pope, not from the bishop. The abbot was free to have his monks ordained by any bishop of his choice, and he was freed from the duty of attending diocesan synods.

Naturally, exemption was not popular with bishops. It deprived them of any power to control or discipline important religious communities within the boundaries of their jurisdiction. Sometimes they fought back. The twelfth and early thirteenth centuries are littered with law suits pursued both locally and at the papal Curia between bishops and self-assertive monasteries; and the monks involved in these litigious duels were not over-scrupulous in their choice of weapons. Forged papal letters were freely used to vindicate claims to exemption, and in the absence of any scientific documentary criticism, they often carried the day. In the famous case over exemption between Evesham abbey and the bishop of Worcester, which was finally determined in favour of Evesham by the pope himself in 1205, the monks produced forged privileges of earlier popes and ancient charters which deceived even the acute legal mind of Innocent III.[38]

Bishops were the more inclined to look askance at claims to exemption from diocesan authority because monasteries were the possessors of parish churches, which involved them in pastoral responsibilities. A monastery acquired churches in a variety of ways – through the ownership of land, by direct donation from a proprietor, and through appropriation. In the early Middle Ages most rural churches were 'proprietory churches' (*Eigenkirchen*), the property of landlords who built and endowed them for the use of their tenants and themselves, and appointed clergy to serve them. Thus when an abbey was endowed with estates, it became the proprietor of the churches that went with the land and, like other landlords, it often erected and endowed new churches on its properties to meet the needs of settlements on newly cleared lands. Monasteries also received churches as gifts; for under the influence of the Gregorian Reform movement many lay landlords were persuaded to relinquish their rights over churches to monks or bishops. Monasteries continued to acquire churches, but from the later years of the twelfth century, under the stimulus of the reforming councils, bishops began to impose conditions upon such appropriations. An abbey seeking to appropriate a parish church was required to make a legal division between the portion of the parish endowments that would be assigned to the monks and the portion needed to support a priest to serve the people of the parish. A fixed proportion of the income from glebe land, tithes, and offerings was thus allocated to maintaining a perpetual vicar, who would reside in the manse and who, once instituted, would enjoy security of tenure.

As a rule, monks did not serve parish churches in their possession. In fact, canon law debarred them from performing pastoral duties. Instead they installed secular clergy to provide the sacramental services for their parishioners. The effect of appropriations was simply to divert income from the parish clergy to the monasteries. The system had its critics, even among monks. St Bernard challenged Peter the Venerable to justify Cluny's possession of parish churches and tithes, since these had been intended for the secular clergy to support the pastoral care: 'theirs is the office of baptizing and preaching and carrying out the other duties that concern the salvation of souls. Why do you usurp them, as you ought to do none of these things?[39] But the exploitation of parochial endowments for a variety of ends, which included the support of royal bureaucrats, episcopal clerks, and university teachers, as well as monks, was too deeply rooted in the structure of medieval society to be eradicated by facile moralisation.

To monasteries that had not obtained exempt status, that is, to the majority of them, the bishop was an ecclesiastical superior with whom they had only occasional contact. They might apply to him to ordain their monks or to license the appropriation of a parish church. More rarely, he might stay under their roof as guest of the abbot or, more rarely still, he might come and inspect them in his capacity as their official visitor. But there was one group of monastic establishments that stood in more constant and immediate relationship to their bishops. These were the cathedral monasteries. Normally, a cathedral church was served by secular clergy who, by the end of the eleventh century were organised as a chapter of canons, with a dean at their head. But in some cases the place of this capitular body was taken by a community of monks. Although this arrangement was to be found in some cathedrals of eastern Germany and Livonia, it was rare outside England. The English monastic cathedrals were the outcome of the monastic revival of the tenth century. They had been brought into existence at the behest of the leaders of the revival, who were monk-bishops and sought to improve their cathedral clergy by forcing them to adopt the monastic life. Thus by the time of the Norman Conquest, the cathedrals of Canterbury, Sherborne, Winchester and Worcester had chapters consisting of Benedictine monks.

It was a model that appealed to some of the newly imported prelates, like Lanfranc of Canterbury and William of St Carilef of Durham, who were monks themselves; and following the Norman settlement it was extended to the cathedrals of Rochester, Durham, Norwich and Ely. Last of all it was adopted at Carlisle, which in 1133 was given a community of Augustinian canons regular. The bishops of Wells and Lichfield, each of whom had a cathedral served by a secular chapter, created second cathedrals served by monks by taking over the abbeys of Bath and Coventry. Theoretically, the bishop discharged the role of abbot towards the monks of his cathedral monastery. But in practice the demands of diocesan business, and his need to surround himself with a corps of clerical assistants and canonists, took him away from the monastic community, and the effective headship of the monastery fell to the claustral prior.

The relationship between cathedral priory and bishop worked fairly well as long as the bishop was himself a monk. But the inherent anomaly of the arrangement became apparent after the middle of the twelfth century, when most bishops were recruited from the ranks of the secular clergy. Tensions developed, which sometimes escalated into bitter confrontations. A common cause of dispute was the bishop's insistence on exercising his abbatial rights by appointing the prior and the senior obedientiaries. The monks resented this intrusion into their affairs by secular clergy, who had no experience of life in the cloister and often showed scant regard for it. Monastic chapters reacted to heavy-handed episcopal paternalism by resisting visitation and asserting their independence in various other ways. Squabbles over the endowments of the see and conflicts over jurisdictional rights were endemic. In the course of time the monks, like the chapters of secular cathedrals, won for themselves a large measure of corporate autonomy. They secured the right to elect their own priors and to govern their own affairs with the minimum of episcopal interference. But the path to this victory was long and it was marked by many sharp skirmishes and litigious battles.

There is a striking sameness about these struggles between cathedral monasteries and their spiritual overlords. The scene varies and the cast changes, but the plot remains much the same. Hugh du Puiset, the son of an aggressive baronial dynasty of northern France, after his election to the see of Durham in 1153, engaged in forty years of strife with the monks of his cathedral over his claims to appoint their prior and his right to custody of the priory's parish churches.[40] And the contest was resumed intermittently under his successors. One of the issues in dispute was du Puiset's restoration of a collegiate church of secular canons at Darlington, which the monks opposed because they saw it as a potentially rival chapter.

It was a similar project that brought several archbishops of Canterbury into collision with the monks of Christ Church cathedral priory. Archbishop Baldwin embarked on a plan in 1186 to found a college of secular canons at Hackington and for the purpose appropriated the income of some of the churches belonging to the priory. After a prolonged struggle, in the course of which the archbishop barricaded the monks in their enclosure, they forced him to abandon his plan. Archbishop Hubert Walter transferred the same project to the manor of Lambeth, which he had acquired from Rochester cathedral priory, and set about building a large collegiate church there with fifty prebends, but the Canterbury monks thwarted this enterprise as well by successfully appealing to Rome. What the archbishops sought was a foundation that would provide canonries for the clerks and canonists they employed in diocesan administration. They were at a disadvantage in having a chapter of monks, which provided them with no means of patronage. But the monks saw the plan for a large collegiate church, endowed out of the properties of the archbishopric and peopled by learned clerks, as a threat to their position; it might prove to be the first step in transferring the chapter's electoral rights, and even the see itself, to the new foundation. And possibly their fears were not entirely groundless. In 1189 they had seen Hugh de Nonant, the bishop of Lichfield, drive his monks out of Coventry by armed force and replace them by secular canons. 'In a couple of months, believe me,' he was reported to have told the king, 'there shall be no monk in any bishop's church in your kingdom, for it isn't right. The monks', he added with characteristic vehemence, 'can go to the devil.'[41]

One of the functions that monastic chapters had in common with their secular counterparts was that of electing the bishop. It was a dangerous privilege, which intermittently placed the monks at the centre of contending political forces. For although by the twelfth century canon law vested the election of a bishop in the clergy of his cathedral church, in practice the chapter's right to elect was circumscribed by the customary claims of the king to make a nomination. A chapter that attempted to ignore or pre-empt the royal choice did so at its peril. It was one such attempt by the monks of Canterbury that precipitated the most famous conflict between the Church and the English monarchy in the Middle Ages. Following the death of Hubert Walter in July 1205, King John intended the archbishopric for John de Gray, the bishop of Norwich, a former judge and royal minister. But the monks endeavoured to pre-empt the decision by secretly electing their own subprior, Reginald, and hastily packing him off to Rome for confirmation. The stages of the ensuing struggle – the rejection of both candidates by Pope Innocent III, the king's refusal to accept the pope's approved candidate, Stephen Langton, and the pope's imposition upon England of the Great Interdict, which lasted from 1208 until 1213 – are too well known to need repeating here.

The point is that the episode, which inflicted much damage on the English Church, was triggered off by the understandable, if myopic, desire of the monks of Christ Church to have a monk as their bishop, preferably one of their own brethren. And they paid heavily for their rash attempt to thwart the royal will. They became the primary target of the king's fury. His agents hounded them from the monastery and seized the property of the priory. Those who were fit enough to travel were driven into exile and took refuge in the abbey of Saint-Bertin in Flanders, where they remained until King John had made his peace with the Church.

The calamity that overtook the monks of Christ Church, and the recurrence of sharp conflicts between monastic chapters and their bishops, illustrate the paradoxical character of the cathedral monastery. Although the monks had the public responsibilities of electing the bishop, and in some cases exercised part of the bishop's spiritual jurisdiction when the see was vacant, they could not provide the administrative services a bishop expected to obtain from members of a secular chapter. Their relationship with a titular abbot who was not a monk was at best ambivalent, and at worst actively hostile. The Benedictine chapters were not, of course, the only capitular bodies that quarrelled with bishops. Conflicts sometimes occurred between bishops and secular chapters bent on asserting their independence. But the special title of the bishop to the pastoral direction of his monks gave their disputes the wounding intensity and destructiveness of a family feud.

The cloister and the schools

Monastic writers of the twelfth century treated the schools as an alien territory. They liked to contrast the snares of the scholastic life with the studious peace of the cloister – 'the blessed school, where hearts are instructed by Christ, and we learn without study or lectures how we ought to live', as Peter of Celle wrote to John of Salisbury, who had found a pleasant place of exile in the city of Paris.[42] The school Peter referred to was the metaphysical one represented by the monastic discipline. But monasteries also had schools in the more literal sense. As long as there were child-oblates, there had to be a school in the cloister and monk-schoolmasters to educate them. On the other hand, formal instruction was rarely provided in the monastery other than for the children who were destined to become permanent members of the community – the so-called *nutriti*. The education of outsiders in the cloister was, in fact, forbidden by the conciliar decrees of the ninth century. An exception might sometimes be made for the children of patrons or noble benefactors. In the 1060s the abbey of Bee for a time opened its doors to secular students attracted by the teaching of Lanfranc; but this seems to have been only a temporary expedient to help defray the cost of the abbey's new buildings.[43] The consensus of monastic legislators was against it.

On the other hand, many of the Benedictine abbeys and priories were proprietors of grammar or song schools, which were conducted in a house outside the enclosure in the adjacent borough. In these cases the monastic body licensed a secular clerk to conduct the school and teach allcomers in return for fees. As a rule, monks did not teach in external schools themselves. In a cottage school of this kind with a secular schoolmaster, instruction can hardly have gone beyond the level of Latin grammar, taught from the primer, basic arithmetic, and knowledge of the service books required to sing the offices in church.

In the twelfth century there was a growing trend to phase out child-oblates, and with them the claustral school. The new orders refused to accept children altogether. Postulants were not admitted under the age of fifteen or eighteen, and were expected to have received their essential literary schooling before they entered the religious life. A number of those who sought admission were *magistri* – men like Lanfranc and Stephen of Tournai, who had studied and taught in one of the higher schools that were adjuncts of cathedrals and were located in cities. St Bernard went out of his way to drag the Paris schools for recruits, and in fact the Cistercians had conspicuous success in attracting schoolmen. But the traffic between the cloister and the schools was only in one direction. Before the middle of the thirteenth century, monasteries in general were disinclined to send their monks to study in the urban schools of the seculars.

The objection was stated in strong language in a letter by Stephen of Tournai. He was writing to dissuade Absalon of Lund from sending his nephew to the schools of Paris: 'as to the plan you intimated in your letter of sending him to the schools of the seculars and the word-merchants, choose another city than Paris in which he is to study, lest under our eyes, in place of the morning and evening sacrifice he should have offered with us, he offers a din of words and an endless clash of disputations'.[44] Stephen had been a schoolman himself, but now he was writing as a canon regular and abbot of Saint-Geneviève on the Mount, where the young man had made his profession as a monk. To send a man to the schools was, as he explained to Absalon, 'repugnant to our institution and custom'; it would be a pernicious precedent for those who came after. 'Wisdom', he adds, echoing Peter of Celle, 'has its own rules in the cloister, where it erects a school of truth.'

Obviously the objection was based in part upon the fear of subjecting young monks to the temptations and distractions of student life in the city; but there was more to it than that. Monastic writers of the twelfth century were profoundly convinced that the intellectual activities of the schools were incompatible with the monk's profession. The root cause of this antipathy was a divergence of purpose and method. A monastery was usually a place of learning. Monks, after all, were committed by the Rule to reading books, and those who had the necessary talent also aspired to writing them. But the literature proposed for reading, both public and private, and the type of books that were produced, were determined by the overall purpose of the monastic life – spiritual growth in the search for God.[45] The literary products of the cloister, whether they were theology in the form of Biblical exegesis, or hagiography, or even history, were designed primarily to provide food for meditation and inspiration for conduct. The object of the scholastic treatise, on the other hand, and of the debates that underlay it, was to advance inquiry and speculation.

The conflicting aims are manifested by the differences of style and method. The divergence had been brought about by the rise of scholasticism, the product of a new intellectual and social milieu. The great expansion of the schools that had begun in the last decades of the eleventh century was associated with the recovery by Western scholars of the lost intellectual capital of the ancient world in the form of Greek and Arabic science and philosophy, made available through the medium of Latin translation. This gradually revolutionised both the content and methods of learning. Aristotle's works on natural science, Greek mathematics and cosmology, and Arabic medicine confronted scholars with a whole new universe of scientific knowledge and speculation, which could not be readily fitted into the traditional academic programme of grammar and Bible studies, and which called in question its hierarchy of values. The books of Aristotle's logic provided a system of rational analysis that could apparently be applied in every field of learning. In the course of the twelfth century the application of dialectic or analytic logic to the materials of study created new sciences of theology and canon law, as well as new secular sciences of logic, jurisprudence, and medicine. And the nerve-centres of the new learning were the law schools of Bologna and the cathedral schools of northern France.

The new learning not only extended the range of the medieval curriculum; it brought about a revolutionary change in the method of study. Medieval teaching was based upon the study of authoritative texts. For theology the basic text was the Bible, and an authoritative guide to Biblical exegesis was provided by the commentaries of the Fathers. This was common ground to both monastic and scholastic theologians. The monk wrote Scriptural commentaries; and the schoolman commented on the text of the Bible in the classroom. But in the schools, the new intellectual tools gave rise to a different type of theological inquiry which employed the disputation as its method.

The scholastic disputation was a system of logical discourse aimed at clarification through the definition of terms. As time went on, collections of *Questiones* – debated problems – raised in the process of commenting on the authoritative text, circulated separately from the text that had prompted them, and finally might be organised systematically to form a *summa* – an independent doctrinal treatise. By the middle of the twelfth century, the new methodology had produced in Peter Lombard's *Four Books of Sentencs* the first of the great syntheses of Christian doctrine that, alongside the Bible, was to form the basis of instruction in the university theology classrooms of the thirteenth century. The *Questio* developed its own techniques and imposed its characteristic form upon scholastic writing. A scholastic treatise uses the vocabulary of Aristotelian logic; it is syllogistic in method and disputatious in its form. Peter Lombard was a proto-scholastic, and his *Sentences* can be read with pleasure and relative ease by anyone with adequate Latin; but the refinement of logical jargon makes the *summa* of a thirteenth-century master something of an obstacle course for the uninitiated reader.

It was precisely this new methodology and the new race of teachers who practised it – the professional *magistri* of the nascent universities – that aroused the misgivings of monastic theologians. They were suspicious of the application of the human categories of analytic logic to the data of Revelation. To teach young men by encouraging them to debate in the schools about the attributes of the Trinity or the nature of Christ seemed an invitation to presumption, pride, and error. Had not Cassian – still the most widely read master of the spiritual life – warned his disciples to receive the teachings of the Fathers like mutes, to be quick to hear but slow to speak, and not to be seduced by those who sought skill in disputation, for such could not enter the arcana of the spirit?[46] The dialectical method, by contrast, thrived upon contradictions between the ancient authorities. The tendency to elevate alongside them the *Sentences* or doctrinal formulations of the leading *magistri* to the status of authorities evoked much scathing criticism from more conservative claustral scholars.

Rupert of Deutz was a spokesman for the traditionalists. As he definitely boasted to his critics, he had received all his education in the cloister, and he had some sharp things to say about those of the brethren who wandered far and wide in search of famous masters, but came only late to discover the unique pearl of Holy Scripture. Commenting on the Rule, he regaled his novices with the story of how, as a young monk, he had climbed the hill to the cathedral school of Laon on a donkey, to beard the two most famous masters of France, William of Champeaux and Anselm of Laon, to defend from Scripture the traditional dogma of the divine will against the blasphemous distinctions formulated by the masters.[47] It was essentially the same complaint that Stephen of Tournai voiced at the end of the century against the novelties and the new *summulae* of the masters of Paris: 'as if the works of the holy Fathers are not enough, they dispute publicly concerning the incomprehensible Deity; they divide and rend the indivisible Trinity; and there are as many errors as there are masters.'[48]

By contrast with the analytical method of the schoolmen, monastic theology – theology written by and for monks – remained literary in form and style, deriving much of its imagery and inspiration from the Fathers, and continued to cling to the traditional modes of Biblical exegesis.[49] This method of exposition, which had been inherited from Christian antiquity, elaborated the 'spiritual', as opposed to the literal sense of the text: an allegorical or moral significance was extracted from persons, things, and events, referred to in both Old and New Testaments. Thus Gregory the Great – the most studied master of medieval exegetes – commenting on the story of Dives and Lazarus in St Luke's Gospel, interprets Dives, the rich man dressed in purple, as signifying the Jewish people, and Lazarus the Gentiles. The ulcers on the skin of Lazarus signify the eruption of sin, and the dogs who lick his sores are the preachers and holy doctors who heal the penitent when he confesses his sins. For Gregory, the spiritual sense was always to be sought behind the letter of the sacred texts.[50]

Treated in this way, a book of the Old Testament like *The Song of Songs*, with its overtly erotic imagery, could be made to furnish a series of homilies on the mystical relationship between the soul and God. This was how it was used in the famous commentary of St Bernard. It was the way in which *lectio divina* had been traditionally understood in the cloister. Its object was to promote prayer. It involved thought, but it differed radically from the analytical approach of the schoolman, which was succinctly summarised in the axiom of Peter the Chanter: 'the discipline of Holy Scripture comprises three things – the exposition by the lecturer, disputation, and preaching . . . nothing is fully understood or faithfully preached unless it has first been masticated by the tooth of disputation'.[51]

The gulf that separated the schools from the monastery would in time be narrowed, if never completely closed. To some extent it was bridged by the new institutes of canons regular, which attracted men like Stephen of Tournai and Andrew of St Victor, who were well versed in the new learning. Not all the work produced in the cloister was untouched by the new methods. The first compilation to apply dialectic to the task of organising the ancient canons of the Church and papal decretals into a systematic treatise was the Concordance of Discordant Canons published about the year 1140. This, which was immediately adopted as a text by the law schools and laid the foundation of a new canonistic science, was the work of Gratian, who was a monk of Bologna.

The expansion of the secular schools and, at the end of the twelfth century, the rise of the universities, signified that intellectual leadership had passed from the cloister. But monastic learning could not remain isolated indefinitely from the intellectual tide that was sweeping through the Western world. The absorption of men from the schools, not all of whom waited until old age before taking the habit, and the challenge of the Mendicant Orders of the thirteenth century, gradually broke down the barriers between the two worlds. In the course of the thirteenth century, the Cistercians and the black monks began sending a small selection of their men to the schools, and established houses of study for them at the universities. These were for monks attending lectures in the faculty of theology. Besides a number of theology graduates, most Benedictine abbeys and houses of canons regular of any size contained a few canonists and civil law graduates who had passed through the law schools of Bologna, Orleans or Oxford.

Although the intellectual apartheid between monks and schoolmen was relaxed in time, the traditional modes of study were still followed and the old classics of ascetical theology were still read in the cloister. The *lectio divina* of the Rule referred as much to public reading in the chapterhouse and refectory as to reading by individuals. Lists of books with passages marked for reading at mealtimes or in the chapter-house, survive from the twelfth and thirteenth centuries; and the choice of literary fare displays an undisturbed adherence to the traditional programme of monastic study. At Saint-Martial of Limoges, at Anchin, at Conches and Saint-Denis, the community continued to be offered a similar diet of the Lives of the Fathers, Gregory's Dialogues, Cassian, Smaragdus on the Rule, and the homilies and Scriptural commentaries of the Fathers from Jerome to Bede.[52] Here and there the homogeneity of the list is lightened by a few items of more recent hagiography, such as the Life of St Francis. But there is a total absence of scholastic theology, or even the work of protoscholastic theologians like St Anselm. If most monastic libraries were by the thirteenth century stocked with scholastic treatises and copies of the Lombard's *Sentences* for private study, in public reading at least, the emphasis is upon edification rather than intellectual nourishment. In a sense, the new learning of the schools, by clarifying the distinction between the natural and the supernatural, between nature and grace, had sharpened the line of demarcation between the cloister and the world.

Notes

1. *Liber Tramitis Aevi Odilonis Abbatis*, ed. P. Dinter, in *CCM* X (1980).
2. *Udalrici Consuetudines Cluniacenses, PL* 149, 633–778; modern edition by B. Albers, *Consuetudines Monasticae* II (Montecassino, 1945); for the text of an eleventh-century English customary, with translation, see *The Monastic Constitutions of Lanfranc*, ed. M. D. Knowles (1951). For modern reconstructions of the monastic day see Joan Evans, *Monastic Life at Cluny 910–1157* (1931); Knowles, *op. cit.*, pp. xxxv–vii,,and *The Monastic Order in England* (1940), pp. 448–71; G. de Valous, *Le monachisme clunisien, op. cit.*, i, pp. 228–93; Noreen Hunt, *Cluny under St Hugh 1049–1109* (1967), pp. 99–123; Janet Burton, *Monastic and Religious Orders in Britain 1000–1300* (1994), pp. 159–61.
3. G. Constable, *The Reformation of the Twelfth Century* (1996), p. 203.
4. *PL* 149, 675–77.
5. *CCM* X, pp. 261–4.
6. *The Letters of Peter the Venerable*, ed. G. Constable (Cambridge, Mass., 1967) i, p. 334.

7. *Abbonis Vita, PL* 139, 393.
8. E. Lesne, *Histoire de la propriété ecclésiastique en France* (Lille, 1938) iv, pp. 298, 330.
9. *PL* 149, 703.
10. Roger Twysden, *Historiae Anglicanae Scriptores* X (1652), p. 1915.
11. Knowles, *Monastic Constitutions of Lanfranc*, p. 10.
12. *Historia Calamitatum*, trans. Betty Radice, *The Letters of Abelard and Heloise* (1974), pp. 71–2.
13. On canonical escape-routes from monastic vows, which were exploited by a few in the later Middle Ages see F. Donald Logan, *Runaway Religious in Medieval England c. 1240–1540* (1996), pp. 42–65.
14. *Constitutions of Lanfranc*, p. 89.
15. *The Account Book of Beaulieu Abbey*, ed. S. F. Hockey (Camden Soc., 4th series 16; 1975), p. 174.
16. *CCM* X, pp. 304–6. On the duties of the obedientiaries at Cluny see Valous, *op. cit.*, i, pp. 123–86.
17. *The Rule of St Benedict*, c. 43.
18. G. Duby, 'Un inventaire des profits de la seigneurie clunisienne à la mort de Pierre le Vénérable' in *Petrus Venerabilis 1156–1956*, ed. G. Constable and J. Kritzeck (*Studia Anselmiana* 40, Rome, 1955) pp. 128–40.
19. U. Berliére, 'Le nombre des moines dans les anciens monastères', *Rev. bén* 41 (1929), pp. 231–61, 42 (1930), pp. 31–42, and 'Le recrutement des moines bénédictins aux XIIᵉ et XIIIᵉ siècles', *Académie royale de Belgique Mémoires*, 2nd series 11 (1924), fasc. 6, gives examples of numerical decline after the eleventh century. R. W. Southern in an interesting and informative discussion in *Western Society and the Church in the Middle Ages* (1970), pp. 233–5, takes these as symptoms of a universal decline. Although I have profited from his discussion, my conclusions are somewhat different. The problem is that in most cases the base-line from which we have to work is extremely uncertain, since figures for the earlier period are mainly derived from the notoriously unreliable statements of hagiographers. The figures compiled by Valous, *op. cit.* i, pp. 211–12, and the figures recorded for English visitations in the thirteenth century, do not indicate any general decline in recruitment to the Cluniac houses. Account must be taken of the fact that both Cluny and Cîteaux imposed a *numerus clausus* on recruitment in order to ensure that each house remained solvent.
20. Valous, *op. cit.*, i., p. 212 n. He queries the alleged number of 400 monks in the time of St Hugh. Hunt, *op. cit.*, suggests a figure of 300.
21. *The Chronicle of Jocelin of Brakelond*, ed. H. E. Butler (1949), p. 44.
22. For this paragraph see W. Urry, *Canterbury under the Angevin Kings* (1967), pp. 153–68.
23. Teryl N. Kinder, 'Blanche of Castile and the Cistercians', *Cîteaux* 27 (1976), p. 3.
24. M.-A. Dimier, 'Mourir à Clairvaux', *Collectanea Ordinis Cisterciensium Reformatorum* 17 (1955), pp. 272–85. On the objections of reformers to accepting late converts see Giles Constable, *Reformation of the Twelfth Century*, pp. 82–3.
25. David H. Williams, *The Cistercians in the Early Middle Ages* (1998), p. 122.
26. Barbara Harvey, *Living and Dying in England 1100–1540: The Monastic Experience* (1993), pp. 179–209. This contains the best modern account of the corrody system, based on the Westminster evidence.
27. J. Hubert, 'Saint-Riquier et le monachisme bénédictin en Gaul à l'époque carolingienne', *Il monachesimo medioevo e la formazione della civiltà occidentale (Settimane di Studio del Centro Italiano di Studi*, IV, Spoleto, 1957), pp. 293–309.
28. G. Duby, *op. cit.* n. 18.
29. *Chronicle of Jocelin of Brakelond*, p. 33.
30. R. A. L. Smith, *Canterbury Cathedral Priory* (1943), p. 142.
31. P. D. A. Harvey, 'The English inflation of 1180–1220', *Past and Present* 61 (1973).

32. The list entitled *Indiculus Loricatorum* is printed in *MGH Constitutiones* I, pp. 632–3; see discussion by L. Auer, 'Der Kriegsdienst unter den Sächsischen Kaisern', *MIOG* 79 (1971), pp. 316–407.

33. Helena Chew, *The English Ecclesiastical Tenants-in-Chief* (1932), pp. 1–36.

34. *Liber Memorandorum Ecclesie de Bernewell*, ed. J. W. Clark (1907), p. 48. On monastic patrons in general see Susan Wood, *English Monasteries and their Patrons in the Thirteenth Century* (1955).

35. W. Erdmann, *Deutsche Königspfalzen* (*Veröffentlichungen des Max-Planck-Instituts für Geschichte*, Göttingen, 1979), pp. 191–9.

36. H.-P. Wehlt, *Reichsabtei und König, dargestellt am Beispiel der Abtei Lorsch mit Ausblicken auf Hersfeld, Stablo und Fulda* (*Veröffentlichungen des Max-Planck-Instituts für Geschichte*, Göttingen 1970), pp. 237–44.

37. V. Fainelli, 'L'abbazia di San Zeno nell'alto medioevo', *Miscellanea di Studi in onore di Roberto Cessi* I (Rome, 1958), pp. 51–62.

38. See the exhaustive account of the Evesham case by C. R. Cheney, *Innocent III and England* (1976), pp. 196–9.

39. *The Letters of Peter the Venerable* i, pp. 81–2.

40. G. V. Scammell, *Hugh du Puiset, Bishop of Durham* (1956), pp. 128–67. On the general problem of relations between secular bishops and their monastic chapters see Knowles, *The Monastic Order in England*, pp. 313–30.

41. *Gervase of Canterbury, Opera*, ed. W. Stubbs (RS 1880), i, pp. 488–9. For the phases of the dispute between the Canterbury monks and the archbishops see C. R. Cheney, *Hubert Walter* (1967), pp. 135–57, and C. H. Lawrence, *St Edmund of Abingdon* (1960), pp. 165–7.

42. H. Denifle and A. Chatelain, *Chartularium Universitatis Parisiensis* I (Paris 1889), p. 24. On this dichotomy see P. Delhaye, 'L'organisation scolaire au XIIe siècle', *Traditio* 5 (1947), pp. 211–68.

43. Margaret Gibson, *Lanfranc of Bec* (1978), pp. 34–5.

44. *Epistolae*, PL 211, 376; reprinted by Denifle and Chatelain, *Chartularium* I, p. 43.

45. On monastic studies, their content and purpose, see the classic study of Jean Leclercq, *The Love of Learning and the Desire for God* (1961, 1978).

46. *Conlationes*, ed. M. Petschenig, CSEL XIll (1886), pp. 408–9.

47. *Ruperti Tuitiensis in Regulam S. Benedicti*, PL 170, 482, cited by M.-D. Chenu, *Nature, Man and Society in the Twelfth Century*, trans. J. Taylor and L. K. Little (Chicago Univ. Press, 1968), pp. 270–1.

48. PL 211, 517.

49. On the tradition of 'spiritual' exegesis in monastic theology see Leclercq, *op. cit.*, pp. 236–86, and Beryl Smalley, *The Study of the Bible in the Middle Ages*, 2nd edn (1952), pp. 1–46.

50. J. Leclercq, 'The exposition and exegesis of Scripture from Gregory the Great to St Bernard' in *The Cambridge History of the Bible*, vol. ii, ed. G. W. H. Lampe (1969), pp. 184–5.

51. *Verbum Abbreviatum*, PL 205, 25.

52. D. Nebbiai-Dalla Guarda, 'Les listes médiévales de lectures monastiques: contribution à la connaissance des anciennes bibliothèques bénédictines', *Rev. bén* 96 (1986), pp. 271–326.

8

MONASTIC REFORM: THE QUEST FOR THE PRIMITIVE

'We appeal to the life of the primitive Church,' wrote Peter the Venerable, 'for what is the monastic life except what was then called the apostolic life?'[1] Peter was defending the observance of Cluny against the onslaught of St Bernard. About the year 1130, when this exchange took place, Peter's sentiments were echoed by Abbot Rupert of Deutz: 'If you will consult the evidences of the Scriptures, you will find that they all seem to say plainly that the Church had its beginning in the monastic life.'[2] The theme had long been a commonplace of monastic literature. Smaragdus stated it in the ninth century: the apostles were monks and the true authors of the cenobitic life.[3] What is new in the twelfth century is not the myth but the apologetic use made of it by both defenders and critics of established practice.

The controversial appeal to the model of the primitive Church sprang from the sharpened historical consciousness of a century that was in the process of rediscovering the lost philosophy and science of the ancient world. By 1080 the law doctors were lecturing on the Digest and Code of Justinian in the Bologna schools; and the whole corpus of Aristotle's logic was known and taught at Chartres by 1140. The revival of intellectual and literary life that occurred in western Europe between 1050 and 1200 took many forms and flowed into many channels; but the common source was the flood of Latin translations that was making Greco-Arabic philosophical and scientific works available to Western scholars. The remote past had come alive again, and it seemed to offer an inexhaustible fund of lessons for those who knew how to interpret it.

The appeal from the present to the remote past was central to the strategy of the Gregorian Reform. It was the avowed aim of the Gregorian party to restore what they conceived to be the discipline and order of the primitive Church. To this end the papal Curia set scholars to work to search libraries and archives for early sources of canon law, and new collections were produced containing 'the ancient law' – the law that governed the Church of the early centuries. At the Roman Council of 1059 Hildebrand, then deacon of the Roman Church, invoked the image of the primitive Church to support his argument that the secular clergy ought to forgo private property and embrace 'a communal life according to the example of the primitive Church'.[4] His history may have been questionable, but the logic could hardly be faulted: if the apostles were monks, then the clergy, who exercised the apostolic ministry, ought also to live like monks. This conviction helped to fuel the drive for clerical celibacy which formed an important part of the Gregorian programme. It also provided the theoretical basis and inspiration for the canons regular – the new hybrid orders of clerical monks that began to appear before the end of the eleventh century.

This search for the order of the primitive Church was close to the heart of the ferment that troubled the monastic world of the twelfth century. New ascetical movements and new orders sprang into existence, all in one way or another expressing discontent with the traditional forms of monastic life. The Benedictine tradition as it was interpreted by Cluny and Gorze no longer satisfied many of those who wanted to become monks. Paradoxically, this spiritual crisis and strange restlessness within the monastic world was the malaise of a society that was getting materially richer. The response of ascetics to the economic expansion of western Europe and the growing affluence of the twelfth century was to idealise voluntary poverty, which now began to assume a critical role in the monastic tradition.[5]

This reaction was partly a protest against the corporate wealth and worldly involvements of the great abbeys; it was also a rejection of a type of community life derived from the Carolingian tradition which imposed a crushing burden of vocal prayer and external ritual and made no concession to the need of the individual for solitude, private prayer, or reflection.[6] In fact, the common theme that runs through all the new experiments in religious life at this period is a quest for disengagement, solitude, poverty symbolised and actualised by the need for manual labour, and simplicity. The thinking of reformers focused upon three models which seemed to be offered by Christian antiquity. One of these was the eremitical life of the Desert Fathers, an obvious model for individuals who had read the early classics of monastic literature. The Benedictine tradition had never wholly lost sight of the anchoritic ideal, which was enshrined in the opening chapter of the Rule. Even Cluny had its hermits, who had been licensed to withdraw from the community of the brethren to remote spots in the Jura and the Pyrenees.[7] In the eleventh century the pull of the desert was felt again and became a major force in Western religious experience.

Another antique model that provided inspiration for many new kinds of monasticism was what men called 'the apostolic life'. This was a fertile idea with a vigorous future before it. It meant different things to different people, but its common source was the life-style of the apostolic community at Jerusalem as it is briefly described in the Acts of the Apostles: 'And they continued steadfastly in the apostles' doctrine and fellowship, and in the breaking of bread, and in prayers. And all who believed were together and had all things in common; and sold their possessions and goods and parted them to all men as every man had need' (*Acts* ii. 41–5). This was the passage invoked by the apologists of the monastic tradition to justify the conventional forms of cenobitic life. To them the essence of the Apostolic Life was life in a religious community, organised for corporate prayer, and based upon the renunciation of personal property. 'What am I to say about these canons or monks, the Apostles?' asks Peter of Celle: 'Jesus taught the discipline of the cloister to the Apostles and the seventy-two disciples. They had no property of their own, but all things in common.'[8]

Peter was a Benedictine monk and a bishop. He was writing in 1179, in old age, from his abbey of Saint-Remi, where he had retreated to nurse his sciatica. He expounded the traditional monastic virtues, and defended them with the conventional arguments. His inclusion of the canons regular in the apostolic troop was a courteous concession to his correspondent, who was a canon of Merton priory. But long before he wrote his book on *The Claustral Discipline*, the appeal to the practice of the apostolic Church had been wrested from the hands of those who were defending existing institutions and was being used to justify new forms of religious life. The Apostles may have been poor, but their primary role, after all, was to preach the Gospel. Evangelisation was coming to be seen as an essential part of the apostolic life. Before the end of the eleventh century, religious movements sprang up in Italy and France which sought to realise this idea by combining poverty with itinerant preaching.

The other model that inspired critics of existing observance was the Benedictine Rule itself. It was the perennial appeal to the primitive document which was regarded as normative. The elaborate ritual and aristocratic life-style of Cluny were contrasted with the relatively simple observance outlined in the Rule and were found wanting. This was the central thrust of St Bernard's attack upon Cluny, which drew a detailed defence from Peter the Venerable:

> How do they keep the Rule who wear furs, who feed the healthy on meat and meat-fats, who allow three or four dishes daily with their bread, who do not perform the manual labour the Rule commands?[9]

The point of Bernard's quill was sharpened by wounded *amour propre* over a cousin who had defected from Clairvaux to seek a less austere home at Cluny. But his argument expressed the mind of growing numbers of dissidents who wanted to discard the developments of Carolingian monasticism and get back to a more literal observance of the Rule. This was the major theme of the Cistercian reform.

The orders of hermits

The first in time was the eremitical movement – the search for solitude. 'O lovely desert, filled with lilies and scattered with flowers, the refreshment of the poor of Christ, the dwelling place of the lovers of God, O chaste and pure solitude, long sought-for and found at last, who has stolen you from me, my beloved?'[10] John of Fécamp's lament for his lost peace voiced the sentiment of a whole generation of ascetics who had gathered new inspiration from reading the Lives and Sayings of the early Egyptian monks. By nature a contemplative, John was a hermit manqué, condemned to end his days in Normandy as abbot of Fécamp. But another from his native Ravenna, the fervent, restless Romuald, succeeded in translating his vision into reality.

A hermitage was not necessarily in a remote and secluded place. Many a parish church of the twelfth and thirteenth centuries supported an anchorite, who lived walled up in a cell attached to the chancel of the building. The individual anchorite was a figure well known to, and respected by, medieval society at all times. But in the eleventh century, ascetics who could not find personal fulfilment in the conventional version of monastic life began to congregate in groups in the secluded mountain regions of central Italy and the forests of northern France. The founding fathers of the Italian eremitical movement were the Greek-speaking Calabrian monk St Nilus, who founded a monastery of the Basilian type at Grottaferrata in the Alban hills, and St Romuald.

Important though he was as the patriarch of the movement, Romuald left nothing of his own in writing, and what we know of him comes from the glowing encomium written a generation later by Peter Damian. An adult convert to the ascetical life, he had taken the habit at the Cluniac abbey of Sant'Apollinare in Classe; but the life at Sant'Apollinare failed to satisfy his fervent quest for self-renunciation, and he left the community in search of solitude. He read the *Lives of the Fathers*, and under their inspiration adopted the life of a hermit, settling first in the Veneto, then in the Pyrenees within the orbit of the abbey of Cuxa; and finally in the hills of Tuscany at Camaldoli. There with the help of Teodaldo, the bishop of Arezzo, he founded a monastery soon after the year 1022.[11] Camaldoli became the mother-house of the first eremitical order to be founded in the West.

The distinctive character of Romuald's institution lay in the fact that it brought together two modes of ascetical life – the cenobitical and the eremitical – and co-ordinated them in the same organisation. At the foot of the slopes was a cenobitical community following the Rule of St Benedict with an austere simplicity. But the *raison d'être* of the monastery was the congregation of hermits living, each in his own hut, higher up among the forested crags. The community provided the nursery, the essential training place, for the solitaries who were to embark on their lonely spiritual conflict. Although it was an arrangement which St Benedict had expressly envisaged, the ethos of Camaldoli, with its severe regime of fasting,

FIGURE 8.1 Camaldoli: the huts of the mountain hermitage

© J. Paul Getty Trust. The Getty Research Institute, Los Angeles (96.P.21)

self-flagellation, and perpetual silence, was more in tune with the desert tradition than with the gentle spirit of the Benedictine Rule. Its attraction was only for a contemplative élite and, although the order endured, Camaldolese monasteries were never very numerous. Some were founded in France and Spain, but Italy remained the chosen land of the congregation.

The same unrest and discontent with traditional observance produced a foundation of a different type at Vallombrosa. This was the work of John Gualberto of Florence, another spiritual refugee, in this case from the abbey of San Miniato above Florence. Like Romuald, Gualberto had fled to the cloister in revulsion from a family feud. After quitting San Miniato, he tried his vocation at Camaldoli for a time; but he decided in favour of a fuller kind of cenobitical life, and his troubled spirit finally found rest in the community that gathered round him at Vallombrosa – Milton's autumnal forest – on the western slope of the Pratomagno hills. It was a completely cenobitical monastery governed by the Benedictine Rule. What distanced it from the practice of older abbeys like San Miniato was the way in which the Rule was scrupulously followed in every detail and in the preservation of strict seclusion from the outside world. This isolation was maintained by the use of lay brothers who were fully professed monks but who did not share the choral duties of the community; their job was to manage the administrative side of the monastery, to do the necessary buying and selling, and to act as an insulation between the monk and secular society. Vallombrosa, like Camaldoli, became the head of a small monastic congregation which had only a few colonies outside Italy. Its main contribution to the Western monastic tradition was the idea of a reversion to a literal observance of the original Rule, and the specialised use of *conversi* or lay brothers recruited from the peasant strata of society, both practices that were to be adopted by the Cistercians with great success.

The most compelling and influential figure in the Italian eremitical movement of the eleventh century was St Peter Damian. He was a child of Romuald's Ravenna. Through the patronage of a clerical relative, he acquired an education in the city schools of northern Italy that made him one of the foremost Latin writers of his generation. Like many great ascetics, Damian is a figure of contradictions. Later, after he had abandoned the schools for the life of the desert, he reacted violently against his early classical education. With that curious intellectual dualism we see in Jerome, he castigates monks 'who join the crowd of grammarians, and forsaking spiritual studies, hanker for the follies of worldly knowledge, who think little of the Rule of St Benedict and find their pleasure in the rules of Donatus'.[12] It is a strange invective from a man who himself wrote not only a powerful and elegant Latin prose, showing all the traces of a grounding in the classical poets, but also some of the best lyrical poetry of the century. He was, in fact, making a promising career for himself as a teacher of grammar and rhetoric when he gave it all up to join the solitaries living at Fonte Avellana in the Apennines. It was one of the foundations inspired by St Romuald; and Damian, who had never known him, was to become Romuald's most illustrious disciple and his biographer.

Damian's evocative strophes on the *Song of Songs* expose the motor nerve of his complex personality. Behind the fierce asceticism and the intense vision of the mystic lay the tortured sensibility of the poet. His ceaseless macerations and his ferocious denunciations of the flesh reflect the long struggle of his own soul. He became the major prophet of the eremitical movement, a teacher and confessor of hermits and mystics. In the *Paradiso* he appeared to Dante as a figure of blinding light, standing in the seventh sphere of the contemplatives. He attracted disciples and founded new establishments for them on the model and following the observances of Fonte Avellana.

The way of life at Fonte Avellana under his direction is described for us by his biographer, John of Lodi, and by his own *Institutes for the Order of Hermits*. It was a regime of great severity which made small concession to human weakness. In the house of the community the brothers occupied cells in pairs; in winter and summer alike they remained barefoot; fasting was almost perpetual: on four days a week there was only a single meal, consisting of bread, salt and water. Higher up the slopes, among the caves and crags, were the eyries of the strict solitaries, who had completed their apprenticeship in the monastery below. They passed the day in reciting the divine office, which was done in solitude at the appropriate hours, reciting the Psalter, manual work and reading. Great austerities were demanded. Damian was a particular enthusiast for the practice of self-flagellation for the purpose of taming the flesh, and he promoted it among his followers. When any of the brethren died, each of the community was enjoined to fast for seven days on his behalf, to receive the whip seven times, and to recite the Psalter for him in its entirety thirty times.[13]

Damian's reputation and powerful pen found him friends among the party of reform at the papal court. He became the friend and correspondent of Cardinal Humbert, Archdeacon Hildebrand, and Hugh of Cluny; and although he recoiled from the hierocratic political doctrine of Hildebrand, he played an active part in the campaign against simony and clerical marriage. His *Book of Gomorrah*, which he wrote in 1051 and dedicated to Pope Leo IX, was a savage indictment of the sexual vices of the Italian clergy and one of the classics of early Gregorian literature. In 1057 he was made cardinal-bishop of Ostia and began to occupy a central place on the stage of public events. But he remained all his life a passionate ascetic and contemplative, and even as cardinal he continued to preach a return to the desert as the surest means of salvation from the corruption of the secular Church.

In Italy at least, the movement Damian so fervently promoted seems to have recruited mainly among the aristocracy and urban patriciate. He himself came of a poor family, but in this he was the exception. Both Romuald and John Gualberto were of patrician origin; and Damian's observations on the hermits of Camaldoli point in the same direction: 'Who would not be astounded at seeing men previously dressed in silken and golden robes, escorted by cohorts of servants, and accustomed to all the pleasures of affluence, now content with a single cloak, enclosed, barefooted, unkempt, and so parched and wasted by abstinence?'[14] Naturally, the ideal of renunciation and voluntary poverty appealed primarily to the children of the rich; it could have little meaning for people to whom poverty and deprivation were the normal condition. Romuald founded a few houses for women, but they played only a small and inconspicuous part in the Italian religious movement of the eleventh century. Significant though it was for the monastic tradition, the revival of the eremitical ideal affected only a small élite within the monastic world. Fonte Avellana in Damian's time contained only twenty monks and fifteen lay servants. All the hermits of the Apennines together must have been vastly outnumbered by the monks of Italy who were following the conventional Benedictine observance.

The Rule and the desert

North of the Alps, the same restless spirit was abroad seeking an outlet in new forms of religious organisation. Eremitical movements appeared in Brittany,

Maine and Burgundy, some of which originated new monastic orders. All these displayed a common inclination to break away from existing forms of monastic and clerical life and restore the practice and ideals of an earlier age. In some cases the aspiration was for a simpler kind of claustral life based upon a literal observance of the Benedictine Rule, a desire to reinstate manual labour and private meditation in the monk's timetable, and recover seclusion from the outside world.

These were the ideals that prompted Robert of Molesme and a group of hermits in the Burgundian forest to found the abbey of Molesme and later, in 1098, to secede from it in search of a wilder and more remote spot at Cîteaux. The same objectives were at the basis of the Order of Tiron, founded by Bernard of Poitiers in 1109, and the Order of Savigny, the mother-house of which was founded by Vitalis, a Norman clerk turned itinerant preacher, some twenty years earlier. In its austere spirit and its literal devotion to the Rule, Savigny resembled the Cistercian Order in many respects. Planted in a secluded valley on the borders of Normandy and Maine, it enjoyed the patronage of the Norman kings, and it rapidly put out colonies in northern France and England until, in 1147, it formally merged with the Cistercians. In that year the Cistercian chapter also received an application for affiliation from a small congregation in the Limousin directed by Stephen of Obazine. This, like others, had grown out of a hermitage, and its austere observance gave effect to Stephen's insistence that his disciples should work with their hands and maintain absolute silence at all times outside the hours of communal prayer.[15]

Tiron and Savigny both represented an attempt to re-create the cenobitical life in accordance with the primitive model of the Benedictine Rule. But in France, as in Italy, the Rule contended in men's minds with those other traditions derived from the literature of the desert and the current understanding of the apostolic life. Before they founded cenobitical communities, both Bernard of Poitiers and Vitalis had experienced the pull of the wilderness and had taken part in the eremitical movement which had found a habitat in the forests of Maine and Brittany. Both of them associated an apostolic preaching mission with the eremitic life. The one role validated the other; as Bernard explained, 'a preacher ought to be dead to the world'.[16]

The most conspicuous leader of the movement was Robert of Abrissel, a Breton by birth, who had taught in the schools and acquired an archdeaconry before he abandoned his clerical career to retire to a hermitage. Robert was the harbinger of a new spring, which came to full flower in the Mendicant Orders of the early thirteenth century. To him the apostolic life meant the total destitution of the hermit combined with the life of the wandering evangelist, calling people to penance. He was a powerful preacher and his message stirred a strange ferment in his hearers. His call to repentance and renunciation was enthusiastically taken up by a throng of disciples, including clergy and laity of both sexes, who joined him in the forest, endeavouring to live, as Robert's hagiographer explained, 'under a rule and according to the custom of the primitive Church'.[17] It was to provide for one of these groups that shortly before the year 1100 he founded the monastery of Fontevrault in the county of Maine.

Fontevrault, which became the head of a small order, was a significant innovation. It was a double monastery, containing men and women. In many ways Robert's ascetical career resembled that of Damian, but he differed from him in this; whether prompted by his devotion to the Blessed Virgin, for which he was famous, or by a greater psychological security, he appreciated the religious aspirations of women converts and welcomed their participation in the penitential movement. The community at Fontevrault consisted of nuns dedicated to the contemplative life and following the Benedictine Rule. To protect their seclusion and provide them with the sacraments, Robert settled alongside them a community of monks, containing both clergy and lay brothers. At the outset, the new foundation contained an omnium gatherum of the penitents Robert had brought in from the woods, including reclaimed prostitutes. He appointed an abbess to rule both the men and the women; and the Rule made it plain that the men occupied a subordinate role in the community. The first abbess, Petronilla de Chemille, was a noblewomen, under whom the house attracted the interest of the ducal family of Anjou, and it soon became a handsomely endowed and aristocratic establishment. In 1189 Eleanor of Aquitaine chose it as the burial place for King Henry II, and in so doing made it the recognised mausoleum of the Angevin dynasty. The rapid spread of the order and the influx of recruits indicate that Robert of Abrissel's revival of the double monastery for the benefit of women answered a substantial social demand.

Fontevrault was a by-product of the eremitical movement in northwestern France. A more radical attempt to institutionalise the solitary life gave birth to the Order of Grandmont. The originator of this was Stephen of Muret, the son of a viscount of the Auvergne. A youthful pilgrimage to the shrines of southern Italy had brought him into contact with groups of hermits living in the mountains of Calabria. It was this early encounter that, as he often told his disciples, inspired him to leave the world and adopt the life of a hermit. Some time between 1076 and 1078 he settled in a deserted spot at Muret in the Limousin.[18] Before long he was joined by other aspirants and found himself the head and spiritual director of a group hermitage. Shortly after his death in 1124 the site of the settlement at Muret was claimed by the Benedictines of Ambaza, and the community he had gathered retreated to a new site at Grandmont among the mountains of La Marche.

Although in its developed form Grandmont provided a community life of shared church, refectory, and dormitory, the spirit of the order, infused in it by the founder, was that of the desert hermitage. Its aim was solitude and a life reduced to the barest necessities as a means to contemplative prayer. The Rule of St Stephen, compiled some years after his death from the reminiscences of his disciples, outlines an austere regime with stress upon simplicity, poverty in clothes and artefacts, perpetual seclusion, and detachment from managerial tasks or from anything else that could disturb the isolation of the cloister. It has an exhortatory quality which clearly echoes the thoughts of the master.[19]

A cultivation of corporate poverty as well as personal indigence was to be a hallmark of the Grandmontine hermits. The Rule forbade them the possession of lands beyond the immediate boundaries of their establishment – 'for when you entered the desert, you abandoned them along with other worldly things' – nor are they to accept the gift of parish churches. For food they were to rely upon alms. Failing other sources of supply, the brethren might go out and beg: 'if, in order to prove you, God has allowed you to come to such poverty that there is no food at all, you may go to the bishop of your diocese and explain your need. If (added the Rule with sturdy realism) he is not willing to help you, after fasting in your cell for two days, two of the brethren may go out, like other poor people, and beg alms from door to door, calling at mills and homesteads. But once you have collected enough for one day's supply, return to your cell.'[20]

This refusal of the normal sources of monastic income and an insistence upon poverty to the point of destitution, coupled with the authorisation of occasional mendicancy and a refusal to hold reserves, anticipates the Franciscan ideal of the thirteenth century. Francis, too, forbade his followers to accumulate reserves beyond the needs of a single day. But for the Franciscans, mendicancy was part of the active evangelical life lived among the people, and it depended upon the existence of a relatively large and well-to-do clientèle that was only to be found in the towns. There was an unreality about the Grandmontine plan to make enclosed monastic communities dependent upon occasional begging from rural communities in sparsely populated areas.

In order to insulate the hermits from all worldly distractions, the community was divided into clerical monks, who devoted themselves exclusively to prayer, and lay brothers or *conversi*, who not only ran the business side of the establishment but directed its internal affairs as well. The Rule avoided, however, the kind of social apartheid that in other orders, like the Cistercians, separated the living quarters of choir monks from those of lay brothers. At Grandmont clerics and *conversi* shared a common dormitory and refectory, assembled together in a common chapter, and both sides of the community were associated in electing the prior who was head of the monastery.

This unusual experiment in egalitarianism proved, however, to have snags. As often happens when 'lay' administrators are given the responsibility of managing the affairs of a professional élite, the lower orders got out of hand and began to push everybody about and to subordinate the spiritual aims of the community to the dictates of their own convenience. The problem was aggravated by the fact that the lay brothers greatly outnumbered the tonsured monks. Friction between the two sections of the order came to a head in 1185–86, when the lay brothers forced the prior of Grandmont, William de Treignac, to stand down and elected a replacement from elsewhere. Pope Urban III had to intervene and clarify the constitutions of the order to ensure that the conduct of the liturgy and presidence over the chapter of faults was reserved to the clerical brethren. But the rebellion of the *conversi* continued, and the problem of authority was not settled until clerical control had been firmly established by the ordinances of Innocent III.[21]

La Marche, where the hermits had settled, was part of the Angevin inheritance that came to Henry II from his marriage to Eleanor of Aquitaine, and he showed great interest in Grandmont and subsidised the building of its monastic church. Under royal patronage the order spread rapidly in France, mainly within the Angevin dominions. The Grandmontines – the *bonshommes* as they were known to their rural neighbours – were imported into England by the wife of the Seneschal of Anjou, the Lady Joanna Fossard, who endowed them with a modest estate in Eskdale. But although a few other foundations followed, the order never attracted the wide support in England that it won in France.

The Carthusians

It was the Carthusians who really succeeded in translating the ideal of the desert hermits into a monastic fortress of stone. It did not happen all at once. The prime mover was Bruno of Cologne, the chancellor and master of the cathedral school of Reims. Haunted, according to his later hagiographer, by the example of the desert hermits, somewhere about the year 1080 he decided to quit the schools and joined the hermits living in the forest of Colan. A few years later, he obtained from Bishop Hugh of Grenoble the gift of a more remote spot high up in a valley of the Alps, where he was installed with a group of fellow hermits. But although Bruno was the patriarch of the Carthusian Order, he was not properly speaking its founder. In 1090 Pope Urban II, who had once been his pupil, summoned him to Rome, and he left for Italy, never to return. He died in Calabria, where he had found a new retreat after escaping from the distractions of the Roman Curia.

Like many of the eremitical experiments of eleventh-century France, the humble hermitage in the Alps seemed bound for extinction when it was joined by a new and dynamic convert from the ecclesiastical fleshpots – Guigo or Guigues du Pin, the dean of Grenoble. In 1109, three years after his arrival, the brethren elected him their prior. It was Guigo who was the architect of the order. He was a man with a wide circle of influential friends and correspondents, which included St Bernard and Peter the Venerable, and through him the hermitage became known, attracted recruits, and began to plant new colonies. In 1132 an avalanche, which killed several of the brethren, forced them to move lower down the valley to the site of the Grande Chartreuse. By this time the endless trickle of friends, pious pilgrims, and curious tourists had started to reach the mountain fastness. Peter the Venerable, who was a great admirer and good correspondent, made an annual visit from Cluny, though the year of the avalanche defeated him: 'as it was the opinion of everyone that no horseman could reach you on account of the huge mounds of snow, I despaired of being able to do it on foot'.[22]

The creation of colonies elsewhere made it urgent to compile some sort of written Rule or customary, and before 1128 Guigo addressed himself to the task and committed the customs of the Chartreuse to writing.[23] In many ways the Carthusians were eclectic. Their practice of mitigating the trials of solitude with some degree of community life had some affinities with Camaldoli. Many of Guigo's customs, including the liturgical instructions, were taken from the Benedictine Rule or from the practice of the black monks. Also, as the order developed, it took some constitutional features from the Cistercians, most notably that of the annual general chapter, which was attended by all the priors, a valuable device for maintaining uniform standards. This practice was begun by Prior Anthelm of the Grande Chartreuse, when he summoned a meeting of all heads of houses in 1141. It remains, though, that the Chartreuse was unique in having successfully domesticated the ideal of the desert in the form of a permanent institution, which never relaxed or compromised its distinctive pattern of life, so that to the end of the Middle Ages it never required the attention of reformers.

The regime differed from other experiments of this kind by creating a group hermitage in which the individual pursued the solitary life within the context of a supporting community. Each monk lived and slept in the solitude of his own cell: 'As water is needful for fish and folds for the sheep,' wrote Guigo, 'let him regard his cell as necessary for his life and salvation.'[24] Originally, the settlement had consisted of separate huts, but before the end of the twelfth century the distinctive Carthusian building-plan had evolved, which remained unchanged in essentials down to modern times. It comprised a series of independent stone cells ranged, like terraced houses, round a covered cloister walk. At the rear of each cell was a small walled-in plot of garden and a private lavatory. Adjacent to the cloister stood the monastic church, the kitchen, refectory, and other offices.

The monks assembled daily in the church for the common celebration of Vespers and the night office; the remaining services of the day were recited by each individual alone in his own cell. Similarly, the single meal of the day that was taken in winter, and the two meals of the summer timetable, were prepared and eaten by each monk in solitude from the materials placed by the kitchener in the hatch of each cell. Community occasions happened only on Sundays and major festivals, when mass was celebrated, a chapter was held, and the brethren sat down together to eat dinner in the refectory. In the afternoon of these days a period of conversation was allowed. This was the only time in the week when the rule of absolute silence was relaxed. The physical austerity of the observance matched the desolation of the natural surroundings. The diet was sparser than St Benedict had allowed: meat was excluded, and on Mondays, Wednesdays and Fridays, bread and water was the rule, though wine was permitted with food. Clothes and bedding were of the coarsest materials; and this spirit of poverty was extended to the monastic church – the customs forbade the use of gold or silver ornaments and vessels other than the chalice.

Obviously, a completely enclosed hermitage could only survive provided others serviced it. For this purpose the Carthusians adopted the practice of Vallombrosa in using *conversi* or lay brothers. It was they who performed the manual tasks, did the necessary buying and selling, and dealt with visitors and guests. The procurator in charge of them, who was an ordained monk, was in effect the business manager of the whole community. They lived in a separate establishment called the lower house, because at the Grande Chartreuse it was situated further down the valley. Guigo assumed they would be illiterate. When the bell rang for the night office they proceeded to their own oratory, and their procurator chanted the office for them while they remained silent, bowing at the appropriate places; for the other offices they recited paternosters in place of the psalms.

The life of the solitary in his cell was organised to fulfil the fundamental purpose of the Charterhouse, which was contemplation. Manual work was encouraged, but as it had to be performed within the confines of each cell and its adjoining plot of garden, it must have been an ascetical exercise, serving a spiritual purpose rather than an economic one. Apart from meditation, reading and vocal prayer, the task that was especially recommended was the making of books. On this subject Guigo, usually laconic in his instructions, is stirred to a glow of enthusiasm: 'let the brethren take care that the books they receive from the cupboard do not get soiled with smoke or dirt; books are as it were the everlasting food of our souls. We wish them to be most carefully kept and to be zealously made.'[25] Guibert of Nogent savoured the report he had heard of Count William of Nevers, who out of devotion to the brethren sent them a gift of silver drinking vessels, which they refused and sent back. So the count, not to be deflected from his purpose, sent them instead a huge quantity of parchment, 'which he knew they would certainly need'.[26]

Monks who could not write when they joined the community were to be taught to do so. Each cell of the Charterhouse was a scriptorium, equipped with parchment, quills, ink-well and ruler. It was not only that the founders, being refugee schoolmen, regarded intellectual pursuits as an integral part of the contemplative life; for Guigo, books had a missionary purpose – they were a means of disseminating the word of God. And in fact copying, illumination, and binding of books was an important service the Carthusians rendered to the ecclesiastical community. We get a glimpse of the process from the letters of Peter the Venerable, who supplied them with codices to copy from the library of Cluny: 'I have sent you the little book or epistle of the Blessed Ambrose against the Proposition of Symmachus. The treatise of St Hilary on the psalms I have not sent, because I found that our copy has the same textual corruption as yours. The letter you sent', he grumbles, 'talked only about books, and was silent about those to whom the books are to be sent.'[27] But the literary traffic was not all one way. 'Send us, if you please, the larger volume of St Augustine's letters, for a large part of ours has been accidentally eaten by a bear.' This pleasing literary correspondence reminds us that the physical solitude of the Charterhouse did not necessarily involve spiritual isolation.

In the nature of the case, it was not a vocation that attracted large numbers. As Bruno wrote sadly from his Calabrian hermitage, 'the sons of contemplation are fewer than the sons of action'.[28] Numbers at the Grande Chartreuse remained small. In Guigo's time there were only thirteen monks and the number of lay brothers was fixed at sixteen, though 'now there are more, for some of them are old and infirm and not able to work, so that on that account we were obliged to take others'.[29] The restriction of numbers was a deliberate policy designed to obviate the need for large-scale endowments, thus preserving poverty and the spiritual fruits of the desert. Charterhouses elsewhere remained similarly small. The growth of the order itself was slow, but remarkably persistent over the centuries. The earliest English foundation was at Witham in Selwood, on the border of Wiltshire and Somerset, which owed its existence to an initiative by King Henry II in 1178. A small and struggling community to begin with, it acquired a new lease of life and some fame from its third prior, the Burgundian Hugh of Avalon, who was elected to the see of Lincoln in 1186. But it was forty-seven years before a second English Charterhouse was founded at Hinton. By the eve of the Dissolution there were only nine Carthusian houses in England. In Europe as a whole, some 216 plantations were made in the course of the four centuries that followed the foundation of the Grande Chartreuse.

The canons regular

The Chartreuse embodied the spiritual experience of the desert in permanent form. That other model of the ascetical life drawn from Christian antiquity – the life of the Apostles or *vita apostolica* – which the Benedictines had long claimed to be the source and origin of monasticism, acquired a new shade of meaning after the middle of the eleventh century, when it was invoked to justify the new religious institute of the canons regular. The canons regular were really a hybrid order of clerical monks, congregations of clergy living under a monastic rule. They represented an effort to give practical effect to the conviction of the Gregorian papacy that the Apostles were monks and that the secular clergy, who had inherited their office, should model their lives upon them. As Hildebrand had said, the proper life for clerks was one in common, based upon the renunciation of personal property 'after the example of the primitive Church'. Damian argued in a tract on *The Common Life of Canons*,[30] addressed to the canons of Fano cathedral, that the call to renounce private possessions and embrace a fully communal life was evangelical, and therefore obligatory upon all clergy serving cathedral and collegiate churches, as opposed to rural clergy for whom it was obviously impracticable.

There was a precedent for Damian's contention in the practice of the Carolingian age. An eighth-century formula for the life of clergy serving collegiate churches existed in *The Rule for Canons* which St Chrodegang had compiled for the clergy of his cathedral church of Metz. This had been given the sanction of imperial approval by the Synod of Aachen in 816 and was widely disseminated. It prescribed for canons a community regime based upon a common refectory and dormitory, and required them to live in an enclosure separated from the residential areas of the laity by locked gates.[31] This code provided a model of observance for many collegiate bodies, but by the end of the tenth century it was widely disregarded. It did not discountenance the ownership of private property, and as the endowments of cathedral churches were partitioned to create prebends for individual members of the chapter, canons built and occupied their own houses within the precincts and communal life gradually lapsed.

The campaign to revive community living and to impose a monastic type of regime upon an important section of the clergy was closely connected with the Gregorian Reform programme. In their concern to end the secularisation of ecclesiastical offices, the reformers sought to separate the clergy from worldly entanglements and to impress upon them the superior character of their sacred calling; and the drive for clerical celibacy was an integral part of this plan. It was perceived that the discipline of community life offered the best hope of achieving these ends. The rejection of personal ownership severed the roots of worldly ambition, and membership of a collegiate society made marriage impossible, but provided a necessary support and companionship. Above all, it was seen to be a faithful imitation of the life of the apostolic Church at Jerusalem as it was described in the Acts. In response to this propaganda, houses of canons regular began to appear before the middle of the eleventh century – groups of clergy, that is, who had renounced private property and lived a fully communal life, observing a monastic timetable and sharing a common refectory and dormitory.

These establishments varied in their origin and recruitment. The movement began in northern Italy, southern France and southern Germany, where it was actively promoted by bishops of the reforming tendency. In some cases the clergy of a cathedral chapter took a spontaneous decision to turn themselves into a community of canons regular; rather more often, they resisted the proposal that they should forgo their private houses and relinquish their wives, and had the canonical regime imposed upon them by an enthusiastic bishop. This was what happened at Lucca, where the objections of the cathedral clergy were overcome by Bishop Anselm, the canonist and future Pope Alexander II.[32] Bishop Altmann of Passau (1056–91) encountered similar resistance when he introduced the new regime in Germany. His foundation at Rottenbuch provided a model for houses of canons regular elsewhere in Bavaria. It was here that Gerhoh of Reichersberg, canon and schoolmaster of Augsburg cathedral, found a refuge from the threats of his pro-imperialist bishop, and learned the new lore and practice of the apostolic life. A feisty publicist for the Gregorian Reform, he was convinced that the renewal of the Church depended upon recalling the clergy to the monastic discipline of the communal life, and became the leading promoter of the canons regular in the province of Salzburg.[33] In several cases, groups of clergy and laity who had experimented with an eremitical type of life, organised themselves into a cenobitical community of canons regular with the help of a sympathetic bishop. The important abbeys of Saint-Ruf – an early foundation established in 1039 on the outskirts of Avignon – and Arrouaise, on the frontier of Flanders and Vermandois, both originated in this way.

What the movement lacked was a rule to provide an authoritative foundation for the apostolic life. It was this need that was met by the so-called Rule of St Augustine. The Rule of St Augustine was one of the great discoveries of the late eleventh century. In the Western monastic tradition its impact was rather like that of the discovery of America on the people of a later age: it had been there all the time, and though it was not precisely what they had been looking for, the world never looked quite the same afterwards. Its implications were absorbed only gradually. The Augustinian Rule influenced all subsequent thinking about the monastic life. It provided, in fact, the formal basis for three major institutions – the canons regular, the Order of Prémontré (a distinct branch of the canons regular), and the Dominicans or Order of Preachers. It also provided the rule for those groups of canons who constituted the male side of some mixed institutions, like the English Order of Sempringham. What was the Rule of St Augustine? Here is a tangled story, which modern scholars have been at some pains to unravel.[34]

After his conversion and baptism in 385, St Augustine lived a communal life with a group of fellow-converts on his estate at Tagaste. On his ordination to the priesthood, he had taken up residence at Hippo, but he continued to follow a monastic life-style; and when he was consecrated bishop, he turned his episcopal household into a monastery, requiring his clergy to renounce private property and live a community life. His sister also entered a religious community, and it was for this sisterhood that Augustine wrote his famous letter of counsel, No. 211, which is a treatise on the virtues of chastity, charity, and concord, here explained as the essential foundation of a religious community. The Rule of St Augustine, as it was known at the beginning of the twelfth century, consisted of this brief exhortatory treatise, in which an unknown hand had made some interpolations and had changed the gender of the recipients to masculine. Joined to this was a more specific *ordo* for a monastery containing instructions on the subject of liturgical prayer, poverty, reading, and silence, which if not the work of Augustine himself, is apparently a document of the fifth century. But the liturgical instructions of this *ordo* were archaic, so in 1118 the canons of Springiersbach obtained from Pope Gelasius II the authority to dispense with that part of it. Thereafter, for the rest of the twelfth century, what passed as the Rule of St Augustine was the doctored version of letter No. 211 – the so-called *Regula Tertia* – together with the shortened *ordo*, known as the *Regula Secunda*.

Here was apparently first-rate authority for the organisation of the apostolic life as it had been lived by the greatest of the Western Fathers at the end of the patristic age. And it suggested that the very essence of the *vita apostolica* was the life of clerks living in a community who had renounced personal property and embraced poverty. Early privileges and charters of endowment in favour of canons regular refer to them living 'in community according to the apostolic life'; but the actual adoption of the Rule of St Augustine by these establishments is an obscure process. References to it occur here and there in the last thirty years of the eleventh century, but it was in the twelfth that it was gradually recognised to be the identity card of the regular canonical life. One of the curious things about it was its generality. In the attenuated form which gained universal acceptance it offered little practical guidance on how to organise a monastery or construct a timetable. For this the various houses of canons regular compiled their own customaries, which drew upon the traditional monastic sources, including the Benedictine Rule and the legislation of Aachen, or borrowed the customs of the Cistercians or other houses of canons.

In essentials the canonical observance was monastic. In fact, for practical purposes the difference between a house of canons regular and a Benedictine monastery would sometimes be hard to define, the more so as by the eleventh century it had become the practice for most Benedictine monks to be ordained. Nor would dress have necessarily been a guide: some congregations of canons wore a black habit like the Benedictines, others wore white. Observances varied from one house to another. All the canonical customaries stress the evangelical ideals of poverty, fraternity, and submission to the will of a superior. In those houses like Arrouaise, which had preserved the eremitic spirit of their origins, the canons maintained strict seclusion from the outside world, and followed an austere observance that included manual labour for all members of the community. This was the pattern of life prescribed by the customs of Arrouaise compiled by abbot Gervase (1121–47), who modelled the practice of his community on the customs of Cîteaux and Prémontré.[35] In other houses sited in less sequestered places, a more moderate regime prevailed, for which Peter Comestor commended them: 'You have discovered honey, that is the life of moderation, which the Philosopher calls golden.'[36] There was the full liturgical round of choral offices, but in some houses the office used was that of the secular clergy, which was shorter than the monastic office. The diet was less austere than that on the Cistercian menu, and intellectual pursuits were favoured in place of manual labour.

It might be expected that, being an order of clergy vowed to imitate the example of the Apostles, the canons regular would be committed to active pastoral work. In some cases they were. Those communities that were attached to a cathedral were inevitably involved in helping the bishop with the government of his diocese. Houses of canons were often given parish churches by lay proprietors as part of their endowment, and occasionally they would perform the pastoral duties themselves rather than delegating the task to secular clergy. But the cure of souls was not invariably regarded as an imperative of the apostolic life in the twelfth century. Many still regarded the renunciation of personal property and community living as the authentic hallmarks of apostolicity. In fact a substantial element in the canons regular refused to be directly involved in the cure of souls and opted, like the abbey of Arrouaise and its colonies, for a life of seclusion from worldly involvements.

The more austere type of observance was adopted by the abbey of St Victor on the outskirts of Paris, a house of canons regular founded in 1110 by the schoolman William of Champeaux. After his bruising encounter with Abelard, William retired from the schools and settled on the Left Bank. There he was joined by new pupils who provided the first community for the new canonical foundation. The canons regular tended to attract and produce scholars and contemplatives, and St Victor, which continued to recruit students of many nationalities from the nascent university of Paris, became a school of ascetical theologians made famous by an extraordinary constellation of scholars. Among them, Hugh and Richard of St Victor stand out in the twelfth century and Thomas Gallus in the thirteenth century, as the foremost expositors of mystical theology to the scholastic world of their time.

The order of canons regular spread by both imitation and colonisation. In England, probably the first clerical community to adopt the observance was that of St Botolph's, Colchester. According to a later tradition, the clergy of this church sent two members to France to study the customs of St Quentin of Beauvais, an important house of canons which had formed its own congregation of daughter houses. St Botolph's had clearly turned itself into a community of canons regular by 1107, as in that year, at the request of Queen Matilda, it sent a party to instruct the priory of Holy Trinity Aldgate, on the edge of the city of London.[37] Matilda and her husband, Henry I, were both enthusiastic patrons of the order, and during the twelfth century it spread rapidly in England. In fact, numbered by its foundations, it became the largest religious order in the country, with two hundred and seventy-four houses, excluding alien priories, as against two hundred and nineteen Benedictine establishments. It was welcomed with the same alacrity and multiplied just as fast in Germany and France.

Besides the attraction of the *vita apostolica* for idealists of the twelfth century, several reasons can be suggested for this proliferation of the canons regular. Many of their houses were quite small. The possibility of making a beginning with a handful of clerks and a correspondingly modest endowment attracted the lay patron with moderate means as well as parsimonious princes. In cases where an existing college of secular clergy formed the basis for a new establishment of canons regular, all that was initially necessary was a rearrangement of existing properties. Their popularity with episcopal patrons is understandable. A house of canons regular could be all the more serviceable to a bishop because it was by definition subject to his jurisdiction and visitation. There were few of the damaging clashes between claims to exemption and episcopal demands for obedience that crop up so frequently in the history of other monastic orders.

Of course, existing collegiate bodies of clergy, entrenched in their territorial prebends, in which members of the local nobility retained a family interest, often offered determined resistance to attempts by reformers to communise their property and abolish their private residences. This was why some enthusiastic bishops who wanted to promote the canonical reform, like Ivo of Chartres and Bartholomew of Laon, were obliged to abandon the plan to impose the change on their cathedral clergy and instead founded new houses of canons regular elsewhere in their episcopal cities.

The label of Augustinian canon regular covered a wide variety of religious establishments, including chapters serving cathedral churches, priories situated in towns, groups of clergy running hospitals or staffing the castle-chapels of princes and nobility; at another extreme, they comprised enclosed communities of contemplatives living according to a severe monastic regime in more sequestered places, like Prémontré in the forest of Coucy or Llanthony in a remote valley of Monmouthshire. Some of the greater houses established their own congregations of daughter-houses linked by a common customary and a loosely knit system of surveillance. The more austere congregations of Arrouaise and St Victor in France, and the less rigorist family of Saint-Ruf, are conspicuous examples of this. In England, both Holy Trinity Aldgate and Merton priory in Surrey headed a group of colonies.

There was no systematic attempt to organise the canons as a whole until after the Fourth Lateran Council of 1215. This decreed that in every province or kingdom those orders that lacked a regular system of general chapters should hold a meeting of heads of houses every three years to regulate their affairs and maintain discipline. Like the Benedictines, the abbots and priors of the canons regular made rather half-hearted efforts to implement this instruction in the following years. In England, after a shaky start in 1216, the difficulty of securing attendance from the heads of so many small and widely scattered houses was such that it was decided to convene separate assemblies for the northern and southern provinces. But this halting and underpowered machinery was not enough to create a unified order. It lacked authority because it was imposed from above instead of growing out of the common will of its constituents. In 1265 the canons of the southern province appointed a committee to draw up a common code of practice or customary that all would observe. This body produced a collection of ordinances which became known as the Statutes of the Park, after Helaugh Park, the meeting place of the chapter that approved them. But successive chapters recorded a general failure to implement the new legislation.[38] In fact, the attempt to enforce a uniform observance upon what was a very disparate collection of religious establishments came to nothing.

The Premonstratensians

The diversity of ways in which men of the twelfth century interpreted the *vita apostolica* is illustrated by the history of the Premonstratensians or Norbertines – a particular branch of the canons regular which took its name from the mother-house

of Prémontré. Their founder, St Norbert, the son of a baron in the duchy of
Cleves, had been a canon of the cathedral of Xanten since his teens. In 1115 he
resigned all his benefices, fled to the solitude, and then adopted the life of an
eremitical preacher like Robert of Abrissel. The canons of Xanten, whom he
attempted to evangelise, gave him a rough time, but he attracted the notice and
sympathy of Bishop Bartholomew of Laon, a zealous bishop of the reform party,
whose chief material monument, besides the replica of his tomb in the cathedral
of Laon, is the great collegiate church of St Martin at the opposite end of the
small precipitous town. Bartholomew wanted Norbert for the headship of St
Martin's, but having failed to persuade him to stay, he was prepared to support
his eremitical experiment and acquired for him the chapel of Prémontré in the
forest of Coucy seventeen miles from Laon. Round this Norbert formed a group
of hermits and preachers, which included laity of both sexes as well as clergy.

According to the narrative of the foundation, on Christmas Day 1121 the
group of Norbert's disciples who had taken up residence beside the chapel of
Prémontré took formal vows to live 'according to the Gospels and sayings of the
Apostles and the plan of St Augustine'.[39] In other words, they adopted the Rule of
St Augustine as the basis for their institute. They agreed to dress in a simple habit
of bleached wool, which was in time to gain them the name of white canons.
For Norbert, as for Robert of Abrissel, the *vita apostolica* meant a combination of
community life organised round the ideal of ascetical poverty with the active
role of a missionary preacher.

The world had not, however, forgotten Norbert in his woodland retreat. He
was well known at the German court and the papal Curia, and in 1125 he was
elected to the frontier archbishopric of Magdeburg, where he succeeded in turning his chapter of secular canons into a community of canons regular. From then
until his death in 1134, he was increasingly absorbed in the creation of missionary communities in the Slav lands, where German settlement was taking place.
When Norbert left his community of Prémontré it had already planted colonies
of its own, and his disciples asked his permission to elect an abbot to succeed
him. The man they chose, Hugh de Fosses, was the real architect of the order:
Norbert was a charismatic preacher but no legislator, and as yet the community
lacked any written customary. It was Hugh who drew up the first statutes and
secured their approval from a general chapter of the white canons.

Because the Rule of St Augustine was a very generic code, it could be developed, as we have seen, in a variety of ways. As Norbert explained to the frightened canons of St Martin's at Laon, his conception of the apostolic life involved
both organised poverty and evangelical preaching. But the statutes compiled by
Hugh de Fosses drew upon both the Cistercian *Carta Caritatis* and the customs of
Cluny, and they slanted the order decisively towards the more enclosed type of
contemplative life that was a feature of the reformed monasticism of the twelfth
century. The observance of the white canons thus included the full round of the
monastic office and the monastic regime of fasting and silence; and, like that of
the Cistercians, their customary allocated a normal place in the daily timetable

to manual labour, an ascetical exercise that was required of all members of the community without exception.[40]

Norbert was a friend and admirer of St Bernard, and it was probably at his suggestion that the legislators of the order drew heavily upon Cistercian practice, so much so, that the white canons reproduced many of the organisational features of the Cistercians. Like them, they developed the practice of summoning all abbots to an annual general chapter held at Prémontré; they also imitated the Cistercian system of filiation, which laid upon the abbot of each monastery the responsibility for visiting and supervising the affairs of its own daughter-houses. Prémontré itself was subjected to the visitation of the abbots of Laon, Floreffe, and Cuissy – the three senior foundations. Also like the Cistercians, the white canons made extensive use of unlettered lay brothers or *conversi* for agricultural work and other manual tasks. The early settlement at Prémontré had, in fact, included lay converts of both sexes as well as clerks, and some of the early foundations of the order were double monasteries; but further development of this arrangement was stopped in 1135 by a command of the general chapter, which decreed that the nuns must remove themselves to separate houses elsewhere.

Like the other Austin canons, because of their relatively modest requirements the Premonstratensians attracted lay patrons and benefactors among the lower aristocracy as well as among bishops, and the order rapidly put out new foundations in northern France, Germany and the Low Countries. It was introduced into England about the year 1143, when Peter of Goxhill, a minor baron of Lincolnshire, endowed the abbey of Newhouse, and imported a group of canons from the county of Guines to start a community. During the following hundred years thirty abbeys of the white canons were founded in England. They resembled the Cistercians not only in their internal regime, but also in the kind of sites they chose for settlement; they tended to gravitate to waste upland areas, which were suitable mainly for animal husbandry. These remote locations, far away from human settlement, like that of the small abbey of Shap just below the Westmorland fells, or Egglestone in Yorkshire, were well suited to the needs of an order that had changed course and made the sanctification of its own members, rather than the evangelisation of secular society, its primary objective.

In its inner story Prémontré provides an example of the divergent interpretations that could be placed upon the *vita apostolica* and the Rule of St Augustine. St Norbert had apparently visualised the canons as an active preaching order, combining a life of apostolic poverty with a pastoral role. His conversion of the chapter of Magdeburg into a body of Premonstratensian canons with pastoral responsibilities inspired a similar change in the cathedral chapters of Brandenburg and Havelberg, and led to a succession of German Premonstratensian bishops. But the legislation of the chapters of 1131–35 set the order on a different course, in which it modelled itself increasingly on Cistercian practice and withdrew from outside commitments. The change of direction was viewed with misgiving by the houses of Saxony, which claimed that their first allegiance was to the successors of St Norbert in the see of Magdeburg rather than to the general chapter of Prémontré. This tension between the two parts of the order remained unresolved, so that for practical purposes the province of Saxony was a separate organisation. Its superiors rarely, if ever, attended meetings of the general chapter during the twelfth century. The full realisation of Norbert's vision of a canonical order following a monastic regime, but committed to an active missionary understanding of the *vita apostolica*, had to await the coming of the Dominican friars – the Order of Preachers – in the thirteenth century.

Notes

1. *The Letters of Peter the Venerable*, ed. G. Constable (Cambridge, Mass., 1967) i, p. 59.
2. *De Vita Vera Apostolica*, ed. E. Martène and U. Durand in *Veterum Scriptorum et Monumentorum Amplissima Collectio* IX (Paris, 1733), 1007. The attribution to Rupert of Deutz is, however, open to doubt. On the theme of the apostolic life see M.-D. Chenu, *Nature, Man and Society in the Twelfth Century*, trans. J. Taylor and L. K. Little (Chicago, 1968), pp. 202–38.
3. *Commentarium in Regulam S. Benedicti*, PL 102, 724.
4. 'Vita communis exemplo primitivae ecclesiae' in J. Mabillon, *Annales Ordinis Sancti Benedicti* IV (Paris, 1707), p. 686. On the place of the primitive Church in the propaganda of the Gregorian Reform see G. Miccoli, 'Ecclesiae primitivae forma' in *Chiesa Gregoriana: Ricerche sulla Riforma del secolo XI* (Florence, 1966), pp. 225–99.
5. On this aspect see the important study of Lester K. Little, *Religious Poverty and the Profit Economy in Medieval Europe* (1978); Brenda Bolton, *The Medieval Reformation* (1983); and J. Leclercq, 'The monastic crisis of the eleventh and twelfth centuries' in *Cluniac Monasticism in the Central Middle Ages*, ed. Noreen Hunt (1971), pp. 217–37.
6. See Boto of Prüfening's complaint that the excess of choral prayer excluded spiritual exercises such as reading and meditation: P. Ström, 'The monk's place in the house of God: the de domo Dei of Boto of Prüfening' in *In Quest of the Kingdom*, ed. A. Härdelin (Stockholm, 1991), pp. 157–75.
7. For an excellent discussion of this theme see Henrietta Leyser, *Hermits and the New Monasticism* (1984).
8. *Pierre de Celle, L'École du cloître*, ed. G. de Martel (Paris, 1977), p. 140.
9. *S. Bernardi Opera*, ed. J. Leclercq, C. H. Talbot, and H. Rochais III (Rome, 1959), pp. 63–108.
10. J. Leclercq and J. P. Bonnes, *Un maître de la vie spirituelle au XIe siècle, Jean de Fécamp* (Paris, 1942), pp. 185–6.
11. The chronology of Romuald's foundation has been revised by G. Tabacco, 'Romualdo di Ravenna e gli inizi dell 'eremitismo camaldolese' in *L'Eremitismo in Occidente nei secoli XI e XII* (*Miscellanea del Centro di Studi Medioevali* IV, Milan, 1965), pp. 73–119.
12. Patricia McNulty, *St Peter Damian, Selected Writings on the Spiritual Life* (1959), p. 104. On Damian and Romuald see J. Leclercq, *Saint Pierre Damian, ermite et homme de l'église* (Rome, 1960).
13. *De Ordine Eremitarum*, PL 145, 333.
14. *Vita Beati Romualdi*, ed. G. Tabacco (Rome, 1957), pp. 55–6.
15. *Vie de Saint Étienne d'Obazine*, ed. and trans. M. Aubrun (Clermont Ferrand, 1970), pp. 56–8.
16. PL 172, 1397, cited by R. I. Moore, *The Origins of European Dissent* (1985), p. 84.
17. For Robert of Abrissel and his following see R. Niderst, *Robert d'Abrissel et les origines de l'ordre de Fontevrault* (Rodez, 1952); Jacqueline Smith, 'Robert of Abrissel, procurator mulierum' in *Medieval Women*, ed. D. Baker (*Studies in Church History, Subsidia* I, 1978), pp. 175–84.

18. Much in the chronology of Stephen's early career is uncertain, as are the details of his stay in Italy, see Carole A. Hutchison, *The Hermit Monks of Grandmont* (Kalamazoo, Michigan, 1989) now the best account of the order, and the discussion of these problems in Leyser, pp. 110–12.

19. The Rule, ed. J. Bequet, *Scriptores Ordinis Grandimontensis* (Turnhout, 1968), pp. 63–99.

20. *Ibid.*, p. 77.

21. J. Bequet, 'Les institutions de l'Ordre de Grandmont au Moyen-Age', *Revue Mabillon* 42 (1952), pp. 31–4; Hutchison, pp. 74–90.

22. *Letters* i, p. 146. Peter also expressed his enthusiasm for the observance of the Chartreuse in his *De Mimculis*, ed. M. Marrier and A. Duchesne in *Bibliotheca Cluniacensis* (Paris, 1614), pp. 1328–30.

23. *Guigonis I Consuetudines, PL* 153, 703; newly edited with French translation by an anonymous monk of the Chartreuse, *Guigues I coutumes de Chartreuse* (Editions du Cerf, Paris, 1984), with good introduction.

24. *Coutumes*, p. 232.

25. *Ibid.*, p. 224.

26. *Self and Society in Medieval France: The Memoirs of Abbot Guibert de Nogent*, ed. and trans. J. F. Benton (Toronto, London, 1984), p. 61.

27. *Letters*, i, p. 47.

28. *PL* 152, 421.

29. *Coutumes*, p. 285.

30. *De Communi Vita Canonicorum, PL* 145, 503–12.

31. Archaeological research has identified numbers of these early communal buildings erected for canons alongside cathedrals of northern Europe: J.-C. Picard, 'Les quartiers canoniaux des cathédrales de France' in *Le clerc seculier au moyenâge* (XXIIᵉ congres de la société des historiens médiévistes de l'enseignement supérieur public, Paris, 1993), pp. 191–202.

32. E. Kittel, 'Der Kampf um die Reform des Domkapitels von Lucca im XI Jahrh.', *Festschrift A. Brackmann* (Weimar, 1931), pp. 207–47. On clerical resistance to the Gregorian decrees relating to celibacy see A. Fliche, *La réforme grégorienne* (Louvain, 1926) ii, pp. 158–62.

33. P. Classen, 'Gerhoh von Reichersberg und die Regularkanoniker in Bayern und Österreich' in *Ausgewählte Aufsätze von Peter Classen*, ed. C. J. Classen and J. Fried (Constance, 1982), pp. 431–56. For the early history of the canons regular see C. Dereine, 'Chanoines, des origines au XIIIᵉ siècle', *DHGE* XII, pp. 353–405, and the studies in *La vita commune del clero nei secoli XI e XII*, 2 vols, *Miscellanea del Centro di Studi Medioevali 3* (Milan, 1962).

34. On the Rule of St Augustine see J. C. Dickinson, *The Origin of the Austin Canons* (1950), pp. 7–25. The most detailed study of the textual problems involved is that of L. Verheijen, *La règie de Saint Augustin* 2 vols (Paris, 1967).

35. L. Milis, *L'ordre des chanoines règuliers d'Arrouaise* (Ghent, 1969), pp. 183–4, 487–9.

36. *PL* 198, 176.

37. *The Cartulary of Holy Trinity Aldgate*, ed. G. A. J. Hodgett (1971), pp. 225–7.

38. See H. E. Salter, *Chapters of the Augustinian Canons* (1920), introduction.

39. *Vita Norberti Archiepiscopi Magdeburgensis*, ed. R. Wilmans, MGH SS XII, p. 683. On the foundation of Prémontré see F. Petit, 'L'ordre de Prémontré de Saint Norbert à Anselme d'Havelburg' in *La vita commune del clero, op. cit.*, i, pp. 466–71. A good English account will be found in H. M. Colvin, *The White Canons in England* (1951), pp. 1–25.

40. *Les statuts de Prémontré au milieu du XIIᵉ siècle*, ed. P. F. Lefèvre and W. M. Grauwen (Averbode, 1978), pp. 8–11.

9

THE CISTERCIAN MODEL

The truth of the letter

Cîteaux, and the order that sprang from it, was the outcome of the same restless search for a simpler and more secluded form of ascetical life that found expression in other new orders in the eleventh century. Like similar movements, it began as a reaction against the corporate wealth, worldly involvements and surfeited liturgical ritualism of the Carolingian monastic tradition. The founders of Cîteaux set out to create a monastery in which the pristine observance of the Benedictine Rule would be restored. As they conceived it, poverty and isolation from the world were integral features of this observance. They drew, in fact, upon a stock of ideas that were current in the monastic circles of their time. But the order that evolved out of their efforts eclipsed all its rivals in the vigour of its growth, the number of its recruits and the brilliance of its reputation.

Our basic source for the new foundation is a brief history called the *Exordium Parvum*, which also survives in a shorter version – the *Exordium Cistercii*. Scholars are divided over the date of these texts, their relationship to one another and to the other early Cistercian documents.[1] In its original form, the *Exordium* was probably the work of the English abbot, Stephen Harding, who was a key figure in the enterprise. It seems, however, to have been enlarged and 'improved' by the generation that followed the founders.

It all began with the secession of a group of malcontents from the abbey of Molesme in the year 1098. The leader of the group was their abbot, Robert of Molesme, who already had behind him a long and restless career as a leader of ascetics. In an earlier phase of his life, he had abandoned his post as abbot of Saint-Michel of Tonnerre to join the hermits living in the Burgundian forest of Colan. They made him their director, and after some years they settled at Molesme. It was agreed that they should follow the Rule of St Benedict. But with time, the advent of new recruits and the growth of endowments brought changes. The rigorists, mainly the veterans who had come in from the forest, complained that the Rule was being diluted. It was not, as apologists later implied, that Molesme had become lax or decadent; what the dissidents wanted was to revive the simplicity and balance of the Benedictine life, which for them meant a return to corporate poverty, symbolised by manual labour, and a location remote enough to save the monks from entanglements with the outside world.[2]

In the end, a party of them about twenty-strong decided to quit the abbey and make a fresh start elsewhere. They persuaded Robert, who first obtained the blessing of Archbishop Hugh of Lyons for the move, to lead them to 'the desert which was called Cîteaux', a remote site some sixty kilometres to the south, given them by the viscount of Beaune. Later apologists of the order applied to it the description of Deuteronomy, dear to medieval hermits, of a 'howling waste and vast solitude'. This settlement, then, was the 'new monastery' – the early sources call it the *novum monasterium* – dedicated to a revival of primitive Benedictine observance. The group of fervent idealists who settled there were primarily in search of seclusion and detachment from worldly ties; they can as yet have had little notion of starting a new order.

For many years the going was hard. The monks left at Molesme protested to the pope about the desertion of their abbot; and Robert was forced reluctantly to return. The organisation of the new settlement was thus left to his two successors, Alberic, who was elected abbot in 1099, and Stephen Harding, who succeeded him in 1109. To begin with, the community at Cîteaux was housed in wooden huts built by the monks themselves. The life was austere and the site was damp and unhealthy. According to the hagiographers, not many new postulants came to fill the thinning ranks, and the experiment seemed in danger of extinction when, in April of the year 1112, the young Bernard of Fontaine knocked on the gate and sought admittance. The son of a landed Burgundian family with aristocratic connections, he brought with him a troop of thirty young men, including several of his brothers, whom he had persuaded to take the habit.

It is arguable that the hagiographers exaggerated the difficulties of the new monastery prior to the arrival of St Bernard. The rapid expansion that followed this infusion of new blood could only have been made possible by a considerable growth of numbers during the previous years. New colonies were founded at La Ferté in 1113, and at Pontigny the following year; and in 1115 Bernard was sent to establish a new community at Clairvaux, of which he was to remain abbot until his death in 1153. Another colony was planned at Morimond in the same year as Clairvaux. As the number of abbeys multiplied, these first four foundations came to acquire a special status in the order as the four 'elder daughters' of Cîteaux, entrusted with the task of visiting and correcting the mother-house. In 1118 both La Ferté and Clairvaux founded daughter-houses, and the nucleus of an order began to emerge.

What was original in the Cistercian Order was its unique constitution. It was this that influenced all subsequent orders and in time coloured the thinking of the Western Church as a whole. The monastic observance of Cîteaux, on the other hand, made no claim to originality. Its avowed aim was the restoration of primitive usage – a reform in the medieval and most literal sense. It was simply a question of getting back to the Rule of St Benedict, which was to be observed to the letter. The early Cistercians wanted to roll back the centuries of monastic development, to discard the circumspect compromises set out in the customaries of the eleventh century, to escape from the world of feudal obligations and to revive what they believed to be the pure simplicity of St Benedict's plan. 'The Rule of St Benedict', wrote Philip of Harvengt, 'has in our times been recalled to the truth of the letter.'[3]

Of course, there is always an element of historical fiction in revivals of primitive usage. The remote past is a dark pool in which reformers see a reflection of their own image. Those of the twelfth century knew even less than we do about the environment and material circumstances of Italian monasteries of the sixth century. There was much in the Rule to justify their desire to escape from secular involvements and seek a more secluded form of religious life; there was rather less foundation in the Rule for the cult of corporate poverty and austerity and the puritanical rejection of all forms of aesthetic expression which came to prevail in the early phases of the Cistercian movement. Whether this fierce spirit of abnegation was implanted by the founding fathers, or was imposed on the order by the dominating personality of St Bernard, it is hardly possible to say.

It was applied to everything – to dress, food, buildings and furniture. In contradistinction to the linen underwear and black habit of the black monks, the Cistercians adopted a coarse habit of undyed sheep's wool, a departure that drew a bitter aside from Peter the Venerable: 'O new race of Pharisees, who to distinguish yourselves from the other monks of almost the entire world, lay claim to a habit of unusual colour, to show that you are white while the rest are black.'[4] The same cult of poverty and simplicity decreed that the ornaments of the monastic church should be as simple as possible and made of wood or iron rather than precious metals. Decorative sculpture was forbidden by the statutes.

This puritanical attitude towards the aesthetic appeal of visual images, which St Bernard expressed so luxuriantly in his invective against the sculptures of Cluny, was reflected in the architecture of the new order. The Cistercians developed their own architectural idiom to express their ideal of the monastic life.[5] Their early churches are devoid of sculpture. They have a flat undecorated west façade and a simple rectangular eastern chevet, and they are without towers. The circular apsidal design with radiating chapels, which the Cluniacs brought to perfection, was abandoned. The new style can be seen in its purest form at Fontenay, a daughter-foundation of Clairvaux, which was built between 1139 and 1147 under the direct influence of St Bernard, its plain façade, stark arcades and bare capitals a visual reproof to the rich figure carvings of the great Cluniac churches. Its impact on the senses of the visitor is one of coolness and immense calm.

FIGURE 9.1 Fontenay Abbey
© Roger Rozencwajg/Photononstop/Corbis

A cardinal feature of the new ideal was the renunciation of anything that could involve the monks in the affairs of the outside world. Cistercian foundations were located with an eye to the preservation of seclusion and strict enclosure. The sites they accepted were generally on deserted and uncultivated land, removed where possible from inhabited settlements. This not only helped to ingratiate them with would-be benefactors, who were more ready to part with uncleared waste; it was also a policy that had a decisive part in shaping the economy of the Cistercian abbeys. In Britain, where they settled in the sparsely populated uplands of Yorkshire and Wales, they turned to sheep farming and wool production on a large scale. In Germany, they played an important part, alongside the Premonstratensians, in clearing and cultivating waste lands on the eastern frontier.

Besides choosing secluded areas in which to settle, the Cistercians adopted a more radical policy of rejecting the customary sources of monastic income, at least to start with. The *Exordium* says that, because such things were not mentioned in St Benedict's Rule, the founders refused to accept possession of churches, altar offerings or tithes, manorial rents, mills or serfs. This total renunciation of the usual means of supporting a religious community proved impossible to sustain for more than a generation. It was prompted by more than a simple desire to avoid secular entanglements; it was the expression of a new zeal for the ideal of collective poverty imitating that of Christ – a new evangelism, which drew its inspiration more from the desert tradition than from a literal understanding of the Rule. As the *Exordium* put it, the monks were the 'new soldiers of Christ, poor men together with Christ the pauper'.[6]

It was the intention that the community should live by the labour of its own hands, as St Benedict had commended. The manual labour prescribed by the Rule was thus restored to a place in the monk's timetable. The morning hours after chapter were assigned to it, and at haymaking and harvest the whole community went out to work in the fields. Cistercian writers stressed the value of work as an ascetical exercise as well as a means of producing food.[7] Nevertheless, they did not mean monks to be just pious agricultural labourers. Liturgically, they remained in the Benedictine tradition. Although they dropped many of the Cluniac ceremonies and accretions to the liturgy, there was still the divine office to sing, including the office of the dead, which was sung on weekdays; there were the daily masses to be celebrated; and time had to be made for private meditation and study. But a part-time labour-force, most of which had not been inured to the physical demands of agricultural work, was inadequate to cultivate land or to tend livestock at any distance from the monastery. To meet this requirement, it was decided at an early stage that the order should both accept lay brothers or *conversi* and employ local hired labour.

As we have already seen, lay brothers were to be found in other monastic institutions of the eleventh century. By definition the *conversus* was a lay convert who had embraced the monastic life as an adult and who, unlike the child-oblate educated in the cloister or the clerical recruit, was usually illiterate. He was a monk in the sense that he took the monastic vows and wore the habit, but he lived a separate existence from the choir monks.[8] Though he attended some of the choral offices, he took no part in singing them. He was chiefly occupied with manual work, serving the community as ploughman, shepherd, carpenter or blacksmith.

The *conversi* were to be found in Cluniac establishments,[9] and they had a special role in the arrangements of Grandmont and the Chartreuse, but it was the Cistercians who developed the use of them in a novel way and on a scale hitherto unknown. Recruited largely from the peasantry, they provided the permanent agricultural work-force of the monastery, leaving the choir monks the necessary leisure for liturgical and private prayer and for reading. For the first two centuries of Cîteaux the institution of lay brothers proved remarkably popular and recruitment remained buoyant. So much was this so that in most Cistercian abbeys the *conversi* formed the larger part of the community. At Rievaulx, at the time of Abbot Ailred's death in 1167, his biographer tells us that the lay brothers numbered five hundred, as against one hundred and forty choir monks.[10] Pontigny at the same period housed three hundred *conversi*, as against one hundred choir monks. At Himmerod in 1224, sixty choir monks were outnumbered by two hundred lay brothers.[11]

Cistercian building plans were specially adapted to house the *conversi* and preserve social apartheid between them and the choir monks. The range of buildings on the west side of the cloister was turned over to their use, providing them with a separate refectory on the ground floor and a dormitory above. At the northern end their quarters gave direct access to the nave of the abbey church, where they congregated for services, separated from the choir monks by a rood screen, for the choir was reserved to clerical members of the community. The same segregation was observed in the cloister, where the *conversi* were confined to the walk on the west side, which was commonly separated from the rest by a wall. We can get a vivid impression of the scale and character of the lay brothers' accommodation in the twelfth century from the surviving west range of Fountains. The astonishing vista of the interior with its petrified forest of piers and vaulting ribs, which housed their refectory and parlour, and the three-hundred-foot-long exterior, bear eloquent witness to the size of the body that gathered there at midwinter and high festivals. The growth of numbers is attested by the stonework of the last nine bays of the southern end, which were added towards the end of the twelfth century to lengthen the dormitory and accommodate a larger refectory.

Not all the lay brothers were housed within the abbey at any one time. With the acquisition of scattered properties and more distant estates, it became impracticable for the monk-labourers to work them while journeying to and fro every day. So the order gradually created a system of local granges, where the brothers could reside while they were occupied on the land. They would return to the abbey on Sundays, where feasible, and for major festivals. The grange was a

FIGURE 9.2 The interior of the lay brothers' refectory at Fountains Abbey (twelfth century)
Photograph by the author

monastic farm settlement. In the twelfth century it probably comprised in most cases little more than a barn and a modest dwelling to house the relays of *conversi* who were sent to work the estate in collaboration with hired workers recruited from the local peasantry. But in the thirteenth century, with the growth of wealth and the waiving of the early rules against accepting manorial rents and serfs, many of the granges grew in size and complexity and became miniature replicas of the parent monastery, with their own dormitory, refectory and chapel, and even a separate chamber to accommodate the abbot when he came to visit the property.[12]

The use made of the *conversi* by the Cistercians has the appearance of a straight-forward exploitation of illiterate peasants for the benefit of the more aristocratic clerical brethren who supplied the majority of the recruits to the cloister. Their inferior social status was underlined by the segregation of their living quarters from those of the choir monks. The two centuries during which the system was at its height were a period of population growth in northern Europe, when rising land values and land hunger were making it hard for increasing numbers of peasants to scrape a subsistence living from the soil. In these circumstances, it is probable that some of those who became lay brothers were bread-converts – men who became monks to obtain regular food and clothing. The discomforts of the monastic regime were no worse than a peasant had to endure in the outside world, and the living quarters were superior to those of a crowded family cottage shared with the livestock. Nor was celibacy necessarily a deterrent for the younger son of a villein, who had no expectation of a share in the family tenement and who for that reason was unable to marry.

To explain the buoyant recruitment of *conversi* solely or even primarily in these economic terms would be a gross oversimplification. The extraordinary tide of religious fervour that swept across Europe towards the end of the eleventh century touched all classes of society. The throngs of people who pressed along the pilgrim routes to lay their petitions at the shrines of the saints included peasants and artisans as well as noblemen and burgesses. It was they who provided the rank and file of the armies that set out in 1096, in response to the pope's invitation, to reconquer the holy places from the infidel. The Cistercians offered a new channel for this religious enthusiasm by opening the monastic vocation to the agrarian peasantry, a class to which it had been largely inaccessible.

Being illiterate, and required by the rule-book, the *Usus Conversorum*, to remain so, the lay brother could not take part in singing the divine office; he made a simple contribution to the spiritual life of the community by being present in the nave of the church during part of the night office, and during the day by regular recitation of a few simple prayers learned by heart.[13] He was required to receive Communion on seven occasions during the year. His major contribution to the effort of the monastery was the labour of his hands. This did not mean, though, that his role in the monastic family was purely economic. Cistercian writers gave manual work a new spiritual significance: it was a necessary part of a life modelled on that of Jesus, and as such it was an obligation for the choir monk as well as for the lay brother. At harvest time they worked in the fields side by side. Caesarius of Heisterbach was moved to join the order by a story of how the Blessed Virgin herself, with St Anne and St Mary Magdalen, had descended in a great flood of light to visit the monks of Clairvaux while they were toiling at the harvest in the valley, and had wiped the sweat from the brows of the monks and fanned them with their sleeves.[14]

This sanctification of manual labour offered the *conversus* an ascetical ideal that was within his grasp. His harsh work was a sacrifice acceptable to God. The point was vividly illustrated in Conrad of Eberbach's tale of a lay brother who dreamed he was ploughing a field. And in his dream he saw that he was not alone: Jesus walked at his side behind the plough, carrying the goad for the oxen.[15]

This ideal, which was held in common by both lay brother and choir monk, was epitomised in the advice Abbot Charles gave Caesarius during his noviciate: 'Brother, if you wish to find peace in the order, let the simplicity of the order suffice you.'[16] Many of the examples placed before the monk by Cistercian hagiography were those of simple people who had, by humility and literal devotion to the Rule, scaled the heights of contemplative prayer, such as the unlettered brothers of Villers, Arnulf and Peter, or the crusader turned monk, like Gobert of Aspremont.[17] It was the same message that was conveyed by the story Caesarius told his novices of the lay brother of Himmerod, the master of one of his abbey's granges, who during the office one night saw the Blessed Virgin enter the choir of the lay brothers, carrying the Christ-child in her arms and proffer the infant to those of the brethren who were rapt in prayer.[18]

The use of the *conversi* as wardens of granges and warehouses as well as manual workmen enabled the choir monks to devote themselves to study and the observances of the Rule without getting involved in the distractions and responsibilities of estate management. It was the same passion for seclusion from the secular world and the fear of incurring outside obligations that led the Cistercians to break away from the monastic tradition of the past, and paradoxically from the Benedictine Rule itself, by refusing to accept child-oblates. There were no boys in the cloister of Cîteaux, and there was little provision for formal schooling, at any rate before the innovations of the thirteenth century. A general chapter held in 1134 conceded that novices or professed monks might learn letters during the periods of the day assigned to reading; but nobody was to be admitted to the noviciate under the age of fifteen.[19] It was all part of a determination to renew the concept of the monastic vocation as a spiritual adventure freely chosen by the individual in response to a divine call. The year-long noviciate, prescribed by St Benedict but waived by Cluny, was revived. Caesarius stiffened the resolution of his novices with endless stories of recruits who fought a heroic and victorious struggle against the efforts of the Devil to make them give up the enterprise they had chosen, though a few, as he admits sadly, yielded and returned to the world, 'like a dog to its vomit'.

One of the reasons for refusing children was a conviction that teaching grammar and the liberal arts was a dangerous distraction from the proper task of the monk. St Bernard quoted with approval Jerome's maxim that a 'monk's business is not to teach, but to lament'. But there was, of course, a school of Cîteaux in a different sense. The Cistercian monastery was a place where men were taught the skills of the spiritual life – in Ailred's phrase, 'a school of love'. And the knot of monks who gathered round him in the evenings at Rievaulx to hear him talk about the spiritual life had something of the quality of a seminar.

The order in fact produced a school of highly articulate writers. St Bernard towers above the rest – the most widely read and influential ascetical theologian of the Middle Ages, who received the posthumous accolade of a Doctor of the Church. But in his wake there was a throng of lesser writers, men whose talent had been fertilised by his torrential literary genius, like William of Saint-Thierry, whose treatise on *The Contemplation of God*, written while he was still a Benedictine abbot and not yet enrolled in Bernard's army, mapped the mystical ascent of the soul to union with God in infused contemplation; or Geoffrey of Auxerre, Bernard's secretary, who became his biographer; or, a generation later, Adam of Perseigne, whose letters to many people outside the cloister as well as to monks came to be regarded as classics of spiritual direction. Many of these disciples and imitators of St Bernard were men like William and Geoffrey, who had been through the schools before taking the habit; but the literary work they produced in the cloister reflects the concerns and the tranquillity of the monastic life rather than the disputatious methods and speculation of the schools. Their preoccupation is with the interior life of the spirit, the states of the soul, and relationship between human and divine love. They were not, of course, alone in this. The same themes were developed by the Victorines and others; but Cistercian writers of the twelfth century contribute a distinctive voice to ascetical literature of this sort.

Growth and recruitment

What has been said about Cistercian observance only in part explains the meteoric success of the new institution. 'Like a great lake whose waters pour out through a thousand streams, gathering impetus from their rapids, the new monks went forth from Cîteaux to people the West,' wrote Conrad of Eberbach.[20] His excited rhetoric is excusable, for it points to a truth: the speed and extent of the expansion were, in fact, extraordinary. Within a generation the obscure and struggling group of recluses at Cîteaux had grown into a mighty order. When St Bernard sought admission in the year 1112, it seemed doubtful whether it had a future. By the time of his death forty-one years later, it had dispatched colonies to all parts of Europe, and there existed three hundred and forty-three abbeys of Cistercian monks, of which sixty-eight had been directly founded from Clairvaux. And the growth continued, if with diminishing momentum, for the following century. By 1500, the men's abbeys numbered seven hundred and thirty-eight and those of the nuns six hundred and fifty-four.[21] In a short time the new order of white monks had wrested from Cluny the moral leadership of the monastic world and had become a powerful force in both ecclesiastical and secular politics. There were Cistercian bishops and 'white' cardinals and even, in Eugenius III (1145–53), a Cistercian pope. What was the explanation of this spectacular success?

One reason was the social catholicity of its appeal, a respect in which it differed from Cluny and from most of the traditional Benedictine establishments. By opening the cloister to peasants and artisans it was able to catch the tide of demographic and economic change that was transforming Western society. But it is less easy to explain the compelling attraction the Cistercian ideal had, not only for the military aristocracy, which had long been a major source of recruitment to the monasteries, but also for the intelligentsia. For the order recruited from the outset among educated clerks and schoolmen; and it continued to do so with some success until the third decade of the thirteenth century, when it quickly lost this catchment area to the new orders of friars.

Part of the attraction must be attributed to the charismatic personality of St Bernard. He was the order's foremost apologist and recruiting officer, and his image was indelibly stamped upon it. To his contemporary admirers he seemed to personify the monastic ideal. For thirty years his was the most eloquent and influential voice in the Western Church. He was the mentor of popes, the counsellor of kings and cardinals, and the maker and unmaker of bishops. His preaching roused the nobility of France and Germany to undertake the Second Crusade. Yet all this activity and his ceaseless literary output represented an extraordinary triumph of the spirit over physical weakness. His tall, slight figure was emaciated by fasting and mortification. 'In him', wrote William of Saint-Thierry, 'the spirit lusted against the flesh with such power that the weakly animal nature sank under the burden.'[22] He suffered from a gastric disorder, of which William spares us none of the nauseating details. He could not keep food down long after eating and so found it necessary to dig a receptacle in the ground beside his stall in choir. For a time his physical presence was so repellent to the brethren that he had to live in separate quarters.

Bernard's fame as a preacher, his reputation for sanctity, and his legendary mortifications gave the Cistercian ideal a publicity it could never otherwise have achieved. Without him the order, had it survived, would probably not have outgrown the dimensions of a small eremitical congregation like that of Camaldoli. Yet the message conveyed in his sermons and letters differed only in its passionate intensity, not in kind, from the traditional summons to the monastic life. In essence it was a call to total renunciation of the secular world, to follow Christ by embracing a life of poverty, austerity and prayer. He was traditional, too, in claiming that those who observed the Rule of St Benedict were reproducing the life-style of the Apostles: 'the Apostles left all and gathered together in the school of the Saviour . . . in hunger and thirst, in cold and nakedness, in toil and fasting. So do you,' he told the brethren, 'and though you are not their equals in merit, you are to some degree made their peers by your practice.'[23] This conviction that the Rule contained a model of the apostolic life was one that Bernard held in common with Peter the Venerable and the Cluniacs. The gravamen of Bernard's complaint against Cluny was simply that it had not adhered strictly to the Rule.

Bernard also worked a well-worn theme in preaching that the cloister provided the only sure route to salvation. For the individual there was only one sort of conversion, and that was to the monastic life, and the call was imperative to cleric and layman alike. It was best to make haste: life was short and precarious. 'I grieve to think', he writes to Master Walter of Chaumont, a young scholar who lingered overlong at the schools,

> of that subtle intelligence of yours and your erudite accomplishments being worn out in vain and futile studies, of you with your great gifts not serving Christ, their author, but things that are transitory. O what if unexpected death should strike and snatch them from you? Alas, what would you take with you from all your toil? What return will you make to the Lord for all he has bestowed on you? He will come, he will come and he will not delay to demand what is his with interest. What will you answer at that dread tribunal for having received your soul in vain?[24]

This appeal relied for its effect upon the common assumption, still not seriously challenged, that the Christian life could only be lived fully in the cloister and that a serious religious commitment meant becoming a monk. It was an assumption that had as yet been hardly eroded by the proliferation of the secular schools and the growing number and diversity of alternative vocations open to educated men. It slowly gave ground in the course of the following hundred years, but it still haunted the university classrooms of the thirteenth century and lingered in the jeremiads of preachers addressing academic audiences.

The theme is the same; only the players are different. What is significant is that in these latter days before the coming of the friars who cast their net over the academic world, when men wanted to preach the duty of abandoning the schools for the cloister, it is the Cistercians they represent as the embodiment of the monastic vocation. Jacques de Vitry tells a Paris congregation the story of a Master of Arts who had a frightening dream in which he was confronted by the tormented soul of one of his pupils who had recently died. The wretched youth was groaning under the weight of a cope covered with beautiful writing, but heavier to bear than the tower of Saint-Germain (under which they were standing): 'these writings', he says, 'are all the vain sophisms you taught me in the schools'. The master wakes in a panic, resigns his magistral chair, and takes the Cistercian habit.[25] The tale must have gained credibility from live examples that would have been known to his audience, like Peter the Chanter, formerly doyen of the Paris theology schools, who ended his days as a monk at Longpont, or Alain of Lille, who left the schools for Cîteaux.

Something of the revivalist note sounded in Bernard's appeal to the young scholar can still be heard in the hagiographers' account of the conversion of Stephen of Lexington, who was to leave his mark on the order as abbot of Clairvaux. He was attending the theology lectures of Edmund of Abingdon at Oxford when in 1221 he decided to throw up his academic career and become a Cistercian. In the hagiographical narratives, the master has a prophetic dream: he sees his school enveloped by a great fire, from which are plucked seven flaming brands. Next morning, still troubled by his fretful vision, he goes to the schools and begins his lecture as usual. But while he is speaking, the Cistercian abbot of Quarr enters the room. At the end of the lecture seven of Edmunds pupils, including Lexington, are moved by his eloquence to approach the abbot and seek admission to the order.[26]

The fact that to educated men a call to the ascetical life presented itself primarily as an invitation to join the Cistercians can be attributed partly to the successful propaganda of St Bernard, and partly to the advantages of a powerful organisation, which enabled the order to promote its image at the expense of its competitors. The ideal was a potent one for an age that was in search of the lost simplicity of the apostolic life. It offered a welcome alternative to the overelaborate and time-consuming rituals and the secular preoccupations of the older monasticism. Its advocates conveyed all the exhilarating sense of taking part in a great movement of reform, which was also a revival of a heroic past. They pushed their case with a single-mindedness which, if it did not repel by its selfrighteous arrogance, persuaded by the force of its conviction. 'You say,' writes Bernard to Peter the Venerable, with an unconvincing plea for fraternal charity between different orders that profess the Benedictine Rule, 'you say, who can see with equanimity the greater part of the world turning away from our old order and converting to the new enterprise of the Cistercians?' The reason for the defections, answered Bernard, was simple: 'we are the restorers of lost religion'.[27] But however attractive the ideal for minds of a certain type, it could not have materialised in a huge and richly endowed order unless it had been promoted and sustained by a strong organisation.

The constitution of the order

The fundamental constitutional law that governed the order was contained in the *Carta Caritatis* – the Charter of Charity. An assembly of the year 1201 decreed that the Charter should be read in entirety at every meeting of the general chapter, and that every abbey should possess a corrected copy of it. In its earliest form this document was said to be the work of the English monk, Stephen Harding, one of the founding fathers, who succeeded Alberic as abbot of Cîteaux in 1108. It was composed at some date before the year 1118, and in the following year it was confirmed by Pope Calixtus II. The actual form of this early text has been the subject of scholarly controversy for the past fifty years.[28] It is now clear that the common version of the Charter that has come down to us contains subsequent interpolations, and that the Cistercian constitution was not a master-plan that sprang fully fledged from a single mind. The successive amendments and additions to the document show that the organisation of the order was articulated gradually over a period of some decades in the light of experience. Something of this structural development is charted by the *Institutes of the General Chapter*, a code of the early regulations compiled by the chapter in 1134.

The remarkable thing about this process of refinement is that it seems to have taken the form of a steady movement from initial autocracy towards a system of representation.[29] At the beginning the structure was monarchic: the abbot of Cîteaux had absolute and undivided powers over his daughter-houses. To ensure that they were kept up to standard in their observance, the abbots of the four elder daughters were required not only to hold their own chapter of faults daily, which was a normal feature of a monastic regime, but also to visit the mother-house once a year and take part in the chapter there, where their faults of omission or commission would be disclosed. It was out of this early arrangement for oversight that the annual general chapter of the whole order developed and, in the course of time, established its position as the sovereign body. In the thirteenth century the Mendicant Orders, more especially the Dominicans, borrowed some features of this model to create an allembracing and completely articulated system of representative government. The Cistercians did not go that far, but in several ways their organisation anticipated the more sophisticated constitutional arrangements of the friars.

The Rule of St Benedict assumes that every abbey is an autonomous society governed by its own elected paterfamilias. The problem that faced the founders of Cîteaux and their successors was how to reconcile this autonomy with the need to preserve standards and ensure uniformity of observance – to keep the original ideal from erosion as new foundations proliferated, many of them in distant lands and less advanced cultures. The model of the centralised Cluniac empire, in which member abbeys were reduced to dependent status, was rejected. The Charter of Charity expressly asserted that the bond which kept the Cistercian abbeys in relationship with one another and with the mother-house was not that of subordination but that of mutual love. Instead, a solution to the problem was found by creating a strong federal framework which ensured strict and uniform observance of the Rule by a system of mutual supervision. The chief agencies in this were the general chapter, attended annually by all abbots or their deputies, and the system of filiation.

It was made the duty of every abbey to oversee the conduct of its own daughter foundations; and this duty was to be discharged by means of regular visitation. As new foundations multiplied, so each abbey which had put out colonies became the head of a family or filiation of daughter-houses for which it had responsibility. The abbot of a mother-house was required to visit the abbeys of his filiation at least once a year. There was a mutuality in these arrangements which is one of the most arresting features of the Cistercian constitution in its fully developed form. The business of the visiting abbot was simply to see that the Rule and the statutes of the general chapter were being observed. He was warned by the statutes not to interfere or do anything that could undermine the authority of the head of the house he was visiting. If, in an extreme case, he had to act against an abbot, he could only do so in consultation with the fellow-abbots of the filiation. The abbots of a filiation also had a role to play when the headship of their mother-house fell vacant: they joined the monks of the head-less monastery to elect a new abbot. This kind of co-responsibility was in time applied to Cîteaux itself, which was at first deemed to be above correction, but was later made subject to supervisory visitation by the abbots of the four elder daughters.

Each filiation thus constituted a distinct family within the order. But these groupings were not geographical provinces like those created by the friars at a later date; they were groups determined by the historical accidents of foundation and patronage, and which therefore cut across national and political frontiers. Many abbots were subject to the supervision of a mother-house in a distant land. In Italy, for instance, the earliest Cistercian foundations of S. Maria del Tiglieto and Locedio, established in the 1120s, belonged to the filiation of La Ferté, from which the colonies had come. Clairvaux also acquired a large Italian filiation through the activity of St Bernard, who sent a party to found Chiaravalle in the contedo of Milan in 1135, which in turn became the mother-house of a cluster of abbeys in Lombardy and the Veneto. Further colonies of Clairvaux were established at Tre Fontane on the Via Ostiense and in the Roman Campagna. In England, the first foundation, at Waverley in Surrey, belonged to the filiation of L'Aumône in the county of Blois. Rievaulx, harbinger of the main Cistercian colonisation of the north, was a daughter-house of Clairvaux, peopled by monks dispatched by St Bernard in 1132 at the request of a Yorkshire baron, Walter Espec of Helmsley. Other English abbeys belonged to the Norman filiation of Savigny.

Although the order had an international structure, individual abbeys were not generally cosmopolitan in their recruitment. Clairvaux in St Bernard's time contained a number of English monks, one of whom, William, served as his amanuensis until he was sent with a party to be the first abbot of Rievaulx. The presence of English monks in French monasteries in the early twelfth century is not surprising, for the landed classes of Anglo-Norman England had territorial and cultural roots on both sides of the Channel, and students from England were to be found at the cathedral schools of northern France. Some of the early Cistercian plantations in England, like Waverley, contained French monks; but once established, they tended to elect native abbots and recruited from the aristocracy and peasantry of their own country, where they quickly put down social roots.

Like the Benedictines before them, the Cistercians soon became an indigenous feature of the English landscape.

It is observable, though, that the system of filiation produced some mobility at the upper levels. The head of an abbey was commonly chosen from the monks of another house within the same filiation. For instance, out of six abbots who ruled Kirkstall between the years 1147 and 1231, all but one had previously been monks of Fountains, which was the mother-house; and one of them, Ralph Haget, after governing Kirkstall for some years, was recalled to be abbot of Fountains.[30] The more energetic and successful abbots tended to be translated upwards through the filiation from one house to another and might eventually be elected to a mother-house overseas.

The career of Stephen of Lexington provides an example of this kind of mobility within the order. His family belonged to the new aristocracy of talent created by the Angevin kings. His father was a royal judge, one of his brothers became steward of the household to King Henry III, and another became first dean, and then bishop, of Lincoln. Stephen's family connections and his own managerial capacities marked him out for rapid advancement when he quitted the Oxford schools to become a monk at Quarr. After two years he was elected abbot of the daughter-house of Stanley, an abbey of which his family had previously been benefactors. Six years later, in 1229, he was translated to the headship of Savigny, which was the mother-house of Quarr; and from there in 1243 he was elected abbot of Clairvaux.[31] But this sequence of honours was unusual. Cistercian communities rarely looked outside their own country for an abbot. What gave the order the complexion of an international organisation was the institution of the general chapter.

The general chapter

The general chapter, which evolved from the regular attendance of the four elder daughter-houses at Cîteaux, was the most distinctive and influential innovation of the new order.[32] It met every year at Cîteaux on the vigil of Holy Cross Day (13 September), and all abbots were under an obligation to attend. Its primary function was to maintain observance of the Rule. In a sense, it was an enlarged chapter of faults – the standard monastic chapter in macrocosm. It received reports, imposed penalties on peccant abbots, reiterated old regulations, made new ones for fresh situations as they arose, and authorised new foundations.

The duty of attendance involved much time and effort for the heads of more distant houses. A journey to Burgundy from central Italy or from the north of England could take five or six weeks. Obviously, a system of surveillance that took an abbot away from his monastery for several months every year was self-defeating. It therefore became necessary, as the order sent colonies to ever more distant areas, to mitigate the demands upon the heads of more remote abbeys. Thus Scottish abbots were permitted to attend in person only once in four years and in other years to send a representative. The same privilege was extended to abbots from Ireland, Portugal and Sicily; and those from Greece and Syria were licensed to come only once every five years.

As the order continued to grow, the increase in numbers attending the chapter posed problems of accommodation, money and procedure. Although no abbot was permitted to bring more than a single monk-secretary and one *conversus* to act as servant, the gathering must have numbered not far short of eight hundred by the middle of the twelfth century; and the housing and feeding of such a huge company of visitors clearly placed a severe strain on the resources of the mother-house.[33] Abbots attending were asked to bring alms to help defray the cost. In the end it became necessary to spread the burden by imposing a levy on all houses for the support of the chapter. The cause also attracted earmarked gifts from princes and magnates. Richard I of England donated the church of Scarborough with its endowments to support the assembly for a period of three days annually;[34] and Alexander III of Scotland put up an annual subvention of £20 sterling.

Meetings of the chapter lasted from seven to ten days. As time went on, the inflated size of the assembly must have made it useless for the transaction of anything but formal business, and it became necessary to set up a steering committee of abbots who were called 'diffinitors' – men appointed to hear cases and make decisions. We find traces of this procedural device already in the chapter acts of the 1140s. The composition of this committee in the thirteenth century is set out in a code of chapter statutes. It consisted of twenty-five diffinitors, and invariably included the abbots of Cîteaux and its four elder daughters; the other twenty were nominated by these five statutory members. It was thus an oligarchic body, which gave the five senior abbots the power to determine the agenda and control the activities of the chapter. The work of the general assembly in practice must have been largely confined to the formal function of ratifying the acts of the diffinitors and transmitting them home.

It is difficult to assess the effectiveness of the chapter as an organ of control. We have no records of attendance, but the chapter ordinances indicate that a number of abbots often failed to turn up. In 1157 the chapter decreed that abbots who had neither come nor sent a representative were to do penance by vacating their abbatial stalls and fasting every Friday on bread and water, until they presented themselves at Cîteaux.[35] The repeated re-enactment of these sanctions against absentees in general, and against named individuals who had in some cases failed to attend for several years, indicate that absenteeism was a chronic problem. Connected with this there was the problem of ensuring that those abbeys that were unrepresented were kept abreast of the regulations.

The acts themselves testify that the enforcement of regulations met with only limited success. For instance, the chapter of 1157 enacted an earlier rule that nobody should be accepted into the noviciate under the age of eighteen. This decree, which contained a principle to which the founders had attached much importance, was reiterated in 1177 and again in 1201, each time with lamentations that it had been breached.[36] Similar admissions of failure appear in the reiterated prohibition of stained glass in the churches of the order.[37] The issue of decrees contradicting previous enactments was not uncommon – probably the result of inadequate record-keeping as much as of divided counsels. Efficiency is not a concept that can be usefully applied to medieval institutions. When all is said, these annual assemblies were a remarkable device for preserving the spiritual cohesion and discipline of a huge organisation with houses in all parts of medieval Christendom.

We have lingered a little over the workings of the general chapter because it represented something new, not only in the monastic tradition, but in the polity of medieval Europe. It made the Cistercians an international order with a cosmopolitan and partly representative legislature. Besides this, it played a role of some significance in Western society as a whole. Before the advent of the friars in the thirteenth century, the Cistercian general chapter and its imitators were the only international assemblies known to Europe, apart from general councils of the Church, which were extremely rare events. These annual meetings of abbots or their representatives from all parts of the Christian world constituted a forum of public opinion and an influential pressure group. The regular journeyings of those attending in effect made every Cistercian abbey a post office and the chapter itself an emporium of news – a whispering gallery of Europe. Many rulers showed they were aware of its possibilities as a medium for disseminating news and propaganda. In 1177 the Emperor Frederick Barbarossa sent the chapter a letter to inform the fathers that he had accepted Alexander III as rightfully being the Supreme Pontiff and that peace had been concluded between him and pope, sensing that in doing so he was notifying the Church at large. In the year 1212 Arnaud Amaury, the archbishop of Narbonne, reported to the chapter the great victory over the Spanish Muslims at Las Navas de Tolosa, in the knowledge that the news would be swiftly relayed to all parts by the returning abbots. In 1245 Pope Innocent IV courted public opinion by sending the chapter a long letter explaining the grounds for his excommunication of Frederick II.

Certain acts of the chapter reflect the widespread esteem the order enjoyed. They record a steady stream of petitions from outside persons – rulers, bishops and lay magnates – requesting spiritual privileges or prayers for some specified intention. The most coveted privilege, which might be granted to benefactors, was that of full commemoration at death. This meant that when the petitioner died, the chapter would notify abbeys throughout the order, and they would celebrate the office of the dead for the deceased. But the clearest testimony to the impression made upon contemporaries by the organisation of the order is the fact that it was copied. The Premonstratensians adopted it in entirety with only a few modifications; the Carthusians convened general chapters from 1141 onwards; in 1200 Cluny also adopted the practice; and the system was carried to its logical conclusion in the organisation of the friars. At the Fourth Lateran Council of 1215, the Cistercian general chapter was accorded the status of an approved model, when Innocent III commended it to all monasteries that lacked a similar organisation of their own, and instructed them to hold assemblies of heads of houses in each province or kingdom every three years.

Criticism and dilution

'O new race of Pharisees': Peter the Venerable's bitter riposte to the Cistercian criticism of Cluny was echoed by others outside as well as within Cluniac circles. The claim of Cîteaux to be the only authentic interpreter of the Benedictine Rule exposed it to the charge of arrogance and self-righteousness. But besides this, there were aspects of the Cistercian phenomenon that aroused apprehension or hostility among some of the secular clergy and the laity. The quest for disengagement took the form of an aggressive and unremitting drive for papal privileges, which exempted the abbeys of the order from episcopal supervision and from other duties and responsibilities. By the end of the twelfth century it was a highly privileged order. It is observable that the manuscript archives of any Cistercian abbey, where they have survived, contain a disproportionate quantity of documents containing grants of exemption and confirmations of privileges.

This privileged position, which was jealously guarded by a succession of Cistercian cardinal protectors at the papal Curia, gained the order no love in those sections of clerical society whose interests had been disregarded or trampled upon in the process. For instance, exemption from the duty of attending diocesan synods, a concession made to the order in 1132 by Innocent II, came to be a source of growing friction with bishops when, before long, the Cistercians waived some of their original principles and started to acquire parish churches. Another privilege which was regarded with envy was that of exemption from payment of tithes due from lands given to the order. Tithes, after all, provided the endowment of parish churches and were intended to support the pastoral care.[38] This aroused much ill feeling later in the twelfth century, and it was in fact made inapplicable to future donations by a ruling of the Fourth Lateran Council.

We come here to one of the curious ironies of Cistercian history. An order that had originated in a protest against monastic wealth and grandeur and had placed apostolic poverty in the forefront of its programme, had by the end of the twelfth century acquired for itself an unenviable reputation for avarice and group acquisitiveness. What was the reason for this disagreeable image? One explanation can be found in the privileged status just referred to. Exemption was never popular with bishops, and the numerous financial immunities enjoyed by the white monks attracted understandable animosity from those members of the clergy and laity who had to shoulder the burdens the monks had managed to avoid. A further reason for mistrust was the fact that the acquisition and successful management of great estates had made the order exceedingly wealthy. In a time of growing land hunger and rising land values, the business acumen the Cistercians displayed in enlarging and consolidating their properties and marketing their produce earned them the envy and dislike of landed families who had been less successful. But at the kernel of the hostile criticism there lay a harsher truth than this.

The rapid expansion of the order had been made possible by a flood of endowments. There was no shortage of aristocratic benefactors in the early decades, and most Cistercian abbeys became large-scale landed proprietors, differing from the older monasteries only in that they exploited their estates largely with their own labour-force instead of leasing them to tenants. And in pursuit of their objective they often displayed a ruthless disregard for the interests of lesser folk who stood in their way. Where they had no use for tenants, either servile or free, they sometimes destroyed existing villages to make way for granges, and evicted the peasant occupiers, who were settled elsewhere. Investigation of the Cistercian settlements in the north of England has verified the charge of the twelfth-century satirist Walter Map: 'they raze villages and churches, and drive poor people from the land'.[39] Their preference for estates they could work themselves brought them many gifts of virgin land; but where it did not, they showed no scruple in creating the kind of estate they wanted by means of depopulation. The claims of peasants could not be allowed to obstruct the ascetic search for the desert. The seamy underside of the Cistercian ideal was the corporate arrogance and institutional egotism that often afflicts religious organisations.

In the course of the twelfth century, the ideal itself was gradually eroded as the early self-denying ordinances proved to be incompatible with the process of expansion. Even in St Bernard's lifetime, it became necessary to compromise over the policy of economic 'purity' – the refusal of seignorial revenues and churches and exclusive reliance upon monastic or hired labour. The incorporation of the Order of Savigny which applied to join the Cistercians in 1147, followed by the absorption of the Aquitainian abbey of Cadouin and its dependencies and of the small congregation of Obazine, together with their original endowments, brought a great mass of manorial revenues, servile tenants, churches and parish endowments, which it was simply not practicable to discard. Bernard himself seems to have approved a similar departure from the founders' principles in 1140 when he negotiated the absorption of the old Roman abbey of Tre Fontane. It, too, was authorised by the general chapter to retain its village, churches and tithes.[40]

Much of the pressure for change came from the needs of efficient estate management. Piecemeal benefactions resulted in scattered properties, some of which were too remote from the monastery to be effectively exploited. At first, the solution to this problem was found by selling such properties or exchanging them for other lands nearer the home-farm. From there it was an obvious step to consolidating the estate by purchasing land that was conveniently situated. The general chapter legislated against this repeatedly from 1180 onwards, but to no purpose. Abbeys with a large surplus of agricultural produce sold it and bought more land with the proceeds.

At Clairvaux a spirit of aggressive enterprise took command with the advent of Abbot Guy in 1193, who vastly enlarged the abbey's property in southern Champagne by purchasing lands, lordships, mills and serfs.[41] The same process can be seen at work in the English abbeys. The abbots of Quarr worked steadily to round off the abbey's estates in the Isle of Wight by purchase, the exchange of more distant properties on the mainland, and the expropriation of debtors, who could be induced to surrender their heavily mortgaged land in return for a corrody or life pension.[42] After 1228 they adopted the practice of leasing properties, including a number of urban properties they had bought in Portsmouth, and rents came to have a growing place in the economy of the abbey. A similar trend has been observed in the case of Sibton abbey in Suffolk, which acquired urban properties in Dunwich and Norwich.[43] The needs of rent collecting and an increasing involvement in trade made it necessary for many abbeys to retain town houses for their own use in major centres of commerce for the purpose of storing and marketing their agricultural produce and wines.

As time went on, economic pressures obliged the rulers of the order to add a monetary dimension to the bond of mutual love envisaged by the Charter of Charity. There were other demands upon the resources of the mother-house besides the annual expense of boarding the general chapter. Among them were the maintenance of proctors at the Roman Curia, the payments involved in litigation and the confirmation of privileges, and the periodic subsidies levied on the monasteries of the order by pope or kings for crusading purposes. The voluntary alms brought by abbots attending the general chapter were insufficient to meet these various demands, which were made more pressing by the inflationary trends of the thirteenth century. In 1250 the general chapter imposed a mandatory tax on all houses of the order to meet its accumulated debts, and this became a regular levy.[44] The income of each abbey was assessed for the purpose; and the father-abbot of each filiation was made responsible for the contributions of his daughter-houses, with powers to suspend abbots who defaulted. The sums collected were delivered to the bursar of Cîteaux at Provins during the biennial fairs.[45]

Thus in the sources of their income, their business methods and their economic attitudes, the Cistercians became indistinguishable from the older Benedictines. The only difference was that they possessed in the lay brothers a domestic, if not always tame, and mobile work-force, which was an important factor in their economic success; and even this peculiarity vanished in the fourteenth century, when recruitment from the peasantry dwindled and eventually dried up altogether. Having begun as a rebellion against the established conventions of monastic life, the Cistercian movement gradually adopted the ways of the establishment it had criticised.

In one respect they moved even further along the road of adaptation. It had been the original vocation of Cîteaux to recall men to the primitive observance of the Rule, in which the essential tasks of the monk were a simplified round of liturgical prayer, work, and study. Between the cloister and the world a new gulf was to be fixed. It was an ideal that accepted learning in St Benedict's sense of *lectio divina* – the study of ascetical theology to provide food for meditation – but it was unsympathetic to the intellectual pursuits of the schools and scholastic methods. The fascination the order exerted over the academic intellect was that of renunciation. But in the thirteenth century the absorption of university masters like the Chanter and Lexington into the ranks of the white monks brought a softening of this early rigorism; for men trained in the liberal and disputatious atmosphere of the schools did not shed their intellectual oudook when they took the habit. So, by a curious paradox, the Cistercians became the first monks to set up colleges for their members in the universities.

The author of the plan to bring the order into contact with the scholastic world of the thirteenth century seems to have been Evrard, the abbot of Clairvaux. He formulated a project of installing a small community of student monks, with a warden and two *conversi*, in a house that the abbey had acquired in Paris; but he died in 1238 before the scheme had got off the ground, and it fell to Stephen of Lexington, the Oxford student and abbot of Clairvaux, to realise it on a larger scale and in a permanent form. Lexington's letters record his growing anxiety over the low state of theological education he had found in many abbeys during the course of his visitations. It was this that moved him to pursue Evrard's plans.[46] In 1245 he obtained the somewhat reserved approval of the general chapter for his project, launched an appeal for endowments, and acquired a plot of waste land called the Chardonnet (place of thistles) near the abbey of St Victor, just south of the modern Boulevard Saint-Germain. Here he had new buildings constructed to house a monastic college.[47] The house, which was for monks attending the schools of the theology faculty, remained under the jurisdiction of the abbot of Clairvaux, who appointed its warden. By 1250 student monks had already taken up their new quarters, and six years later the first Cistercian incepted as a master and began teaching in the faculty.

The college was to be only the apex of a plan to create an organised system of studies for the Cistercian order, imitating that of the Dominican Friars. The general chapter which authorised the Parisian house of studies also decreed that every abbey should have a school (*studium*), and that at least one abbey in every ecclesiastical province should constitute a *studium* of theology. This revolution in Cistercian policy seems to have been brought about by a small pressure group of university schoolmen, who succeeded in pushing through their plans with the aid of powerful friends at the papal court, the most influential of whom was the English Cistercian cardinal, John Tolet. The endorsements on the papal privileges for the new college show that he was an active promoter of Lexington's enterprise.

The attempt to turn the Cistercians into a student order provoked a backlash from more conservative abbots, who felt that the principles of the founding fathers were being betrayed. In some places Lexington's appeal for funds fell on stony ground. 'It has not hitherto been the custom', wrote Abbot Arnulf of Villers grimly, 'for monks to leave their claustral exercises, which most befit their profession, in order to give themselves over to the study of letters; as St Bernard says, a monk's business is not to teach, but to lament.'[48] He would make no contribution to funding the college. The critics demanded a victim, and despite Cardinal Tolet's efforts to protect him, Abbot Stephen was deposed. But his fall did not bring about a reversal of his policy. His college of the Chardonnet at Paris continued to flourish; and in 1287 the general chapter decreed that every abbey having twenty monks should maintain one of them at the university. By this time the order had houses of study at the universities of Oxford, Montpellier and Toulouse; and the Benedictines were following where the Cistercians had led the way.

The entry into the new scholastic world of the universities was one of many ways in which the early principles of Cîteaux were modified in response to a changing social environment. The white monks did not make a great impact on the academic world. After 1240 men with intellectual aspirations were much more likely to join the friars. Yet, thanks to the strength of its organisation and its spiritual cohesion, the order preserved high standards of observance in most of its houses, and for much of the thirteenth century it continued to attract the admiration and patronage of the high aristocracy. Richard of Cornwall, brother of King Henry III, lavished some of his immense fortune on founding a Cistercian abbey at Hailes, which became his own mausoleum and that of his family. In France, Louis IX and the queen-mother, Blanche of Castile, founded new abbeys and enriched others with generous donations. The most favoured royal foundation was the abbey of Royaumont, close to the royal manor of Asnières-sur-Oise. It received its endowment in 1228, fulfilling a request made in the will of Louis's father, Louis VIII, and monks were brought from Cîteaux to people it. Louis demonstrated his devotion for the monks of Royaumont by personally assisting in the construction of their buildings and, whenever possible, by joining them in choir and chapter.[49]

The high reputation of the order continued also to be demonstrated by the favour of reforming popes. It was to the Cistercians that Alexander III turned for preachers and missionaries to combat the Albigensian heresy in southern France. Innocent III entrusted the overall direction of the mission to Arnold Amaury, the abbot of Cîteaux. But significantly, the prelatical style of the Cistercian abbots failed to make much impression on the sectaries, whose leaders – the *perfecti* – were conspicuous for their asceticism and voluntary poverty, as well as for their skill in debate. Before the end of the thirteenth century, much that was distinctive in the Cistercian vocation had been lost. In its heyday it had summoned the aristocracy and the intellectual élite of Europe to a new spiritual adventure. But the compromises that followed in the train of wealth and influence made the voice less compelling. A new European intelligentsia was emerging, and it looked to other forms of religious life for the fulfilment of its ideals.

Notes

1. There has been much scholarly debate about the original form of the Cistercian documents since the classical edition of the texts by P. Guignard, *Les monuments primitifs de la règle cistercienne* (Dijon, 1878). The text of the *Exordium* was reedited by J. de la Croix Bouton and J. B. Van Damme in *Les plus anciens textes de Cîteaux: Commentarii Cistercienses Studia et Documenta* II (Achel, 1974). A good summary of the critical problems, with bibliographical references, will be found in C. Waddell, 'The *Exordium Cistercii* and the *Summa Cartae Caritatis*' in *Cistercian Ideals and Reality*, ed. J. R. Sommerfeldt (Kalamazoo, Michigan, 1978), pp. 30–61. For general accounts of the order see L. J. Lekai, *The White Monks* (Okauchea, Wisconsin, 1953); M. D. Knowles, *The Monastic Order in England* (1940), pp. 209–26; D. H. Williams, *The Cistercians in the Early Middle Ages* (1998), which contains a comprehensive bibliography.
2. See J. Leclercq, 'The intentions of the founders of the Cistercian Order' in *The Cistercian Spirit*, ed. M. B. Pennington (Shannon, 1970), pp. 88–133.
3. *PL* 203, 87D. See on this theme Giles Constable, 'Renewal and Reform in religious life' in *Renaissance and Renewal in the Twelfth Century*, ed. R. Benson and G. Constable (1982), pp. 37–67.
4. *The Letters of Peter the Venerable*, ed. G. Constable (Cambridge, Mass., 1967) I, p. 57.
5. On the aesthetics of Cistercian architecture see P. Fergusson, *The Architecture of Solitude* (Princeton, 1984).
6. *Exordium Parvum, op. cit.*, p. 77.
7. See the interesting discussion of this point by C. J. Holdsworth, 'The blessings of work: the Cistercian view' in *Sanctity and Secularity*, ed. D. Baker (*Studies in Church History* 10, 1973), pp. 59–76.
8. Early versions of *Usus Conversorum*, the lay brothers' customary, do not regard them as monks, restricting the term 'monk' to the choir monks: J. A. Lefèvre, 'Les traditions manuscrits des *Usus Conversorum*', *Collectanea Ordinis Cisterciensium Reformatorum* 17 (1955), pp. 85–97.
9. On the large number of *conversi* at Cluny in the time of St Hugh see W. Teske, 'Bernardus und Jocerranus als Mönche von Cluny' in *Beiträge zur Geschichte der Konversen im Mittelalter* (*Berliner Historische Studien* 2, 1980), pp. 9–24.
10. *The Life of Ailred of Rievaulx by Walter Daniel*, ed. F. M. Powicke (1950), p. 38.
11. M. Toepfer, *Die Konversen der Zisterzienser. Untersuchungen über Ihren Beitrag zur mittelalterlichen Blüte des Ordens* (Berlin, 1983), pp. 53–4, who finds a few bourgeois and landowners among the *conversi* of the German abbeys at the end of the twelfth century. The origin and function of the *conversi* have been the subject of much discussion, see the basic investigation of K. Hallinger, 'Woher kommen die Laienbrüder?' in *ASOC* 12 (Rome 1956), pp. 1–104; and J. Dubois, 'L'institution des convers au XIIᵉ siècle. Forme de vie monastique propre aux laïcs', *I Laici nella Societas Christiana dei Secoli XI e XII* in *Miscellanea del Centro di Studi Medievali* 5 (Milan, 1968), pp. 183–261.
12. Colin Platt, *The Monastic Grange in Medieval England* (1969); Williams, *op. cit.*, pp. 276–92.
13. The *Usus Conversorum* decrees that from September until Maundy Thursday those *conversi* sleeping in the abbey are to be woken by the bell in time to attend the second and third nocturns of Matins; in the summer months, as they have no siesta, they only rise in time for the dawn office of Lauds. At the day hours, they recite prayers at their workplace: Guignard, *op. cit.*, p. 279. An ordinance in the Refectorer's accounts for Beaulieu Abbey records that the *conversi* resided in the abbey on 87 days of the year, including days for bleeding every quarter: *The Account-Book of Beaulieu Abbey*, ed. S. F. Hockey (1975), pp. 144–45.
14. *Dialogus Miraculorum*, ed. J. Strange (Cologne, 1851), i, p. 24.

15. This was one of many stories of the heroic age of the order collected by Conrad of Eberbach in his *Magnum Exordium*, ed. B. Griesser, *Series Scriptorum S. Ordinis Cisterciensis* II (Rome, 1961), pp. 243–4.

16. Strange, *op. cit.*, i, p. 340.

17. Simone Roisin, *L'hagiographie cistercienne dans le diocèse de Liège au XIIIe siècle* (Louvain, 1947), pp. 28–72.

18. Strange, *op. cit.*, ii, p. 15.

19. Guignard, *op. cit.*, p. 272. The minimum age for admission was subsequently raised to eighteen.

20. *Magnum Exordium*, p. 79.

21. The expansion in terms of filiations is shown by the *Atlas de l'Ordre Cistercien* of F. Van der Meer (Paris and Brussels, 1965). For the statistics, correcting previous calculations, see the article by F. Vongrey and F. Hervay, 'Notes critiques sur l'Atias de l'Ordre Cistercien' in *ASOC* 23 (1967), pp. 115–52. The figures for the women's houses are less sure than those for the men's because the status and observance of some nunneries are difficult to establish.

22. *Vita Prima, PL* 185, 250. For modern studies of St Bernard see *Mélanges Saint Bernard: XXIVe Congrès de l'Association Bourguignonne des Sociétés Savantes* (Dijon, 1953); A. H. Bredero, 'Études sur la *Vita Prima de Saint Bernard, ASOC* 17 (1961), 18 (1962); G. R Evans, *The Mind of St Bernard of Clairvaux* (1983).

23. *S. Bernardi Opera* VII, ed. J. Leclercq and H. Rochais (Rome, 1974), pp. 261–3.

24. *Sermo XXII, PL* 183, 595; cited by M. H. Vicaire, *L'imitation des apôtres. Moines, chanoines et mendiants, IVe–XIIIe siècles* (Paris, 1963), p. 30.

25. T. F. Crane, *The Exempla of Jacques de Vitry* (1890), p. 12; cf. C. H. Haskins, *Studies in Medieval Culture* (1929), p. 50. For other university sermons on the same theme see, for example, *Les sermons universitaires parisiens de 1230–31*, ed. M. M. Davy (Paris, 1931), pp. 292, 295.

26. C. H. Lawrence, *St Edmund of Abingdon: A Study in Hagiography and History* (1960), p. 251.

27. *Epistolae, PL* 182, 414.

28. The text of the 'vulgate' or commonly received version is given in *Statuta Capitulorum Generalium Ordinis Cisterciensis*, ed. J. Canivez I (Louvain, 1933), pp. xxvi–xxxi. A text of the alleged early version, the *Carta Caritatis Prior*, was edited by J. de la Croix Bouton and J. B. Van Damme in *Les plus anciens textes de Cîteaux, op. cit.*, ii, pp. 132–42. For an English translation of the 'vulgate' version see D. Douglas and W. Greenaway, *English Historical Documents* II (1953), pp. 687–91. For discussion of the textual problem see M. D. Knowles, *Great Historical Enterprises and Problems in Monastic History* (1963), pp. 197–222; P. Zakar, 'Die Anfange des Zisterzienserordens', *ASOC* 20 (1964), pp. 103–38; C. Waddell in *Cistercian Ideals and Reality* (1978), pp. 30–61.

29. See comments of J. B. Van Damme, 'Les pouvoirs de l'Abbé de Cîteaux aux XIIe et XIIIe siècles', *ASOC* 20 (1964), pp. 47–85.

30. M. D. Knowles, C. N. L. Brooke and Vera London, *Heads of Religious Houses in England and Wales 940–1216* (1972), p. 136.

31. C. H. Lawrence, 'Stephen of Lexington and Cistercian university studies in the thirteenth century', *JEH* 11 (1960), pp. 164–78.

32. The best account of the workings of the general chapter is that of J. B. Mahn, *L'Ordre cistercien et son gouvernement* (Paris, 1951). The chapter acts were edited by J. Canivez, see n. 28 above.

33. It has been estimated that the chapter-house at Cîteaux after the rebuilding of 1193 had accommodation for about 300: L. J. Lekai in *Cistercian Ideals and Reality, op. cit.*, p. 20.

34. C. H. Talbot, 'Cîteaux and Scarborough', *Studia Monastica* 2 (1960).

35. Canivez I, *op. cit.*, p. 61.

36. *Ibid.*, pp. 62, 84, 264.

37. *Ibid.*, pp. 70, 91.

38. See on this question G. Constable, *Monastic Tithes from their Origins to the Twelfth Century* (1964).

39. R. A. Donkin, 'Settlement and depopulation on Cistercian estates during the twelfth and thirteenth centuries', *Bulletin of the Institute of Historical Research* 33 (1960), pp. 141–65.

40. The general chapter authorised the retention of such properties in 1153: Canivez I, pp. 43–5, 51–2; see discussion by L. J. Lekai in *Cistercian Ideals and Reality, op. cit.*, pp. 4–26.

41. R. Fossier, 'La vie économique de l'abbaye de Clairvaux 1115–1471', *École des Chartes, Positions des théses* (Paris, 1949), pp. 57–63.

42. S. F. Hockey, *Quarr Abbey and its Lands* (1970), pp. 72–94. C. H. Holdsworth remarks on the same trend towards leasing lands and acquiring serfs in *Rufford Charters* I (Thoroton Society, 1972), pp. xxxiii–lxxix.

43. *Sibton Abbey Cartularies and Charters*, ed. Philippa Brown (Suffolk Record Society, 1985), pp. 121–2; cf. R. A. Donkin, 'The urban property of the Cistercians in Medieval England', *ASOC* 15 (1959), pp. 104–31.

44. Canivez II, *op. cit.*, p. 21.

45. A. O. Johnson and Peter King, *The Tax Book of the Cistercian Order* (Oslo and Bergen, 1979), pp. 22–8; Peter King, *The Finances of the Cistercians* (Kalamazoo, Cistercian Publications 85, 1985).

46. *Registrum Epistolarum Stephani de Lexinton*, ed. B. Griesser, *ASOC* 2 (1946), pp. 45–8.

47. C. H. Lawrence, 'Stephen of Lexington', *op. cit.*, P. Dautrey, 'Croissance et adaptation chez les cisterciens au treizième siécle: les débuts du collège des Bernardins de Paris', *ASOC* 32 (1976), pp. 122–98.

48. *Chronica Villariensis Monasterii*, ed. G. Waitz, *MGH SS* XXV, p. 208; cited by E. de Moreau, *L'Abbaye de Villers-en-Brabant aux XIIe et XIIIe siècles* (Brussels, 1909), pp. 116–17.

49. J. Richard, *Saint Louis, roi d'une France féodale* (Paris, 1983), pp. 148–9.

10

THE NEW MONASTICISM VERSUS THE OLD

The simple austerity of the early Cistercian observance and the fervour of its evangelists, combined with a dynamic central organisation, brought the order spectacular success. But the success was won at a price and brought its own penalties. Traditionalists felt threatened by the widespread acclaim accorded the white monks. The Cistercian claim to have revived the pure and undiluted observance of the Benedictine Rule implied an unfavourable judgement upon the religious life-style of the Cluniacs and other black monks; and there were enthusiasts in the new order who were eager to throw stones at Cluny and all it stood for. Smouldering resentment towards the revivalists, and wounded *amour propre*, were inflamed by the flight of recruits from one organisation to the other.

Partisans on both sides, reformers or traditionalists, gleefully capitalised on such converts, some of whom travelled in both directions before finally setting down. One of these was Amadeus of Clermont, the lord of Hautrives, who entered the Cistercian abbey of Bonnevaux with his son; but finding the work regime too harsh and the education of his son neglected, he deserted and went to Cluny. But there, says his Cistercian biographer with a whoop of triumph, he was stricken with remorse over the delicate food he was offered and the gorgeous mass vestments made of silk and studded with gems: 'Alas, alas, what have I done? With such things as these did Dives abound who, as Scripture testifies, is buried in hell.' So he tore off his vestments and fled.[1]

St Bernard and Peter the Venerable

It was one such defection that was the signal for the outbreak of the famous controversy between the Cistercians and the Cluniacs. The opening salvos took the form of literary exchanges between St Bernard and Peter the Venerable; but others joined the debate, which continued to rumble for the rest of the twelfth century. Essentially, it was a confrontation between the ideals of the new monasticism and the unyielding traditions of the old. The fugitive whose departure lit the fuse was Bernard's young cousin, Robert of Châtillon. The lad had been recruited to Clairvaux, but finding the life too hard, had quitted the abbey during Bernard's absence and gone to Cluny, where he was made welcome. About the year 1120 Bernard wrote him a letter which was at once an impassioned appeal to return to the fold and a scathing indictment of Cluniac practice. Like all such letters of that period, it was intended for a wider readership than that of the immediate recipient. It was in fact a polemical tract, designed to publicise the case of the reformers against Cluny, and that in the most offensive terms. The credulous boy, he suggests, had been deceived. 'The preacher of a new Gospel entices him; he commends gluttonous feasting; he damns frugality; voluntary poverty he calls misery; fasting, vigils, silence and manual work he calls madness . . . He is led to Cluny, is cropped, shaved and washed; the dirty peasant clothes are taken off, and he dons precious new garments, and he is received into the community with how much honour and triumph . . . O good Jesu, how much is done to encompass the perdition of one little soul!'[2]

The chronology of the ensuing debate is not entirely clear. The major manifesto on the Cistercian side was St Bernard's *Apologia*, which appeared in 1125.[3] Composed at the suggestion of William of Saint-Thierry, an abbot and sympathiser who was later to join the Cistercian camp, its avowed purpose was to rebut the charge that the white monks were denigrating Cluny. As a polemical tract it is a masterpiece, written with rhetorical artistry, immense verve and controlled passion. Bernard begins with a disarming avowal of his admiration for Cluny. But then, while pretending to rebuke the uncharity of his own monastic brethren who snipe at Cluny, he places in their mouths arguments in their own defence which expose everything he regarded as most reprehensible in the Cluniac observance: the excess of food and drink and its ridiculous delicacy, the well-made and expensive clothes and the precious bed-covers, the pomp of abbots riding abroad with huge retinues, the vast churches of the order and the extravagance of their ornaments. In short, it appeared that Cluny was not faithful to either the letter or the spirit of the Benedictine Rule.

It would, of course, be a mistake to accept Bernard's invective as a literal description of life at Cluny. With some justice it has been categorised as a caricature.[4] Paradoxically, a more comprehensive and sober summary of the Cistercian case is to be found in a famous letter Peter the Venerable wrote to rebut the charges.[5] This makes no reference to Bernard's *Apologia*, and it is not clear whether Peter wrote before or after Bernard's tract. He, too, was well versed in the ancient art of rhetoric, and he adopted the classical dodge of seeming at the outset to side with his opponent. Thus he sets out the case for the prosecution before embarking on its refutation.

The curious thing about Peter's letter is that he states the charges of his opponents more effectively than he answers them. Most of his replies tacitly admit the substance of the accusations, while resorting to unashamed special pleading in order to parry them. For instance, to the charge that Cluny broke the Rule by practically dispensing with the noviciate and admitting postulants to membership of the monastic community with the minimum delay, he appeals to the example of Christ when he called the disciples: 'When Our Lord said to them "come follow me", did he stipulate that they should delay their conversion for a year? Should we obey the Rule of St Benedict and deny the Gospel?' In reply to the objection that Cluny had abandoned the manual work prescribed by the Rule, he invokes the underlying intention of St Benedict's admonition, which was to forestall the dangers of idleness. The Cluniac brethren, he argues, fulfil the spirit of the command by other kinds of work – by prayer, reading and added psalmody: 'are only rustic works acceptable to God? If corporal works are preferred to spiritual works, Mary (the model for contemplatives) would not have chosen to sit at the Lord's feet listening to him and allowed her sister Martha to do the serving on her own.'[6]

Other charges are met by equally unconvincing answers. His adversary's objections to the high quality of the food and the wide choice of dishes available to the monks of Cluny are not met by denial; they are circumvented by appealing to a general discretion that the Rule allows the abbot to vary the recommended diet to obviate harshness or discontent. As to their right to possess the tithes and offerings of parish churches which, as Bernard pointed out, were intended to support the clergy engaged in the pastoral care, canon law rightly permitted the appropriation of parish churches to monasteries, for monks also served the faithful by their prayers, psalms, tears and almsgiving. Indeed, adds Peter with a sideways swipe at the secular clergy, monks possess these things more justly, for many clerks were now to be seen neglecting their spiritual duties and the salvation of their flocks in order to pursue temporal gain.[7]

The speciousness of these arguments is all the more striking because it stands out in marked contrast to the cogency and clarity with which Peter expounds the opposition case. He sounds like an unhappy barrister who is less than fully convinced of his client's honesty. The reason for this apparent malaise is not far to seek. As head of the Cluniac empire, he felt bound to defend its reputation. But at heart, humanist though he was, he was a man of the new monastic era. He understood the fresh winds that were stirring the complacency of the monastic world. He appreciated the eremitical life, he admired the Chartreuse, and he sympathised with the ascetical ideals of the reformers.

The clearest evidence that in his inmost self Peter acknowledged the case of the reformers is to be found in the changes he endeavoured to introduce at Cluny. He embarked on the programme soon after he assumed the abbacy. In 1132, a few years after his first exchange with Bernard, he summoned a chapter of some two hundred priors of the congregation to consider proposals for greater austerity. These and subsequent ordinances, of which he compiled a list in 1146,[8] restored a stricter regime of fasting and abstinence from meat, forbade expensive indulgence in clothing and bed-covers, extended periods of silence, and excluded secular clerks and lay people from the cloister. The reasons he gives for these changes tacitly concede the substance of some of Bernard's charges. But Peter had probably been moved to pursue reform not so much by the Cistercian polemic as by his own inner conviction and by similar initiatives taken by other reformers among the black monks.

Many of the changes related to trivial matters, such as the banning of animal fat for cooking vegetables on Fridays. Taken as a whole, they suggest that there had been some degree of relaxation at Cluny in the time of St Hugh, but they hardly justify Bernard's colourful descriptions of high living. On one of the more significant issues that Bernard had raised, Peter compromised. He recognised that the one-year noviciate prescribed by the Rule had been reduced to as little as a week, and that as a consequence many unsuitable people had been admitted. But rather than reinstating the year of probation, he settled for a compulsory noviciate of one month before a monk was admitted to profession. Possibly the compromise was dictated by the poor state of his abbey's finances: the day of a recruit's profession was a time of gifts.

Peter's efforts to harden the ascetical regime at Cluny met with some internal resistance. Ordericus Vitalis, the chronicler, attended the chapter of 1132 and recorded his disapproval. He had been dispatched by his parents to Saint-Evroul as a tearful child of ten, had spent his life in the cloister and grown old in the established ways. He saw the new proposals as an attempt to rival the Cistercians and other 'seekers after novelties'. When in writing his chronicle he came to describe the secession of the reformers from Molesme, he let the opponents of the move speak for those like himself who clung to the conventional interpretation of the Benedictine Rule: 'We prefer the well trodden paths. Why should we be driven into the deserts of Paul and Antony? St Benedict sent St Maur to Gaul to introduce the Rule . . . he did not introduce the customs of Egypt. St Benedict says that all things are to be done with moderation.'[9] Many would-be reformers met with similar resistance from their brethren, and even with violence. As Abbot Suger observed over the efforts to reform Sainte-Geneviève at Paris, 'irregular canons will never consent to become regular canons except by force'.[10]

Reformers and traditionalists

Behind the wrangling over the interpretation of the Rule lurked a deeper confrontation between the traditional monasticism, with its relatively humane and gentle ascesis, its elaborate liturgical rituals, and its manysided involvement in the society and public life of its time, and on the other hand the more austere spirit of the new orders, which drew their inspiration from the primitive desert tradition and sought to institutionalise the quest for poverty, of which manual labour was the symbol, simplicity, and detachment from the outside world. These ascetical ideals inspired the Premonstratensians, the Grandmontines, the disciples of Stephen of Obazine, and the more austere congregations of canons regular, as well as the Cistercians.

The spirit of the new monasticism was incapsulated in a widely circulated letter of William of Saint-Thierry. The letter was addressed to the Carthusians of Mont-Dieu, where William had been a guest. In them he believed he had discovered 'the perfection of the Christian religion that seemed closest to heaven, which had perished from the world but had now been found again'. He recognised in their life-style the model of the Fathers of the Thebaid, who made themselves simple cells, where they occupied themselves with contemplation, in profound poverty (*altissima paupertas*), silence, and total seclusion from mankind. He urged them to persist in their imitation of the Fathers by working with their hands – not to sustain the body, but to preserve their spiritual fervour. They should not be discouraged by those who cavilled at the novelty of their observance (the only hint of asperity in William's discourse), for they have renewed the life-style of the primitive Church.[11]

The smoke thrown up by the polemics can easily obscure the fact that the propagandists of the reformed monasticism shared with their more traditionalist opponents a large area of common ground.[12] Both parties held that the monastic life lived in faithfulness to the Rule represented the most perfect realisation of the Christian ideal. William's manifesto for the eremitical life was copied and read in Cluniac as well as Cistercian houses. Many of the leading spirits among the black monks were moved by the appeal to the model of the primitive Church and recognised the need for a more austere observance. It was in response to this appeal that in 1131 abbots of the black monks in the province of Reims convened a general chapter to meet at Saint-Rémi in order to review their observance. There they ordained a series of regulations bearing on silence in the cloister, the period of the monastic fast, abstinence from meat, and the curtailment of additions to the divine office in the interests of a slower and more devout performance. They also proposed to hold regular annual meetings to ensure that these new standards were maintained.[13]

Their efforts at reform upset traditionalists and drew a remonstrance from the papal legate, Cardinal Matthew of Albano. Matthew was himself a Cluniac monk. He had been prior of Saint-Martin-des-Champs at Paris before Pope Honorius II raised him to the purple, and under his regime the house had been noted for its strict observance as well as for its generous hospitality to the outside world.[14] In his letter to the abbots of Reims he applauded the zeal of the reformers, but he defended the customs of Cluny against these rigorist and ill-conceived demands: 'Moses shaved his hair in places, but you have not known how to shave superfluity; you have performed a radical amputation.'[15] As a Cluniac he was passionately opposed to the proposed curtailments of the liturgy and objected to the imposition of almost perpetual silence – more restrictive, it seemed, than that imposed by the customs of the Charterhouse. The abbots, however, were unabashed and sent a barbed rejoinder: 'We profess we have vowed to obey the Rule of St Benedict, not the customs of Cluny. Whence is this new Gospel from the legate of the Apostolic See? This Gospel is indeed that of the lord Matthew, not that according to Matthew the Evangelist.'[16]

The controversy between the rigorists and the traditionalists outlived Matthew and St Bernard, but some of the passion went out of it after their time. Later tracts, like the famous *Dialogue* between a Cluniac and a Cistercian of the 1160s,[17] are couched in the more detached tones of academic debate. In practice, rivalry was softened by mutual appreciation and recognition of a common inheritance. This fact is attested by the records of confraternity. Arrangements made between monastic communities to provide liturgical commemoration for one another's members on death frequently ignored institutional boundaries. In the time of Peter the Venerable, both Cistercian and Carthusian communities entered into confraternity with Cluny, indicating that even in reformist circles a value was placed upon Cluniac intercession.[18] Forty-two years after Peter's death, Cluniac observance was given a striking testimonial from St Hugh the Carthusian, then bishop of Lincoln. On his way to revisit the Grande Chartreuse, Hugh broke his journey at Cluny and spent three days with the community. His biographer, Adam of Eynsham, reported his enthusiastic approval of all that he found there: 'Truly, if I had seen this place before I had fallen in love with the Chartreuse, I should have become a Cluniac monk.'[19]

In time the legitimacy of individual migrations from the traditional houses of the black monks to one of the more austere new orders was recognised by authority and embodied in canon law. A decretal of Pope Innocent III, authorising a monk of Durham cathedral priory to transfer himself to Cîteaux, stated once and for all the principle that a monk could be released by his own monastery provided that the reason for his leaving was his desire to join a stricter order (*ordo arctior*).[20] This rule was obviously open to interpretation, but it was mostly invoked to justify a transfer to the Cistercians or the Carthusians.

Occasionally, a transfer from an easier-going establishment to the Carthusians was imposed upon an individual by higher authority as a punishment for a grave offence. In 1238 the prior of Canterbury Cathedral priory was disciplined in this way by the visiting papal legate on account of his involvement in the forgery of a privilege that St Thomas Becket was alleged to have granted the priory.[21] In this case the cardinal legate was using the Charterhouse as a penitentiary. Behind Pope Innocent's edict of permission lay eighty years of contention over the migration of discontented individuals. The debate between the reformers and the traditionalists gradually flagged and faded away because developments on the Cistercian side, as well as intransigeance on the other, deprived it of any meaning. In the following century, the claims of rival monastic groups to be the authentic exemplification of the apostolic life were subjected to a new and more radical challenge by the orders of mendicant friars.

Notes

1. M.-A. Dimier, 'Un témoin tardif peu connu du conflit entre cisterciens et clunisiens' in *Petrus Venembilis 1156–1956: Studies and Texts Commemorating the Eighth Centenary of his death*, ed. G. Constable and J. Kritzeck (Rome, 1956), p. 93. For an account of the controversy see A. H. Bredero, 'The controversy between Peter the Venerable and Saint Bernard of Clairvaux', *ibid.*, pp. 53–71, and *Cluny et Cîteaux au XIIᵉ siècle* (Amsterdam, 1985); M. D. Knowles, *The Historian and Character* (1963), pp. 50–75.
2. *S. Bernardi Opera* vii, pp. 1–11.
3. *Ibid.*, iii, pp. 63–108. For an English translation M. Casey, *Cistercians and Cluniacs: St Bernard's Apologia to Abbot William*, with excellent introduction by Jean Leclercq (Kalamazoo, Michigan, 1970).
4. Leclercq, *ibid.*, p. 25.
5. *The Letters of Peter the Venerable*, ed. G. Constable (Cambridge, MA., 1967), i, pp. 52–101.
6. *Ibid.*, pp. 70–1.
7. *Ibid.*, pp. 81–2.
8. *Petri Venerabilis Statuta*, ed. G. Constable, J. D. Brady and D. C. Waddell in *CCM* VI (1975), pp. 21–106. See G. Constable, 'The monastic policy of Peter the Venerable', *Colloques internationaux du Centre National de la Recherche Scientifique*, No. 546 (Paris, 1975), pp. 120–42.
9. *The Ecclesiastical History of Ordericus Vitalis*, ed. M. Chibnall, iv (1973), p. 313.
10. *Oeuvres Complètes de Suger*, ed. Lecoy de la Marche (Paris, 1865), p. 255, cited by G. Constable, *The Reformation of the Twelfth Century* (1996), p. 112. As abbot and rebuilder of Saint-Denis, Suger was conversant with the ideals of the reformers and was a benefactor to a number of Cistercian and Premonstratensian foundations: Lindy Grant, *Abbot Suger of St-Denis* (1998), pp. 185–90.
11. *Un traité de la vie solitaire*, ed. M.-M. Davy: *Études de Philosophie Médiévale* (Paris, 1940), pp. 72, 73, 117.
12. A point emphasised by Constable, *The Reformation of the Twelfth Century*, pp. 135–6.
13. A summary of the ordinances of 1131 and the ensuing letters between the abbots and Matthew of Albano were printed by U. Berlière, *Documents inédits pour servir à l'histoire ecclésiastique de la Belgique* I (Maredsous, 1894), pp. 91–110.
14. U. Berlière, 'Le cardinal Mattieu d'Albano', *Rev. bén* 18 (1901), pp. 113–40, 280–303. On his hospitality at Saint-Martin-des-Champs see *PL* clxxxix, 920.
15. Berlière, *Documents*, p. 100.
16. *Ibid.*, p. 107.
17. For this and other treatises of the kind see A. Wilmart, 'Une riposte de l'ancien monachisme au manifeste de Saint Bernard', *Rev. bén* 46 (1934), pp. 296–305; Watkin Williams, *Monastic Studies* (1938), pp. 61–74.
18. As pointed out by Constable, *The Reformation of the Twelfth Century*, pp. 170–1, who observes that the disciplined life of Cluny and its prestige 'made it seem as a rival rather than an opponent to the reformers'.
19. *Magna Vita Sancti Hugonis*, ed. Decima Douie and Hugh Farmer (1961–2), ii, p. 175.
20. *c.18. X iii, 31*. See comment of Berlière, 'Innocent III et les monastères bénédictins', *Rev. bén.* 32 (1920), p. 35.
21. C. H. Lawrence, *St Edmund of Abingdon: A Study of Hagiography and History* (1960), p. 163.

11

A NEW KIND OF KNIGHTHOOD

Of all the new forms of monastic life that emerged from the religious ferment of the twelfth century none was more original or seemingly more paradoxical than that of the Military Orders. These were orders of knights, dedicated to fighting the infidel, who were also fully professed monks. They look like a contradiction in terms. Admittedly, ascetical writers were much given to using military imagery, but the warfare they referred to was spiritual combat, not the warfare of this world. Monks and clergy were forbidden by the canons to have any part in the shedding of blood. How could fighting and killing with carnal weapons be reconciled with the Gospel of peace and love? Professionally, the monk and the warrior stood at opposite poles. The reconciliation of these incompatible occupations in the orders of fighting monks can only be understood in the context of the crusading movement from which they sprang.

The scruples of the early Church on the subject of warfare continued to haunt the minds of medieval moralists and left their mark on the penitentials. In a fallen world the profession of arms might be necessary, but it was dangerous to the soul. Although it was lawful in certain conditions for a Christian to engage in warfare, the individual who did so was not exonerated from the moral guilt of killing his enemies. He had still committed a sin that called for repentance and satisfaction. Burchard of Worms, the eleventh-century canonist, devotes a whole chapter of his Decretum to the penances appropriate to 'those who commit homicide in a public war'.[1] The traditional tariff required the performance of three Lents – three periods of penance each lasting forty days – for every victim the penitent had slain. Thus, despite the fact that William the Conqueror had obtained the prior approval of the pope for his invasion of England, the year after the battle of Hastings a papal legate arrived and imposed carefully graduated penances on all the Norman and Breton knights who had fought in the battle.

What made possible the creation of hybrid institutions like the Military Orders was the lifting of this sinful stigma from prowess in arms. Such a change in attitude was in fact brought about in the course of the eleventh century by the emergence of a new ideal of Christian knighthood. The status of the knight was gradually transmogrified: from being a professional hit-man operating on the edge of the moral law, he was slowly transformed by ecclesiastical thinking into a Christian warrior fighting in the service of the Church, a champion of the defenceless against the unbridled power of the wicked. We can see the genesis of this change already in tenth-century liturgical formulas for the blessing of warriors and their weapons.[2] It derived impetus too from the early peace movements, like the Peace of God, which were encouraged by the Cluniacs. These were attempts to limit the destructiveness of private warfare by persuading members of the knightly class to observe certain codes of conduct towards non-combatants and to defend the property of churches. Popes of the eleventh-century reform, from Leo IX to Gregory VII, refined the idea of chivalry by offering spiritual privileges to those who used their arms in defence of St Peter and his successors in the see of Rome. But the decisive agency in bringing about the change was the First Crusade.

In a sermon preached at Clermont on 18 November 1095, Pope Urban II summoned the chivalry of France to an armed pilgrimage in order to rescue Jersusalem and the other Holy Places from the hands of the infidel. And to all who participated in the enterprise he offered an indulgence – a remission, that is, of the canonical penance due for their sins. Although the precise terms of this indulgence are uncertain, there can be no doubt about the interpretation placed upon crusading indulgences by the theologians and canonists of the twelfth century: they sanctioned the principle of a holy war. In such a war, killing an enemy, provided he was an infidel, was not a materially sinful act requiring penance; on the contrary, it was a positively meritorious act, which remitted the temporal punishment due for sin. Death in such a war carried the rewards of martyrdom. 'The knight of Christ need fear no sin in killing the foe,' wrote St Bernard: 'he is the minister of God for the punishment of the wicked. In the death of a pagan a Christian is glorified, because Christ is glorified.'[3]

The crusading indulgence represented a landmark in the medieval theory of Christian warfare. It proposed a new vocation of Christian knighthood. It diverted the aggressive and acquisitive instincts of the military aristocracy into a holy war against Islam; and in so doing it sanctified the profession of arms. The Military Orders – the societies of ascetical warriors or monk-knights – were the product of this crusading ethos. They were professionally dedicated to the holy war; and in them Christian knighthood found its apotheosis. They offered knights and sons of the baronage the fulfilment of their religious aspirations by becoming monks without having to abandon their zest for physical activity or their skills in mounted warfare. St Bernard, who presided at their inception, saw in them the ideal means of salvation for those laymen who showed no aptitude for the traditional type of monastic life.

The Templars

Although the Order of Hospitallers had a longer pre-history, the Knights of the Temple were the first to be constituted as a Military Order. They were called into existence by the needs of the Latin Kingdom of Jerusalem. Thanks largely to divisions among the rulers of the Muslim states in the Middle East, the First Crusade had ended in spectacular success. In 1099, after capturing Antioch, the Franks stormed Jerusalem. In the wake of the army, the leaders of the contingents created a group of Frankish principalities; and in the following twenty years these territories were extended by further conquests.

Yet the Latin Kingdom and its satellite principalities of Antioch, Tripoli and Edessa maintained only a tenuous foothold on the fringe of the Muslim world. They were subjected to periodic attacks of mounting weight, and they suffered from a chronic shortage of manpower. At the end of the campaign many crusaders returned home, and later crusades did little to replenish the Frankish settler population. The majority of pilgrims to the Holy Land were also birds of passage. It was the inability of the settler population to police the roads and protect pilgrims from brigands and Muslim raiders that persuaded a knight of Champagne, Hugh de Payns, to form a standing militia for the purpose. Towards the end of the year 1119 he and eight other companions of the same class, who were residing at Jerusalem, formed themselves into a religious society for the purpose of defending pilgrims *en route* to the holy places. King Baldwin II of Jerusalem, evidently perceiving the potential value of this small association, took them under his wing and assigned them quarters in the royal palace adjacent to the Dome of the Rock, known to the Franks as the Temple of the Lord.

Hugh de Payns seems to have conceived from the outset that his group of knights would be soldier-monks.[4] They took vows of chastity and obedience, followed some form of community life, and assisted at the divine office sung by the canons regular who served the church of the Holy Sepulchre. The plan was an intelligible development of crusading ideology; for the crusade was a pilgrimage. In the early stages of the movement it may have offered alluring prospects of plunder and territorial gain to some of the participants; but to others, and to the churchmen who preached it, the rewards it offered were primarily spiritual ones. It was an ascetical exercise, a supreme act of self-denial, which rendered satisfaction for sins. The privations and dangers of the long journey across hostile territory were to be endured in a spirit of mortification. Battles and sieges were preceded and accompanied by prayer and fasting. It was in fact a form of penitential life, of limited duration, undertaken for the love of God.[5] Thus it realised, though in a different way, the essential principle of monasticism. To give it permanent institutional form in a special monastic order involved bridging only a small mental gap.

In the autumn of 1127 then, Hugh de Payns sent to Rome to seek papal authorisation for this novel kind of monastic institution, while he himself set out for France to solicit donations and recruits. For official approval he was referred to a council of prelates which met at Troyes in January 1129, under the presidency of the papal legate, Cardinal Matthew of Albano.[6] The council approved the plan, and the composition of an appropriate rule was entrusted to St Bernard. The Rule of the Temple, as it emerged from Bernard's committee, clearly owes much to the Benedictine Rule, of which it contains verbal echoes, and also to the observances of the Cistercians. It bears traces, too, of the aggressive and elitist spirituality that is such a marked feature of the early Cistercian movement: 'If any knight out of the mass of human perdition wishes to renounce the world',[7] runs the formula for the reception of novices, echoing Bernard's invective against the gaudy panoply of secular knighthood.

The observance prescribed by the Rule is unremittingly monastic and cenobitic. The knights are bound by vows of personal poverty, chastity, and obedience. They are to dress soberly, to wear short hair, and to avoid all association with women – the white gown they wear is to be an outward sign of chastity. They sleep fully clothed in a common dormitory, and eat in a common refectory. They are to be present at the singing of Matins and all the canonical hours, but an exception is made for those away on active duty or tired out by their military activities; these are allowed to recite paternosters in place of the offices. It is apparent that, being laymen, they are expected only to hear the offices, not to sing them; that was to be the role of the clergy attached to the order. Similarly, the Rule makes no provision for individual reading. Instead, the brethren listen to a clerk reading to them at mealtimes and other assemblies. They are bound by the monastic regime of fasts and vigils, with relaxations made necessary by the demands of their military role: they eat twice daily, and meat is allowed three days a week. Another standard feature of the monastic timetable included with modification is the chapter of faults, which is to be held weekly on Sundays, wherever at least four of the brethren are residing together.[8]

Socially, the order reproduced the class structure of secular society. There were two classes of brethren – the knights who were recruited from the military aristocracy, and the sergeants, or serving men, of humbler origin. No postulant was acceptable into the ranks of the knights or was entitled to wear the white mantle unless he could prove his descent from a knightly or armigerous family. At the beginning, the brethren depended upon the canons regular or members of the secular clergy for liturgical and sacramental services. But after the order had gained official recognition, it recruited chaplains of its own, who were fully incorporated as ordained members. It also found employment in its houses for a growing workforce of cooks, servants and artisans.

At the outset, the attraction of recruits to such a novel kind of monastic vocation and the search for endowments required a special effort of propaganda. Hugh de Payns, in a letter written for the comfort of the brethren back at Jerusalem, refers to critics of their profession who question the legitimacy of an institution of warrior-monks – subtle tempters who urge the knights of Christ to lay down their arms.[9] It was in order to confound such critics and to publicise the new order that Bernard wrote one of his most powerful and emotional propaganda tracts – *In Praise of the New Knighthood*:[10] 'there is word abroad of a new kind of knighthood, arisen lately, one that fights flesh and blood as well as the spirits of wickedness in high places'. They dwell in the Temple of Solomon; and their way of life bears all the marks of evangelical perfection. 'How blessed are the martyrs who die in battle. Rejoice, brave athlete, if you live and conquer in the Lord; but exult and glory all the more if you should die and be united with the Lord.'

Enthusiasm for the crusading enterprise, to which Bernard appealed, and concern for the safety of the Latin Kingdom of Jerusalem brought the order a flood of donations and bequests from princes, prelates and lay landowners. The most spectacular gift came from Alfonso I of Aragon, who was eager to enlist the knights in the *reconquista* of the Iberian peninsula from its Muslim rulers. In his will of 1131, three years before his death, he bequeathed his entire kingdom jointly to the canons of the Holy Sepulchre, the Hospital at Jerusalem, and the Knights of the Temple.[11] Although other claimants to Alfonso's kingdom prevented his last will from being implemented, the settlement negotiated with his successors left the Templars with vast territorial possessions and castles in Aragon and Catalonia, and a tenth of the royal revenues. Thus within a few years of the Council of Troyes Hugh's small brotherhood grew into a large and wealthy international order. It received the ultimate seal of papal approval in the privilege *Omne datum optimum*, issued by Pope Innocent II in 1139.

The bull gave the order a privileged status. It was allowed its own oratories and burial grounds, it was exempted from payment of tithes from its lands, and it was removed from the jurisdiction of diocesan bishops and made directly subject to the pope. As it acquired estates, it erected houses and churches in the West; and by the middle of the twelfth century its constitution had been articulated. The head of the order was the Grand Master, to whom all the brethren took an oath of absolute obedience. He was elected by an electoral committee set up by a special meeting of the general chapter of the order. The lands and houses of the order were grouped in provinces, each of which was directed by a master and a commander. The individual house was called a preceptory, and its head a preceptor. Probably many of these preceptories, some of which have left no trace except a place-name, were of a quite modest size, housing only a handful of knights – not so much military establishments as depots for the management of estates and the transfer of the proceeds to the fighting brethren in the East.

The concept of an order of fighting monks, once it had gained acceptance and official blessing, proved infectious. Other orders of chivalry sprang up, inspired by the example of the Templars. In Spain and Portugal, where the reconquest of the peninsula from the Moors was a major political preoccupation of Christian rulers, the Orders of Calatrava and Alcantara were formed under royal patronage in the middle years of the twelfth century, and adopted many features of the Templars' observance. The Order of Santiago, created in Leon in 1170, was another spiritual stepchild of the Templars, though it differed from the model in being less a religious order than a pious confraternity of knights, whose members continued to live as married men.[12] The most illustrious contemporary and rival of the institute of the Temple, however, was the Order of Hospitallers, or Knights of St John of Jersusalem.

The Hospitallers

They began as a fraternity serving a hospice for poor and sick pilgrims at Jerusalem. Some twenty-five years before the launching of the First Crusade, a group of pious merchants of Amalfi had built, or perhaps simply restored, the Benedictine monastery of St Mary of the Latins on a site adjacent to the Holy Sepulchre. In order to provide for the increasing flow of pilgrims, the monks built a hospice, dedicated to St John the Baptist.[13] This was staffed by a fraternity whose members, like the monks, were Italians, and who took monastic vows. In 1099, when the crusaders took Jerusalem, the master of this establishment was an Italian, probably an Amalfitan, named Gerard, who was clearly an administrator of vision.

Gerard grasped the opportunities opened up by the Frankish conquest and settlement. He persuaded the first ruler of the Latin state, Godfrey of Lorraine, and his successor, King Baldwin I, to endow the Hospital with lands and city properties in the newly conquered territories. He also extended his organisation by establishing daughter-hospitals in, or close to, the ports of Italy and southern France, from which pilgrims embarked for the Holy Land. The brotherhood of the Hospital began now to attract substantial donations of land in Italy, Spain, and France. The Latin patriarch of Jerusalem, himself an Italian, granted it exemption from payment of tithes on its properties. And in 1113 Gerard succeeded in obtaining from Pope Paschal II a bull which recognised the Hospitallers as a distinct religious order, ruled by their own Master, and subject directly and solely to the jurisdiction of the pope.

The twelfth-century Rule of the Hospitallers, which cannot be dated with any certainty, drew its inspiration from the Rule of St Augustine; and the observances of the order were those of the canons regular. It was not at first a Military Order. It was primarily a charitable organisation devoted to the care of sick and indigent pilgrims. Its membership included both clerics and lay brethren, but not as yet professional warriors. The decision to undertake a military role was taken by Raymond du Puy, who succeeded Gerard as Master on the latter's death in 1118. As a Frenchman, Raymond cannot have been impervious to the example presented by the newly fledged Order of the Temple, created by the knighthood of Champagne. But what prevailed upon him to change course was apparently the military need of *Outremer*.

The Latin principalities suffered from a chronic shortage of manpower. There was urgent need to reinforce their defensive capability with a standing army of professionals. This was just the service that a Military Order, richly endowed and constantly attracting recruits of high quality from overseas, could provide. The Hospitallers were thus drawn into an active military role by the predicament of the society they were serving. This process seems to have begun in 1123, when a body of the brethren formed an emergency corps of mounted soldiers to help repel the Fatimid invasion from Egypt. After this, they were given an increasing number of military assignments alongside the Templars. They began to supply armed contingents for the king's campaigns, and they were called upon to garrison castles. In 1136 King Fulk entrusted them with the newly constructed castle of Bethgibelin, commanding the approach to the Muslim port of Ascalon; and Count Raymond of Tripoli gave them the great frontier fortress of Crak des Chevaliers to man. By 1180 the order possessed twenty-five castles in Palestine.

The reorientation of the order under Raymond du Puy meant adding to it a regular establishment of knights. It came to resemble the Templars in having a membership divided into knights, sergeants, and clerics, and a domestic labour force of hired servants. Like the Templars, too, the knights of the Hospital were lay monks, bound by vows of personal poverty, chastity and obedience. They lived a life in community, and followed the full monastic round of the choral offices, which were sung by the chaplains. Their distinctive badge was a white cross worn on the surcoat, corresponding to the red cross worn by the Templars. By the middle of the century, the order had acquired a network of establishments and vast estates in many parts of Europe. Its possessions were divided into provinces – called priories – and commanderies; and a substantial part of their yield was exported every year to support the fighting brethren in *Outremer.* The central government of the organisation, which was in the hands of the Grand Master, assisted by a prior and five senior officers, was located at Jerusalem until 1187. Following the disastrous defeat of Hattin by Saladin that year, and the subsequent collapse of the Latin Kingdom, the Hospital transferred its headquarters to the castle of Margat on the frontier of Tripoli.

Decline and fall

The Military Orders were products of the crusading movement of the twelfth and thirteenth centuries. They personified the aggressive thrust and self-confident expansion of Western Christendom. The Knights of the Temple and the Knights of St John found their identity as defenders of the Latin states in Syria against the counter-attack of Islam; and their fortunes inevitably waxed and waned with the rise and decline of *Outremer.* They had been born in the euphoria that accompanied and followed the First Crusade. The failure of later crusades to succour the Latin kingdom, culminating in the fall of Acre to the Mamluks in 1291, and widespread disillusionment with the crusading ideal, deprived them of their chief *raison d'être.* Their predicament was symbolised by the fact that the Grand Masters of both orders were fatally wounded during the defence of the city.

The débâcle left them exposed to the animosity of their critics, of whom they had acquired many. The Hospitallers gained a new lease of life by capturing the island of Rhodes from the Greeks in 1308, and making it their new headquarters. They had, in any case, never abandoned their more pacific task of maintaining and staffing hospitals, and this gave them a more lasting social role. The Templars suffered a less happy fate.

Through their extensive international organisation, which was engaged in the regular transfer of large sums of money to the East, the Templars had gained a subsidiary role as international bankers. They financed crusaders, made credit arrangements for travellers, and lent money to kings. They provided valuable banking facilities for the kings of both England and France. At London, the New Temple, which the order erected off the Strand, was used by the royal exchequer in the thirteenth century as a storehouse for the revenue; and the Temple at Paris discharged a similar function for the king of France. The military brethren not only offered strongholds for safe deposit; they also provided a kind of medieval Securicor service to guard monies in transit.

These services did nothing, however, to ingratiate the order with public opinion. Its corporate arrogance was notorious. Its exemption from all jurisdiction other than that of the pope alienated the ecclesiastical hierarchy and rendered it impervious to any form of secular control. Its vast territorial wealth made it a tempting prey to an indigent prince. When King Philip IV decided to plunder it in 1307, it found few friends to plead for it. Philip's destruction of the order was executed with an accomplished ruthlessness, cynicism and cruelty, that evoke a comparison with the worst villainies of the modern police state: the dawn swoop, the conditioning of the prisoners by threats and torture, the preposterous confessions extorted from the Grand Master and others, and the burning of those who retracted. A feeble attempt by Pope Clement V to set up an independent inquiry was brushed aside; and the approach of a royal army was sufficient to persuade the pope to issue a bull on 22 March 1312 declaring the order dissolved. A further papal mandate ordered its property to be transferred to the Hospitallers; but a significant share was retained by the French crown.[14]

Many factors contributed to the tragedy that overtook the Temple – the growth of royal absolutism, the weakness of the papacy, and not least, the irresponsible conduct of the Templars themselves. But in a sense they were the natural scapegoats for the collapse of the crusader states in the East, with whose destiny they had become identified. This did not mean, however, that Western society had rejected the ideal of the crusade. There was still work for a military order. The Knights of the Teutonic Order, which had been created in the Holy Land in the wake of the Third Crusade, found a new field for their activities in conquering the pagan Prussians and Lithuanians. After the fall of Acre, they transferred their headquarters first to Venice, and then to Marienburg on the Vistula, and established themselves as a major territorial power in eastern Europe.

Notes

1. *PL* 140, 770.

2. C. Erdmann, *Die Entstehung des Kreuzzugsgedankens* (Stuttgart, 1935), p. 73. This seminal work translated by M. W. Baldwin and W. Gofart, *The Origin of the Idea of Crusade* (Princeton, 1977), contains the fullest modern discussion of the changing ethic of warfare in the Middle Ages; but see the critique of J. Riley-Smith in *The First Crusade and the Idea of Crusading* (1986), pp. 1–30.

3. *De Laude Novae Militiae* in *S. Bernardi Opera*, ed. J. Leclercq, C. H. Talbot, and H. Rochais, III (Rome, 1959), p. 217.

4. G. de Valous, 'Quelques observations sur la toute primitive observance des Templiers' in *Mélanges Saint Bernard* (XXIVᵉ congrès de l'association bourguignonne des sociétés savantes, Dijon, 1953), pp. 32–40. The best account of the origins and organisation of the Templars is now that of Malcolm Barber, *The New Knighthood: A History of the Order of the Temple* (1994).

5. J. Riley-Smith, 'Crusading as an act of love', *History* LXV (1980), 177–92.

6. On the revised date and circumstances of the council see Barber, *op. cit.*, pp. 8–10, 13–20.

7. H. de Curzon, *La Règle du Temple* (Paris, 1886), c. 11, p. 23.

8. *Ibid., p. 215.*

9. J. Leclercq, 'Un document sur les débuts des Templiers', *Revue d'histoire ecclésiastique* LII (1957), pp. 81–90.

10. *S. Bernardi Opera* III, pp. 213–39.

11. Barber, *op. cit.*, pp. 27–31.

12. On the rise of the Spanish military orders see A. Forey, *The Military Orders from the Twelfth to the early Fourteenth Centuries* (1992).

13. For the origin and constitution of the Hospitallers the authoritative account is that of J. Riley-Smith, *The Knights of St John in Jerusalem and Cyprus 1050–1310* (1967).

14. The episode is admirably reconstructed by Malcolm Barber, *The Trial of The Templars* (1978).

12

SISTERS OR HANDMAIDS

Frauenfrage – the question of the sisters

'Finally,' wrote the twelfth-century canon of Liège, 'we shall return to women who lead the eremitical life, rising to be holy nuns, and to those who sweetly take up the yoke of Christ with holy men or under their guidance.'[1] But the promised supplement to his little book on *The Orders and Callings of the Church* was either never written or it has been lost. This is a pity, because the canon's views on the place of women in the monastic movement of his time would have been instructive, especially as he was based in Liège, where women played an unusually prominent part in the religious life of that period. Few woman wrote about it themselves, and this makes the mental world of the nunneries hard to penetrate. There was the rare prophetess, like St Hildegarde of Bingen, whose spiritual experience was transmitted from the Rhineland to other parts of Europe by means of a voluminous correspondance; but there is a dearth of the kind of narrative writing that tells us about the inner life of many of the men's establishments. For the most part, the experience of religious women of the Middle Ages is communicated to us by celibate males; and they were rarely adequate spokesmen.

The nunneries of the early Middle Ages not only offered women the chance to pursue the ascetical life; they attracted endowments because they performed an important social role in providing a haven for the daughters and widows of the aristocracy for whom no suitable marriage could be found. The women who entered them, and the families that placed them there, expected them to enjoy the society of their own kind. Many of them were thus aristocratic and socially exclusive communities. If girls of humbler origins were admitted at all, it was only in the capacity of servants. The superior of Remiremont priory in Lorraine decreed that before the nunnery accepted a girl of unknown lineage, three knights known to the convent must be asked to testify on oath that both her parents were the offspring of armigerous families above reproach.[2]

In any case, the need for a postulant to bring a dowry to support her in the religious life must have been an obstacle to recruiting women from landless families. The canonists accepted the propriety of the age-old custom by which a gift of property was offered to a monastery to help meet the cost of feeding and clothing a recruit; but to exact a gift as a condition of admission was simony. 'It is one thing to make a voluntary offering,' observes Gratian, 'it is another thing to pay an exaction.'[3] The Lateran Council of 1215 singled out nunneries as common offenders: 'the stain of simony has so infected many nuns that scarcely any are received as sisters without a price'.[4] Such depravity was to be punished by the expulsion of the offenders to do penance in a more austere order. Nevertheless, whatever the decretists said, many women's foundations of the eleventh and twelfth centuries were small and poorly endowed. They could not afford to accept new members unless they brought additional income with them, and the prohibition of gifts or contracts to secure admission proved impossible to enforce.[5]

Consequently, the majority of nuns came of aristocratic or knightly families. Hildegarde defended this exclusiveness, which was still a feature of most nunneries in the twelfth century: 'what man would keep his whole flock in a single pen? There should be discrimination; otherwise, if different people are congregated together, the flock may be rent asunder through the pride of those who are socially superior and the shame of those who are of a different class; for God differentiates between people both on earth and in heaven.'[6] This last observation was a rejoinder to an ingenuous remark by the abbess of Andernach that the Lord had chosen poor fishermen to found his Church, and that the Blessed Peter himself had confessed that God was no respecter of persons.

Where lists of those professed are available, research has revealed that a significant proportion of the inmates were either married women or widows.[7] Some of those who took the veil during the lifetime of their husbands were casualties of the matrimonial chess-game played by the aristocracy in pursuit of male offspring. Some were refugees from a marriage that had become intolerable. Others were wives of men who had entered a monastery themselves, having obtained the consent of their spouses. In most cases other than the last, a sense of vocation was probably not the primary motive for entering the religious life.

In the early Germanic world noblewomen enjoyed a higher political status and a greater power of disposing of themselves and their property than they came to possess at a later period. This relative independence was reflected in the masterful government of double monasteries by the royal abbesses of Merovingian Gaul and Anglo-Saxon England. They ruled both the men and the women of their communities with the self-assurance that was their birthright. But in the different world of the tenth and eleventh centuries the independence of women, both outside and inside the cloister, diminished. An aristocratic society, whose legal arrangements and modes of thought were conditioned by the military fief, reduced women to a strictly subordinate role. And the inferiority of their status was reinforced by the male chauvinism of the Latin Church. Not only sacramental acts but all ecclesiastical functions, including teaching, were confined to men. Had not the writer of the Epistle to Timothy said, 'Let a woman learn in silence with all submissiveness. I permit no woman to teach or to have authority over men'?

A clergy that was required *ex professo* to be celibate tended to stress the moral and intellectual weakness of womankind. Ascetical literature was written largely by men, and to the male ascetic woman appeared primarily in the guise of the temptress. Paradoxically, the elaboration of the cult of the Blessed Virgin Mary did nothing to counteract this image, for the doctrine of the Immaculate Conception, which was gaining ground at this period, exempted her from the taint and consequences of original sin and thus detached her from the normal experience of the human race.

This change in the position of women was reflected in their declining role in the monastic world. By the tenth century many of the early women's abbeys had vanished from the map. Some had been taken over by canons.[8] Houses of canonesses survived and new foundations were occasionally made, because they continued to serve a social purpose for the higher aristocracy who felt the need to provide protection and supervision for their unmarried womenfolk. Thus in tenth-century Germany the Ottonian dynasty showed an active interest in the nunneries of Herford, Gandersheim and Quedlinburg, which housed the daughters of the Saxon aristocracy and were governed by royal princesses. Quedlinburg, the foundation of Queen Matilda, the mother of Otto I, became, in fact, the chosen mausoleum of the dynasty. Similar considerations moved the Countess of Anjou in 1028 to found the aristocratic nunnery of Roncerey at Angers. But the double monastery of an earlier age disappeared under a tide of clerical disapproval. When it reappeared in the eleventh century it was in a changed form: no abbess or prioress had jurisdiction over monks; and the nuns were usually subject to the supervision of male founders or deputies appointed by them.

Women, in fact, played a largely subordinate role in the initiatives that launched the major ascetical revivals of the tenth and eleventh centuries. These were movements initiated and led by men and sponsored by patrons who were interested in creating male monasteries. Those women's houses that were founded in their wake were few and undistinguished by comparison with the plethora of important foundations for monks. It was not necessarily that fewer women were attracted to the religious life or even that their social circumstances precluded such initiatives. The problem lay partly in the mentality of the monastic reformers, who regarded contact with women as a hazard to their souls to be avoided at all costs, and who were therefore reluctant to assume the responsibility of directing nuns.

The other side of the problem was the attitude of the lay patrons. The lay donor who endowed a monastery hoped to reap spiritual benefits from his gift, and the most highly valued of these was one that women could not provide – women could not celebrate mass. Medieval piety increasingly emphasised the expiatory value of the mass. So as it became the normal practice to ordain professed monks to the priesthood, and the institution of the private mass enabled all to offer mass daily, patrons were increasingly eager to sponsor communities of monks, who would continually plead the merits of Christ's passion on behalf of their forgetful benefactors.

The subordinate role of women in the monastic revival is evident in the first Cluniac foundation for nuns. It came late in the day, when the Cluniac empire already numbered its colonies in hundreds. In fact, the movement was approaching its climacteric when St Hugh decided in 1056 to create a house for women at Marcigny in the region of Autun. He persuaded his brother, Count Geoffrey of Semur, to give the necessary land. Family *pietas* was a major motive: Hugh's primary purpose was to provide a religious retreat for his own mother and for the wives and female relatives of men who had been persuaded to become monks at Cluny. Count Geoffrey himself ended his life as a monk of Cluny, and Marcigny provided a home for his sister and daughter.[9]

Marcigny was an establishment for ninety-nine nuns headed by a claustral prioress – the office of abbess was reserved for the Blessed Virgin herself, as a sign of which an abbatial stall was always kept empty for her in choir. They were to follow the customs of Cluny, with the proviso that the nuns must be strictly enclosed at all times. The house had some of the features of a double monastery, for Hugh established in the vicinity a small community of twelve monks from Cluny to provide the necessary sacramental services and help with business management. But the spirit of the foundation was very different from that of the double monasteries of earlier times: the nuns were placed under the supervision of the prior, who was the director of both communities and who was appointed by the abbot of Cluny.[10] Marcigny was an aristocratic nunnery, and it remained so. The Countess Adela of Blois, daughter of William the Conqueror and mother of King Stephen, who had inherited her father's imperious will, was one of several members of ruling dynasties who took the veil there. Nevertheless, Hugh clearly judged it inappropriate that the ladies should be allowed to run their own affairs and organise their own religious life without male supervision.

Marcigny, with its rigid enclosure – what Peter the Venerable called its 'jocund prison' – and strict rule of life, was the prototype of a cluster of Cluniac nunneries that were founded in France, Italy, England and Germany in the following fifty years. Many of them were small. None of them was endowed on the lavish scale of the greater men's abbeys. Marcigny itself was in straitened circumstances when the mother of Peter the Venerable sought admission. The postulant was, of course, expected to bring a dowry with her when she entered, but nuns could not touch the generosity of patrons as easily as the monks could.

But for all their modest scale, these satellites of the Cluniac empire went some way to meeting the religious aspirations of women who wanted a more secluded and devout way of life than they could find in the older houses of canonesses like Faremoutiers or Essen.

A widespread and growing demand for new forms of monastic life suited to the needs of women made itself increasingly felt, especially in northern Europe. St Benedict, after all, had legislated for men. 'What provision would he make for women', mused Heloise, 'if he laid down a Rule for them like that for men?' In 1129 she and the nuns in her charge had accepted Abelard's invitation to occupy the vacant settlement of the Paraclete in the woods of Champagne after losing their home at Argenteuil. It was at his insistence that she had taken the veil at Argenteuil after their love had ended in tragedy. Now as prioress she wrote to him as the refounder of their community to ask him to prescribe a rule suitable for women.[11]

The Benedictine Rule, she explained, could not be observed by women at all points. Its instructions on dress were inapplicable to them. So too were the references to manual labour: it was not the practice for nuns to work in the fields. And how could a woman perform the duties the Rule assigns to the abbot? – it would be inappropriate and dangerous for her to entertain guests at her table, especially male guests. In general, she argued, women were the weaker vessels, and the asperities of the Rule should be mitigated to accommodate them – 'enough if we live continently and without possessions, wholly occupied by the service of God, and in doing so equal the leaders of the Church themselves or religious laymen or even those who are called canons regular'. Like them, nuns should be permitted to eat meat, drink a little wine, and wear linen next to their skin.

Abelard responded to this appeal with two long and rambling letters of instruction.[12] Over food, fasting, and sleep he conceded mitigations; what mattered was moderation in all things. He would not have them drink wine though – 'a sensual and turbulent thing, entirely opposed to both continence and silence'. If they must drink it, let it be diluted with at least a quarter of water. For the rest, his prescriptions reflect the preoccupations and assumptions that were common to the monastic reformers of his age. Strict enclosure, perpetual silence, and a location secluded from the world were essential for the religious life. Away with those monks who on the pretext of offering hospitality change the solitude they had sought into a city – 'thus they have returned to the world, or rather, brought the world to them'. The religious vocation was a call to the desert. He shared, too, the ideas of his contemporaries about the need to provide male support and supervision of women's establishments. The seclusion of the nuns was to be protected by an adjacent house of monks. The nuns should have their own superior, but both communities were to be subject to the head of the men's house.

The problems with which Heloise confronted Abelard were experienced by other founders of the new orders of the eleventh and twelfth centuries. Women as well as men responded eagerly to the new ideas of the *vita apostolica*, the call to embrace voluntary poverty and the privations of the eremitical life for the sake of the kingdom of God. The preachers of the new ascetical movement, who had sought solitude in the forests of Craon and Councy, found themselves the centre of colonies of enthusiastic disciples of both sexes. But it was inconceivable that women should be allowed to assume an active role in the apostolic life as it was now being interpreted. Ecclesiastical tradition disqualified them from preaching; and social convention, which accepted the mendicant holy man, would be outraged by the spectacle of groups of female mendicants. Their unchastity would be taken for granted. 'They say', wrote Marbod sternly to Robert of Abrissel,

> that these women are disciples and followers of your peregrinations. They say you have numbers of women distributed in guest-houses and inns, whom you have deputed to serve the poor and pilgrims. Divine and human laws are both clearly against this association. Sin began with a woman and it is through her that death comes to all of us. Without doubt, you cannot long be chaste if you dwell among women.[13]

Marbod, sometime schoolmaster, archdeacon and finally bishop of Rennes, wrote some appalling verses *On a Whore*, which reveal him as a professional misogynist. But his warning to Robert voiced a conviction that was widespread among both clergy and laity that the only safe place for a woman who had no husband was behind the high walls of a nunnery or perpetually immured in an anchorhold.

The presence of substantial numbers of women in his following obliged Robert of Abrissel to establish a stable residence for them at Fontevrault. This, as we have seen, was a double monastery in which a small group of monks had a subordinate role, serving an aristocratic community of nuns. The aristocratic flavour of the order, which had been assured by the abbess Petronilla, was reproduced in its three English houses of Westwood, Nuneaton and Amesbury in the twelfth century, all of which owed their foundation and endowment to members of the higher nobility, enjoyed royal patronage, and recruited members from the ladies of the court.[14]

Norbert also solved the problem of his female devotees by creating double monasteries. At Prémontré he set up a house for women adjacent to that of the canons. But male ascendancy here permitted the sisters only a subservient role. They attended the church when the canons sang the hours; otherwise they were assigned such humble tasks as serving the hospice for the poor and washing and darning the clothes of the male community. Their status resembled that of the lay brothers in the Cistercian abbeys. The more aristocratic sisters, who could not be expected to do such menial work, were probably allowed to live in the house as recluses.[15]

Despite these limitations, the recruitment of women remained surprisingly buoyant and for some years there was a proliferation of double monasteries, especially in the Low Countries. By the middle of the century, Herman of Tournai claimed, with an exaggeration born of enthusiasm, that there were a thousand sisters living at Prémontré and its immediate dependencies, and that the order contained ten thousand of them.[16] But Marbod's strictures were echoed by misogynists within the order as well as outside it, and a move began to jettison the female communities. In 1138 Pope Innocent II took the canons to task for failing to support the sisters adequately out of the common endowments, of which no small part had accrued to the order through the women recruits.

The pope's remonstrance was probably connected with the fact that at about this time the general chapter, under the guidance of Norbert's successor, Hugh de Fosses, took a decision to suppress the double monasteries. This did not mean that the women were extruded from the order. The chapter merely decreed that they must live in totally separate establishments well distanced from the parent abbey. The nuns were required to pack their bags and find accommodation elsewhere. Those at Prémontré had some difficulty finding a permanent home. The bishop of Laon built them a new convent at Fontenelles; but a little later they appear to have moved on to Roziéres. Those of the Flemish abbey of Tongerloo were found accommodation in the distant parish of Euwen, where the abbey had some property.

In some ways the upheaval may have improved the status of the nuns. They ceased to be humble handmaids servicing communities of men, and became fully fledged religious communities with ends of their own. They became, in fact, canonesses, singing the liturgical offices and following the same monastic regime as the men's houses. But their autonomy was still limited: the parent abbey in each case continued to supervise their affairs by means of a *praepositus* or prior whom the abbot appointed for the purpose. There are also indications that they paid a heavy price for this semi-independence. The letters of Innocent II and his successors suggest that the parent abbeys, which retained control over the joint endowments, adopted an increasingly niggardly attitude towards supporting their female dependencies after they ceased to provide the canons with material services. In the end, mistrust and a desire to be rid of the financial burden moved the leaders of the order to adopt a policy of complete disengagement. In 1197 or 1198 the general chapter took the decision to admit no more women to the order. This decision, which was ratified by a rescript of Pope Innocent III,[17] condemned the female branch of the Premonstratensians to a process of gradual extinction.

The Norbertines were not the only species of canons regular to offer a vocation to women in the early stages. The Flemish abbey of Arrouaise had a large community of canonesses attached to it during the years of its expansion under the dynamic direction of Abbot Gervase (1121–47), though here the nuns formed an independent establishment rather than part of a double monastery. And this arrangement of parallel establishments was adopted by other abbeys of the Arrouaise congregation.[18] But here too the early promise of a dual order succumbed to the same forces that had disinherited the Norbertine nuns. Economic pressure, which was intensified by the growing influx of female postulants, persuaded the chapter of the order first to impose limits upon the size of the women's communities and then, in the thirteenth century, to discard them altogether. Thus from 1140 onwards the new orders increasingly adopted a policy of apartheid towards their female branches. In view of this trend, it is all the more interesting that one religious organisation for women besides Fontevrault was successfully launched in the twelfth century and maintained its course in the teeth of the prevailing wind. This was the English order founded by St Gilbert of Sempringham.

St Gilbert and the Order of Sempringham

Unlike most monastic innovators, Gilbert was neither a hermit nor an ascetic in search of his own vocation. He was an educated secular clerk, the son of a Norman knight settled in Lincolnshire and an English mother. After a spell in the *familia* of the bishops of Lincoln, he was content to retire to the family patrimony and serve the two parish churches in his father's gift. His order grew out of his efforts to meet the needs and aspirations of a small group of young women in his parish who sought a refuge in the monastic life. He began by building them a house and cloister against the north wall of his church, where they could live in seclusion in the manner of anchoresses. The fact that Gilbert's provision met a widely felt social need is indicated by the interest and support he attracted from several baronial and knightly families of the area and from his old patron, Bishop Alexander of Lincoln. After a modest start, grants of land began to tumble in and a new foundation followed.

At an early stage the problem of organisation had to be faced. Gilbert does not seem to have envisaged an order of double monasteries to begin with. His first foundations coincided with the Cistercian plantations in the north, which were attracting much interest in clerical circles. He was in touch with Abbot William of Rievaulx, and intended his nuns to follow a modified form of Cistercian observance. His own position as a secular clerk directing a monastic congregation was anomalous. The obvious solution was to disembarrass himself of his spiritual progeny by affiliating them to the Cistercian Order. With this in mind, he approached the general chapter of Cîteaux in 1147 and asked it to assume responsibility for his nascent order, which at that date comprised the nunneries of Sempringham and Haverholme. But the Cistercians had no desire to be involved with the affairs of more women's houses, and Gilbert's request was refused.

It may have been the practice of Fontevrault that suggested the plan he adopted. For, after returning empty-handed from the chapter of Cîteaux, he set about associating small communities of canons regular with each convent to serve the sacramental needs of the nuns and to assist with the management of their property. The characteristic Gilbertine monastery thus contained communities of both men and women occupying separate quarters on either side of the conventual church. The canons sang the hours in their own oratory and celebrated mass for the nuns in the conventual church; the nuns recited the hours in their own choir. From the first, Gilbert had recruited lay brothers among impoverished local peasants and artisans to act as bailiffs for the nuns as well as to hew and carry for them, and lay sisters to cook and perform other menial tasks. Gilbert's thirteenth-century biographer likens the order to the chariot of Aminadab:

> It has two sides, one of men, another of women; four wheels – two of men, both clerks and laymen, and two of women, lettered and unlettered. Two oxen draw the chariot – the clerical and monastic discipline of the Blessed Augustine and the holy Benedict. Father Gilbert guides the chariot over places rough and smooth, over the heights and in the depths. The way by which they go is narrow, but the path leads to eternal life.[19]

We do not, in fact, know much about the internal life of the Gilbertine houses in the early years. Gilbert's original constitutions have been submerged in a medley of later ordinances.[20] The developed institutes insist upon a rigid segregation of the two communities. Even in the conventual church they were hidden from the sight of each other by a longitudinal screen, and at mass, communion was passed through a turn-table. But the grisly story of the nun of Watton suggests that in the earlier days contact between the sexes was less rigidly debarred than it later became. She was able to contrive lovers' meetings with a lay brother on the premises for some time before they were discovered and she was found to be pregnant. The nuns vented their rage on the body of her lover with a horrible act of revenge.[21] This incident, and the trouble with the lay brothers in the 1160s, may have resulted in a less flexible regime of segregation. Before the advent of the canons, it had been the practice of the lay brothers to attend the night hours in the nuns' church, but this was later stopped.

The rebellion of the lay brothers of Sempringham in 1166–67 illustrates the difficulties that beset an attempt to revive double monasteries in the twelfth century. The ringleaders were two brothers whom Gilbert had entrusted with managerial responsibilities and who probably felt they had lost status through the arrival of the canons. After being punished by him for misconduct, they daringly went to the papal Curia at Sens and laid charges against the order. The most serious accusation alleged grave sexual lapses resulting from the close proximity of nuns and canons in the Gilbertine houses. This attack came close to success: the conspirators returned from the Curia with letters from Pope Alexander commanding Gilbert to rehouse the canons and nuns in completely separate and properly distanced establishments. But Gilbert had powerful friends and admirers who rushed to the defence of his order. Five English bishops picked up their pens to rebut the charges and reassure the pope that the nuns and canons lived in strict segregation; the legate, Hugh Pierleoni, visited Sempringham and wrote a glowing testimonial;[22] and – the most cogent argument of all – King Henry gave the pope to understand that he would confiscate the endowments of the order if any such radical change was made.[23] And so the double monasteries survived.

In his old age Gilbert took the habit of the canons regular himself, and in 1175–76 he resigned the direction of his order to Roger, the prior of Malton. At his death, the order contained nine double monasteries and four houses that were for canons only. All save two of these foundations were in Gilbert's native Lincolnshire. Six more houses were founded in the following century. Although Gilbert's plan had been vindicated, the rebels had touched a sensitive nerve. The scandal of the nun of Watton was common knowledge in the north of England, and possibly there had been other but less notorious cases. The pope's readiness to respond to charges brought by a couple of disgruntled runaways indicated the conviction of many churchmen that men and women could not be associated in the religious life without hazard to chastity.

This early crisis in the order left its mark in the severity of the statutes regulating the enclosure of the nuns. The internal affairs of each house were directed by three prioresses, who ruled the community by turns. The canons were denied all access to the nuns except for the purpose of administering extreme unction to a dying sister. The ordinances contain elaborate instructions for the making and custody of the turn-table, the sole point of communication through which advice and funds could be passed. Even at mass the celebrant was hidden from the sisters by a screen. The only meeting point was the general chapter of the order, which assembled annually at Sempringham. This was attended by prioresses as well as by the priors of the male communities; but the nuns were required to travel in a covered cart, so that they could neither see about them nor be seen. This preoccupation with keeping the two sides of the order from contact with one another had one advantage for the nuns. They were left with a rare degree of autonomy in the running of their own affairs. They had control of the monies and the conventual seals, and the prioresses were answerable only to the Master of the order, that is to Gilbert himself and his successors.

The Cistercian nuns

In rejecting Gilbert's overture the general chapter of Cîteaux was following a policy to which it continued to cling until the beginning of the thirteenth century. The early Cistercian ethos was hostile to any arrangement involving contact with women and the order refused to accept responsibility for the pastoral care of nuns. Abbots were forbidden to bless female novices, and the statutes fiercely debarred female visitors from the cloister. But as time went on, the success of the Cistercian ideal in attracting female disciples created a problem of growing dimensions. Gilbert's nuns were not alone in their desire to be associated with the

Cistercian Order. The Order of Savigny, when it merged with Cîteaux in 1147, brought with it a cluster of affiliated convents of women, and these continued to be supervised by the abbot of Savigny, who was thereafter a Cistercian prelate.

Elsewhere in Europe, many nunneries were modelling their observance on the customs of Cîteaux. Yet the governing body of the order steadily declined to undertake their pastoral care. It has been observed that until 1191 the official acts of the general chapter omit any reference to the existence of this large company of female fellow-travellers.[24] Individual abbots gave encouragement to new foundations for women and helped with advice; but the order refused to incorporate them into its organisation. Being excluded from the official structure and direction of the order, some groups of nunneries following Cistercian customs made a move to form a parallel organisation of their own. Before the end of the twelfth century the Cistercian abbesses of Castile were meeting in annual chapters at Las Huelgas, and the Burgundian nunnery of Tart was convening the heads of its daughter-houses to an annual chapter.[25]

In the end, the stance of benevolent detachment became impossible to maintain. The growing demand by nuns and their aristocratic patrons for association forced the order to take cognisance of the women's houses. It may have been the pressure from Alfonso VIII of Castile on behalf of the royal nunnery of Las Huelgas that eventually overcame the reluctance of the general chapter. He was determined that his foundation should be recognised as a daughter-house of Cîteaux; and he was a valuable patron whom it was not easy to refuse. Further pressure came from the decision of the Premonstratensians in 1198 to admit no more nunneries to their order, which left more and more communities looking to Cîteaux for guidance and support. 'After this,' wrote Jacques de Vitry, 'the nuns who professed the religion of the Cistercian Order multiplied like the stars of heaven and vastly increased . . . convents were founded and built, virgins, widows, and married women who had gained the consent of their husbands, rushed to fill the cloisters.'[26]

Jacques himself, who was an Austin canon regular, had seen seven abbeys of Cistercian nuns constructed within a short period in his own corner of the diocese of Liège. So, early in the thirteenth century, the general chapter yielded to this clamorous demand and began to acknowledge that some nunneries had been incorporated into the order. In 1213 it enacted the first of many statutes to regulate their observance. This ordinance laid down a rule of strict enclosure and underlined the responsibility of abbots to supervise those women's houses that had been affiliated to their abbeys.

Only seven years after this first effort to bring some of the nunneries under the official control of the order, the general chapter decreed that no more women's abbeys should be incorporated.[27] The prohibition was reiterated in more drastic form in 1228: 'if any convent of nuns not yet associated with the order or not yet built wishes to imitate our institutes, we do not forbid it; but we will not accept the care of their souls or perform for them the office of visitation'.[28] There were probably a variety of reasons for this *volte-face*, chief among them the sheer scale of the problem. There were many women's houses that had been sailing under the Cistercian flag without being subject to the disciplinary constraints of the Cistercian organisation. Many years later the abbot of Cîteaux complained to the dean of Lincoln that the abbesses of six named English nunneries were wearing the Cistercian habit and were claiming the privileges of the order though they did not belong to it.[29] The bishop of Lincoln testified in their favour that they were, in fact, following Cistercian observance.[30]

During the thirteenth century, Cistercian nunneries multiplied at an extraordinary rate, especially in Germany and the Low Countries, where they greatly outnumbered the men's abbeys.[31] It proved an impossible task to exercise effective supervision over such a multitude of different establishments. The chapter acts reveal the difficulties encountered by the order in trying to impose its disciplinary control over them. Aristocratic ladies, accustomed to managing their affairs in relative freedom, did not take kindly to the constraints of a highly disciplined organisation that was governed by men. Abbots attempting to carry out a visitation of their affiliated nunneries sometimes found the doors barred against them.[32] The chapter repeatedly referred to the need for the stricter enclosure of both nuns and their abbesses. In 1298 it complained that the order was being dishonoured by nuns who roamed freely outside the cloister.[33]

In 1250 the chapter received a report on the abbey of Colonges which disclosed a situation that was far from being unique. Colonges in Burgundy was a daughter-house of Cîteaux. When the headship of the house fell vacant, two abbots of the filiation went to supervise the election of a new abbess. But the prioress refused to surrender the seals or carry out instructions. The two abbots therefore excommunicated her and retreated. Having got them out of the way, the convent proceeded to elect one of their own number as abbess and installed her.[34] A year later, the general chapter had made no headway with the problem and despairingly reported the excommunication of the nuns to the bishop. The same chapter that received the complaint against Colonges excommunicated another nun who was conducting herself as abbess of Blandecques.[35] The problem of controlling these recalcitrant nunneries was obviously made more difficult by the fact that they were unrepresented in the sovereign body of the order. Abbesses were not allowed to attend the general chapter; and women of high birth were disinclined to submit to dictation by a distant body of men who showed scant understanding of their problems. When visitors informed the abbess and convent of Parc-aux-Dames of the chapter decrees of 1242, the nuns signified their annoyance by stamping their feet and clapping and finally by walking out of the chapter-house.[36]

These difficulties, and the fear of incurring financial liability for communities without adequate endowments, explain the reaction of some sections of the order against the incorporation of women's houses. But the prohibition of 1228 evidently did not reflect a consensus, for it failed to stick. In the Low Countries the Brabander abbey of Villers continued to promote the foundation of Cistercian nunneries and to provide them with spiritual direction in the 1230s.[37] Moreover, the general chapter continued to accede to requests for the affiliation of new foundations made by influential patrons. In 1248 it bowed to a request from Queen Margaret of France for the incorporation of her abbeys of Le Lys and Vaux de Cernay.[38] In 1250 the dowager Countess of Arundel, Isabella d'Albini, persuaded it to accept her foundation for nuns at Marham in Norfolk.[39]

These convents that were incorporated into the order were supervised by the father abbot of the filiation to which they belonged. When abbot of Savigny, Stephen of Lexington was an assiduous visitor of the Savigniac nunneries in the 1230s, and the injunctions he issued in the wake of his visits provide a few glimpses of life inside these establishments.[40] The nuns of Mortain are reminded of the obligation to renounce all personal property and are warned of the fearful penalties for being caught, alive or dead, with personal belongings. In the future no nun is to be allowed a cell of her own. The number of maidservants must be kept within the financial means of the house. When they are hired by the prioress, they must swear to remain chaste while in service, and not to relay gossip from the outside world or to tell tales about the nuns outside the convent. Postulants are not to be admitted to the noviciate until they are nineteen; but the convent may continue to take in and educate girls of twelve and upwards[41] – a ruling plainly contrary to the ordinances of the general chapter. The nuns of Moncé in the Touraine are sternly forbidden to offer hospitality to goliards or other vagabonds pretending to be priests or to ribald laymen. Whenever any such rascals are admitted, the portress and the lay sister in charge of the guest-house are to be put to penance on bread and water and to be whipped in chapter.[42] A corner of the veil is lifted upon a community of gentlewomen, accustomed to a rather relaxed version of Cistercian observance, relieved of chores by paid servants, and appreciative of outside entertainment.

Besides making regular visitations, the parent abbey supplied its dependent nunneries with groups of monks – lay brothers as well as priests – who lived in quarters adjacent to the nuns' enclosure and provided them with sacramental services and administrative support. Lexington's rules for the monks residing at the Savignac convents imply arrangements not unlike those of the Gilbertine double monasteries. The two communities observed the same horarium in parallel. When the bell rang for Vigils in the nuns' church, the monks had also to rise and recite the office in their own oratory. They celebrated mass in the nuns' church, but they were not permitted to remain there when mass had ended. Neither the prior nor the monks were to enter the nuns' cloister; when they needed to speak to the prioress or the cellaress, they had to do so in the public eye at the parlour window.[43] Generally, these groups of monks attached to Cistercian nunneries seem to have been quite small. Lexington's statutes for Monce assign the house four priests and two *conversi* to serve thirty nuns. Their head was a prior, who was responsible for regulating the expenditure of the whole establishment.

It is understandable that many abbots were reluctant to enter into these arrangements for the spiritual care of nuns, which involved separating groups of monks from their own communities for more or less prolonged periods.

A new experiment: the Beguines

The official attitude of the order may have placed some brake upon the affiliation of women's houses, but it did nothing to impede the creation of new religious communities for women, which continued to multiply, especially in northern France, Germany and the Low Countries. Some of these modelled their observance on that of the Cistercians; others adopted a freer, more experimental type of religious life. It was these latter groups that contemporaries called Beguines.

The Beguines, like the Cistercian nuns, were a product of the extraordinary spirit of religious fervour that swept through certain sections of Western society in the twelfth and thirteenth centuries. They were groups of lay-women living in the towns of northern Europe and in some rural areas of Swabia, who came together to practise a new form of religious life. They were not affiliated to any religious order, nor did they follow any recognised monastic rule. The movement probably owed its recruits to the social exclusiveness of the nunneries; possibly it represented a conscious and widespread rejection of the affluent image and formalism of the established orders. But there was more to it than this. Its piety was rooted in the cult of voluntary poverty and the current ideas of the apostolic life, but it flowered in a very different soil. In northern Europe it was an urban phenomenon.[44]

The leaders of the movement were recruited largely among the daughters and widows of the newly affluent bourgeoisie of the northern cities – women like Marie d'Oignies, mystic and doyenne of the Flemish Beguines, whose patrician family of Nivelles was infuriated and frightened by her determination to renounce all her property. And whereas the traditional forms of monastic life had sought salvation in the desert, the Beguines found the milieu for their religious life in the towns. In this they resembled the friars, with whom they soon came to be linked. Like the Franciscans, they were inspired by a new kind of vision formed in the uncomplicated minds of lay Christians – a vision of the evangelical life or literal imitation of the life of Christ. In his biography of Marie d'Oignies, Jacques de Vitry tells us that she was consumed with a desire to follow the Gospel and make herself a beggar, 'so as naked to follow the naked Christ'.[45]

It began with groups of devout women living in the world, in some cases remaining at home in their own families, who used a town church as a focus for their association and engaged in works of charity. By the beginning of the thirteenth century, they had begun to form communities occupying houses in the towns of northern France, Flanders, Brabant, and the Rhineland, and in rural areas round Lake Constance. They took no irrevocable vows, but simply made an engagement to observe celibacy while they lived in community. A condition of membership was the renunciation of personal wealth and the cultivation of a humble and frugal life-style. They attended mass and the canonical hours in the local parish church. They supported themselves by their own work, mainly by weaving, sewing and embroidery; and they moved freely about the streets serving the needs of the poor and the sick. Some groups resorted to organised begging as a means of support.

The rapid spread of the Beguines is one of the most arresting religious phenomena of the later Middle Ages. As they gradually secured recognition from the authorities of church and state, Beguinages sprang up everywhere in the northern towns. In some cases the houses were purchased out of funds brought to the communities by new members; in others, buildings were donated by members of the ruling nobility. By the end of the thirteenth century, Namur contained five Beguinages, and Cologne, the biggest and most populous of north German cities, had witnessed fifty-four such foundations. In Brussels, where the Beguines enjoyed the patronage of the dukes of Brabant, they were allowed to appropriate the chapel of La Vigne to their use, and they secured a right to have their own chaplains and their own burial ground. Here, as in other towns of the Low Countries, they came to constitute a separate enclave within the city.

Some impression of the size and layout of these establishments of pious women can be gained from the Beguinages that are still to be seen at Bruges and Louvain and some other Belgian cities. Although most of its existing houses date from the seventeenth century, the Great Beguinage of Louvain still presents the dimensions and the essential aspect of the medieval settlement – a small township within the town, containing its own streets, gardens, church and collegiate buildings, separated from the surrounding city by a high encircling wall. Certainly not all Beguine communities acquired such spacious accommodation, but everywhere in the course of the thirteenth century the informal sisterhoods of the early days had been translated into organised communities with permanent conventual buildings.

Why were so many women attracted to the movement? The relatively free regime of the Beguinage, which offered its members a total surrender to God through a life of prayer and active service to their neighbours, clearly met the spiritual aspirations of women who had heard the call to the apostolic life. As a social phenomenon, the explanation for its huge success must lie in the demography of the northern cities. The escalating demand by women both for nunneries and for alternative forms of ascetical life indicates a population imbalance. The number of marriageable women must have significantly exceeded the number of available men. Such an imbalance can be easily accounted for by normal female longevity and the inroads made upon the male population by warfare, the hazards of merchant travel, and clerical celibacy. Just as the nuns and canonesses had provided a home for the ladies of the landed classes for whom no suitable marriage could be found, the Beguinages, in turn, offered a refuge to the surplus daughters and the widows of the wealthier bourgeoisie. Nor were they

FIGURE 12.1 The Grand Beguinage, Louvan, Belgium (thirteenth to seventeenth centuries)

© Sander Claes/Alamy

only a haven for the unmarriageable. The religious life offered an escape, usually the only escape, for girls who found themselves forced by their families into a marriage they did not desire. Being the children of affluent families, they were readily attracted by the ascetical ideal of voluntary poverty and also, no doubt, by the relative absence of institutional constraint that characterised the life in the Beguinages.

It was Jacques de Vitry who first trumpeted the virtues of the Beguines at the papal Curia. As an Augustinian canon, he had lived for a year as the neighbour, disciple and confessor of Marie d'Oignies, and once made a bishop, he strenuously defended the new communities of women against their detractors and persuaded Pope Honorius III to authorise their way of life. After Marie's death in 1213 he wrote her Life for the benefit of Bishop Fulk of Toulouse, so that he could show the ascetical sectaries of the Languedoc what a real holy woman was like. Jacques saw the Beguines, in the way that reforming popes saw the friars, as a sign of fresh hope for a Church beleaguered by heresy and weakened by the ignorance and vices of the secular clergy.

There were other educated and zealous churchmen who took the same view. According to Eccleston, Grosseteste, when he was lecturing to the Franciscans at Oxford, warned them that there was an even higher form of holy poverty than the mendicancy they practised, which was to live by the labour of one's own hands, 'wherefore he said that the Beguines have attained the highest perfection of holy religion, for they live by their own labour and do not burden the world with their demands'.[46] It was a striking testimonial from one of the greatest schoolmen of the thirteenth century. He was echoed by Master Robert of the Sorbonne, who daringly opined that the Beguines would fare better at the Last Judgement than many of the masters and theologians of Paris.[47]

Yet despite this enthusiastic promotion, the women's movement encountered much hostile criticism from both the laity and the more conservative sections of the clergy. The spectacle of laywomen, without the sanction of any religious order, engaging in an active apostolic role was offensive to both male chauvinism and clerical professionalism. From the first they were suspected of heresy – the name 'Beguine' originally denoted a heretic; and although for the most part they were neither heretical nor anticlerical, the individualistic and intensely affective piety they cultivated aroused the misgivings of ecclesiastical authorities. The laity, observed William of Saint-Amour, hammer of the friars, belonged to that order of the Church that stood in need of perfecting by the ministrations of the clergy.[48] The mystical experiences and direct illumination ascribed to laywomen like Marie d'Oignies or Hadewijch, the Beguine of Nivelles, could be seen by the legalistic as posing a threat to the hierarchical organisation of divine grace. It was the chronic conflict between the religion of authority and the religion of the spirit.

Before the middle of the thirteenth century the reaction had set in. Criticism focused upon the lack of inclaustration or clerical supervision and upon the scandalous behaviour of female mendicants. In 1233 a provincial synod at Mainz attempted to stop the practice of begging by some Beguines: they were not to run about the streets; they must remain in their houses, live by the work of their hands, and be directed by the parish clergy.[49] Another synod held at Frizlar in 1244 alleged frequent sexual lapses among younger Beguines and ordained that for the future no woman should be admitted to their communities under the age of forty.[50] The attitude of many of the clergy towards them was tersely summed up by Bruno, bishop of Olmutz, thirty years later: 'I would have them either married or thrust into an approved order.'[51]

In the end the conflict was resolved by a compromise. The Council of Vienne in 1312 censured 'certain women, commonly called Beguines, who lose themselves in foolish speculations on the Trinity and the divine essence . . . these women promise obedience to nobody, and they neither renounce their property nor profess any approved Rule'. Their way of life was permanently forbidden. But this was without prejudice to 'those faithful women who wished to live as the Lord shall inspire them, following a life of penance and living chastely together in their hospices, even if they have taken no vow'.[52] In other words, the Beguines would be tolerated as long as they stayed in their convents and accepted clerical supervision. Female vagrancy and similar antics were not acceptable. Most Beguinages, in fact, attached themselves to houses of Franciscan or Dominican friars, who supplied them with spiritual directors and confessors.

In its tamed form the Beguinage survived the onslaught of its critics and persecutors. In many of the cities of the Rhineland, northern France and the Low Countries, it remained an established and respected institution, providing a home for the sick and destitute as well as for the sisterhood. In a limited sense the Beguines represented a movement of women's liberation. Even after their wilder manifestations had been suppressed, their informal associations offered unmarried women a greater degree of freedom and initiative than was allowed them either in a traditional convent or in a lay family. Their simple piety based upon study of the vernacular Bible and their cultivation of mystical experience, which in the writings of Hadewijch of Antwerp was expressed in the erotic imagery of the *Brautmystik* or 'bridal' mysticism, placed them alongside the friars as preachers and exponents of a new kind of religious experience. It was a distinctively feminine spirituality, individualistic and intuitive, which focused upon the humanity of Christ and sought to identify with his sufferings by mortification of the body.[53]

Notes

1. *Libellus de Diversis Ordinibus et Professionibus qui sunt in Aecclesia*, ed. G. Constable and B. Smith (1972), p. 5.
2. M. Parisse, *Les nonnes au moyen-âge* (Le Puy, 1983), p. 132.
3. *c.2 D causae I Q.ii.*
4. *Mansi*, XXII, p. 1051; C. *40 X, De Simonia, V, 3.*

5. J. H. Lynch, *Simoniacal Entry into Religious Life, 1000 to 1260* (Ohio, 1976), pp. 203–24, This study provides a survey of the legislation on the subject and of the problems of enforcement.

6. *Epistolae, PL*, 197, 337–8. See now *Letters of Hildegard of Bingen*, 3 vols ed. J. L. Baird and R. K. Ehrmann (1994–2004).

7. See, J. Verdon, 'Les moniales dans la France de l'ouest aux XIe et XIIe siècles' in *Cahiers de civilisation médiévale* XIXe année, No. 3 (1976), pp. 247–63. M. Verdon found that at Ronceray widows and married women comprised 30 per cent of the community; at Holy Trinity, Caen, they comprised 25.9 per cent of those with identifiable names, and at Marcigny more than half of those professed in the period 1055–1136, whose names are ascertainable.

8. Mary Skinner, 'Benedictine life for women in Central France, 850–1100' in *Distant Echoes: Medieval Religious Women*, ed. J. A. Nichols and L. T. Shank (Kalamazoo, 1984), p. 90.

9. *Le cartulaire de Marcigny-sur-Loire*, ed. Jean Richard (Dijon, 1957), pp. 15–17.

10. On Marcigny see G. de Valous, *Le monachisme clunisien* (Ligugé, Paris, 1935) i, p. 383; Noreen Hunt, *Cluny under St Hugh 1049–1109* (1967), pp. 186–94.

11. The text of Heloise's letters and Abelard's replies were newly edited by J. T. Muckle and T. P. McLaughlin in *Mediaeval Studies* (Pontifical Institute of Toronto) xvii (1955), pp. 240–81, and xviii (1956), pp. 241–92. For a good modern translation see Betty Radice, *The Letters of Abelard and Heloise* (Penguin, 1974), pp. 159–269. The authenticity of the letters has been questioned by some historians. Authentic or not, they represent twelfth-century views of the role of women in the religious life. See also, on the intellectual equipment of Heloise, Peter Dronke, *Women Writers of the Middle Ages* (1984), pp. 107–43. For her response to Abelard's advice on monastic life at the Paraclete see M. T. Clanchy, *Abeland: A Medieval Life* (2002), pp. 251–63.

12. Radice, *op. cit.*, pp. 180–269.

13. *Marbodi Redonensis Episcopi Epistolae, PL* 171, 1481–2. On Robert's relations with women disciples see Jacqueline Smith, 'Robert of Abrissel, procurator mulierum' in *Medieval Women*, ed. D. Baker (*Studies in Church History, Subsidia* I, 1978), pp. 175–84.

14. Sally Thompson, *Women Religious. The Founding of English Nunneries after the Norman Conquest* (1991), pp. 121–4.

15. E. Erens, 'Les soeurs dans l'ordre de Prémontré', *Analecta Praemonstratensia* V (1929), pp. 6–26. The status of women in the order is examined at length by H. Lamy, *L'abbaye de Tongerloo depuis sa fondation jusqu'en 1263* (Louvain, 1914), pp. 93–101.

16. *De Miraculis S. Marie Laundunensis, AA SS June* I, pp. 865–6.

17. *Die Register Innocenz III*, I, ed. O. Hageneder and A. Haidacher (Graz-Vienna-Cologne, 1964–8), pp. 286–7.

18. L. Milis, *L'Ordre des chanoines reguliers d'Arrouaise*, 2 vols (Bruges, 1969), pp. 502–29.

19. A critical text of Gilbert's *Vita* will be found in R. Foreville and G. Keir, *The Book of St Gilbert* (1987), pp. 1–133. The best account of the order is now that of Brian Golding, *Gilbert of Sempringham and the Gilbertine Order, c. 1130–1300* (1995).

20. Printed in *Monasticon* VI, 2, after p. 947; see the critical observations of Raymonde Foreville, *Le livre de Saint Gilbert de Sempringham* (Paris, 1943), pp. xi–xii.

21. G. Constable, 'Aelred of Rievaulx and the nun of Watton' in *Medieval Women*, pp. 205–26.

22. *Papsturkunden in England*, ed. W. Holtzmann (1952) III, no. 231.

23. For an account of the whole incident see Golding, pp. 40–51.

24. On the early Cistercian nunneries see L. J. Lekai, *The White Monks* (Okauchea, Wisconsin, 1953), pp. 237–44; Sally Thompson, *Women Religious*, pp. 94–112.

25. A. Dimier, 'Chapitres généraux d'abbesses cisterciennes', *Cîteaux* 11 (1960), p. 272.

26. *The Historia Occidentalis of Jacques de Vitry*, ed. J. F. Hinnebusch, *Spicilegium Friburgense* 17 (Fribourg, 1972), p. 117.

27. *Statuta Capitulorum Generalium Ordinis Cisterciensis*, ed. J. Canivez, I (Louvain, 1933), p. 517. On the bearing of this decree see Sally Thompson, 'The problem of the Cistercian nuns in the twelfth and thirteenth centuries' in *Medieval Women*, pp. 227–52.

28. Canivez, II, p. 68.

29. *Cal. Close Rolls 1268–72*, 301.

30. Sally Thompson, *Women Religious*, pp. 105, 109.

31. For the figures see F. Vongrey and F. Hervay, 'Kritische Bemerkungen zum Atlas de L'Ordre Cistercien von F. Van der Meer' in *ASOC* 23 (1967), pp. 137–8.

32. See, for example, the cases reported to the general chapter in 1243 and 1244: Canivez, II, pp. 272–3, 281.

33. *Ibid.*, III, p. 293.

34. *Ibid.*, II, pp. 357–8, 375.

35. *Ibid.*, II, p. 359.

36. *Ibid.*, II, p. 272.

37. Simone Roisin, 'L'efflorescence cistercienne et le courant féminin de piété au XIIIe siècle', *Revue d'histoire ecclésiastique* 39 (1943), pp. 342–78.

38. Canivez, II, p. 331.

39. *Ibid.*, II, p. 364.

40. Bruno Griesser, 'Stephen Lexington, Abt von Savigny, als Visitator der ihm unterstehenden Frauenklöster', *Cistercienser-Chronik* 67 (1960), pp. 14–34.

41. *Registrum Epistolarum Stephani de Lexinton*, ed. Bruno Griesser, *ASOC* 8 (1952), pp. 234–47.

42. *Ibid.*, p. 240.

43. *Ibid.*, pp. 253–7.

44. Recent research has revealed numbers of rural Beguinages in the area round Lake Constance in the thirteenth century, possibly to be explained by commercial links with the Rhineland: A. Wilts, Beginen im Bodenseeraum, *Bodensee Bibliotek* 37 (Thorbecke, 1994).

45. *AA SS June* V, 557. On the rise and development of the Beguines the classic study is that of Herbert Grundmann, *Religiöse Bewegungen in Mittelalter*, 2nd edn (Berlin, 1961). See also E. W. McDonnell, *The Beguines and Beghards in Medieval Culture* (Rutgers, 1954); and R. W. Southern, *Western Society and the Church in the Middle Ages* (1970), pp. 318–31. On Marie d'Oignies and other leaders of the movement see Brenda Bolton, 'Vitae Matrum: a further aspect of the Frauenfrage' in *Medieval Women*, pp. 253–73, and the same author's valuable study *The Medieval Reformation* (1983), pp. 87–90.

46. *De Adventu Fratrum Minorum in Angliam*, ed. A. G. Little (1951), p. 99.

47. Grundmann, *op. cit.*, p. 305.

48. *De Periculis Novissimorum Temporum*, ed. E. Brown in *Fasciculus Rerum Expetendarum* (1690) II, pp. 18–41. William's attack was aimed chiefly at the ministry of the friars, cf. Chapter 13 below, but he singled out the Beguines for particular condemnation.

49. Grundmann, *op. cit.*, p. 326.

50. *Ibid.*, p. 326.

51. *Ibid.*, p. 337.

52. Schroeder, pp. 388–9; *Clement, de religiosis domibus, III, xi, c.l.*

53. A. Vauchez, *La spiritualité du moyen-âge occidental* (Paris, 1994), pp. 157–64.

13

THE FRIARS

The orders of mendicant friars which appeared in the early years of the thirteenth century represented a new departure, a radical breakaway from the monastic tradition of the past. By adopting a rule of corporate poverty and refusing to accept endowments or to own property they discarded impedimenta that had long been regarded as indispensable to any organised community of monks. But their rejection of property and reliance upon begging to support themselves were only the outward signs of a more fundamental change of spirit. The Mendicant Orders broke free from one of the most basic principles of traditional monasticism by abandoning the seclusion and enclosure of the cloister in order to engage in an active pastoral mission to the society of their time.

Preaching and ministering to the people was the *raison d'être* of the friars; and the message they brought was different. They demonstrated that it was possible for a committed Christian to live in the world of men, yet not be of the world. Assurance of salvation need no longer be sought by flight from the human hive or by attachment to the shirt-tails of an enclosed spiritual élite; those who lived in the world, whatever their status, could fulfil the demands of the Christian life by sanctifying the ordinary duties and humdrum tasks of their estate; all that was needed was that they should repent and base their lives on the Gospel.

It was a necessary condition of this missionary programme that the old monastic principle of stability should be dispensed with. It was one of the favourite charges brought against the friars by their more conservative opponents that they were *gyrovagi* – the wandering monks for whom the ultimate curse of St Benedict had been reserved. Unlike the monk, who was bound to the house of his profession, the friar was mobile. Supported by an organisation that was international and cosmopolitan, he moved from house to house and from province to province at the dictates of his superiors for the purposes of study, preaching, or administration. But although the Mendicant Orders embodied a revolutionary concept of the religious life, they had antecedents; the roots of the plant that flowered so prolifically in the thirteenth century lay in the religious experience and the social changes of the previous hundred years.

As we have seen, the cult of voluntary poverty and the ideas of the apostolic life had found expression in various new forms of religious life in the course of the twelfth century. There was a growing recognition that a mode of life modelled upon that of the Apostles should involve not only the renunciation of worldly goods but also a commitment to active evangelism. It was this perception that stirred individual ascetics like Norbert of Xanten and Robert of Abrissel to combine mendicancy with the role of the itinerant preacher. However, their vision of the *vita apostolica* was a personal one which they did not succeed in communicating to the institutions they founded; both the Order of Fontevrault and the Premonstratensian canons conformed in fact to the accepted norms of monastic organisation. It was later in the century that the cult of voluntary poverty combined with the apostolic preaching of 'metanoia', or interior conversion, to inspire a more revolutionary form of religious life which was adopted by a number of more or less organised groups of preachers roving the towns of France and northern and central Italy. The early friars were only the most conspicuous and successful of these groups of zealots. To understand the dynamics of these new religious associations we need to look at the social environment from which they sprang.

The social context

In the century and a half before 1200 western Europe had experienced a prolonged period of economic and demographic expansion which had both solvent and stimulating effects upon the religious life. As commercial wealth and industrial activity grew, urban populations increased and the physical area of many towns was enlarged. In northern Italy and Flanders, where a thriving textile industry was organised on a capitalist basis, and in the Rhineland, several cities underwent an expansion to a point where they had begun to attain the dimensions of a modern town. Rapid urban growth, the expansion of international trade, the rise of a new bourgeoisie deriving its wealth from commerce, and the creation of an international community of learning which gave birth to the first European universities, all tended to break down the isolation of local communities and to produce a society that was more mobile, more critical and, at the upper levels, more affluent than before. It is a truism that city populations provided the most fertile seed-bed for religious dissent and anticlericalism. Recent studies have suggested that in the thirteenth century scepticism about some of the fundamental dogmas of faith was commoner even among the rural peasantry than was once believed. Nevertheless, the closely regulated and enclosed society of the rural manor exerted on the individual an almost irresistible pressure to conform, whereas town living, with its relative freedom from customary constraints, its political turbulence and the constant stimulus of economic competition, fostered a more critical mentality and provided readier opportunities for the communication of new ideas.

Another feature of economic growth was the emergence of a literate section of the laity. Literacy was ceasing to be a clerical monopoly. Commercial activity on any scale demanded of its practitioners at least a degree of formal literacy; and, in fact, by the end of the twelfth century the ability to read and write the vernacular, and to a lesser extent Latin, was quite common in the larger Italian towns. Well-to-do merchants sent their sons to the city schools, while their wives and daughters attended classes where they learned to read the Latin Psalter. The rise of an articulate town-dwelling laity, critical of the intellectual and moral shortcomings of the clergy, brought to the surface the tension between the traditional assumptions of monastic spirituality and the aspirations of lay people newly awakened to a sense of their Christian vocation.[1] As we have seen, the activities of itinerant preachers and the new religious congregations of the twelfth century had initiated a widespread renewal of the Christian life which drew its inspiration from the New Testament.

These aspirations of the laity presented the medieval Church with a pastoral challenge it was ill-equipped to meet. The diocesan and parochial structure of the Western Church had developed to serve the needs of a rurally based population. Its clergy, apart from an educated élite which was absorbed by the schools and the ecclesiastical bureaucracy, were largely recruited locally from the ranks of the free peasantry, and educationally most of them were only a little above the level of their rustic parishioners. The numerous churches that were to be found in bigger towns were generally appropriated to monasteries or collegiate bodies and were too poorly endowed to attract the services of educated clerks. The predicament of the thirteenth-century Church was rather like that of the British railways in the mid-twentieth century – its layout reflected the economic and social needs of an earlier age. Of course, the analogy can be pushed too far. In the thirteenth century the majority of the population still resided in the countryside; but the significant growth points were the towns, and thenceforward modes of Christian piety and forms of the ascetical life would be determined by the religious experience of townsmen.

It was this gap in the pastoral equipment of the Church that the friars were to fill with such brilliant success. Thomas of Celano, the biographer of St Francis, tells that Pope Innocent III had a dream the night after his first encounter with Francis. In his dream he saw the Lateran basilica (the mother-church and head of all the churches of the West) tottering on the point of collapse, when a little man, obviously a beggar and wearing a habit of sackcloth and a belt of cord, crossed the piazza and shored up the edifice with his back.[2] The dream had a symbolic reality that was to be vindicated by history. As Innocent perceived, in the new world that was emerging the Church was facing a major crisis. Heresy was widespread. In the

Languedoc the Catharist heresy had taken root under the patronage of the landed classes and was organised as a counter-church with its own hierarchy. The towns of northern Italy had long been nurseries of various heretical sects, against which the secular clergy could make no headway. The bourgeoisie and the swelling population of artisans offered a ready audience for freelance itinerant preachers who moved along the trade routes in increasing numbers. New and radical forms of lay piety were appearing, which drew their inspiration from first-hand study of the New Testament, parts of which were now circulating in unofficial vernacular translations, and which posed a potential threat to the hierarchical structure of the Church. The question was whether this unruly flood of enthusiasm could be channelled and made to serve the cause of orthodoxy. Innocent was playing for high stakes when he gave his qualified approval to certain groups of mendicant lay preachers, but it was a gamble that succeeded.

New evangelists

The friars were only one among several groups of itinerant evangelists. The common inspiration of these groups came from a fresh and more radical interpretation of the apostolic life. Poverty, voluntarily embraced, was an essential part of it; and so was the idea of a preaching mission to proselytise the unconverted. But a new dimension was perceived in the old ideal. Authentic discipleship was now seen to be modelled upon the earthly life of Jesus as it was revealed by the Gospels – the imitation of Christ. The mental leap was easier for the literate layman in search of a paradigm of Christian perfection, whose mind was unencumbered by the medieval traditions of Biblical exegesis. It was a rediscovery of the literal sense of the Gospel.[3] In fact, the initiative in forming groups of evangelists came in many cases from the more affluent and articulate sections of the urban laity.

The founder of one such group, which in many ways anticipated the Franciscans, was Waldes, a wealthy cloth merchant and banker of Lyons. Strangely moved by hearing a *jongleur* in the street narrating the story of St Alexius – the rich young nobleman who was said to have renounced his bride and his patrimony on his wedding night and embraced poverty for the love of God – Waldes sought the advice of a schoolman about changing his way of life. The master he interrogated referred him to the Gospel injunction: 'If you would be perfect, go, sell what you possess and give to the poor, and you will have treasure in heaven; and come, follow me' (Matt. xix. 21). Moved by this advice, Waldes embarked upon a spectacular act of renunciation.

House and lands were settled on his aggrieved wife – her consent to her husband's spiritual odyssey seems not to have been sought – his two daughters were given a dowry and placed in a convent of the Order of Fontevrault; and the rest of his fortune was given away, some of it in the form of cash which he distributed to the poor in the streets. This done, he set off on a career of itinerant preaching, supporting himself solely by begging. In a short time he began to acquire disciples who adopted his way of life. Called to account for his activities at a legatine synod held at Lyons in 1181, he made a profession of orthodox faith, and explained that he and his followers had vowed themselves to absolute poverty, refusing to hold reserves of money, food, or clothing: 'nor will we accept gold or silver, or anything from anyone, except only food and clothing for the day'.[4] Most of his followers, the Waldenses or Poor Men of Lyons, who subsequently, in the face of clerical hostility, drifted into a radical anti-sacerdotal position, were drawn from the same social milieu. It was the class that produced St Francis of Assisi, the son of a rich cloth merchant, and his first disciples, and the leading spirits of the Humiliati in northern Italy.

The Humiliati were a religious fraternity, dedicated to the new style of apostolic life, which had gained a substantial following in the cities of Lombardy and the Veneto. Their members sought to realise in their lives what they believed to be the life-style of the apostolic Church, represented by voluntary poverty or at least frugality, simplicity in food and dress, penitential discipline, regular prayer, and preaching. Jacques de Vitry, ever a sharp-eyed reporter of the religious scene, noticed their success in recruiting among the urban patriciate, some of whom joined their celibate communities, while others remained in their own homes with wives and families, but 'living in the religious state and persevering in sobriety of life and works of mercy'. He also noticed that their members, though laymen, had been authorised to preach: 'their brethren, both clerks and literate laymen, have authority from the supreme pontiff, who has confirmed their rule, to preach, not only in their own congregation but also in the city squares and secular churches'.[5]

The decision of Pope Innocent III to authorise lay preaching legitimated an extraordinary breach in the sacerdotal professionalism of the medieval Church. Admittedly, he hedged the permission about with a proviso that the lay brethren should confine themselves to spiritual exhortation and avoid questions of dogmatic and sacramental theology;[6] but even with this limitation a significant frontier had been crossed. To more conservative churchmen lay preaching usurped the function of the official ministry; it was synonymous with subversion and heresy, and the initial reaction of authority had been to stamp on it. Thus both the Humiliati and the Waldenses were included, along with heretical sects, in a general condemnation by Pope Lucius III in 1184. It was left to the shrewd intelligence and inspired pragmatism of Innocent III to rehabilitate the Humiliati and to reconcile the orthodox section of the Waldenses led by the Spanish priest Durandus of Huesca and Bernard of Prim.

In their spirit and organisation the Humiliati bore some resemblance to the orders of friars. They associated voluntary poverty with evangelism; and their organisation, as it was approved by the pope, comprised three orders, the first consisting of tonsured clerics, the second of lay people living the cenobitical life under a quasi-monastic regime, and the third of lay disciples pursuing a life of regular devotion in their own homes; both the second and third orders earned their keep by working at manual crafts. Where the friars differed was in pursuing a more radical ideal of poverty. In Milan and other cities of northern Italy the communities of Humiliati enjoyed the security of well-endowed conventual houses. St Francis would have none of this. The scheme of evangelical perfection he proposed to his followers involved organised destitution; they were to join the ranks of the holy beggars who were becoming a scourge of the ecclesiastical establishment.

The friars came, then, on an urban scene that had grown accustomed to the visitation of wandering preachers and wild prophets and to the sight of unkempt and threadbare evangelists. They were part of this scenario themselves, and they might well have proved as ephemeral as the rest. The fact that they persisted and expanded into a Europe-wide organisation can only be explained, in human terms, by the peculiar genius and unique vision of their founders and by the shrewdness of the ecclesiastical authorities who perceived their possibilities and gave them support. The two first and greatest of the Mendicant Orders originated in the early years of the thirteenth century, and they grew side by side in a kind of symbiosis, though their antecedents and the circumstances of their origin were very different. The Dominicans were founded by an Augustinian canon, and from the outset they were a clerical order, which retained many of the features of the canons regular and had discernible roots in the twelfth-century ideology of the apostolic life. The Franciscans, on the other hand, owed their origin to the literal and uncomplicated but intense vision of a layman.

Franciscan origins

To his followers St Francis was a figure of momentous significance in world history. St Bonaventure identified him with the sixth angel named in the Apocalypse and credited his order with a messianic role, inaugurating a new phase in the Christian dispensation. This belief in the cosmic significance of Francis inspired an outpouring of hagiographical writing and reminiscence in the decades after his death. The complex interrelationships of these sources, the difficulty of distinguishing what is original from what is derivative, of disentangling genuine eye-witness report from pious fiction, have always posed serious critical problems for the historian.

The problem is aggravated by the fact that, as time went on, Francis became a sign of contradiction to his followers. Within four years of his death the leaders of the order sought a papal ruling which declared his death-bed Testament to the brethren to be without binding force, and provincial ministers were ordering copies of it to be burned. Later in the century the order he had inspired was rent by controversy over the meaning of his life and teaching, especially over his uncompromising ideal of poverty; and eventually the conflict between the 'Spiritual' party – the rigorists for absolute poverty, who claimed to be the authentic custodians of the founder's message – and the less radical 'Conventuals' ended with the Spirituals being driven into schism.

These dissensions, which became a lasting and tragic feature of Franciscan history, present a critical problem for the student of St Francis because at an early stage they infected the hagiographical tradition. What is probably the most widely known image of the poor man of Assisi, the Poverello, is derived from the *Little Flowers* – the *Fioretti*. The publication of this work, a classic of early Italian literature, in English translation enchanted the religious imagination of Victorian England, and even today it retains much of its freshness and power. Yet it is a relatively late and partisan source – a collection of anecdotes and legends which assumed its existing form in the Marches of Ancona in the fourteenth century. It represents the beginning of the movement – the idyllic Franciscan morning of the Umbrian countryside – as it was seen through the eyes of the Spirituals, and it is deeply tinged with their preconceptions and disappointments.

This conflict colours most of the sources. Brother Thomas of Celano, who wrote the earliest Life of St Francis, was commissioned to do so by the pope; and although it uses the language of official hagiography, it has the merit of having been begun in 1228, only two years after the death of Francis, so that it was composed before the outbreak of troubles in the order had tainted the wells. But Celano's second Life, produced sixteen years later, has significant omissions and changes of contour which clearly reflect the pressure of subsequent events. The wonderful cycle of frescos with which Giotto, or his pupils, embellished the walls of the upper basilica at Assisi drew their subject matter from the Life of the saint by St Bonaventure. This was the work of a man who was deeply involved in reconciling the conflicting viewpoints. It was commissioned by the general chapter of the order in 1260 and was accorded the status of the official biography; and in its omissions and sandpaperings it bears the unmistakable marks of the official hagiographer. Following its acceptance, order was given that the two earlier Lives by Celano should be destroyed. Even the great basilica itself, which Brother Elias had built over the tomb of St Francis, became a rock of offence. A later anecdote in the Spiritual tradition tells that Brother Leo, the old disciple and friend of St Francis, visited Assisi, and seeing a marble collecting vase which Elias had put out to receive contributions to the building fund for the basilica, was filled with rage and indignantly smashed the offending object with his stick.

To some extent the chronic controversy over Franciscan poverty has infected modern historians as well as the medieval biographers. Paul Sabatier, who published the classic modern biography in 1894, saw the early history of the movement in terms of an inevitable conflict between the pure religion of the spirit, represented by St Francis, and the religion of authority, represented by Ugolino – the cardinal protector of the infant order, who later became Pope Gregory IX and sought to translate the charismatic movement into traditional legal structures. Thus the original ideal of Francis was progressively diluted and smothered by the institutional Church. This viewpoint, which has been adopted by several modern scholars, derived some support from those sources that transmitted the tradition of the Spirituals.

FIGURE 13.1 Giotto's fresco showing St Francis and his brothers kneeling before Pope Honorius III, who is handing him a copy of the second Rule (the '*Regula Bullata*').

© Prisma Archivo/Alamy

All this means that anyone who sets out to describe the personality and teaching of St Francis must recognise that the enterprise is fraught with difficulties and subject to limitations. But the task is not impossible. In the search for the historical Francis through the thicket of the literary sources, the surest compass is provided by a handful of Francis's own writings, including the first and second Rules and the precious Testament, dictated on his deathbed, and with these the first Life by Celano.

Francis was a child of one of the turbulent urban societies of the twelfth century. His father, Pietro Bernardone, was a rich cloth merchant or draper of Assisi. As a son of a well-to-do bourgeois family, Francis took his place among the children of the chivalric class and the patriciate of the small hill town. Enchanted, like many Italian youths of his time, by the dreamworld of chivalric romance, he aspired to the accolade of knighthood; and with this in view he set out in the spring of 1205 to join the crusade led by Walter of Brienne to expel the remnants of German imperial power from southern Italy. But at Spoleto he was stopped by a dream which he believed to convey a divine message and also perhaps by misgivings about his physical and mental aptitude for mounted warfare, and so abandoned the expedition and returned home. The ignominy of this failure and the loss of his juvenile dreams of fame proved to be the first stage of his conversion to the religious life.

We do not know, we can only surmise, how his mind encountered and absorbed the various ascetical ideals that were abroad at the beginning of the thirteenth century. His education had begun and ended at the school of San Georgio at Assisi. Two surviving letters in his own hand, one of which is preserved in a reliquary in the *sacro convento*, show that he had an elementary grasp of Latin and could write it, if in a crude form. He also spoke French, the lingua franca of the medieval merchant class, though a companion remarked that he did not speak it at all well.[7] He was not a bookish man, either in his youth or in later life; but at any period, ideas that are widely current can be absorbed without recourse to books. Francis travelled in connection with his father's business and helped in the family shop, and it is probable that in the course of his journeys he encountered the Humiliati or other exponents of the apostolic life. His lifetime coincided with a climactic period of the Italian eremitical movement; and as a traveller he could hardly have failed to hear of the hermitages in the wooded hills of Umbria and Tuscany. All these offered models for a man in search of his religious vocation.

His early struggles after he had renounced the family home and the life-style of his class indicate that his mind was at first captivated by the eremitical ideal. In the early stage of his spiritual saga he lived as a hermit in caves and ruined churches, begging his food. Before long, he acquired a group of disciples from the young men of Assisi; and when he took them to Rome to seek papal approval of their way of life, a perceptive cardinal suggested that he could best fulfil his thirst for spiritual perfection as a hermit. Celano reports a significant discussion the party had on their way home; they had stopped overnight in a deserted spot

among the tombs outside the town of Orte – a scenario recalling the Life of
St Anthony the Hermit – and they discussed 'whether they ought to live among
men, or betake themselves to solitary places'.[8] Despite the spiritual attractions
of the desert, Francis decided for the active role of the evangelist; but he recognised the dilemma of those who were drawn to the contemplative life, and he
composed a brief and simple Rule for the brothers who lived in hermitages.[9] In
his later years, the compulsion of the solitary life of prayer reasserted itself, and
he increasingly withdrew with a few companions to a hermitage in the caves of
Fonte Colombo or the fastness of Mount Alverna.

While he was still in search of his vocation, the pull of the desert was superseded in his mind by another and more compelling idea. This was the concept of
the apostolic life which, as it was now coming to be widely understood, involved
poverty and an active preaching mission. Celano pinpoints for us the moment
when the idea took hold of his mind with overwhelming force. It was sometime
after his act of renunciation, when he was attending mass at the chapel of St
Mary of the Angels – the Portiuncula – outside Assisi. It was the feast of St Mat-
thias, and the Gospel lesson of the day was from Matthew, chapter 10, describing the sending out of the disciples: 'Preach as you go, saying "The kingdom of
heaven is at hand." . . . Take no gold, nor silver, nor copper in your belts, nor a
staff; for the labourer is worthy of his food.' Celano says that when Francis heard
this, he cried, 'This is what I want; this is what I am seeking'; and he immediately
removed his shoes, made a tunic of roughest material, and began to preach to all
the need for repentance.[10]

This model of the apostolic life had been the inspiration of other lay pietistic
movements of the twelfth century, including the Waldenses and the Humiliati.
They, too, had embraced an austere life of poverty and devoted themselves to
preaching. But Francis proposed for himself and his followers a more radical ideal
than these. Their poverty was to be more absolute; the brethren were to reject even
the common ownership of the primitive apostolic Church; they were to wander
through the world, sleeping in borrowed barns and shacks, and performing casual
labour or, if need be, begging for their daily food. How Francis understood the
way of life he adopted and taught his disciples can be most directly stated in his
own words; it was the literal imitation of the earthly life of Christ as depicted by
the Gospels: 'This is the life of the Gospel of Jesus Christ which Brother Francis
asked to be permitted him by the Lord Pope Innocent' begins the Second Rule. In
the Testament he declared that this conformity to the model of the homeless Christ
was not something he had been taught by somebody else; it was an ideal that had
come to him directly from God: 'The Most High revealed to me that I ought to
live according to the model of the Holy Gospel'; and again, in the Rule:

> The brothers shall appropriate nothing to themselves, neither a place nor
> anything; but as pilgrims and strangers in this world, in poverty and
> humility serving God, they shall with confidence go seeking alms. Nor

need they be ashamed, for the Lord made himself poor for us in this world. This is that summit of most lofty poverty which has made you, my most beloved brothers, heirs and kings of the kingdom of heaven.[11]

For Francis, this organised destitution, the refusal to own houses or touch money or accumulate reserves, was not just a missionary expedient or a means to an end; it was itself the *via salutis* – the literal imitation of the earthly life of Christ, who had nowhere to lay his head. The sole model for his fraternity was to be the life of Christ as communicated by the Gospel accounts. According to Celano, the first draft of a Rule he submitted to the pope caused consternation at the Curia: it contained nothing but a collection of texts from the four Gospels. This literal understanding of the Bible was characteristic of Francis. He had received the education of a layman, and throughout his life his modes of thought and his language continued to be that of the laity. His vision was always direct, literal and concrete, uncomplicated by the conceptual analysis of the clerk who had been through the schools. His apprehension of God was not through analytical language but through concrete symbols – the painted crucifix in the church of San Damiano, which spoke to him and commanded him to restore the church; the living crib at Greccio; and the seraph he saw in prayer, which left on his body the physical stigmata of crucifixion. Symbols like these expressed a new orientation of Western religious sentiment, marked by a personal devotion to, and identification with the humanity of Jesus, a concern with the circumstances of his earthly life, and a compassionate participation in his sufferings. They expressed a form of direct religious experience, which was no longer confined to an enclosed spiritual élite and which the teaching of the friars was to make available to the ordinary Christian living and working in the secular world. Its inspiration came from a rediscovery of the literal sense of the Gospel.

'Why you?' asked Brother Masseo of St Francis one day. 'Why you? The whole world seems to go after you, to listen to you, to obey you. Yet you are not handsome; you are not a man of great learning or wisdom; you are not of noble birth. So why is it you whom the whole world desires to follow?'[12] Masseo's mystified inquiry pointed to a fact that had profound and ever-widening implications for the history of Western Christianity. The instant popularity of the cult of St Francis and the enthusiasm with which the friars were welcomed in the cities of Europe derived their impetus from the resonance the Franciscan message had for all classes of the laity. The religious movements of the twelfth century, in particular the preachers of the apostolic life, had made numerous lay people aware that their state did not necessarily debar them from a life consecrated to God, even though marriage or worldly responsibilities prevented them from entering the cloister or seeking priestly ordination. The lesson transmitted by St Francis was that it was possible to live the Gospel, to practise the imitation of Christ, while living in the everyday world; the disciple of Christ could renounce the world, but continue to live in it. In the Testament Francis recalled his meeting with a leper and added that 'after this I did not wait long before leaving the world'. For him the process of 'leaving the world' was interiorised; it did not mean entering a monastery; it meant renouncing worldly values and ambitions and adopting a penitential life of prayer and service to the needy. The only Rule to be followed was the Gospel. This was a form of religious life to which all were invited whatever their condition. In the search for his own identity Francis had discovered and revealed that of the lay Christian.[13]

In its genesis the Franciscan movement was a lay initiative which had sprung from an urban environment. More than in the countryside, great disparities of wealth and poverty were made conspicuous by the crowded conditions of medieval town life. Meditation upon the Gospel and the spectacle of luxury in the midst of destitution had led Francis to reject the values of the new urban aristocracy. A sense of guilt was suggested by the fierceness with which he forbade the brethren to touch money. Their voluntary destitution identified them with the most deprived sections of society. But although they recruited members from all social groups, their chief attraction was understandably for the more affluent middle class and the clerical intelligentsia.

Voluntary poverty is not an ideal that has much appeal for those who are born poor. It is cetainly a mistake to regard the friars as an incorporation of down-and-outs. Francis himself and the apostles of the movement were almost all children of well-to-do families of Assisi. Salimbene, himself a Franciscan of the second generation, observed in his invective against the secular clergy that

> there are many in both orders of friars who, if they had been in the world, would have possessed the prebends they hold, and perhaps much better, for they are just as nobly born, as rich, powerful and learned as they, and would have been priests, canons, archdeacons, bishops and archbishops, perhaps even cardinals and popes, like them. They should recognise that we have given up all these things to go begging.[14]

The Friars did have some early success in recruiting among artisans, but broadly speaking, Salimbene's boast was justified. Their ideal of evangelical poverty attracted substantial numbers of followers from the aristocracy and the urban patriciate. Their most spectacular trawl was among the students and masters of the universities, a triumph fraught with momentous consequences for the future development of the order.

At the beginning, Francis and his followers were an intimate fraternity of nomadic preachers – a few, like Brother Sylvester, clerics, but most of them laymen – who moved from town to town in central Italy; they dossed down in borrowed accommodation, like their first hut at Rivo Torto; they preached in the market-squares, attended mass in the churches, and did manual jobs or begged for their keep. The outward sign of their poverty was the crude material of their habits, secured round the waist with a cord, and the fact that they went barefooted. Francis did not call them monks but Friars Minor or Little Brothers (*Fratres Minores*), a name intended to signify their very lowly status – the term *Minores* was used in the language of the Italian communes to mean the lowest class of people. The theme of their preaching was the need for repentance and penance for sins. It was one that would have found a ready response in the penitential associations that had sprung up in many Italian towns. When the brothers who went to preach in the March of Ancona were asked by the local people who they were, they answered 'we are the penitential men of Assisi'.[15] In 1209 Francis took his ragged company to Rome and persuaded Innocent III, not without misgivings, to sanction their activities. Although he does not seem to have formulated any organisational plan at this date, it was, in fact, the first step in the creation of a new religious order.

As numbers grew, it became the practice of the brethren to assemble at intervals and camp round the tiny church of the Portiuncula – a building lent them by the Benedictines of Subasio – where they held a chapter. It was at the Whitsun chapter of 1217 that the decision was taken to launch the brothers on a universal mission. In this and the following years parties were dispatched to the countries beyond the Alps, provinces were defined, and provincial ministers were appointed to supervise them. The composition and style of the party that later founded the English province was characteristic. On 10 September 1224 a group of nine, consisting of four clerics and five lay brothers, all of them barefooted and penniless, landed at Dover, having been ferried across the Channel by the monks of Fécamp. Four of the party were Italians, including their leader, Agnellus of Pisa, and three were Englishmen, including the only priest in the group, Richard of Ingworth; two were recent recruits, still in the noviciate. They made their first settlement at Canterbury in a room lent to them below the school-house; from there they quickly moved on to London, where they were lent a house on Cornhill by the sheriff, John Travers; and quite soon two of them, Ingworth and Richard of Devon, proceeded from there to Oxford.

The urban populations were the chosen mission field of the friars; and it was in the towns of northern Europe that the apostolate of the Franciscans began to take shape. As it did so, the paradox inherent in the idea of St Francis came to the surface and disturbed the order with a prolonged crisis of identity. The attempt to reconcile absolute poverty with the practical needs of a pastoral ministry involved heroic gymnastics of conscience. How could the friars preach and administer the sacraments if they possessed no churches? How could preachers and priests be educated for their task if they had no books (costly commodities in the medieval world) and no rooms in which to study? And how could any of these essentials be acquired without funds?

In the official Rule – the so-called *Regula Bullata*, which was sanctioned by Pope Honorius III in 1223 and which represented Francis's third attempt to draw up a plan for the order – he had expressly forbidden the brethren to own buildings or to touch money. The practical problems posed by this prohibition forced the provincial ministers in 1230 to seek a papal interpretation of the Rule from Gregory IX, which in effect mitigated its force: they were permitted to appoint a *nuntius* or 'spiritual friend' as a trustee to receive and hold money on behalf of the brethren, to whom they could apply to pay for necessities;[16] they were thus enabled to accept gifts of money, notably the legacies that were showered upon them by grateful penitents. The papal privilege *Quo elongati* authorising this concession represents the beginning of the inevitable retreat from St Francis's uncompromising ideal of absolute poverty.

The observance of poverty was not the only problem. The primitive fraternity had been largely lay in its inspiration and membership. There was no distinction of status between clerical and lay members. We do not know precisely when Francis himself was ordained; possibly he was tonsured by the pope in 1210, but he never proceeded beyond the diaconate.[17] Brother Elias, the chosen disciple to whom Francis handed over the direction of the order, remained a layman throughout his life. Agnellus of Pisa, the first English provincial minister, was a deacon when he arrived in England, and showed a marked reluctance to accept priestly ordination. But the whole concept of a lay ministry conflicted with the sacerdotal professionalism of the medieval Church. As Salimbene, himself an ordained friar, remarked, the hordes of idle lay friars he met in the Italian friaries were useless for the vital pastoral tasks of hearing confessions and dispensing the sacraments. For this there was need of priests.

Moreover, as the Friars Minor expanded and made settlements in the towns of northern Europe, they came under the direct influence of, and in competition with, the Order of Preachers. In Paris, Cologne, London and Oxford, they found the Dominicans already established; they came up against an order that, like them, was dedicated to poverty and preaching, but which was almost entirely clerical and had a clearly defined missionary purpose and a fully articulated representative constitution of a kind that St Francis had never envisaged. The problem was accentuated by their success among the scholars of the northern universities, which brought the Franciscans an influx of highly educated clerics. These tensions culminated in a conflict with the minister-general, Brother Elias, and led to his deposition.

In the tradition of the Spirituals, Elias was cast for the role of the Judas who betrayed the ideal of St Francis.[18] Certainly, his life-style during his generalate laid him open to criticism: accustomed by virtue of his position to socialising with the great, he seems to have acquired a taste for grandeur, and abandoned any personal effort to observe the spirit of Franciscan poverty. Salimbene refers indignantly to his plump palfreys, his retinue of page-boys, and the private cook who accompanied him on his travels.[19] But other and more significant charges were laid against him. The attack on his regime came from the northern provinces, and it was mobilised by a group of friars who were clerks and university graduates, the most prominent among whom was the English scholar Haymo of Faversham. The indictment contained the charges that he had governed the order autocratically and had failed to convene a general chapter for many years, and that he had persistently appointed lay brothers to positions of authority as guardians of houses and provincial ministers. There is no doubt that in promoting lay friars and refusing to accord ordained brothers a privileged status he was acting in accordance with the mind of St Francis; and his paternalistic regime was also faithful to the founder's notions of authority and religious obedience. But the disapproval of the ministers prevailed, and after presiding over a stormy meeting of the general chapter in 1239, Pope Gregory IX deposed him. His overthrow was quickly followed by a reappraisal of the constitution and objectives of the order. Leadership passed to the graduate clerical members, and lay brothers were debarred from holding office. In fact the Friars Minor had been subjected to a clerical takeover from within. In the ensuing phase of constitution-making they came under the powerful influence of the Dominican Order, to which we must now turn.

The Order of Preachers

The Order of Preachers differed in both its genesis and its spirit from the early Friars Minor. From the start, it was a clerical and learned order, a stepchild of the canons regular, in which everything was subordinated to the needs of a pastoral mission. It grew out of the situation of the Languedoc, where the founder had become involved in preaching against the heresy of the Cathars. Dominic was a Castilian priest of aristocratic birth – a late tradition connects him with the noble Spanish family of Guzman.[20] He had been educated at the schools of Palencia, and he was a canon of Osma cathedral, the chapter of which had been reconstituted as a community of canons regular living according to the Rule of St Augustine. It was in 1203, when accompanying his bishop, Diego of Osma, on a diplomatic mission, that he made his first direct acquaintance with the pervasive strength of the Catharist heresy in the society of the Languedoc.

At this time the task of combating the Albigensian heresy had been assigned by the pope to the Cistercians; but they had had little success. On their way home in 1206, Dominic and Diego encountered the Cistercian legates at Montpellier, and decided to add their efforts to the enterprise. At this point Peter Ferrandus, Dominic's biographer, records a significant conversation between the two parties of missionaries: Diego and his young canon argued that the Cistercian abbots were hampered by their prelatical style and large retinue; only practitioners of the *vita apostolica* vowed to poverty could hope to secure a hearing as authentic preachers of the Gospel; it was a question of competing with the *perfecti* – the spiritual élite of the Catharist sect, who were famous for their austerity and self-denial.[21] Since the early twelfth century the apostolic life had been understood to be the life of the itinerant preacher, without visible property and dependent upon alms for his food. The two Spaniards persuaded the abbots to join them on these terms; the bishop set the tone by sending his servants and clerks home with the horses. The party then set out on foot on an itinerant preaching tour, holding public debates with the Cathar leaders at Servian and Béziers and other towns of the Midi.

It has often been said that the Dominicans borrowed the ideal of absolute poverty – the rejection, that is, of even corporate ownership and the practice of mendicancy – from the Franciscans; but this is an oversimplification. Francis and Dominic admired one another; acording to Celano's second Life, they met in Rome in the house of Cardinal Ugolino. But the mendicant idea was adopted by Dominic and Diego independently at a time when they could scarcely have heard of Francis. To them it was simply the practical application of the twelfth-century notion of the *vita apostolica*, a perfectly familiar concept to Dominic, the Augustinian canon regular. In the case of the Dominicans we can see quite plainly the link with current doctrines of the apostolic life, which we can only suspect in the case of the Franciscans. Where the Franciscan example may have influenced the policy of the Order of Preachers was over the question of corporate ownership. Dominic acquired houses in Toulouse, where he founded an establishment to train preachers, and Bishop Fulk of Toulouse assigned them a portion of the tithes in his diocese. But the first general chapter of the order, which was held at Bologna in 1220, renounced all its properties in Toulouse and decreed against the acceptance of any properties other than churches or any revenues for the future. Thus a year before his death, Dominic had persuaded his order to opt for corporate poverty and to commit itself to mendicancy. It is possible, though we cannot be sure, that this decision was prompted by the example of the Friars Minor.

Diego returned home to die; but Dominic continued his preaching and pastoral ministrations in the Midi throughout the grim years of the northern crusade against the Albigenses and the social upheaval that followed it.

Bishop Fulk, himself a Cistercian and former abbot, had come to regard Dominic's preachers as the best hope of salvaging what was left of the orthodox Church in his diocese, and in the autumn of 1215 he took Dominic to Rome to seek Innocent III's authorisation of a new order devoted to preaching. They were kindly received at the Curia, and letters confirming the properties held at Prouille were obtained without difficulty; but over the proposal for an order of preachers the pope temporised.[22] Preaching and the licensing of preachers were *ex professo* the function of bishops; to vest it in a monastic body seemed anomalous; all the more so as canon law debarred monks from ministering in public churches.

Besides this objection to the plan, a new one was presented by the Fourth Lateran Council which was then assembling. Apparentiy out of a desire to stem what now seemed to be an uncontrollable flood of religious experiment, the fathers of the council in due course decreed that, owing to the multiplicity and confusion of orders, nobody was to found a new one; anyone desiring to found a new fraternity was instructed to adopt an existing rule that had already been approved.[23] Faced with this check to his plan, Dominic returned to Toulouse to discuss the matter with the brethren. The solution they adopted was the obvious one: they placed themselves under the Rule of St Augustine, to which Dominic was already vowed. This left him free to plan the organisation of the order as he thought best. Papal confirmation obtained from Pope Honorius III in 1216 did no more than recognise the existence of the fraternity and confirm its possessions at Toulouse. It did not ratify any specific rule comparable to that of the Friars Minor. The arrangements subsequently enacted by the general chapters, which gave the order its remarkable constitution, were never confirmed by the papacy; nor was confirmation sought: officially, the Order of Preachers was simply a branch of the canons regular.

When Dominic approached the Curia, his fraternity was still engaged in preaching in the Languedoc. But in 1217, in a chapter held at Toulouse, he anounced the decision to disperse. There was a diaspora of the Toulouse community; some were dispatched to Paris, some to Spain, and some to Bologna. The Preachers were thus launched on a universal mission, a fact proclaimed by a bull of Honorius III issued in 1218, which commended the brethren to prelates everywhere and invoked support for their preaching efforts. The selection of Paris and Bologna as early objectives highlighted an element in Dominic's strategy that was to be vigorously pursued by his successors: his friars not only sought to provide for the theological education of the preachers; they made it their aim to capture the leading intellectual centres of their time.

One of the talents St Dominic had – one that St Francis conspicuously lacked – was a capacity for organisation. The earliest comprehensive body of statutes governing the life of the Friars Preachers was enacted by the general chapter of 1228, and it was codified by Raymond of Penaforte during his mastership (1238–40), but the plan it embodied was largely the creation of Dominic himself. In their domestic observance the Preachers retained the marks of their monastic origin. As a canon regular, Dominic had followed the usages of Prémontré, and he imposed these on his new order, including choral recitation of the divine office at the canonical hours, a daily chapter of faults, and the Premonstratensian penitential code. The monastic periods of fasting were observed and the monastic rule of silence was kept everywhere in the house and at all times except in privileged places.

Obviously, a plan to reconcile a strictly regulated monastic regime of liturgical prayer, silence and seclusion with the activities of a pastoral mission presented problems. Mitigations were necessary to allow the preachers freedom to operate outside the cloister and to release lectors and their pupils for study and practice in the skills of disputation. Thus the monastic tradition of manual labour was discarded; the statutes decreed that the offices were to be sung 'shortly (*breviter*) and succinctly so that the brethren be hindered as little as possible in their studies';[24] and any prior was authorised to dispense friars of his house from attendance at the offices for the sake of study, lecturing or preaching. The chapter gave friars studying at Paris to equip themselves for lectorships a general dispensation to absent themselves from the non-festive offices on weekdays, with the exception of Compline. That exception was indicative of a spirit of adaptation: the short office of Compline that ended the monk's day and inaugurated the hours of the Great Silence, was converted by the Preachers into a public service; sung at an hour of the day when most people's work was finished, it attracted many towns-people to the churches of the friars.

If the internal observance of the Dominican friaries was firmly anchored in the monastic tradition, the constitution of the order embodied a revolution in the practice, if not the theory, of government. It gave effect to the principles of representation and responsibility to an extent then unknown in either ecclesiastical or secular government. At every level the superiors of the Order of Preachers were not only elected by the brethren; they were made responsible for the conduct of their office to their constituents. The basic unit of the organisation was the individual convent or priory. Its head, the prior, was elected by his brethren in chapter. They also elected a companion, a *socius*, to accompany their prior to the annual meeting of the provincial chapter, and it was part of his role to carry a report on the state of his community and the conduct of their superior to the assembly.

The order was divided into territorial provinces, and the head of each – the provincial prior – was elected by a special session of the provincial chapter; this consisted of the heads of individual houses together with two representatives elected for the purpose by each priory. The provincial prior was answerable to the chapter. As the provincial chapter was usually a large body, the Dominicans quite early adopted the Cistercian practice of delegating business to a steering committee, in this case of four 'diffinitors', chosen by a poll of the chapter on the opening day; and this committee could receive complaints against the provincial and, if necessary, suspend him from office.

Dominic had determined from the outset that the sovereign body of the order should be a general chapter. It met every year at Whitsun, alternating in the early years between Bologna and Paris, but thereafter in various places chosen by itself. The general chapter had, of course, been a feature of some monastic organisations for nearly a century. Where the Dominican chapter differed was in its representative character. It consisted of the Master-General, who presided, and one 'diffinitor' elected by the chapter of each province. As the order had established only thirteen provinces before the year 1300, the general chapter must have been a relatively small and effective body. For two successive years, only these elected representatives of the provinces attended, reinforced by a small group of friars who held the prestigious office of Preacher-General; but in the third year the provincial priors attended the chapter instead. This nice balance between the representative and official elements was strengthened by a proviso that any new statute must have secured the assent of three consecutive chapters before it acquired the force of law. This requirement not only insured against hasty and ill-considered legislation; it also allowed the official element to exercise a veto.

There was also another severely practical reason for these arrangements which we, in the days of air and motorway travel, can easily overlook. Perpetuating the example set by St Dominic, the statutes insisted that friars should manifest the spirit of poverty and place themselves on the level of the most indigent classes of society by always travelling on foot. No exceptions were allowed for longer journeys; the general chapter of 1255 ordained that priors or other brethren who were unable to make their way to the chapter on foot should stay at home.[25] Travel to the general chapter from the more distant provinces had therefore to be reckoned in months rather than days. A journey from England to Bologna on foot would have taken anything from eighty days to four months. If provincial priors had been required to attend every year, they would have spent most of their time on the roads and away from the provinces they were supposed to govern.

The head of the order, the Master-General, was himself elected by an enlarged session of the general chapter. Although he might hold office until resignation or death, the statutes made him answerable to the chapter for his stewardship; the diffinitors had the power to correct him or, in the case of heresy or grave misconduct, to depose him; they were warned, however, to proceed with utmost caution in such an eventuality.[26] In fact, although a Master sometimes resigned on account of ill health, as Humbert of Romans did in 1263, most incumbents of the office held it for life.

In order to ensure that the decrees of the sovereign body were observed and standards maintained, a system of regular visitation was devised. For this four friars were chosen annually by each provincial chapter to visit all the priories in their territory and report; and every third year visitors were appointed by the general chapter. Here then was a completely articulated system of representative government, which apparently sprang fully fledged from the minds of St Dominic and his successor, Jordan of Saxony, in the years 1220–28. It succeeded, in a way that no other monastic rule had done, in giving institutional form to the ascetical principle of obedience to a superior without recourse to paternalism or prelacy. It proved to be a model that influenced many other ecclesiastical organisations, and not least that of the Friars Minor.

The Franciscans worked out their constitutional arrangements more slowly. To his followers St Francis was a pillar of fire, but he was no legislator. The process of legislation only began in earnest after the fall of Elias in 1239, and it was completed by the code which St Bonaventure compiled and presented to the general chapter at Narbonne in 1260.[27] Much of the Franciscan structure of government was borrowed from the Dominicans, including the system of provincial chapters, and election to office. But although their debt to the sister order is obvious, the arrangements of the Friars Minor fell short of the thoroughgoing system of representation that the Dominicans had created. Their general chapter met only every third year, and their General Minister was left with less fettered powers of direction. Moreover, the process of democratic election to office operated only at the higher level; at the lower level, the guardians of friaries were designated by the provincial ministers, and so, too, were the heads of the custodies, the subordinate regions into which provinces were divided. Something of the paternalistic spirit in which the primitive order had been governed still survived in the constitutions of 1260.

The mission of the friars

The friars set out to evangelise the new world of the cities. 'There', explained Humbert of Romans, 'preaching is more efficacious because there are more people, and the need is greater, for in the city there are more sins.'[28] Themselves the product of the new urban society, they preached the Word to people whose language and mental habits they knew and understood. Initially, they made for the larger and long-established cities, the major centres of commerce and exchange. It was there that the size of the population offered a ripe field for the evangelist and the existence of surplus wealth made it possible to support groups of missionaries who depended upon alms-giving for their livelihood; there also could be found a reservoir of young people free from seignorial bondage, from which the mendicant apostles hoped to recruit new members.

They found these conditions in the rich and turbulent city republics of central and northern Italy, the commercial and episcopal cities of the Rhineland, the Paris basin and the Low Countries, and in some of the smaller but prosperous towns of England. For the Dominicans, and to a lesser extent for the Friars Minor, a desire to recruit among the educated was one of the factors determining their choice of venue. For this reason the university towns of Bologna, Paris, and Montpellier were among their primary objectives. In England, while both orders made for London, their decision to settle in Oxford immediately afterwards was probably influenced less by the commercial importance of the town, which was a small one by continental standards, than by the attraction of the schools, which offered a promising hunting-ground for recruits. In the early phases of settlement the residences of the friars consisted of disused and not always salubrious dwelling houses lent them by individual merchants or by the borough corporations, who generally welcomed them with enthusiasm; more often than not they were located in the suburbs outside or in close proximity to the town walls, for within the walls of the older cities property was hard to find and expensive. In Germany and England it was not unusual for their conventual buildings to be integrated with the mural fortifications.

'The harvest was great of those who lacked the doctrine of salvation', wrote Bonaventure, but suitable labourers were few.[29] The friars captured a market that was relatively neglected. The success they had with their city congregations was the result of their effectiveness as preachers and confessors. For many of the church-going laity a homily had long since ceased to be part of their normal experience. Few of the parish clergy had enough education to offer their people doctrinal or moral instruction; the many small churches to be found in the older towns were either private chapels or were appropriated to monasteries, and were too poorly endowed to attract the services of educated clerks. This was the gap in pastoral provision that the friars were able to fill with resounding success. It was their achievement to lead a revival of popular preaching that was just beginning. In their hands, sermon-making became a new art, which was inculcated in their schools and disseminated through their writings.[30] To help the preacher perform his task they produced a large body of didactic literature, ranging from the theoretical treatise, like the *Art of Preaching* by the Dominican Thomas of Wales, to collections of model sermons and sermon-aids, such as the books of *Exempla* – collections of anecdotes which a preacher could use to enliven his sermon and catch the attention of his congregation.

Lively and well-argued sermons were calculated to make an irresistible impact upon congregations containing significant numbers of merchant families and professional people, long starved of pulpit oratory. But it was not only superior technique and lively performance that enabled the friars to grip the attention of their audiences. An even more important factor in their success was the message they brought: to lay people dissatisfied with their role as passive spectators of liturgical observances and hungry for guidance in personal religion, who could find no outlet for their spiritual aspirations in the existing structures of the Church, they offered new possibilities of active participation. By both their teaching and example they pioneered the idea of the devout life for the laity – a Christian life of prayer and sacrifice, not modelled upon that of monks or dependent upon the vicarious merits acquired for them by professional ascetics, but one modelled upon the supreme paradigm of Christ and lived fully in the world. It was a hopeful message that contrasted with the pessimism of the traditional monastic spirituality, which regarded the monk as the only truly committed Christian and offered only a tenuous hope of salvation to the married laity.

Those lay people who were stirred by the teaching of the friars to ask how they could respond to the call of the evangelical life without deserting their worldly responsibilities were offered fulfilment in the penitential fraternities, some of which acquired the status of Third Orders – lay religious orders incorporated into the orders of the Mendicants: 'there are many', observed Humbert of Romans, 'who say they cannot perform penance in the world; nor do they wish to enter religion, which they cannot do on account of being married; but lo, divine providence has ordained so as to remove all excuse of this kind; there exists in the midst of the world a way of doing penance which has been approved by the pope and distinguished by many graces and privileges, which is adopted by the brethren called brothers of penance . . . Many people of high birth, both men and women, most of all in parts of Italy, have adopted this kind of life.'[31]

What the friars offered was a new theology of the secular life: personal sanctification was within the reach of those engaged in secular occupations – even for merchants, whose calling was generally censured by ascetical theologians. The new orientation is exemplified by the popularity of a genre of sermon that had made its first tentative appearance in the twelfth century – sermons *ad status*, addressed to the particular spiritual needs of different classes and occupations: sermons for knights, merchants, scholars, servants, masters, rulers, married people, and so forth. This was a genre of preaching in which the friars excelled. Humbert of Romans included in his *Instruction of Preachers* a series of model sermons of this type suitable for lay townsmen, for those living in rural communities, for members of confraternities, merchants attending fairs, and rulers of cities, as well as various categories of religious. An interesting feature of this preaching, which is only now receiving attention from scholars, is a more appreciative and optimistic approach to the theme of marriage and married love, a subject that in the past had often evoked virulent misogyny from ascetical writers. 'Our Order', the Dominican Henry of Provins reminded his brethren, 'is the work of a mere mortal; but it was God who himself instituted the order of marriage . . . at the time of the flood, the Lord showed his preference by saving married people.'[32]

The counterpart of evangelical preaching was the hearing of confessions. 'There are some preachers who totally refuse to hear confessions,' wrote Humbert disapprovingly; 'these are like farmers who gladly sow, but are unwilling to reap any harvest'[33] – the preacher's aim was to rouse his hearers to repentance and contrition. This was the other area in which the friars achieved remarkable success. They were greatly in demand by the laity as confessors and spiritual directors in royal and aristocratic courts as well as in the city market-places. Both Henry III and Louis IX of France kept Franciscan and Dominican friars constantly in their entourage to serve as confessors and counsellors. This popularity can be partly explained by the fact that the friars gave their men training in the discipline of the confessional; but the phenomenon had a more complex root than that, one that is hinted at in Chaucer's gibe at the friar confessor:

> He was an esy man to yeve penaunce
> Ther as he wiste to han a good pitaunce.

Chaucer's crack was a half-truth, the product of a century of bitter polemic between the Mendicants and the secular clergy. The fact was, the friars made themselves the chief exponents and practitioners of a new school of moral theology, which had been developed in the schools of Paris. It was a form of casuistry, in the proper sense of the word, which escaped from the straitjacket of the old penitentials with their fixed tariff of punishments, and placed greater emphasis on the circumstances and intentions of the penitent.[34] Its application made, of course, greater intellectual and psychological demands upon the confessor than the older system, and it was easily open to misunderstanding and misrepresentation.

Student orders

A pastoral mission to the literate and relatively sophisticated people of the towns, as well as disputation with the élite of the Cathars, demanded both mental agility and a thorough theological education. Dominic and Jordan of Saxony, who succeeded him as Master-General in 1222, had perceived this from the outset. For this reason Jordan directed his best efforts towards recruiting postulants from the university classrooms. 'Your prayers for the scholars of Padua have been heard,' he wrote triumphantly to Diana d'Andolo, superior of the nunnery at Bologna, 'twenty of them have entered our order.'[35] In 1226 he was at Paris, preaching to the schoolmen, and reported a fine crop: 'Within four weeks of our arrival, twenty- one brethren entered, among whom were six Masters of Arts, and the rest bachelors.'[36] 'At the studium of Oxford, where I am at present,' he wrote, 'the Lord has given us great hopes of a good catch';[37] and in the event his hopes were realised; his preaching to the university in November 1229 brought a flush of recruits, including masters as well as students.

Behind the drive to recruit men from the universities was an awareness of the pressing need to provide instructors to educate the brethren and train them for their task. The Preachers had to be a student order if they were to accomplish their objects. 'Study', observed Humbert, 'is not the end of the order, but is most necessary to secure its end, namely preaching and the salvation of souls, for without study neither can be accomplished.'[38] Every priory, therefore, had its classroom, where all members of its community except the lay brothers were required to attend lectures daily and to take part in practice disputations. It was an obligation imposed on every young friar as soon as he had completed his year's noviciate; and the general chapter constantly urged priors to chivy their young recruits into applying themselves to their studies. To provide systematic schooling, the Dominican Order as a whole was organised as a kind of disseminated university.

At the base of the organisation was the priory school with its own lector. The statutes decreed that no priory might be established without a minimum complement of twelve friars, one of whom had to be a theologian competent to instruct the brethren. The lector's task was to lecture to his community on the Bible, the Biblical *Histories* of Peter Comestor, and to provide an introduction to dogmatic theology by giving cursory lectures on the *Sentences* of Peter Lombard.[39] In addition he was enjoined to lecture using as his text the *Summa de casibus* – a treatise on penance and confession by the Spanish friar Raymond of Penaforte.

As the testimonial letters of Pope Honorius had made clear, the mission of Dominic's friars was to hear confessions and counsel penitents as well as to preach. Those who were going to hear confessions had to be well instructed in the problems of moral theology; and for those of the brethren who were not going to proceed to a university or one of the higher schools – the majority, in fact – the instruction had to be given in their own priory. It was for their guidance that in the 1220s a number of lectors put together treatises on confessional practice, of which Raymond's *Summa* was the most famous. Initially composed in 1225 for the use of the brethren in Spain, in its revised form it was adopted as the classical manual of instruction throughout the order, and remained in use .until it was superseded by the *Summa* of John of Freiburg in the fourteenth century. In the early years it proved difficult to provide adequate staffing of schools at priory level, as the expansion of the order outran the supply of ready-made graduates who could act as lectors. The education of a theologian was a long process. The general chapter of 1259 remarked that in some provinces there were priories without lectors; and the visitors were told to search out vacancies and to commandeer the services of any friars who were qualified to teach.[40]

What was provided in the priory schools was Bible study and a basic grounding in the principles of dogmatic and moral theology, reinforced by practice in debate. At a more advanced level, a study of the logical works of Aristotle – 'the books of the heathen', as the statutes refer to them distastefully – was an indispensable preparation for the study of scholastic theology. The Aristotelian logic formed part of the university Arts curriculum, but the friars refused to allow their men to attend the Arts course in the turbulent and dissolute society of the universities. Instead they provided the necessary courses in specialist schools of their own. In the course of time, the Dominicans developed special centres to meet all their needs. Within each province a number of priories were given the status of major schools – *studia solemnia* – with a larger teaching staff to teach the subjects of the Arts curriculum. In the later decades of the thirteenth century, we find provincial chapters designating houses in each vicariate or visitation, some to be schools of logic, some to provide instruction in natural philosophy, and others to offer more advanced courses in theology. The chapters also appointed the lectors to these senior schools.

Those who were groomed for lectorships were sent to one or another of the provincial schools to follow courses in logic, natural philosophy and theology. Some might proceed no further; but the ablest went on to study theology at a *studium generale* – one of the order's 'general schools' situated in a university centre. These formed the apex of the order's scholastic structure. The earliest of them to be established – and the most prestigious – was the school of Paris, the famous priory in the rue Saint Jacques, to which each province was entitled to send three of its picked men. In order to reduce the pressure on the Paris house and to meet the increasingly voracious demand for lectors, the general chapter of 1247 instructed the provincial priors of England, Germany, Lombardy and Provence, to set up a general school in their provinces, to which other provinces might send a quota of two students each, and this led to the creation of general schools at Oxford, Cologne, Bologna and Montpellier. By the year 1300 additional centres of advanced study had been established at Florence and Barcelona. In due course, men with the aptitude for scholarship would be authorised to incept as masters in the theology faculty of the university. This co-ordinated academic system was an extraordinary construction without parallel in the Middle Ages. It was superior to any educational provision that existed for the secular clergy or the laity.

The Franciscans moved into higher education more slowly and at first more reluctantly. There can be little doubt that St Francis never envisaged such a move and that he would have been opposed to it. Celano reports him as saying 'My brethren who are led by curiosity for learning shall find their hands empty on the day of retribution.'[41] A studium set up at Bologna during his absence in 1219 failed to secure his approval, and it was only saved from closure by the intervention of Cardinal Ugolino, the Protector of the order. Francis's misgivings were shared by some of the disciples of the first generation. 'O Paris,' lamented Brother Giles, 'thou hast destroyed Assisi.'[42] But the leaders of the next generation, like John Parenti and Haymo of Faversham, recognised that learning was imperative if the order was to fulfil its pastoral mission. Hugh of Die, the fiery Provencal friar, who became famous as the expositor of the prophecies of Joachim of Fiore, argued that no one was better fitted to expound the Gospel than the university master who was also a friar.[43]

The decision to enter university teaching and the world of scholarship seems to have been taken at Paris in the 1230s, when the English theologian Alexander of Hales sought admission to the Friars Minor; he already held a chair of theology, and he was permitted to continue lecturing in the faculty without interruption, thereby giving the order a foothold in the academic association. At Oxford, where Franciscans arrived in October 1224, they were at first taught by a succession of secular masters, the first and most distinguished of whom was Robert Grosseteste, who had some years earlier been head of the Oxford schools. It was not until 1247 that a Franciscan incepted as a doctor in the theology faculty. This was Adam Marsh, who was already a Master of Arts when he joined the order. After this, the English Franciscan province rapidly developed a scholastic structure closely resembling that of the Dominicans. Its organisation was largely the result of collaboration between Adam Marsh and the provincial ministers who picked and groomed suitable men to be lectors in the friaries throughout the province.[44]

Both the Mendicant Orders thus created an articulated international system of advanced education. Compared with the secular schools this system had another important advantage besides that of superior organisation. In the secular schools men taught for a few years and moved on. University teaching was not regarded as a career for life; the need to acquire a benefice, to repay patrons, the competition for pupils, and the expectation of a career at the higher levels of Church or state, constantly drew men away from the schools in early middle-life. But when a man became a friar, he opted out of the race for preferment. At the schools he was freed from such preoccupations and able to pursue scholarship with a detachment and security hardly open to his secular colleagues; and if he was successful, he might be left by his order to spend his whole life teaching and in the pursuit of truth. These were propitious conditions for original intellectual work. They go some way towards explaining the fact that in the thirteenth century, the classical age of scholastic theology, it was the friars who produced the most original and creative scholars. The Dominicans Albertus Magnus, Aquinas, and Kilwardby, and the Franciscans Alexander of Hales, Bonaventure, and Duns Scotus, were not only men of creative genius who dominated the intellectual world of their time; they left behind them a huge mass of written work – the fruit of academic leisure and security – which is of permanent and universal significance.

The complaint of the clergy

To begin with, relations between the friars and the secular clergy were fraught with ambiguity. In some places their settlement was greeted with mistrust if not hostility. But the more zealous and discerning prelates welcomed their assistance. Grosseteste, after he became bishop of Lincoln, wrote to the provincials of both orders asking them to supply him with friars who could be used to preach and hear confessions during his diocesan visitations. But as the Mendicants expanded their pastoral activities, began building their own churches, and moved into the schools, they came increasingly into collision with the interests of the secular clergy, and much of the early good will evaporated. Their success as preachers and confessors siphoned congregations away from parish churches, and of course with the people went the flow of offerings and pious bequests, which were diverted into the trust funds administered for the friars. Many of the great urban preaching churches of Europe, like Santa Croce in Florence, embellished with frescoes and paved with the monuments of the civic aristocracy, bear eloquent witness to their success in winning the patronage of the city populations of the thirteenth century. The mounting tension was brought to the boil after 1250, when the friars obtained from Innocent IV a privilege permitting anyone, who so desired, to be buried in one of their cemeteries. This breached what had hitherto been a lucrative and jealously guarded monopoly of parish churches.

Many of the secular clergy now began to regard the friars as a threat to their status and livelihood; and their cause found an articulate voice among the secular masters of the university of Paris. Here the dispute began as a straightforward conflict of interests. Papal decree had limited the number of chairs in the theology faculty to twelve at any one time, three of which were reserved to canons of the cathedral. By the process we have seen, the Mendicants had gained control of three chairs, and looked likely to gain a fourth. The brilliant success of the Mendicant teachers necessarily reduced the opportunities open to the secular masters of the faculty – the friars were capturing too large a share of this restricted academic market.

In the face of what they perceived to be a growing threat to their prospects, the regent masters in theology decided upon concerted action to curb the invasion of their territory by the Mendicants. In February 1252 they approved a statute ordaining that each religious order should be restricted to conducting a single school and to a single master of the faculty. This ordinance proved to be the opening salvo of a bitter struggle that continued for many years. But the conflict was more than a squabble over academic posts. The friars were in the university, but not exclusively of it, and they tended to take lightly their obligations towards the academic corporation.

The flash-point came in the Lent of 1253. Following a brawl in which a student had been killed by the city watch and others imprisoned, the university in a hastily convened congregation responded by a suspension of teaching and a threat to secede from Paris unless it received immediate redress from the city authorities. The friars, however, refused to take part in the demonstration or to suspend teaching; they were therefore excommunicated and expelled from the university by their enraged colleagues. What had begun as an 'industrial dispute' now developed into a violent controversy, which brought into focus some of the deepest tensions and most revolutionary developments in the structure of the medieval Church.

The leading spokesman of the secular masters was the Burgundian theologian William of Saint-Amour, who enjoyed the security of prebends at Mâcon and Beauvais. William did not confine his attack to the academic activities of the friars; he challenged their right to exercise any form of pastoral ministry. In his tract *Concerning the Perils of the Last Days*, which he put out in 1255, he took his stand on the theory that the diocesan and parochial structure of the Church was founded upon the Apostles and was of divine ordinance. In this divine dispensation the secular clergy alone were entrusted with the cure of souls, and this was something that no one, be he pope or anyone else, had authority to change. Taking a leaf from the *Hierarchies* of the Pseudo-Denys, he argued that it was the exclusive role of the superior priestly order to perfect and instruct others; monks (a category in which he included the friars) belonged, like the laity, to the inferior order of those who required to be perfected by pastoral ministrations of the clergy; they could not perform an office that belonged to their superiors. Moreover, mendicancy, he argued, was contrary to the example of Christ and the express instructions of St Paul. The friars were therefore false prophets who, in view of their begging activities, should be classed with common thieves.[45]

In the face of this attack, the friars invoked the authority of the pope, who had sanctioned their ministry, and took refuge behind a paralysing barrage of papal privileges – a strategy plainly contrary to the declared will of St Francis, who had warned the brethren against postulating privileges from Rome, even for their own protection. They also produced replies to William which expounded a different system of church order. One of these was written by the English Franciscan Thomas of York; others also joined the fray, most notably Bonaventure, who was at the Paris house of the Franciscans waiting to incept as a doctor in the theology faculty. To confute William of Saint-Amour, the Mendicants produced an apologia based upon an extreme papalist doctrine: the pope was not only the universal bishop; he was everyman's parish priest, and as such he could delegate his parochial responsibilities to whom he chose; and he had chosen to delegate them to the friars.[46] Thus the controversy resolved itself into two conflicting ecclesiologies: that of William of Saint-Amour based upon a static hierarchy and the indefeasible rights of local churches within their territorial boundaries; and that of the friars – a dynamic theory, which reflected the rising power of the centralising papacy, and regarded the Church as a single social organism emanating from the pope. It was a theory adapted not only to developments in the organisation of the Church; it also reflected the social and economic changes of the thirteenth century, when the isolation of local communities was being eroded by the agents of the central power, the growth of international trade, and the rise of an international community of learning.

William's tract was condemned by Rome, and he was forced to retire from the schools. But his defeat did not end the controversy; the attack on the friars was renewed a decade later by Gerard of Abbeville, who denounced the Franciscan doctrine of evengelical poverty from the university pulpit. This drew from Bonaventure his *Apologia Pauperum* – the classical vindication of the Mendicant ideal as a literal imitation of Christ, who was deemed to have lived in absolute poverty. The university of Paris was the cockpit for a quarrel that continued with growing intensity elsewhere. Secure under papal protection, the friars went from strength to strength. In 1281 a Franciscan pope, Martin IV, issued them with the privilege *Ad fructus uberes*, which authorised them to perform all pastoral functions in any diocese or parish without seeking consent from the local ecclesiastical authorities. This represented the high-water mark of their privileges, and it led to a prolonged and bitter struggle. In France, the bishops made repeated efforts to get the bull annulled.

After a decade of wrangling, it was Boniface VIII who in the end devised the terms of a truce with the bull *Super Cathedram*, promulgated in 1300. This decreed that friars might only preach in parishes with the consent of the incumbent; that provincials of the friars should present a number of their members to the bishop, who would license them to hear confessions in his diocese; and that though the friars might accept requests for burial in their cemeteries, a quarter of the mortuary dues and bequests were to be reserved for the parish priest. This proved to be a workable settlement. Papal support saved the mission of the friars; and they in turn made themselves the foremost exponents of the papalist ecclesiology of the thirteenth century. As centrally governed international orders, devoted to Rome and to the preservation of orthodox faith, they corresponded exactly to the needs of a papacy that was in the process of creating a centralised system of church government and law.

All the same, the conflict with the secular clergy left a long residue of bitterness, and echoes of the dispute continued to reverberate in England and elsewhere down to the Reformation. In the fourteenth century, regardless of papal privileges and *Super Cathedram*, and notwithstanding the regular licensing of Mendicant confessors by bishops, writers of manuals of instruction for the parish clergy still questioned whether a penitent who confessed to a friar had fulfilled the canonical requirements for absolution: he would be safer to repeat the confession to his own parish priest in accordance with the decrees of the Fourth Lateran Council. The friars emerged victorious, but not unscathed. The grievance of the clergy lived on in popular literature. Chaucer's friar – the confidence trickster who sold easy penances and traded on the credulity of pious women – and Langland's four orders guilty of 'glossing the Gospel' for their own advantage, were stereotype lampoons derived, by a process of literary descent, from the bitter polemics of thirteenth-century Paris.

The place of the nuns

Like the earlier preachers of the apostolic life, both Francis and Dominic attracted women followers as well as men. Dominic's first foundation in the Languedoc was the convent of Prouille for women converts. One of Francis's earliest and most illustrious converts was Clare of Assisi. A girl of aristocratic family, she quietly slipped away from the family home one night in the spring of 1211 and made her way to the Portiuncula, where she took vows to follow Francis in the practice of poverty and the imitation of Christ. Jacques de Vitry, who was in Italy in 1216, observed groups of sisters called Minoresses, who worked alongside the Friars Minor ministering to the sick and destitute in the towns, but who lived apart in their own residences.[47] Francis assigned to Clare and her sisterhood the restored church and house of San Damiano just below the walls of Assisi. But if he contemplated any active collaboration by his women disciples in the ministry of the friars, the pressure of social convention and ecclesiastical disapproval must have disabused him. The Rule that Cardinal Ugolino, acting as Protector and patron of the Friars Minor, gave to Clare and her disciples in 1219 provided for a regime of strict enclosure modelled on the Rule of St Benedict.[48] The ideal of voluntary poverty for the sake of Christ was not a male monopoly, but female mendicancy seemed unthinkable as a way of religious life; so Ugolino's Rule reiterated the call to personal poverty, but authorised the sisters to hold property in common.

This was not how Clare understood her discipleship of St Francis. She, who called herself the 'little plant' (*plantula*) of our blessed father Francis, had promised him to live in absolute poverty 'according to the perfection of the holy Gospel'. In the end, she herself composed a new Rule for the sisterhood at San Damiano, applying to them the words of the Second Rule of St Francis – 'the sisters are to appropriate nothing for themselves, neither house, nor place, nor anything': they were to possess no property, either directly or through any intermediary.[49] With the help of the Cardinal Protector, confirmation of this was obtained from Innocent IV in August 1253, two days before her death. It was, however, a personal privilege that was not applicable to other convents of the order. Until the end, the extreme poverty and simplicity of the living conditions she maintained at San Damiano continued to provide an instructive example to a generation of friars who had never known St Francis. Cultivated poverty indeed remained a hallmark of the order of Poor Clares, but in other respects they became an enclosed monastic order of the traditional type.

The Dominican sisterhood developed in a similar way. St Dominic seems to have accepted the fact from the beginning that his women converts would be strictly enclosed, and he gave them a fully monastic constitution based upon the customs of Prémontré. The crucial question which would determine their ethos was that of their relationship to the friars. For a period both the Dominican and Franciscan nuns came close to being cast off by their parent orders of friars, and suffering the same fate as St Norbert's nuns in the twelfth century. The Dominican general chapter of 1228 ordered the friars to discontinue their priestly ministry to the women's houses on the grounds that it diverted them from their apostolic mission. Only Dominic's own foundations of Prouille and St Sixtus at Rome succeeded in winning exemption from this ruling. It was only after decades of struggle that the needs of the women's convents gained recognition from the Master, Humbert of Romans (1254–63) and the nuns obtained from Pope Clement IV a constitution that accorded them full status as an associate order of the Friars Preachers.[50] The Clares had to overcome the same reluctance of the friars to assume responsibility for their direction. The reluctance was understandable: the preoccupation of the friars was with the evangelisation of the urban laity, and the duty of counselling numerous communities of nuns seemed a diversion from this apostolic task. It was an inescapable paradox that the two Mendicant Orders, which had broken out of the monastic tradition of enclosure and segregation from the world, originated two female contemplative orders which observed a regime of strict enclosure.

Other Mendicant Orders

The new version of the religious life created by the Friars Minor and the Preachers deeply affected the way that thirteenth-century people thought about the Christian vocation. No subsequent religious organisation could wholly escape their influence. Several groups of penitents adopted some features of their organisation as well as the practice of mendicancy. Among these were the Trinitarians or Mathurin friars, an order of canons dedicated to ransoming Christian captives from the Muslims. They were a product of the apostolic movement of the twelfth century, who in fact predated the Friars Minor and the Dominicans by some years, but in their adoption of the evangelical life and their organisation took their model from the Friars Preachers. Other new orders that adopted the organisation of the Mendicants and abandoned claustral enclosure to engage in pastoral or social work, were the Servites, a small Italian order originated by a penitential fraternity in Florence, the Friars of the Cross or Crutched Friars, who were mainly engaged in running hospitals, and the Friars of the Sack, an expansive order of Mendicants that enjoyed wide success with the town-dwelling laity of the thirteenth century.

Alongside these and other smaller and more ephemeral groups of friars, there sprang up in the wake of the Mendicant mission a multitude of para-orders, consisting of fraternities of lay people, who engaged in a life of piety and works of charity while continuing to live in their own homes and plying their trades or professions. The Franciscan Tertiaries – the so-called Third Order of St Francis – was a confraternity of this kind. Its members bound themselves to attend mass regularly at the churches of the Friars Minor, to dress humbly, to 'avoid dishonourable feasts and shows', to recite the divine office according to the Franciscan breviary, where possible with the friars in church, and to subscribe regularly through the elected officers of the fraternity to the relief of the poor. They were prescribed a rule by Pope Nicholas IV in 1289. This, and a similar Third Order created by the Dominicans, realised in institutional form the message of the Mendicants that personal sanctification was accessible to those living in the secular world. Besides these satellite organisations, two other major religious bodies fell under the spell of the mendicant ideal and produced two orders of friars which came to rival the Dominicans and Franciscans in scale and esteem. These were the Carmelites and the Augustinian Friars.

The Order of Our Lady of Mount Carmel emerges from legend into history towards the end of the twelfth century, when groups of hermits, expatriates from the Latin West living in Palestine on the slopes of Mount Carmel, began to form an organisation that attracted the attention of the ecclesiastical authorities. At some point in the first decade of the thirteenth century, in response to their request, the Latin patriarch of Jerusalem, Albert of Vercelli, provided them with a brief Rule: they were to confine their settlements to deserted places, to occupy separate cells, to assemble together only for a daily mass in their common oratory and to meet on Sundays for a weekly chapter, and they were to work with their hands. Possibly because it later became a focus of contention in the order, the original text of this eremitical Rule has been lost.

In the 1230s a diaspora began. Impelled by the collapse of the Latin kingdom of Jerusalem and the menacing attitude of the Muslim conquerors, the hermits migrated in several groups to the West, forming new settlements in Sicily, Italy, Spain, France and England. Most of what is known of this phase of Carmelite history comes from the occasional references of Franciscan chroniclers. It is the Franciscan Thomas of Eccleston who tells us that the first contingent to reach England from the East was brought by Lord Richard de Gray of Codnor in the years 1241–42, on his return from crusading in Syria.

Initially these immigrants from the waste places of Palestine sought out remote areas where they could pursue their contemplative way of life in solitude. The earliest English settlements were in such isolated spots as Aylesford in the yet unpopulated Kentish Weald and Hulne in Northumberland. But in less than ten years strains became apparent. Younger recruits, unhindered by recollections of life on the holy mountain, and sensitive to the apostolic ideals of their time, pressed for change. They wanted the order to adopt an active role of preaching and study, following the example of the friars, which would engage them in a pastoral mission to the towns. In this identity crisis the initiative was taken by a general chapter meeting at Aylesford in 1247, which decided to petition the pope to have Albert's Rule modified. There seems to be no historical basis for a much later tradition, embalmed in Carmelite hagiography, that the lead in supplicating the change was taken by an otherwise obscure brother named Simon Stock.[51]

At the request of the chapter, Innocent IV set up a commission of inquiry, consisting of the theologian Cardinal Hugh of St Cher and William, bishop of Tortosa, both of whom were Dominicans, who might be expected to sympathise with the desire of the Carmelite hermits to emulate the friars; and on the basis of their report the pope issued in 1247 the constitution *Quae honorem conditoris*, which made slight but significant changes in the original Rule.[52] It authorised the order to make new settlements in any convenient places, including by implication the towns; and it approved various cenobitical practices such as taking meals in common. This opened a new road to those who wished to take it. The order now adopted a fully cenobitical pattern of observance and an active pastoral role; and in the course of the next decade it began to establish houses in or on the fringe of cities. The earliest statutes that survive – those of a general chapter held at London in 1281[53] – show the order modelling its structure on that of the Dominicans, holding annual provincial chapters, and also imitating the scholastic organisation of the Friars Preachers. The London ordinances provide – apparently for the first time – for a Carmelite *studium generale*, a house of advanced studies at the university of Paris, to which were to be sent those who had the ability to serve as lectors, two from each province, to study theology.[54]

Such a radical reorientation of the character and aims of the order was bound to meet with internal resistance from more conservative members. The struggles of the decades following the reappraisal of 1247 are largely hidden from us by the poverty of the sources. Some of the brethren, who found the pace of change too slow, transferred themselves to the Friars Minor; some who were altogether opposed to it fled to the Cistercians. For a brief moment the heart-searchings and tensions that accompanied the change of direction are vividly illuminated by a curious tract entitled *An Arrow of Fire* (*Ignea Sagitta*) which appeared in the year 1270. This was an encyclical letter addressed to the brethren by the retiring General of the order, Nicholas Gallus. It is a last plea from an old man for the order to retrace its steps and return to the desert. He had, he explained, been roused from sleep by the cold wind of adversity – 'would it had blown through my garden twenty years earlier'. Now religion, which flourished in the holy solitude, has been abandoned and perverted by her sons:

> Perhaps they will answer, 'it was never our intent to resist the divine will, but rather to follow it. For we desire to build up the people of God by preaching his Word, hearing confessions and counselling, so that we can be useful to ourselves and our neighbours. For this reason, a most just one, we fled the solitude of the desert to settle among the people in the cities, so as to perform these tasks.' O foolish men! I will show you that in the city you accomplish none of this, but that in time past in the solitude you accomplished it all . . . What is this new religion discovered in the

cities? . . . Tour the provinces, go to and fro among superiors, and tell
me, how many have been found in the order who are fit and sufficient to
preach, to hear confessions and counsel the people, as is proper for those
who dwell in towns?[55]

This strange valediction from a man who had been entrusted with the direction
of his order for several years suggests that a significant number of the brethren
believed that the changes made since 1247 had been a mistake. Nicholas's tearful
jeremiad is evidence of the internal stresses engendered by the process of turning an association of hermits into an order of mendicant friars. But those who
felt as he did were increasingly isolated; the tide of change was now irreversible.
Twenty-four years after his lament, the statutes of a chapter held at Bordeaux
reveal that the White Friars (as they became known on account of their white
habit) had become an articulated order divided into twelve provinces, governed
by regular general and provincial chapters, and possessing an elaborate scholastic
structure to promote advanced studies.

The Austin Friars were an offshoot of the Italian eremitical movement and in
this respect their origin was similar to that of the Carmelites, but better docu-
mented. They grew out of an amalgamation of groups of hermits living in Lombardy, Tuscany, and the Romagna. The thirteenth-century popes displayed a
constant anxiety to harness and control the anarchic tendencies of these religious
movements, and in 1244 Innocent IV, himself a canonist of no mystical temper,
instructed Cardinal Richard Annibaldi to organise the hermits of Tuscany into
a regular order. This he did, giving them a constitution, accrediting them to the
Rule of St Augustine, and appointing a Superior General to govern them.

In north Italy the most conspicuous body of hermits was a congregation of
penitents founded by St John Buoni (d. 1249), a layman of Mantua, and called
after him the Bonites. Influenced by the example of the Franciscans, they adopted
a life of preaching and mendicancy, an initiative that drew from Pope Gregory
IX a protest that they were poaching on the territory of the Friars Minor. The
canonisation process of Buoni in the years 1251–54 attracted widespread notice
and brought many new recruits, and the need to rationalize the various competing groups of mendicants became pressing. So, acting on the instructions of Pope
Alexander IV, Cardinal Annibaldi summoned leaders of the groups to a meeting
in the church of S. Maria del Popolo in Rome in the year 1256, and ordained
an act of union, bringing together the Augustinian Hermits of Tuscany, the
Bonites, the Williamites, and the hermits of Ancona called the Brettini, into a
single Mendicant Order, and directing their mission to the townspeople of Italy.
The bull *Licet Ecclesiae Catholicae*, by which Pope Alexander ratified this union,
formally constituted the Order of Friars Hermits of St Augustine.[56]

Following the example of the Tuscan hermits and the Bonites, the new order
of friars took the Rule of St Augustine as their spiritual identity card, and they
modelled their constitution on that of the Dominicans. The prior of the Bonites,

Lanfranc Septala, became their first Prior General. Thus the Austin Friars, like the Carmelites, moved from their hermitages into the towns, and followed the Franciscans and Dominicans into the scholastic world of the universities. In the last forty years of the century they founded priories in the towns of Spain, Germany, France, and England; but their centre of gravity remained in Italy, from where they had sprung. Italy, including Sicily, contained eleven of the twenty-four provinces into which the order was divided by the fourteenth century. Of the eight men who held the office or acted as General before 1300, all but one were Italians; and it has been estimated that in the fourteenth century more than half the membership of the order was based in Italy.

Both the Carmelites and the Austin Friars, then, originated as groups of monks or lay penitents pursuing the eremitical life. Their conversion into orders of friars bears witness to the powerful impact of the evangelical ideal upon the consciousness of religious people in the thirteenth century. Once the notion gained currency that the authentic imitation of Christ involved an active ministry of preaching or service, as well as voluntary poverty, it proved impossible to withstand. But the change in each case involved a radical reorientation which, however gradual, could not be accomplished without stress. Corporate poverty long remained a contentious issue: many of the fraternities that had been merged in the Austin Friars owned properties that had been donated by well-wishers or their own members; but more radical groups urged that these modest homes should be disposed of. In both orders the attraction of the solitary life of the contemplative continued to make itself felt.

To some extent the Austin Friars succeeded in accommodating the eremitical vocation. In Italy, their spiritual homeland, they never wholly lost touch with their hermitages, where a few groups continued to live. The greatest and most famous of these was the hermitage of Lecceto, situated in an ilex forest some miles from Siena. From time to time it received recruits who felt a desire to retire from the active life of the order. One of these was an English friar, William Flete, a Bachelor of Theology from Cambridge, who later became the friend and amanuensis of St Catherine of Siena. In 1359 he obtained the General's permission to retire to Lecceto as a recluse. Twenty-one years later William wrote to his brethren of the English province. He had, he explains, been afraid to write earlier for fear of reawakening old affections long since dormant. Now the burden of his message was that they should not travel about to attend chapter meetings or university inceptions; nor should they frequent towns or villages, but stay in their cells: 'in the cell is peace; outside it nothing but strife'.[57] This advice was obviously at odds with the Mendicant interpretation of the religious life; but by Flete's time the eremitical ideal could be contained within the framework of the order, as it had been by the Franciscans, without posing a threat to its missionary enterprise.

The continuing hostility of many of the secular clergy towards the friars, which had found expression in the fierce polemic of William of Saint-Amour, was intensified by the expansion of Mendicant church-building and the proliferation of new Mendicant Orders and their satellite lay associations. Their anxieties were constantly voiced by visitors to the papal Curia. In 1245 the Franciscan Adam Marsh, who had accompanied Grosseteste to the Curia and stayed on for the Council of Lyons, wrote home to his Provincial to report that many bishops were planning an onslaught on the friars at the Council, with a view to curtailing their privileges or even securing their total abolition.[58] In fact, Pope Innocent IV was prevailed upon to rescind some of their privileges, but the threat to their existence was headed off. The attack was, however, renewed by the bishops who assembled for the Second Council of Lyons in 1274. Gregory X yielded to episcopal pressure and framed a constitution which, in effect, suppressed several smaller orders of friars, and this was approved by the Council.

The conciliar decree *Religionum diversitatem*[59] invoked the canon of the Fourth Lateran Council prohibiting the foundation of new religious orders, and abolished all that had been founded since that date (i.e. 1215), unless they had been approved by the Apostolic See; those that had been approved were to accept no more recruits nor acquire new houses; they were thus condemned to slow extinction. The decree was specifically aimed at those orders that lacked endowments and depended upon begging for their livelihood. But the decree excepted the Franciscans and Dominicans from its application on account of their 'evident usefulness to the Church'. As more recent arrivals, the Carmelites and Austin Friars were clearly more vulnerable; but, with benign casuistry, the decree stated that their foundation had predated the Council of 1215; they were therefore allowed to continue until 'we ordain otherwise concerning them'. Whatever Gregory's ultimate intentions towards them, the favour of his successors ensured their continued existence and growth. On the other hand, the Friars of the Sack and several smaller Mendicant Orders were slowly extinguished by the operation of the decree.

Notes

1. Cf. A. Vauchez, *La spiritualité du moyen-âge occidental* 2nd edn (Paris, 1994), pp. 124–30.
2. Thomas de Celano, *Vita Secunda S. Francisci* (Quarrachi, 1927), p. 141. Early Dominican sources which also have the story of the pope's dream identified the beggar with St Dominic.
3. On this theme see M-D. Chenu, 'Moines, clercs, laïcs au carrefour de la vie évangelique', *Revue d'histoire ecclésiastique* 49 (1954), pp. 59–89; reprinted in *Nature, Man, and Society in the Twelfth Century*, trans. J. Taylor and L. K. Little (Chicago and London, 1968), pp. 202–38.
4. A. Dondaine, 'Aux origines du Valdéisme: une profession de foi de Valdes', AFP xvi (1946), pp. 191–235. The primary source for the career of Waldes is the chronicler of Laon in *MGH* SS, XXVI (1882), pp. 447–9, who is, however, confused about the date of Waldes' conversion, which evidently occurred in 1176. For good modern discussion of the Waldenses see Lester K. Little, *Religious Poverty, and the Profit Economy in Medieval Europe* (1978), pp. 120–8; and Brenda Bolton, *The Medieval Reformation*, (1983), pp. 55–61.

5. *The Historia Occidentalis of Jacques de Vitry*, ed. J. F. Hinnebusch (Fribourg, *Spicilegium Friburgense* 17, 1972), p. 145. On the social origins and development of the Humiliati see H. Grundmann, *Religiöse Bewegungen im Mittelalter*, 2nd edn (Berlin, 1961), pp. 70–79; and Brenda Bolton, 'Innocent III's treatment of the Humiliati', *Studies in Church History* 8 (1972), ed. G. J. Cuming and D. Baker, pp. 73–82.

6. 'ita quod de articulis fidei et sacramentis ecclesie non loquantur': *Vetera Humiliatorum Monumenta*, ed. G. Tiraboschi II (Milan, 1776), p. 133.

7. *Legenda Trium Sociorum*, 10; Habig, p. 899.

8. Thomas de Celano, *Vita Prima S. Francisci* (Quarrachi, 1926), p. 28.

9. L. Pellegrini, 'L'esperienza eremitica di Francesco e dei primi Francescani', *Francesco d'Assisi e Fmncescanesimo dal 1216 al 1226 (Atti del IV Convegno di Studi Francescani*, Assisi, 1977), pp. 281–313. For the *Regula pro Eremitoriis data* see K. Esser, *Die opuscula des Heiligen Franziskus von Assisi* (Grottaferrata, Rome, 1976), pp. 405–12; trans. Habig, pp. 72–3.

10. Celano, *Vita Prima*, p. 19. On the changing understanding of the 'apostolic life' see besides Chenu, *op. cit.*, M. H. Vicaire, *Limitation des apôtres, moines, chanoines et mendicants, IVᵉ–XIIIᵉ siécles* (Paris, 1963).

11. *Regula Secunda* in *Opuscula S. Patris Francisci* (Quarrachi, 1904), pp. 68–9; trans. Habig, p. 61. Translations of this and other documents will be found in Rosalind Brooke, *The Coming of the Friars* (1975).

12. The *Fioretti*, Habig, pp. 1323–3.

13. On the implications of Francis's teaching for the laity see M. D'Alatri, 'Francesco e i laici' in *Ricerche Storiche* 13 (1983), pp. 613–33; Prospero Rivi, *Le Origini dell' Ordine Francescano Secolare* (Rome, 1988), pp. 83–92.

14. *Cronica Fratris Salimbene de Adam*, ed. O. Holder-Egger *MGH SS* (1913), p. 418. On the social catchment area of the Franciscans see Grundmann, pp. 157–69.

15. From the *Legenda Trium Sociorum*, Habig, p. 926; cited by G. G. Meersseman, *Dossier de L'ordre de la pénitence au XIIIᵉ siècle (Spicilegium Friburgense* 7, Fribourg, 1961), p. 3.

16. *Bullarium Franciscanum*, ed. J. H. Sbaralea I (Rome, 1759), pp. 68–70.

17. See discussion of this point by Michael Robson, *St Francis of Assisi: The Legend and the Life* (1997), p. 77.

18. The generalate of Elias has been the subject of important studies by E. Lempp, *Frère Elie de Cortone: Collections d'études et documents* (Paris, 1901), and Rosalind Brooke, *Early Franciscan Government* (1959), pp. 83–105, 137–67.

19. *Cronica Fratris Salimbene*, p. 157.

20. The best modern accounts of St Dominic and the origins of the order are those of M. H. Vicaire, *St Dominic and his Times*, trans. K. Pond (1964); W. A. Hinnebusch, *A History of the Dominican Order, Origins and Growth to 1550* (New York, 1965); S. Tugwell, *St Dominic* (Strasbourg, 1995); P. Manndonet, *Saint Dominique, l'dée, l'homme et l'oeuvre*, 2 vols (Paris, 1937) was a seminal work that is still valuable.

21. For the organisation of the Cathars see A. Dondaine, 'La hiérarchie cathare en Italie', *AFP* 19 (1949), pp. 280–312; 20 (1950), pp. 234–324; W. L. Wakefield, *Heresy, Crusade and Inquisition in Southern France 1100–1250* (1974).

22. In his chronicle Peter Ferrandus reports that 'the pope was difficult over this': *Cronica Ordinis*, ed. B. M. Reichert, *MOFPHl*, p. 323.

23. *c.9, X De Religiosis, in, 36*; Schroeder, p. 255.

24. *Constitutiones Antique Ordinis Fratrum Predicatorum*, ed. Fl. Denifle *ALKG* I (Berlin, 1885), p. 197.

25. *Acta Capitulorum Generalium Ordinis Praedicatorum*, ed. B. M. Reichert *MOFPH* I, p. 77.

26. Denifle, *Constitutiones Antique*, pp. 214–15.

27. *Statuta Generalia Ordinis Narbonae 1260, Assisii 1279, Parisius 1292*, ed. M. Bihl, *AFH* 34 (1941), pp. 13–74.

28. Humbert de Romanis, *De Eruditione Predicatorum:* ed. M. de la Bigne, *Maxima Biblioteca Veterum Patrum* XXV (Lyons, 1677), p. 491.

29. *Questio xix: Cur fratres frequentius predicent in oppidis* in S. Bonaventurae, *Opera Omnia* VIII (Quarrachi, 1898), p. 370. Bonaventure's authorship of this *questio* has been questioned, but it is accepted as probably authentic by B. Distelbrink, *Bonaventurae Scripta, Authentica, Dubia vel Spuria, critice recensita* (Rome, 1975), p. 51.

30. For the art and literature of sermon composition by the friars see D. L. d'Avray, *The Preaching of the Friars* (1985); M. E. O'Carroll, *A Thirteenth-Century Preacher's Handbook* (Toronto, 1997).

31. *De Eruditione Praedicatorum, op. cit.,* pp. 474–5.

32. Lecoy de la Marche, *La chaire française au moyen-âge* 2nd edn (Paris, 1886), pp. 429–30.

33. *De Eruditione Praedicatorum* II, p. 79.

34. On the new moral theology developed by the Paris schoolmen see O. Iottin, *Psychologie et morale aux XIIe et XIIIe siècles* III (Louvain, 1949), pp. 329–535.

35. *Beati Iordani de Saxonia Epistulae,* ed. A. Walz, *MOFPH* XXII (1951), p. 4.

36. *Ibid.,* pp. 38–9.

37. *Ibid.,* pp. 19–20.

38. *Opera Omnia* II, p. 41.

39. On the curriculum of the provincial schools see M. Michele Mulchahey, *First the Bow is Bent in Study: Dominican Education before 1350, Studies and Texts* 132 (Toronto, 1998), pp. 219–350.

40. Reichert, *Acta Capitulorum Generalium* I, p. 100.

41. Celano, *Vita Secunda* c. 147; Habig, p. 518. The ambiguity of Francis's attitude to the place of learning in the order is stressed by E. Frascadore and H. Ooms, 'San Francesco e la cultura' in *Bibliografia delle Bibliografie Francescane: AFH* (1964–5), pp. 5–7.

42. There are various versions of Brother Giles's dictum, cf. *Dicta Beati Aegidii Assisiensis* (Quarrachi, 1905), p. 91, and *Chronica XXIV Generalium Ordinis: Analecta Franciscana* III (Quarrachi, 1897), p. 86.

43. *Hugh of Digne's Rule Commentary,* ed. David Flood, *Spicilegium Bonaventurianum* XIV (Grottaferrata, 1979), p. 187.

44. C. H. Lawrence, 'The letters of Adam Marsh and the Franciscan school at Oxford', *JEH* 42, No. 2 (1991), pp. 218–38.

45. 'De Periculis Novissimorum Temporum' in Edward Brown's *Fasciculus Rerum Expetendarum* (London, 1690) II, pp. 20–22. The fullest modern account of this dispute is that of M.-M. Dufeil, *Guillaume de Saint-Amour et la polémique universitaire parisienne, 1250–59* (Paros, 1972).

46. *Manus que contra Omnipotentem tenditur* in Max Bierbaum, *Bettelorden und Weltgeistlichkeit an der Universität Paris* (Munster, 1920), pp. 37–168. On the ecclesiological implications of this controversy see C. H. Lawrence, *The Friars* 2nd edn (2013), pp. 152–65.

47. *Lettres de Jacques de Vitry,* ed. R. B. C. Huygens (Leiden, 1960), pp. 71–8.

48. Ugolino's original rule for the Clares is lost, but as Pope Gregory IX he reissued it in revised form in 1239, see J. R. H. Moorman, *A History of the Franciscan Order from its Origins to 1517* (1968), pp. 38–9.

49. Text of the Rule with French translation in *Claire d'Assise: Écrits,* ed. M. F. Becker, J. F. Godet and T. Matura (*Sources chrétiennes,* Paris, 1983), pp. 142, 146; English translation in *Francis and Clare, the Complete Works,* ed. R. A. Armstrong and I. C. Brady (1982).

50. R. Creytans, 'Les constitutions primitives des soeurs dominicaines de Montargis', *AFP* (1947), pp. 41–84.

51. On the doubtful credentials of St Simon Stock and the problems of the early sources for Carmelite history see K. J. Egan, 'Toward a historiography of the origin of

the Carmelite province in England' in *Carmel in Britain*, ed. P. Fitzgerald-Lombard (Rome, 1992), I. pp. 86–119.

52. M.-H. Laurent, 'La lettre *Quae honorem conditoris*', *Ephemerides Carmeliticae* (Florence, 1948), pp. 5–16.

53. L. Saggi, 'Constitutiones capituli Londinensis anni 1281', *Analecta Ordinis Carmelitarum*, n. s., 15 (1950), pp. 203–45.

54. *Ibid.*, p. 240. By 1324 the general chapter named eight *studia generalia* of the order, including one at London for the English province and one at the papal Curia: *Acta Capitulorum Generalium Ordinis Fratrum B. V. M de Monte Carmelo*, ed. G. Wessels (Rome, 1912), p. 53.

55. *Nicolai Prioris Generalis Ordinis Carmelitarum Ignea Sagitta*, ed. A. Staring, *Carmelus* 9 (Rome, 1962), pp. 278–9, 281, 283.

56. *Bullarium Ordinis Eremitarum S. Augustini*, ed. B. Van Luijk, *Augustiniana* 14 (Louvain, 1964), pp. 239–41.

57. Aubrey Gwynn, *The English Austin Friars in the Time of Wyclif* (1940), pp. 195–6.

58. *The Letters of Adam Marsh*, ed. C. H. Lawrence, 2 vols (2004–09), pp. 214–15.

59. Mansi XXIV, col. 134.

14

EPILOGUE: THE INDIVIDUAL AND THE COMMUNITY

Most of the forms of the religious life we have described persisted in the later Middle Ages and beyond. But when we enter the fourteenth century we see signs that the traditional version of the cenobitic life, as it was represented by the Benedictine abbeys and priories, was being eroded by a process of general decay. The most obvious symptom of this malaise was a decline in the number of monks. A gradual reduction in numbers had been in evidence since the early years of the thirteenth century. In part, this was a consequence of the phasing-out of child-oblates and a general trend to raise the age of admission. Also a proportion of those who would in the past have entered the cloister were attracted instead to the Mendicant Orders. But in many cases falling numbers were not so much the result of dwindling applications as of a restrictive policy pursued by the monks themselves.

Under the pressure of economic difficulties, many abbeys of black monks took a decision to impose a limitation on the size of their community and to restrict the number of recruits. In 1200 Abbot Hugh V of Cluny decreed that, because many houses of the order were burdened by excessive numbers, no new postulants were to be admitted for the following three years except to fill vacancies created by death. Moreover, lay postulants, rustics, and aged persons were no longer to be accepted.[1] It was a drastic reversal of the missionary strategy pursued by St Odo and St Hugh. At some point this freezing of the existing situation was made permanent: records of the visitations of the English Cluniac houses carried out in the thirteenth century show that a fixed quota of members – a *numerus clausus* – that was not to be exceeded had been imposed on every house of the order.[2]

This policy of limitation was widely adopted elsewhere. The abbot and monks of Fleury decided in 1299 to fix their numbers at forty-five.[3] In 1234 the abbey of Corbie agreed on an optimum number of forty. The monks of Montéliou, in the south of France, fixed their number at thirty-seven in 1340, and agreed on a procedure for the future selection of postulants. The abbot was to choose a postulant to fill the first place to fall vacant; the convent would choose candidates for the next two vacancies; the abbot would fill the next one, and so on alternately.[4] There was a similar arrangement at the Norman abbey of Mont-Saint-Michel, where the community decided in the thirteenth century to fix numbers at forty, so as to keep within its income. There seems to have been no shortage of applicants for the limited number of places available: in the fourteenth century, the lay nobility were eager to nominate relatives and protégés; and the abbot was issuing letters expectative, accepting postulants but imposing delays of four, five or six years before they were admitted to the noviciate.[5]

An anxiety to maintain institutional grandeur and domestic living standards at a time when real income was falling was the main reason for holding down numbers. But it was not the only one. As has been seen, many of the German abbeys boasted of their aristocratic exclusiveness; the only postulants they would admit were the sons and daughters of the freeborn nobility. Reichenau was a case in point. In the past it had contained a community of upwards of ninety; in 1339 it had only eight or ten monks. Pope Benedict XII, who castigated them for their neglect of the divine office, made no doubt that their policy of social exclusiveness was the cause of their decline in numbers.[6]

A variety of unfavourable conditions conspired to create the economic difficulties that beset so many of the older abbeys in all parts of Europe in the later

FIGURE 14.1 Reichenau Abbey, showing the exterior from Strabo's garden (ninth and tenth centuries)

Photograph by the author

Middle Ages. Clearly, bad management played a part in many cases. La Charité was reported to be in a desperate financial plight early in the thirteenth century because, finding its income seriously eroded by the grant of too many corrodies, it had, like many other houses, resorted to the money-lenders to make good the shortfall. At the same period, Vezelay was also sinking under a burden of debt, having been ruined by a simoniacal abbot, who had dilapidated the abbey's properties in order to enrich his relatives.[7] But mismanagement was not the only nor the most intractable problem. Falling income and dilapidations were themselves signs of dwindling social support for the traditional form of Benedictine monasticism. The abbeys had ceased to attract significant new endowments and, like other landlords, they suffered from the effects of the agricultural recession of the fourteenth century. There were many reasons for this shrinkage of support. The phasing-out of child-oblation deprived the Benedictine houses of their usefulness as repositories for the surplus children of the landed classes. And the adult recruit, if he was highly motivated towards the ascetical life, was likely to be drawn off by the Cistercians or the friars. In general, the life-style of the Benedictine monasteries of the later Middle Ages had some attraction for the sons of the gentry or of the burgher class who were in search of security and status; but it offered no challenge to a fervent aspirant in search of spiritual fulfilment.

Much has been written about the relaxed discipline in the monasteries of this period.[8] There are widespread indications of a drift away from strict observance of the Rule. It was not a question of scandalous vice – though cases were not unknown – so much as a general dilution of community life in favour of the individual. The most conspicuous breaches in the cenobitic principle were over privacy and individual ownership. In many houses the common dormitory was replaced by individual chambers; monks received a cash allowance from the common fund with which they could buy clothes, books, and a few luxuries; and the constraints imposed by the customary rules of enclosure were greatly relaxed. Monastic life in these conditions resembled that of a college of secular clergy. In some abbeys the process was pushed to its logical conclusion by dividing up the property of the house into prebends to support individual monks.

The decline in numbers and the disintegration of community life were accelerated in the second half of the fourteenth century by the catastrophes of war and plague. The bubonic plague – the Black Death – that swept through Europe in 1348–49, and recurred at intervals, left some communities unscathed, but devastated others. St Albans lost forty-nine monks, including the abbot; the ancient German abbey of Echternach had its community reduced to seven by the plague. The Benedictines were not, of course, the only religious communities that were severely hit by plague; mortality was heavy among the friars because their urban locations and their faithful ministry to the sick and dying made them especially vulnerable. But unlike the Mendicant communities, those of the Benedictine houses rarely seem to have made good their losses. War also took its toll in some parts of Europe. In the course of the Hundred Years War, many French abbeys and priories were looted and burnt, either by the combatants or by roving companies of freebooters, and communities of monks were dispersed.

One of the features of a declining regard for monastic observance in the higher ranks of church and society was the practice of commendam. This was the conferment of the title and income of an abbot upon a beneficiary who was not a monk but a secular prelate or even a layman. Usually, the commendatory abbot received the headship of an abbey for life, and he would be an absentee. The post was simply a source of income; according to his disposition, he might or might not display any interest in the community of monks for which he was nominally responsible. It was a device used by the Avignon popes and their successors to increase the emoluments of the cardinals. The plight to which it might reduce a monastery is exemplified by that of the ancient Roman abbey of St Paul's-Without-the-Walls. In 1409 it contained only six monks, two of whom were absent. Its abbot was a secular cleric, a cardinal in fact, who had received it in commendam from the pope, and who enjoyed its revenues while residing in his palace in another quarter of the city. Any semblance of regular observance in the abbey had long since ceased.[9]

In the fifteenth century, the practice of appointing commendatory abbots, though unknown in England, became widespread in France, Italy, and Spain. In 1516 a concordat between King Francis I and Pope Leo X reduced the practice to a regular system of exploitation, by which the king would nominate those who had served him well to vacant abbeys and the pope would ratify his choice. Like most abuses, it was a symptom rather than a cause of malaise. It reflected the diminished social esteem for the Benedictine form of cenobitical life; and it was facilitated by the internal situation of the abbeys. The abbot had long since been a prelate with secular responsibilities outside the monastery, living apart from his monks in a palatial residence, and deriving his income from a separate portion of the monastic estates. Where, as was often the case, he was presiding over a much-reduced group of monks who had adopted the easygoing life-style of a college of secular clerks, the spiritual character of his charge had become largely invisible. In these conditions an abbacy could be regarded as a sinecure, or at best an ecclesiastical benefice like any other, and it was ripe for picking by patrons who wished to use it for their own purpose.[10]

The spectacle of total decay presented by some of the ancient abbeys was not universal. In all parts of Europe Benedictine houses continued to exist where a decent – if not inspiring – standard of regular life was maintained. If judged by the letter of the Rule, they might be found wanting; yet it is hardly meaningful to contrast their observance with that of a much earlier age, when the demands and expectations of society were very different. Some idea of the internal life and social role of these establishments can be gained from recent studies of the cathedral priory of Durham and the abbey of Westminster in the fifteenth century.

At Durham numbers continued to be maintained at about seventy, of whom some forty were resident at the priory, and the rest were living in the nine dependent cells of the house, or at Oxford, where the priory possessed a college for its own monks and others of the northern province.[11] Recruits, who generally entered the cloister in their late teens, were drawn mainly from the merchant and professional classes and lesser landowners of the region. They were professed after a brief noviciate, and proceeded by the canonical stages of lesser orders to priestly ordination. Many of them were sent to study at the Oxford college. A high proportion of them could expect to be employed as obedientiaries in one of the priory's administrative posts during their active lifetime. The regular round of choral office was maintained, and besides this, there were the daily community masses and the numerous private masses said for benefactors at the side-altars. Otherwise, the prevailing attitude to collective obligations seems to have been fairly relaxed. Once professed, monks were not bound to eat in the refectory, though the quantity and quality of the food provided may have been an inducement to do so; for the community lived well.

Like their Durham brethren, the monks of Westminster Abbey had a life made comfortable by an army of servants, and enjoyed a quantity and quality of food and drink on a par with the fare to be found in the outside world on the tables of the gentry and urban patriciate.[12] Here, as in many other Benedictine houses by this date, half the community in rotation ate outside the refectory in a separate dining-room, where a decree of Pope Benedict XII permitted the eating of meat in contravention of the Benedictine Rule except during the fasting periods of Lent and Advent. The very generous helpings of food and ale revealed by the kitchener's accounts were augmented on the numerous feast days and anniversaries by delicacies like salmon, pike and conger eels, and on these days wine was served.

The picture of fifteenth-century Durham that emerges from the records is suggestive of one of the wealthier Oxford colleges of the nineteenth century, when the statutes still required dons to be celibate. Prior John Wessington, who presided over the monastery from 1416 until 1446, kept up a state that a Warden of All Souls might have envied. His lodgings within the priory complex comprised eight rooms, including chapel and hall, where he entertained important visitors. The state bedroom was regally decorated with plush hangings calculated to impress secular guests; his collection of silver plate, stored in the buttery, was engraved with his arms; the stables housed two horses for his exclusive use, and his stud of horses was good enough to attract the envious eyes of noblemen. The monks of his community were invited in rotation to sample the fare at his table, which included such luxuries as salmon, oysters, Malmsey, and dates. It is understandable that there was no shortage of nominations for vacant places in the priory. It offered an agreeable life in palatial surroundings, combining religious observances with opportunities for study. It also provided a variety of openings for a man with organisational talents, and the possible rewards of prelacy at the summit of a successful career.

Periodic attempts were made to restore a more literal observance of the Rule in the Benedictine houses. Some of these reforms were imposed by external authority; others burgeoned on the old stock itself. The papacy concentrated its efforts upon organisational changes that were designed to preserve standards. Innocent III showed much concern for the promotion of religious life in the cloister, which he regarded as part of his mission to renew the universal Church. Perceiving that the supervision of the exempt abbeys posed a special problem, he ordered the heads of the exempt houses in Italy, France, and England to meet in regional chapters to regulate their affairs; but there is no clear evidence that his instructions were carried out.[13]

The example of the Cistercian general chapters suggested the best means of achieving adequate self-regulation and lasting reform. It had already been adopted in 1200 as a regular feature of government by the Cluniac congregation under the leadership of Abbot Hugh V – a zealous reformer bent on reviving the pristine observance of Cluny.[14] With this model in mind, Pope Innocent used the Fourth Lateran Council of 1215 to ratify a decree imposing similar arrangements upon all houses of monks and canons that were not already members of a congregation with a general chapter of its own. Within each kingdom or ecclesiastical province, their heads were to hold a chapter of their order every three years; they were bidden to elect one or more of their number to preside over the assembly, and were instructed to take advice from Cistercian abbots on procedure. These provincial chapters were to discuss plans for the restoration of regular observance. An important item of their agenda was to be the appointment of 'religious and circumspect persons' from their midst to conduct visitations of the monasteries of their province, both the men's houses and the nunneries, in the pope's name, and correct whatever they found amiss.[15]

These were hopeful plans, but they yielded only meagre results. The attempt to impose regulations by means of a general assembly conflicted with the jealously guarded autonomy of the Benedictine abbeys and was all but defeated by their deeply rooted conservatism. The difficulty of overcoming the forces of calculated inertia can be gathered from what happened in England. The heads of houses in the Canterbury province held their first chapter at Oxford in the winter of 1218–19.[16] The abbots of St Albans and Bury St Edmunds were elected presidents and various reforms were decreed, which were to be enforced by visitors appointed by the chapter. But after this promising start, the drive for reform lost momentum. The next chapter, summoned in 1222, ended in fiasco as one of the president abbots failed to turn up. The third meeting, held at Northampton three years later, was attended by only fifteen heads of houses out of more than sixty who should have come. The chapters continued to meet, but attendance remained poor. During the following hundred years, the constant reiteration of injunctions about silence in the cloister, the need for abbots to share the life of their monks in choir and refectory, the elimination of private possessions, and abstinence from meat, indicate that the zealots were fighting a losing battle. Cluny, as undisputed head of its congregation, was in a stronger position to enforce reforms; nevertheless, the records of the Cluniac general chapters tell a similar story of chronic absenteeism on the part of many priors, and the failure of visitors to remedy the chronic problems of relaxed observance and monastic debt.[17]

Many of the changes and relaxations that had become an accepted part of the Benedictine life were formally acknowledged and regularised by a series of constitutions issued by Pope Benedict XII in 1336. Himself a Cistercian, the most austere of the Avignon popes, he recognised the need for adaptation of the traditional Benedictine observance in response to different social pressures. In many ways the role of the Benedictine monks had changed. Their intercessory function was undercut by the growth of chantries served by the secular clergy; those who felt a strong vocation to the ascetical life were looking for fulfilment elsewhere, either in the eremitical orders or in newer kinds of religious organisation which allowed greater scope to the individual; men with intellectual interests were either absorbed by the schools or drawn off by the friars. What the Benedictine abbeys offered their recruits was security, social status, and a career similar to that of the secular clergy without the distraction of pastoral responsibilities.

The constitutions of Benedict XII acknowledged these conditions.[18] They mitigated some of the asperities of the Rule, authorised a reduction in accretions to the liturgical offices that had been added in the early Middle Ages, and laid down rules to ensure that the education of monks was not inferior to that of the secular clergy. Every Benedictine establishment was required to provide a qualified master to lecture to the brethren on grammar, logic, and rhetoric – the basic subjects of the university Arts curriculum; and abbots were to send at least one out of every twenty monks to university. This last requirement did no more than place the stamp of official approval upon a practice that had been gathering momentum during the previous eighty years. In the course of the thirteenth century, Cluny and Fleury had both established monastic colleges at Paris, alongside the Cistercian College of Saint-Bernard, and the chapter of the English black monks had provided for the foundation of Gloucester College at Oxford, which was to be joined in the fourteenth century by Durham College for monks from the northern province, and the studium of Rewley Abbey for Cistercians. The old dichotomy between the cloister and the schools, so fiercely preached by St Bernard, was forgotten; the monk-graduate was becoming a familiar feature of the scholastic landscape.

In contradistinction to this relatively relaxed version of the Benedictine life which had now gained official approval, a number of groups endeavoured to revive a more austere and literal observance of the Rule. One of these was the Olivetan congregation of the fourteenth century. Its founder, Bernard Tolomei (d. 1348) of Siena, had retired with two friends in search of solitude on Monte Oliveto to, a forested promontory twenty-two miles south of Siena, before he turned to the cenobitical life of the Benedictine Rule. In time, Tolomei's hermitage gave birth to a new congregation of abbeys, distinguished by the severity of their observance: the regime involved a sparse diet without meat, continuous silence, and regular manual work. Standards were maintained through a system of strict supervision exercised by the mother-house. In order to ward off the threat of commendatory appointments which had caused havoc elsewhere, Olivetan customs debarred life appointments and required abbots to be elected for a term not exceeding four years.

The Olivetans were largely an Italian group. By 1400 the congregation had eighty-three houses in Italy, and in the fifteenth century they provided the inspiration for another observant congregation which stemmed from the reformed abbey of Santa Giustina of Padua. Here, too, abbots were appointed for a fixed term, normally for three years, and the autonomy of individual houses was curtailed by a general chapter, which appointed all superiors. In 1505 the reform of Santa Giustina was adopted by the abbey of Monte Cassino, an accession that brought the congregation added prestige and changed its name to that of the mother-house of the Benedictine world. North of the Alps, a movement to revive strict observance of the Rule began with a reform of the ancient Austrian abbey of Melk, which imported monks from Subiaco in 1419.

These drives for monastic revival had their successes, but inevitably they fell short of achieving a universal impact; for, by the fourteenth century, the number of monastic foundations in existence vastly exceeded the needs of those few men and women who were moved by a personal vocation to the ascetical life. Moreover, those who were in search of such a commitment were turning away from a version of monasticism that no longer seemed to meet their requirements. It was not simply a problem posed by relaxed observance; the crisis of cenobitic monasticism in the later Middle Ages had deep roots in the religious psychology of the period. The rise of urban populations had created a new reservoir of recruits to the religious life; and the piety of townspeople, like their social attitudes, was more individualistic, more introverted and more critical, than that of people whose experience was dominated by the immemorial routines and collective work of the countryside. The Benedictine life of the tenth and eleventh centuries was a closely structured life dedicated to collective ritual. It imposed upon the individual an unremitting burden of vocal prayer and exterior observances in a community environment, which allowed no opportunity for solitude and left little time or energy for private meditation or introspection. Dissatisfaction with this pattern of observance had impelled numbers of people in the twelfth century to break away from existing religious institutions and search for a new kind of regime that was simpler and freer, in which the individual could develop a more inward life of his own. It was the growth of this more individualistic piety, the quest for personal religious experience, in the later Middle Ages that diverted the enthusiasm of the devout away from the structured life of community observances that was associated with traditional Benedictine monasticism.

One of the signs of this trend in late-medieval Western spirituality was the flowering of mystical writing, but it was not only the mystics who experienced a desire for solitude and greater individual freedom; many of the relaxations in the regime of the older abbeys, such as the jettisoning of additions made to the divine office in former times, the acceptance of private apartments and opportunities for study, were a concession to this desire. But the clearest sign of this flight from the spiritual constraints of the older type of cenobitical life was the rise of new eremitical congregations like the Celestines. The Celestine Order took its name from Pope Celestine V who, before he became pope in 1294, had founded a group of hermitages in central Italy. He himself was so ill at ease in the world of affairs that he was easily prevailed upon to abdicate the papacy and retreat to his hermit's cell. Another indication of the same trend was the small but steady growth in the number of Carthusian foundations made in the fourteenth and fifteenth centuries. It was an outward and visible sign of the spiritual kinship between the eremitical ideal and the religious individualism of the townsman that at this period patrons of the Carthusians began to erect Charterhouses in the centre of cities like London, Paris, and Cologne.

In the course of the fourteenth century, groups devoted to reviving the rigours of pristine observance appeared among the friars as well as in the monastic world. Here, too, by a curious paradox, the revivalist movement began as a quest for solitude. The first Franciscan Observants settled in a mountain hermitage at Brugliano, in the region of Foligno, in 1334, having obtained for their experiment the blessing of the Minister-General. Their leader, Giovanni della Valle, apparently accepted the premiss of the outlawed Spirituals who held that the absolute poverty enjoined by the Rule of St Francis could be faithfully observed only in the desert. With the support of the papacy and the sympathy of some of the Ministers-General of the order, the movement overcame an early setback and slowly spread, so that by 1391 there were twenty-two Italian Observant hermitages, where the Rule was followed in all its literal rigour and simplicity. A parallel movement appeared in the Touraine; but the major expansion of the Observants, which turned them into an autonomous and separate branch of the Friars Minor, occurred in the fifteenth century. It was brought about by the inspirational preaching of men like St Bernardino of Siena and St Giovanni Capistrano, who reconciled the austerities of the eremitical ideal with the Mendicant tradition of missionary activity and scholarship.[19]

The quest of the individual for a more intense interior life of the spirit and disillusionment with the traditional structures of the monastic orders took their most striking form in a religious movement that gained rapid ground in the towns of Holland and North Germany in the last two decades of the fourteenth century. The originator of this movement, which became known as the *devotio moderna*, was Gerard Groote, the son of an affluent cloth merchant in the Dutch town of Deventer.[20] After graduating in Arts at Paris and picking up prebends at Aachen and Utrecht, Groote was apparently launched upon a conventional clerical career when, in 1374, he threw it all up in order to try his vocation with the Carthusians of Munnikhuizen. But having been ordained to the diaconate, he concluded that he was not cut out for the solitude of the Charterhouse and left the monastery. The rest of his life was spent as a preacher and the spiritual director of a growing company of disciples. His fierce denunciations of clerical vice and worldliness gained him few friends in the ecclesiastical hierarchy, and in the end, a year before his death, he was forbidden to preach.

The message he gave his followers can be gathered from their reminiscences and from his own autobiographical writings, letters of direction, and sermons. Although he had been fired by contact with John Ruysbroek of Groenendael, the greatest of the Flemich mystics, and had translated some of his writings, Groote's own teaching bore no resemblance to Ruysbroek's profound analysis of the unitive experience of the contemplative. What he taught was a simple affective piety, based upon devout reading of the Scriptures, and regular meditation upon the human life of Christ. It was a plain man's version of the spiritual life, not given to theological speculation and suspicious, if not contemptuous, of intellectual analysis. What mattered was interior conversion, the renunciation of personal wealth and ambition, and a humble perseverance in everyday tasks. The main road to perfection lay in voluntary poverty, both material and spiritual. These were the conditions he found lacking in many monastic houses of the time. Some of his hottest invective was provoked by the spectacle of convents in which nuns were allowed to enjoy a personal income allotted them by relatives.[21]

The communities of men and women that stemmed from Groote's spiritual crusade embodied this ascetical programme. He had made over his parental house in Deventer to a sisterhood whose way of life was not unlike that of the Beguines. They took no vows and wore no distinctive dress; members of the community were free to leave when they wished; they elected their own superior annually and earned their livelihood by taking in hand-work. The first of the men's communities was formed with the help of one of Groote's disciples, Florence Radewijns, who held a vicarage in the church of St Lebwin at Deventer. Radewijns's house in Enghe Street became the residence of the founding community of what became known as the Brethren of the Common Life. In the following years similar groups sprang up in many of the towns of the Low Countries and North Germany.

Although the Brethren of the Common Life followed a strict regime of prayer and work, in most other respects they differed from any of the traditional religious orders. In accordance with Groote's mistrust of binding religious vows, they maintained a free association unconfined by vows or any recognised Rule. They included both clergy and laymen on the same footing, and they adopted no distinctive religious habit. Like most ascetical teachers, Groote was convinced of the spiritual value of manual work; in any case, work of some sort was necessary to support a community, even in the frugal style of men devoted to evangelical poverty. Possibly it was his own well-attested enthusiasm for books – it was the only form of impedimenta he refused to forgo – that suggested the most suitable kind of gainful occupation for the Brethren. At all events, book production, the copying, illumination, and binding of texts became, along with teaching the young, their favoured task. It was a trade well suited to their needs: it could be pursued in a place apart from the world, and in silence; and in the cities of northern Europe there was a buoyant market for the product.

The customs of the Brethren reveal a simple unceremonial regime, which combined some of the outward features of the old monasticism with a greater degree of personal independence.[22] They recited (the word used in the customary is 'read') the canonical hours in common; but the emphasis was upon the interior prayer-life of the individual. Systematic meditation upon prepared themes was practised at intervals throughout the day: 'When roused from sleep, I rise at once and begin to meditate upon the theme to be prepared . . . at 7 o'clock I go to the work allotted me, concentrating upon meditating the theme.' Each works, studies, and prays in his own cell. There is no binding rule of silence, but frivolous or useless conversation is to be avoided: 'It is expedient for me to avoid distractions throughout the day; therefore I do not wish to leave my cell without cause, nor to go looking for an occasion to talk with guests or strangers, except when advised.' The day closed with supper, followed by Compline. The last act before sleep was the private examination of conscience.

As had happened to the Beguines, groups of men and women living a communal life without vows or affiliation to any recognised religious order aroused the suspicion and hostility of the clerical establishment. It was possibly in order to neutralise criticism from this quarter that Groote formed a plan to establish a community of canons regular. There was nothing in this that was inconsistent with his principles. Although he denounced the failings of monks and nuns, he was moved by zeal, not contempt, for the monastic life; his letters show that he directed many devout people to the cloister. The Rule of St Augustine, with its generalised precepts about chastity, mutual charity, humility and obedience, and its lack of specific regulations, clearly commended itself as an appropriate formula for the kind of community that had gathered round Radewijns. The project materialised in 1387, after Groote's death, with the foundation of a house of Augustinian canons at Windesheim, near the town of Zwolle. The nucleus of the establishment was formed by a group of Brethren of the Common Life, who decided to bind themselves by taking formal vows.

Groote's mission thus originated two parallel and closely linked movements, one consisting of communities of devout men and women practising the common life without obedience to any formal rule, plying a trade or teaching children, and living in the world of the small northern towns, yet spiritually apart from it; the other a monastic congregation which, outwardly at least, conformed to the traditional norms of a religious order. In the end it was Windesheim that did more to disseminate and perpetuate the spirit of the *devotio moderna;* for it became the mother-house of a large congregation, whose daughter-houses in Germany, France, and the Low Countries far outnumbered the humble communities of the Common Life.[23] By the year 1500, eighty-seven monasteries had been incorporated into its family, and many more had come under its influence.

The form of piety practised and taught by Windesheim was what it had received from Groote and Radewijns – a spirituality based upon a systematic meditation upon the human life of Christ and preoccupied with the interior life of the individual: 'Seek a suitable time of freedom to yourself; as someone has said, "Whenever I have been among men, I have come back diminished as a man".'[24] 'Be watchful and diligent in the service of God, and meditate frequently on why you came hither.'[25] It was a practical, emotive piety, which inculcated the virtues of humility and hiddenness from the world, and was generally impatient with learning and speculation: 'Quietly relinquish an excessive desire for knowledge, for therein is to be found great distraction and deception.'[26] 'What advantage to you is it to dispute profoundly concerning the Trinity, if you lack humility?'[27]

These were commonplaces of the school, which found their most famous expression in the *Imitation of Christ* by Thomas à Kempis (c. 1380–1471).[28] Thomas became a canon of the Windesheim congregation at Zwolle, and his book was really designed for the instruction of novices under his care. Its central theme is the interior life nurtured by devout meditation on the human life and passion of Christ. Conceptually it was not original – Thomas was well read in St Bernard and the classics of medieval spirituality – but it exudes the essence of the *devotio moderna*, and it outlived its immediate purpose to become a classic of Christian literature.

'If anyone should ask you to what religious order or rule you belong,' wrote Stephen of Muret to the brethren of Grandmont, 'tell him to the rule of the Gospel, which is the fountain-head and origin of all rules.'[29] To the modern observer of the medieval centuries, the most astonishing thing is the rich variety of religious institutions that sprang from meditation upon an identical premiss. These varied forms of monastic and para-monastic organisation provided an institutional framework for every type of religious experience between the two poles represented, on the one hand, by the total isolation of the hermit, and, on the other, by the active pastoral mission of the Mendicant Orders.

As we have seen, the claims of the eremitical and the cenobitical life were not mutually exclusive. The Benedictine abbeys trained and sent out hermits from their communities; the Order of Camaldoli institutionalised the practice; and the Carthusians reconciled the vocation of the solitary with his need for the support of a community. Even St Francis, whose disciples were cast into the urban society of their time, provided a Rule for those friars who wished to withdraw to a hermitage. As St Benedict had appreciated, the individual who moved out of a religious community to live in solitude was not necessarily demonstrating discontent with the cenobitic life. He might be moved to become a recluse by a process of personal spiritual development that could only find ultimate fulfilment in solitude, away from the closely structured regime of the community.[30]

Nevertheless, the decay of many ancient monastic establishments, accompanied by new experiments in community living, point to a prolonged crisis in the religious life of the later Middle Ages. This crisis was only part of a turmoil that afflicted the ecclesiastical world as a whole; for there was always a dialectic between monasticism and the world the monk had abandoned. The forms taken by religious institutions at different periods were conditioned by the demands and expectations of the society that supported them. The great social and economic changes that overtook Western society from the thirteenth century onwards, especially the growth of urban populations and the wider dissemination of literacy among the laity, produced a new kind of religious sentiment, which experienced the ascetical vocation as primarily a search for individual fulfilment. For many people among both the clergy and the educated laity, the traditional forms of the cenobitic life did not seem to offer a way of satisfying this aspiration. Orthodox critics as well as heretics accused the monks of idleness and excessive wealth. This dissatisfaction was deepened by disillusionment with the institutions of the secular Church, whose claims to spiritual authority were weakened by a manifest failure of hierarchical leadership, culminating in the disaster of the Great Schism.

A few sought refuge in the hermit's cell. Some found fulfilment of their ideal in free religious associations like the Brethren of the Common Life. Others, of whom St Catherine of Siena and St Briget of Sweden were conspicuous examples, found a way to realise their contemplative vocation as lay people living in the secular world. Both Catherine and Briget were mystics, who assumed a prophetic role in the affairs of the Church during the critical years of the Avignon papacy and the outbreak of the Great Schism. Although Briget was inspired in the end to create a new religious order which aimed at a combination of the contemplative life with an apostolic ministry, for much of her life she, like Catherine, pursued an austere contemplative life while standing outside the organised religious institutions of her time.[31] 'My cell', wrote Catherine, 'will not be one of stone or wood, but that of self-knowledge.' The monastic bodies that continued to flourish were those that succeeded in accommodating this quest for personal identity.

The crisis of the fifteenth century was not a terminal disease, for both the eremitic and the cenobitic forms of monastic life survived the storms of the Reformation and both are still with us. But monasticism survived by undergoing an exterior and interior transformation. Because associations devoted to the celebration of liturgical ritual no longer met the religious demands of society or provided convenient homes for its surplus children, and because the number of monastic establishments greatly exceeded the needs of those few who had a personal vocation to the ascetical life, social and economic support fell away; the number of monasteries dwindled, and monastic property was transferred to other purposes. In England, the process was a catastrophic event, engineered by the government and involving many personal tragedies. Within the cloister itself, there was a necessary adjustment between the needs of the individual and the claims of the community. Such adaptations were made inescapable by changes in the outside world; a Rule designed for monks in late antiquity or in the twelfth century could not be applicable in every detail to recruits of a later age, whose intellectual and psychological formation was very different. As Stephen of Muret had observed, no Rule was absolute except that of the Gospel, which was the starting-point of the monastic ideal.

Notes

1. *Statuts, chapitres généraux et visites de l'Ordre de Cluny*, ed. G. Charvin, I (Paris, 1965), pp. 42, 43.
2. *Ibid.* I, pp. 275, 383, 386, 451. For the English visitations see G. F. Duckett, *Visitations of the English Cluniac Foundations* (1890). In each case the visitors report the number of monks in the house and refer to instances where the 'prescribed number' has been exceeded or not kept up.
3. Figures from U. Berlière, 'Le nombre des moines dans les anciens monastères', *Rev. bén* 41 (1929), 231–61; 42 (1930), 19–42.
4. U. Berlière, 'Le recrutement dans les monastères bénédictins aux XIIIe et XIVe siècles', *Académie royale de Belgique, classe des Lettres, Mémoires* XVIII (1924) fasc. 6, p. 13.
5. Nicole Simon, 'L'abbaye au XIVe siècle' in *Millénaire monastique du Mont-Saint-Michel*, ed. J. Laporte (Paris, 1966) I, pp. 174–9.
6. Berlière in *Rev. bén.* 42 (1930), p. 21. Cf. the discussion of the aristocratic element by F. Rapp, 'Les abbayes, hospices de la noblesse: l'influence de l'aristocratie sur les couvents bénédictins à la fin du moyen-âge' in *La noblesse au moyen-âge*, ed. P. Contamine (Paris, 1976), pp. 167–74.
7. U. Berlière, 'Innocent III et les monastères bénédictins', *Rev. bén.* 32 (1920), p. 38.
8. For example P. Schmitz, *Histoire de l'Ordre de Saint Benoît* III (Maredsous, 1948), pp. 63–86; M. D. Knowles, *The Religious Orders in England* II (1955), pp. 167–74.
9. I. Schuster, *La basilica e il monastero di S. Paolo fuori le Mura* (Turin, 1934).
10. For the history of commendam see *Dictionnaire de Droit Canonique*, ed. R. Naz III (Paris, 1942), pp. 1029–85.
11. For this and the other details of Durham see R. B. Dobson, *Durham Priory 1400–1500* (1973).
12. For this paragraph see Barbara Harvey, *Living and Dying in England 1100–1540: The Monastic Experience* (1993).
13. On Innocent's zeal for monastic reform see M. Maccarone, *Studi su Innocenz III* (Italia Sacra 17, Padua, 1972), pp. 223–337; Brenda Bolton, 'Via ascetica: a papal quandary' in *Monks, Hermits, and the ascetic Tradition*, ed. W. J. Sheils (*Studies in Church History* 22, 1985), pp. 161–91.
14. Hugh's statutes were edited by Charvin, *op. cit.*, I, pp. 40–52. All priors were required to attend a chapter annually at Cluny on the second Sunday in Lent.
15. Mansi XXII, 999–1002.
16. For this and subsequent chapters see *Chapters of the English Black Monks*, ed. W. A. Pantin (Camden Society, 3rd ser., xlv, xlvii, and liv, 1931–37)
17. Charvin, I. pp. 66–7; II, pp. 39, 59, 60, 67, 133, 358.
18. Summarised in Pantin, *Chapters*, II, pp. 230–2.
19. For an account of the Franciscan Observants see D. Nimmo, *Reform and Division in the Franciscan Order, 1226–1538* (Rome, 1987).
20. On Groote see T. P. Van Zijl, *Gerard Groote, Ascetic and Reformer* (Catholic University of America, *Studies in Medieval History*, n.s. 18, 1963), and the authoritative study of Georgette Épinay-Burgard, *Gerard Grote, 1340–84, et les débuts de la dévotion moderne* (*Veröffentlichung des Instituts für europäishe Geschichte* 54, Mainz 1970); his sermons are edited by J. G. J. Tiecke, *Werken van Geert Groote* (Gronigen, 1941); his letters by

W. J. M. Mulder, *Gerardi Magni Epistolae* (Antwerp, 1933). For the Brethren of the Common Life see E. F. Jacob, *Studies in the Conciliar Epoch* (1943), pp. 121–38.

21. *Epistolae* No. 45, p. 177.
22. *Consuetudines Fratrum Vitae Communis*, ed. W. Jappe Alberts (*Fontes Minores Medii Aevi* 8, Gronigen, 1959) for the following quotations.
23. By the end of the fifteenth century most of the houses of the Brethren of the Common Life had become collegiate churches served by canons; the movement was thus assimilated through the congregation of Windesheim to the more traditional monasticism: R. R. Post, *The Modern Devotion* (*Studies in Medieval and Renaissance Thought* 3, Leiden, 1968), pp. 467, 555.
24. Thomas à Kempis, *De Imitatione Christi* i, c. 20.
25. *Ibid.*, i, c. 25.
26. *Ibid.*, i, c. 2.
27. *Ibid.*, i, c. 1.
28. Because the *imitation* is a very derivative work, the authorship of Kempis has been disputed by some scholars; see a judicious summary of the question by Giles Constable, *Three Studies in Medieval Religious and Social Thought* (1998), pp. 239–42.
29. Prologue to the Rule of St Stephen: *Scriptores Ordinis Grandimontensis*, ed. J. Bequet (Turnhout, 1968), p. 67.
30. Cf. the observations of G. Constable, 'Eremitical forms of monastic life', *Atti della settimana internazionale di Studi Medioevali a Mendola 1977* (Milan, 1980), pp. 263–4.
31. Cf. observations on the religious mentalités of the fourteenth century and the position of women saints and mystics in relation to religious communities, by André Vauchez, *La sainteté en occident aux derniers siècles du moyen-âge* (Rome, 1981), pp. 439–40.

GLOSSARY

Advocate lay protector and legal representative of a monastery.

Advowson the right of a patron to present a clerk to an ecclesiastical benefice.

Almoner officer of a monastery entrusted with dispensing alms to the poor.

Ambulatory aisle or passage encircling the choir of a church.

Anchorite a solitary or hermit.

Antiphoner a choir book containing the music for the canonical hours.

Apostolic life the manner of life followed by the Apostles in the primitive Church, especially as understood in the eleventh and twelfth centuries.

Appropriation legal act by which a parish church with its endowments were donated to a monastery, which appointed a vicar or chaplain to perform the pastoral duties.

Apse semicircular or polygonal east end of a church, terminating the chancel.

Arch-cantor early title for choirmaster in a greater church.

Archdeacon subordinate of a bishop with responsibility for supervising the diocesan clergy and holding courts within the territory of his jurisdiction.

Ashlar large blocks of dressed stone used in building.

Austin the English form of the name 'Augustinian' as in 'Austin Friars', i.e. friars following the Rule of St Augustine.

Benedictional a liturgical book containing formulas for blessing people and objects.

Benefice   a permanent ecclesiastical living.

Breviary   a book containing the complete text of the divine office for every day.

Calefactory   warming-room in a monastery.

Canonical hours   the services sung or recited at the eight fixed times of the day; cf. *Opus Dei,* **Office**, etc.

Canonical penance   periods of penitential discipline, usually expressed in days or years, imposed for various sins as set out in the ancient penitentials, q.v.

Canons regular   communities of clergy following a monastic Rule, especially the Rule of St Augustine.

Capitulary   term used for the written decrees or instructions issued by the Carolingian rulers of Gaul and emperors.

Capitulum   Latin term for a chapter, e.g. of the Bible or of the Rule of St Benedict, and hence for the daily assembly in a monastery at which a chapter of the Rule was read, cf. **Chapter**.

Cartulary   a book or register in which were entered copies of the charters or deeds relating to the lands, churches and other properties of a monastery or of any other establishment.

Casuistry   a system of moral theology which takes full account of the circumstances of penitents and formulates rules for particular cases.

Catharist   term applied to the dualist heresy of the Middle Ages which regarded the flesh and the world of physical phenomena as intrinsically evil.

Cellarer   the monastic officer responsible for the general provisioning of his community and storing its goods.

Cenobitical   relating to monastic life in community, as opposed to the life of hermits; cf. **Eremitical**.

Chancel   the eastward section of a church, containing the main altar and choir.

Chancery   the secretarial office of a king or bishop.

Chantry   an endowment to provide for the celebration of masses and the office of the dead for the soul of the founder and for the souls of other designated beneficiaries.

Chapter   (i) the daily assembly of a monastic community at which a chapter of the Rule was read, faults were confessed, and business was transacted; (ii) a body of clergy serving a cathedral.

Chapter-house   the special hall in a monastery, normally situated adjacent to the church on the east side of the cloister, where the daily chapter was held.

Chevet the east end of a church, comprising chancel and apse.

Circatores the roundsmen at Cluny and some other monasteries, whose function was to perambulate the premises at intervals to ensure that the Rule was being observed and that nothing irregular was taking place.

Claustral prior the abbot's second in command, responsible for the internal observance of the monastery.

Co-arb co-heir of the founder of a Celtic monastery – the usual position of the abbot of an Irish monastery.

Collegiate church a church served by a corporation or college of clergy, of which a cathedral is one type.

Commendam in the later Middle Ages, the practice of granting the headship of a monastic house and the income that accrued from the office as a perquisite to a secular clerk or bishop, who normally resided elsewhere.

Compline a short service, the last of the day offices, which terminates the monastic day; it signalled the beginning of the Great Silence – the night hours in which talking was forbidden.

Confraternity association with a monastic community granted to monks of another monastery or to a lay person, conferring a special commemoration in the prayers of the community and a share in its spiritual privileges.

Conventuals name given to that section of the Franciscan Order that accepted the need to modify the practice of absolute poverty enjoined by St Francis, so as to build churches and permanent friaries (cf. **Spirituals**).

Conversus (i) an adult convert to the monastic life, as opposed to one reared in the monastery from childhood; (ii) a lay brother, especially a Cistercian lay brother, see Chapter 9.

Corrody a pension, in the form of board and lodging, or food, or money, granted to a lay person by a monastery, often purchased by the beneficiary for himself and his spouse. Hence 'corrodian' – the recipient of such a favour.

Crossfigill an ascetic exercise practised by Celtic monks, involving standing in prayer with arms outstretched in the form of a cross for long periods.

Custodian in the Franciscan Order, the head of a custody, the subdivision of a province.

Customary (i) a book setting out in detail the practice of a particular monastery, with instructions for the celebration of the divine office and for the other activities of the monastic day; (ii) a compilation recording the manorial customs, obligations of tenants, and rents due from an estate.

Dean   (i) in early monastic use, a monk appointed by the abbot to supervise a group of ten brethren; (ii) at Cluny, a monk officer in charge of one of the abbey's granges; (iii) in general ecclesiastical use, the head of a cathedral chapter; also the senior priest and supervisor of a rural deanery or group of parishes.

Decretal   a papal letter, or part of one, containing a decision on a point of ecclesiastical law.

Decretum   a common title for a collection of canon law, arranged thematically, in use from the eleventh century onwards.

Demesne   that part of an estate that a landlord retains in his own hands and exploits directly, as opposed to parts of the estate that are leased to tenants.

Devotio moderna   a form of individual piety that originated in the Low Countries in the late fourteenth century and is associated with the teaching of Gerard Groote of Deventer (1340–84) and the Brethren of the Common Life, see Epilogue.

Diffinitors   a term used by the Cistercians and the Dominicans for those members of the general chapter who were chosen to draft legislation and steer the assembly.

Diploma   technical term for an elaborate type of charter used in the early Middle Ages to confer land or privileges, characterised by a pious and lengthy preamble and concluding with anathemas against those who infringe or diminish the gift.

Dorter   the monk's dormitory.

Dowry   in monastic use, a gift of land, property or an entrance fee, usually exacted by a religious community as a condition of accepting a new member; a postulant was generally expected to bring an endowment for his support, but canon law forbade its exaction as a condition of admission.

Eigenkirche   the German expression for a church in private ownership or proprietory church – the condition of most rural churches in the early Middle Ages.

Eremitical   relating to the mode of monastic life followed by hermits either singly or in groups, from the Greek *eremos*, meaning a desert, as opposed to monastic life in community, cf. **Cenobitical**.

Eucharistic prayer   the central prayer of the mass.

Evangelical counsels   recommendations found in the Gospels to embrace celibacy, poverty, and obedience as a means to attain spiritual perfection – the subject of the vows that formed the basis of monastic life.

Exemption   a privileged status obtained by some monasteries which freed them from the jurisdiction of their local bishop and made them directly subject to the pope.

Familia   the household establishment of a bishop or abbot, consisting of his clerks and domestic servants.

Filiation   a monastic organisation that made each abbey responsible for supervising its daughter foundations; hence a group of abbeys linked in this way to a common mother-house, a system developed by the Cistercians, see Chapter 9.

Florilegia   an anthology, especially one of patristic texts; such collections were widely used by scholastic theologians.

Frater   the monks' refectory.

Garth   the open central space, normally a quadrilateral, enclosed on four sides by a cloister.

General chapter   an assembly comprising the heads or representatives of all houses, or of all provinces, of a religious order.

Glebe   land constituting the endowment of a parish church.

Goliards   a medieval term for vagrant clerks and ribald rhymesters who wrote scurrilous verse.

Grange   a monastic farm settlement at some distance from its parent abbey, supervised by a monk and staffed by lay brothers, created to cultivate one of the abbey's estates.

Guardian or warden   in the Franciscan Order, the superior of a friary.

Gyrovagi   wandering monks or clergy who lived a life of professional guests (a pejorative term used by St Benedict and subsequent medieval writers and legislators).

Indulgence   a commutation of a certain period of canonical penance, usually expressed in days, authorised by a bishop, enabling penitents who had repented and confessed their sins to substitute for part or all of their penance some specified acts or works of charity, such as a visit to a shrine or a contribution to the building of a church or hospital.

Infirmarian   monk in charge of the monastic infirmary.

Infirmary   part of a monastery, commonly situated to the east of the main complex, which housed the monks who were sick or too old and infirm to take part in the normal monastic round.

Interdict   a canonical sentence laid upon a territory or an establishment, ordering the administration of the sacraments and all public liturgical rites and the ringing of bells to cease until such time as the sentence was lifted; the baptism of infants and the absolution of the dying were normally excepted from the operation of the ban.

Introit   the opening verses of Scripture, varying according to the day, sung at the beginning of mass.

Judge-delegate   a prelate, senior priest, or monastic superior, commissioned by the pope to hear and determine an ecclesiastical case or legal action locally in its country of origin.

Lauds   the service of the divine office immediately following Matins, usually sung at dawn. (Confusingly, it is often called 'Matins' in medieval texts.)

Laura   a type of eremitical settlement first found in Palestine and Egypt, in which the cells or caves of the ascetics are clustered round a common centre.

Laus perennis   a practice, found in some Gallic monasteries of the seventh century, by which successive choirs maintained a continuous round of psalmody throughout the day and night.

Lectio divina   'sacred reading', meaning the reading of the Scriptures and the Fathers prescribed by the Rule of St Benedict as one of the most important occupations of the monastic timetable.

Lectionary   a book containing the lessons that formed part of the mass liturgy and the divine office.

Lector   (i) 'reader', i.e. one ordained to the minor order of lector; (ii) the monk entrusted with reading the lessons in church or refectory; (iii) in the usage of the Mendicant Orders, a qualified lecturer or teacher of theology accredited to a friary.

Legate   an ambassador, usually a cardinal, dispatched by the pope to a territory with plenary powers. (Some archbishops, including the archbishops of Canterbury, claimed to be *legati nati* or standing legates in virtue of their office.)

Legenda   'legends', viz. readings or lessons from the Lives of the saints, especially those used in the second Nocturn of Matins on saints' days.

Liber vitae   a book kept in a monastery, often placed on the altar, recording the names of benefactors and all those who had a particular claim on the intercessory prayer of the monks.

Martyrology   a list of the martyrs, read during the office of Prime.

Master-General   the elected head of the Order of Preachers or Dominican Friars.

Matins   the first office of the day, sung during the night, commonly called Nocturns in medieval texts.

Mendicant Orders   the orders of friars, so called because they refused to own property and supported themselves by begging.

Mensa the part of a monastic estate that was allocated to the direct support of the community.

Metanoia a term used in ascetical literature for interior conversion involving the orientation of the personality towards God.

Minister (i) in Franciscan usage, the head of a province of the order; (ii) also Minister-General, i.e. the head of the whole order.

Minor orders the four lesser orders to which a man might be ordained, i.e. those of acolyte, lector, exorcist, and doorkeeper, as opposed to the three 'major orders' of priest, deacon, and subdeacon. In medieval canon law celibacy was required only of those in major orders.

Minorite a Friar Minor or Franciscan.

Mixed rule an expression denoting monastic practice, especially that of the seventh century, by which religious communities followed observances taken from several Rules, especially those from the Rules of St Benedict and St Columbanus, rather than any single Rule.

Nocturns sections of the office of Matins. In the monastic office each Nocturn consisted of three psalms followed by four lessons; on important festivals Matins comprised three such Nocturns and thus included twelve lessons. In medieval texts Matins is commonly called Nocturns.

Nones the liturgical office sung at the ninth hour of the day, i.e. around 2.30–3 p.m.

Noviciate the period of training undergone by a recruit before taking monastic vows; the Rule of St Benedict prescribed a noviciate of one year before a recruit was permitted to make his profession.

Nuntius in Franciscan usage, an intermediary or trustee authorised to receive and hold monies donated to the friars, which might be used to fund building or to purchase basic necessities.

Nutritus a monk reared in a monastery from childhood (see **Oblate**), as opposed to a *conversus* – an adult convert to the monastic life.

Obedientiary a monk in charge of one of the administrative departments of a monastery, such as the cellarer, sacrist, or infirmarian.

Obit a commemoration, often in the form of mass, celebrated on the anniversary of a person's death, especially for deceased benefactors and members of a religious community.

Oblate a person given in childhood to a monastic community by his parents, to be brought up as a monk; the practice of child-oblation is already referred to in the Rule of St Benedict.

Octave   the eighth day, or the period of eight days counting inclusively, that followed a liturgical festival.

Office   or 'divine office', the services sung or recited at the canonical hours of the day. The monastic office was somewhat longer than the office sung in secular churches.

Official   a legal officer appointed by a bishop or an archdeacon to perform certain acts on his behalf. In the thirteenth century the bishop's Official was president of the diocesan consistory court.

Opus Dei   'the work of God' – the expression used by St Benedict to refer to the divine office (see **Office**). The Rule states that it must take precedence over all else in the monastic timetable.

Opus signinum   a crude type of mosaic paving used in Roman houses in late antiquity.

Orders   the various grades of the Christian ministry, see **Minor orders**.

Ordinal   a liturgical book containing the rites used to confer orders.

Ordo   (i) a book of directions describing the ceremonies for the celebration of mass and other liturgical rites; (ii) a book setting out the order of the divine office for every day of the year.

Pallium   a yoke-shaped band of white wool, embroidered with crosses, worn by the pope and also conferred on archbishops, symbolising in the latter case the delegation to them of metropolitan jurisdiction over the other bishops of their provinces; it was conferred by the pope and normally had to be collected from Rome in person or by special envoys.

Paruchia   in the usage of the early Celtic Church, the area and the churches, including distant territories, over which a monastery had spiritual jurisdiction.

Peculiar   a parish or other area subject not to the bishop in whose diocese it lies, but to the jurisdiction of a bishop or some other ecclesiastical body in another diocese.

Pelagian   relating to the heresy of Pelagius *(c.* 354–*c.* 419), who denied the transmission of original sin and emphasised the primacy of human endeavour in achieving salvation.

Penitential   (i) a treatise setting out the penances or acts of satisfaction appropriate to various sins, which a penitent was required to perform after he had repented and confessed to a priest; (ii) part of a Rule prescribing penances for breaches of monastic discipline.

Pittances   extra dishes of superior quality served in a monastery on festivals and anniversaries, for which benefactors often bequeathed funds.

Placebo et dirige   the first words of the opening antiphons of Vespers and Matins in the office of the dead; hence, in medieval usage a common term denoting the office of the dead.

Polyptique   term for an early type of estate survey recorded in writing.

Postulant   a person seeldng admission to a religious order.

Prebend   a portion of the estate of a cathedral or collegiate church allocated to a canonry in such a church to provide the occupant with a stipend; the prebend took its name from the estate appropriated to it.

Precentor   a cathedral dignitary responsible for the choir and the liturgical arrangements in the cathedral church.

Preceptory   a house of the Knights Templars.

Prime   the office sung or recited at the first hour of the day.

Prior   (i) in an abbey the second in command or officer next in rank after the abbot; (ii) the superior of a monastery that did not have the status of an abbey – in the case of a nunnery, the prioress.

Proctor   a legal representative of any person or community able to act for them in the ecclesiastical courts.

Proprietory church   a church in private ownership, the property of a landlord or of a monastery – the condition of most rural churches in the early Middle Ages (see *Eigenkirche*).

Provincial   in the Mendicant Orders, the superior in charge of a province of the order, called in the case of the Friars Minor a 'Provincial Minister', and by the Dominicans a 'Prior Provincial'. The name and office have been adopted by many subsequent orders, e.g. the Jesuits.

Quadragesima   literally 'the fortieth day': the Latin term for Lent, a period of approximately forty days (in fact forty-six days) before Easter.

Rector   the incumbent of a parish living entitled to receive the great tithe. Where a parish church had been appropriated to a monastery (see **Appropriation**), the monastery became the corporate rector of the church.

Reeve   an officer placed in charge of a borough or, on a manor, a peasant foreman appointed to superintend the peasant labour force.

Refectory   the dining-hall of a monastery.

Regularis Concordia   the concordance or code of monastic rules compiled for the English Benedictine abbeys in the year 970.

Reliquary   a vessel or container, often of precious metal and richly ornamented, used to house the relics of a saint.

Rere-dorter   the latrines of a monastery, so called because they were usually situated at the back or far end of the dormitory.

Retro-choir   part of a church at the east end of the choir, behind the high altar; in cathedral churches the area was often the location of the shrine of a saint.

Sacramentary   a type of liturgical book used in the early Middle Ages, containing the prayers recited by the celebrant of the mass and other sacraments; the lessons and verses sung by the choir were contained in separate books.

Sacrist   the monk officer responsible for the care of the altars, sacred vessels, and the fabric of the church, and also for the care of shrines in the church.

Scapular   part of a monk's dress, consisting of a broad band of cloth, open at the sides and hanging down front and back, worn over the habit.

Scholasticus   the clerk or teacher in charge of a cathedral school, called in some cathedrals the chancellor.

Scriptorium   the room in a monastery where writing was done and manuscripts were copied.

Secular canons   clergy serving a cathedral or other collegiate church, who were not subject to a monastic rule and possessed private property.

Sext   the service sung or recited at the sixth hour of the day, (i.e. about midday).

Socius   literally 'companion'; among the friars, a fellow-friar chosen to accompany the provincial to chapter meetings, or to accompany a friar on a preaching mission.

Spirituals   the name attached to that section of the Franciscans that refused to modify the instructions of St Francis on absolute poverty and claimed to be the authentic interpreters of his message, as against the **Conventuals**.

Studium generale   a term which appeared in the thirteenth century, denoting a school of universal status, used especially of universities. In canonical theory it indicated a privileged status that could only be conferred on a school by the pope or emperor. Its special mark was the theoretical right of its graduates to teach in any other school of Christendom without further examination (the *ius ubique docendi*).

Stylite   an ascetic who lived on top of a pillar.

Temporalities   the landed estate and other properties belonging to a church or religious community, especially the estates of a bishopric in respect of which the bishop owed secular duties to the king and which would be exploited by agents of the crown during the vacancy of the see, as opposed to 'spiritualities' i.e. those properties and functions of a bishopric or monastery that were subject to the exclusive jurisdiction of the Church.

Terce   the service sung or recited at the third hour of the day, i.e. about 9 a.m.

Tertiary   a member of a Third Order, i.e. of a confraternity of lay people attached to the friars, following a Rule which bound them to various religious observances, including recitation of the day hours of the divine office, see Chapter 13.

Tithe   a tenth part of the produce of the land and the product of labour which had to be paid to every parish church. Monasteries generally secured exemption from payment of tithes from their land.

Tithing   (i) any group of ten persons; (ii) in early monastic usage, a group of ten monks supervised by a monk officer called a dean — it was a means of devolving command in large religious communities; (iii) in early secular law, a tithing was a recognised group of neighbours to which all free men were bound by law to belong.

Tonsure   a ritual clipping of the hair of the head by which a young man received clerical status, normally performed by a bishop.

Translation   (i) in the case of a bishop, his transfer from one see to another, a change which in classical canon law could only be authorised by the pope. (ii) The term was also used to describe the process by which the bodily remains of a saint were removed from their tomb to a place of greater honour above or behind the altar of a church. Originally, it was an act that signified canonisation; from the early thirteenth century, it was a solemn act carried out following a declaration of canonisation by the pope.

Troper   a musical book containing chants used in the liturgy other than those contained in the antiphoner.

Vespers   the liturgical office sung at evening, otherwise called Evensong.

Vicar   the incumbent of a parish church which has been appropriated to a monastery or to some other religious body; the vicar, who was responsible for the pastoral care of the parishioners, received a fixed portion of the parish endowments and offerings, and enjoyed security of tenure, hence a 'perpetual vicarage', meaning a benefice of this kind sanctioned by the bishop.

Vigils   in early monastic literature, the term for Matins, i.e. the office sung during the watches of the night.

Vita Apostolica   see **Apostolic life**.

GROUND PLAN OF THE CISTERCIAN ABBEY AT ROCHE

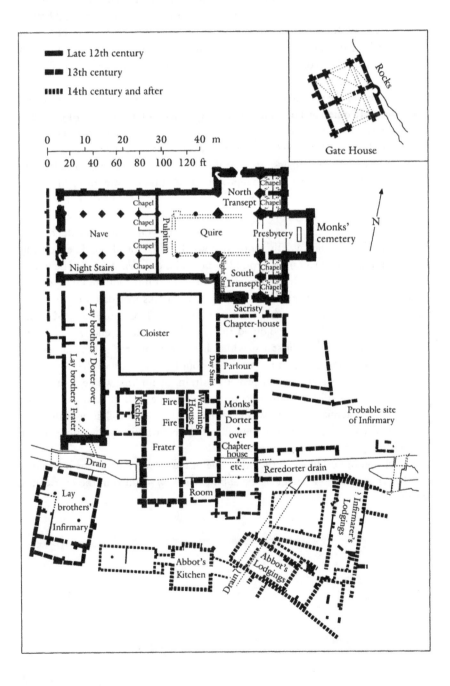

- ▬ Late 12th century
- ▬▬ 13th century
- ⦚⦚⦚ 14th century and after

0   10   20   30   40 m

0 20 40 60 80 100 120 ft

Rocks

Gate House

Chapel

North Transept

Chapel

Chapel

Monks' cemetery

N

Chapel

Nave

Pulpitum

Quire

Presbytery

Chapel

Night Stairs

Chapel

Night Stairs

Chapel

South Transept

Chapel

Sacristy

Cloister

Chapter-house

Lay brothers' Dorter over

Day Stairs

Parlour

Lay brothers' Frater

Kitchen

Fire

Warming House

Monks'

Probable site of Infirmary

Fire

Dorter

Frater

over

Chapter-house

etc.

Drain

Reredorter drain

Lay brothers'

Room

? Infirmarer's Lodgings

Infirmary

Abbot's Kitchen

Drain

Abbot's Lodgings

The plan of Roche Abbey, near Sheffield in Yorkshire, illustrates the standard layout of a Cistercian monastery. The abbey was founded in 1147 by two members of the lesser baronage, Richard de Bully of Tickhill and Richard FitzTurgis. It was colonised by monks of the Cistercian Order from Newminster in Northumberland, which itself had been colonised from Fountains Abbey as recently as 1138. Roche was thus part of the first wave of Cistercian settlement in the north of England. It was one of the more modestly endowed Cistercian houses of Yorkshire, containing towards the end of the twelfth century some twenty choir-monks and about sixty lay brothers.

The layout of the monastic buildings of Roche presents a standard plan which can be seen at Fontenay, Fountains, and many other Cistercian sites. In its essentials it derived from the classical plan of the Benedictine monasteries. This uniformity of design reflects the fact that the general chapter of the order supervised the foundation of new abbeys, and would only authorise occupation after the buildings had been inspected and approved. The buildings are grouped on the south side of the abbey church round a quadrilateral, of which the open space in the centre – the cloister garth – is surrounded by a covered cloister-walk. The range of buildings along the west side of the quadrilateral, which like the church was constructed in the twelfth century, housed the lay brothers. Their dining hall and living room was on the ground floor, and their dormitory ran the whole length of the range above. In the east range the most conspicuous building on the ground floor was the chapter-house, where the monks met daily for monastic business. The monks' dorter (or dormitory), on the floor above, extended the full length of the range and adjoined the church at its north end. Access from the dorter was by the night stairs, which led down into the south transept of the church. The rere-dorter (the latrine) juts out from the end of the dormitory over the running stream which provided drainage for the whole monastery. The monk's frater (dining hall) was on the south side and, in accordance with the standard Cistercian pattern, was set at right-angles to the cloister-walk. The kitchen and warming house on either side of it were originally the only parts of the building provided with a fireplace.

The cluster of buildings on the other side of the stream include the infirmary and the separate establishment of the abbot, which was added in the fourteenth century.

INDEX